Cabinets, Ministers, and Gender

T0347630

Cabinets, Ministers, and Gender

CLAIRE ANNESLEY, KAREN BECKWITH, AND
SUSAN FRANCESCHET

OXFORD
UNIVERSITY PRESS

OXFORD
UNIVERSITY PRESS

Oxford University Press is a department of the University of Oxford. It furthers
the University's objective of excellence in research, scholarship, and education
by publishing worldwide. Oxford is a registered trade mark of Oxford University
Press in the UK and certain other countries.

Published in the United States of America by Oxford University Press
198 Madison Avenue, New York, NY 10016, United States of America.

CIP data is on file at the Library of Congress
ISBN 978-0-19-006900-1 (pbk.)
ISBN 978-0-19-006901-8 (hbk.)

1 3 5 7 9 8 6 4 2

Paperback printed by Marquis, Canada
Hardback printed by Bridgeport National Bindery, Inc., United States of America

Contents

Preface

Women today face unprecedented opportunities to participate in governments and elected assemblies. In just two decades, women's presence in the lower houses of parliaments around the world has nearly doubled.[1] Gender parity cabinets, that is, cabinets with an equal number of female and male ministers, have appeared in all the major regions of the world, from Europe to Latin America to Africa. In October 2018, Ethiopian prime minister Abiy Ahmed appointed a cabinet that was "half female, in an unprecedented push for gender parity in Africa's second-most-populous nation."[2] A few countries, including Costa Rica, Finland, and Spain, have appointed cabinets in which women hold a majority of portfolios. In June 2018, Spanish prime minister Pedro Sánchez appointed a cabinet with a female supermajority of 11 women and six men.[3]

In many cases, women have been included in cabinet in greater magnitude than in parliament (Beckwith 2014) and women's inclusion in cabinet has come faster than women's election as heads of government, as heads of state, or as members of parliaments. While rapid gains in women's parliamentary representation can be explained by the spread of gender quotas to more than 130 countries around the world (Krook 2009; Krook and Zetterberg 2016; Tripp and Kang 2008), the same is not the case for women's cabinet representation. There are no formal rule changes that legally require leaders to appoint more women to cabinet, no electoral systems that reserve cabinet seats for women, and no financial incentives for leaders or parties to select more women as ministers. In the absence of any legal requirement to do so, presidents and prime ministers around the world are appointing historically high proportions of women to their governing teams, and more leaders than ever

---

[1] In January 1999, the global average for women in lower houses of parliament was 13 percent; by January 2019, the figure was 24 percent. See *Women in National Parliaments*, Inter-parliamentary Union, http://archive.ipu.org/wmn-e/arc/world010199.htm.

[2] Paul Schemm, "In Ethiopian Leader's New Cabinet, Half the Ministers Are Women," *Washington Post*, October 16, 2018.

[3] Susan Franceschet and Karen Beckwith, "Spain's Majority Female Cabinet Embodies Women's Global Rise to Power," *The Conversation*, July 13, 2018, http://theconversation.com/spains-majority-female-cabinet-embodies-womens-global-rise-to-power-98433.

are taking the bold step to appoint fully gender-equal cabinets. Gender parity cabinets are recent, increasing, and global; in democracies, all-male cabinets are exceedingly rare.

What explains the recent increase in numbers of women in cabinets? Why do some presidents and prime ministers appoint ever-larger proportions of women to cabinets, while others continue to appoint smaller numbers of women? Why, in the same country, is a cabinet with few women succeeded by a cabinet with many women, without major economic, social, or cultural changes, but sometimes with a change of party— including a change to a more conservative governing party?[4] *Cabinets, Ministers, and Gender* was sparked by these global trends and seeks to answer these questions.

Cabinets, Ministers, and Gender offers a cross-time, cross-country, qualitative analysis of women's cabinet inclusion in seven democracies in Australia, Europe, and North America. Although increases in women's inclusion in cabinet are relatively recent, explaining this trend required us to consider a much broader historical framework, given that for several decades, cabinets everywhere had been composed entirely of men. The disappearance of all-male cabinets came early in Germany—the last was in 1957—but much later elsewhere. In the United States, for example, the last all-male cabinet was President Ronald Reagan's first-term, post-election cabinet appointed in 1981, while in Australia, Labor prime minister Paul Keating appointed his country's last all-male cabinet in 1993.

Answering why women's cabinet representation has grown over time but with different patterns cross-nationally challenged us to examine the process by which cabinets are constructed. We developed a model for understanding how cabinets are formed, in the interaction between *selectors* (presidents, prime ministers, and other actors empowered to select cabinet ministers) and *ministrables* (those who are both eligible and qualified for inclusion in cabinet). Our model takes into account system-level and party-specific rules. We examine formal rules (written, legally enforceable, with sanctions) and informal rules (often well-known, but sometimes private and invisible, but nonetheless powerful, with political or social sanctions for non-compliance). We present this model in Chapter 2, where we also explain our methodology,

---

[4] For example, the last Australian all-male cabinet, appointed by Labor prime minister Paul Keating in 1993, was succeeded in 1996 by Liberal prime minister John Howard's post-election cabinet, which included two women.

data collection, and case selection. Chapters 3 through 7 explain in detail how these actors and rules intersect to shape the cabinet formation process generally and, in each of our country cases, specifically.

Rules of cabinet formation, whether formal or informal, may appear as neutral and universally applicable. In Chapters 8 through 10, we demonstrate how these rules themselves are gendered and how they intersect to produce gendered outcomes, generally and in each of our specific country cases. *Cabinets, Ministers, and Gender* focuses on the process to show where and how gender enters into the recruitment of ministers and formation of the cabinet team, and what the different consequences are for women and men.

The book concludes by summarizing our findings in terms of the timing, magnitude, and persistence of women's cabinet inclusion. We present in detail our concept of the "concrete floor," defined as the minimum proportion or number of women for a cabinet to be perceived as sufficiently representative and legitimate. This concept captures the process by which cabinets have been re-gendered to include ever greater numbers of women. The concrete floor helps to explain why presidents and prime ministers have not reverted to appointing all male-cabinets and, in most cases, have refrained from appointing significantly fewer women to cabinet than their predecessors. We further believe this concept provides a strategic foothold for feminist activists who want to increase women's presence in national politics, specifically in cabinets and shadow cabinets. We conclude the book by identifying the practical political implications of our findings.

Cabinets, Ministers, and Gender does not answer all questions for all countries in regard to the gendered process of cabinet formation. First, we focus on a specific subset of country cases: Australia, Canada, Chile, Germany, Spain, the United Kingdom, and the United States. These are countries where we were confident of our language skills, had access to national media reports, were able to secure interviews with party and political elites, and were confident that the data we collected were reliable. As a result, the book's country cases do not include semi-presidential systems, such as France, nor any of the Nordic countries, where gender parity cabinets came earlier and are more common. Our cases exclude non-democracies, although such countries have included women in cabinet (e.g., Cuba). The extent to which our model of cabinet formation and our empirical findings apply to such cases will be known when future scholars (including ourselves) investigate the gendered process of cabinet formation in other countries and into the future.

Our project does not consider gendered differences in portfolio allocation (Krook and O'Brien 2012).[5] Recent research has turned attention to women's appointment as defense ministers (Barnes and O'Brien 2018) and foreign affairs ministers (Bashevkin 2018); there is still little research on women's access to appointment as treasury ministers.[6] The gendered nature of specific cabinet posts is an important research question, but it is not addressed in *Cabinets, Ministers, and Gender*. Nor do we consider the policy implications of women's cabinet inclusion (Annesley and Gains 2010; Atchison and Downs 2009). Answering questions about policy outcomes and their relationship to numbers of women and men in cabinets would have required a different methodology and database. As important as research on portfolio allocation and policy impact is, this was simply beyond the scope of our project. We hope that *Cabinets, Ministers, and Gender* can provide a foundation for comparative public policy scholars to address the implications of increasing numbers of women in cabinets and particularly the policy consequences of gender parity cabinets.

Finally, the time frame for our data concludes in 2016. *Cabinets, Ministers, and Gender* does not include analysis of the US cabinet appointments in 2017, following the 2016 presidential election. Theresa May's post-election cabinet following the 2017 UK general elections is similarly outside the scope of this book, as is the cabinet, with a super-majority of female ministers, formed by Spanish prime minister Pedro Sánchez after the 2018 elections. We leave these cabinets and the process of their formation for further, future research.

---

[5] We discuss variation in such appointments in Chapter 9 but do not consider the extent to which these are powerful, central, and exclusionary.

[6] Among our seven cases, no woman has ever held the position of minister of finance (Australia, Canada, Chile, Germany, Spain), chancellor of the exchequer (UK), or US secretary of the treasury in the time period under investigation.

Acknowledgments

Cabinets, Ministers, and Gender is the culmination of an international feminist research project. We are feminist political scientists based in three different countries, first inspired to work together by a workshop on feminist institutionalism organized by Professor Louise Chappell in March 2010 in Sydney, Australia. Later that year, our plan to undertake this project took shape over discussions at the annual meetings of the American Political Science Association, in Washington, DC. Since that beginning, we have met multiple times in six different countries (the United States, the United Kingdom, Italy, Spain, Canada, and Sweden) to construct the research design, to develop the model of cabinet formation, to identify where and how the cabinet construction process might be gendered, to organize a cabinets database, a media database, and an interview database, and to discuss, in comparative perspective, cross-national differences in procedures, conventions, and outcomes.

No research project of this scope can be completed without the support of others, and our project was no exception. This book would not have been possible without the graciousness and willingness of many people who, despite leading enormously busy lives, were willing to grant interviews and discuss at length the intricacies of cabinets, gender, and executive politics in their countries. Although we cannot name them here, we thank them for sharing their knowledge with us. Susan Franceschet would also like to thank the following people in Chile and Spain for being willing to discuss politics with her and also for help in identifying potential interviewees: María Bustelo, María de los Angeles Fernández Ramil, Emanuela Lombardo, Marcela Ríos Tobar, Juan Rodríguez Teruel, and Tània Verge. Claire Annesley would like to thank Louise Chappell, Sandra Kolnik, and Caroline Adams for their assistance with organizing some interviews.

Our students were also important to the progress of our work; they collected and organized media data and constructed cabinet histories for our seven countries. Karen Beckwith worked with CWRU undergraduates Olivia Ortega, Kirsten Costedio, Rita Maricocchi, and Gillian Prater-Lee; their work was funded by the CWRU Department of Political Science's

Undergraduate Research and Mentoring Assistantship Program. Research assistance for Susan Franceschet was provided by Elizabeth Pando Burciaga and Mariana Hipólito Ramos Mota and was funded by Canada's Social Sciences and Humanities Research Council, and Claire Annesley received research assistance from Emmy Eklundh and Tomas Maltby at the University of Manchester and Adam Ahmet at the University of Sussex.

Along the way our research has received crucial financial support from a variety of sources. At the outset, we were fortunate to be awarded a European Consortium for Political Research Sessions grant, allowing us to spend five days in May 2011 at the European University Institute in Fiesole, Italy, hosted by Professor Peter Mair, a colleague and a friend, whom we thank now and whom we still miss. Professor Isabelle Engeli, now at the University of Bath, joined us at the EUI; her contributions at this stage were key to the development of the project. We also benefited from the serendipitous presence at the EUI of Professors Melinda Adams and John Scherpereel, with whom we spent an afternoon discussing our project and their related research on gender and cabinets.

At the conclusion of our project, with a nearly finished book manuscript in hand, we had the privilege of being invited to convene a manuscript workshop at the University of Uppsala in Sweden. Receiving the 2016 Johann Skytte manuscript workshop award allowed us to bring together 15 international scholars of executive politics, gender and politics, and institutionalism, for a four-day critical discussion of our manuscript in draft. We particularly thank Professor Elin Bjarnegård, University of Uppsala, for organizing the workshop, and those who came from around the world to participate: Meryl Kenny, Matthew Kerby, Vivien Lowndes, Diana O'Brien, Juan Rodríguez Teruel, and John Scherpereel. We also thank participants from Sweden: Christina Bergqvist, Josefina Erikson, Lenita Friedenvall, Cecilia Josefsson, Thomas Persson, Pernilla Tuneberger, and Pär Zetterberg.

In addition to the ECPR and the Johan Skytte Foundation, the American Political Science Association supported our work with two research grants, one from the Fund for the Study of Women and Politics and the other from the Presidency Research Fund. Susan Franceschet's field research in Chile and Spain was funded by an Insight Grant from the Social Sciences and Humanities Research Council of Canada (SSHRC); she also benefited from a Calgary Institute of Humanities Fellowship in 2014 and spent 2016 as a Visiting Professor at the University of Sussex. Claire Annesley received funding from the University of Manchester's Investing in Success and Strategic Investment schemes (2012, 2014). Karen Beckwith's research was supported by funds associated with her endowed Chair, funded by the former Flora Stone Mather Alumnae Association and, for undergraduate research assistance, by the CWRU Department of Political Science. In the early stages of our project, we were also encouraged by, and honored with, the 2011 Carrie Chapman Catt Prize, awarded by the Catt Center for Women and Politics, Iowa State University, for significant research on women and politics.

Along the way, we have presented our research at numerous international conferences, workshops, and universities in Canada, Chile, Japan, Spain, Sweden, the United Kingdom, and the United States. Specifically, we presented papers from our work in progress at multiple annual meetings of the American Political Science Association, the Midwest Political Science Association, the ECPR Joint Sessions of Workshops, the biennial European Conferences on Politics and Gender, and several workshops associated with Georgina Waylen's European Research Council project "Understanding Institutional Change," which served as a friendly but rigorous venue for feedback on our work in progress. We have also benefited from the opportunity to present our work as lectures or seminars at various universities, including the University of Minnesota and Rice University in the United States; Birkbeck, University of London, Queen Mary, University of London, University of East Anglia, University of Cambridge, University of Newcastle-upon-Tyne, University of Bristol, and University of Sussex in the United Kingdom; Pompeo Fabra University in Spain; Diego Portales University in Chile; and Ochanomizu University in Japan.

Throughout this project, we have also received extensive feedback, critique, and encouragement from our colleagues, peers, and students around the world, who have been generous and unrelenting in their attention to our work. For this, we are immensely grateful. For interest in and support of our project from the early stages, we are grateful to Professors Louise Chappell (University of New South Wales), Sarah Childs (Birkbeck, University of London), Francesca Gains (University of Manchester), Mary Fainsod Katzenstein (Cornell University), Fiona Mackay (University of Edinburgh), Rainbow Murray (Queen Mary, University of London), Peter Siavelis (Wake Forest University), and Georgina Waylen (University of Manchester). Despite shamefully short notice, Professors John Scherpereel (James Madison University) and Laurel Weldon (Simon Fraser University) wrote letters of support for our second APSA Centennial Grant. Conversations with Melinda Adams, Lisa Baldez, Gretchen Bauer, Maria Escobar-Lemmon, Christina Ewig, Meryl Kenny, Vivien Lowndes, Lanny Martin, Carol Mershon, Diana O'Brien, Brenda O'Neill, Jennifer Piscopo, John Scherpereel, Leslie Schwindt-Bayer, Michelle Taylor-Robinson, Gwynn Thomas, Melanee Thomas, Laurel Weldon, Christina Wolbrecht, and Christina Xydias also challenged us and enriched our work; we thank them for their patience and their insights. Karen Beckwith is grateful to Professor Matthew Hodgetts, CWRU, for some very last-minute research assistance and an invigorating discussion about Canadian cabinet formation on a late Friday afternoon. Susan Franceschet is grateful to all her colleagues at the University of Calgary, and particularly to David Stewart, who was always willing to share his vast knowledge of Canadian politics, and Jack Lucas, who helped us enormously with a strategy to visually present the patterns in our data. Claire Annesley is grateful to her colleagues and friends at the University of Manchester and University of Sussex.

We thank the anonymous reviewers of the book manuscript and two article manuscripts for providing detailed, rigorous, critical comments that shaped and improved our book. We are enormously grateful to Angela Chnapko at Oxford University Press whose enthusiasm, professionalism, and continued support for our work enabled us to get to this stage. We hope we have vindicated our reviewers' and Angela's faith in us, as we strove to incorporate their insights into the final manuscript.

Finally, we recognize that we are standing on the shoulders of giants, whose excellent comparative work on women and cabinets precedes our own, of whom there are many. We recognize and thank, in particular, Rebecca Howard Davis, author of *Women and Power in Parliamentary Democracies* (1997), and, more recently, Maria Escobar-Lemmon and Michelle Taylor-Robinson, who wrote *Women in Presidential Cabinets* (2016). Their work provides the foundation for this book. In short, we thank all those who have contributed to *Cabinets, Ministers, and Gender*, across these several years (and we apologize to those whose contributions we may have failed to recognize here). Whatever flaws remain this book cannot be attributed to them and are our sole responsibility.

Cabinets, Ministers, and Gender could not have been written by a single scholar; it took the three of us. The collaboration required to produce this book forged our strong feminist friendship. Across the past several years, in meetings, Skype sessions, and emails, we have celebrated personal milestones—promotions, new jobs, new grandchildren—and have listened to concerns about domestic politics, our work, and our families. Although we will miss the project meetings, we are thankful for our enduring friendship.

Claire Annesley would like to thank Rorden Wilkinson for his rock-solid love and support; she dedicates this book to their children Holly and Ewan. Karen Beckwith is profoundly grateful to her family—nuclear and extended—for their support, helpful distraction from work, patience, tolerance, and celebration at this book's completion. She dedicates this book to her grandchildren, Lila, Graham, and Hunter. Susan Franceschet is deeply grateful for the boundless support, love, and friendship of Antonio Franceschet, and dedicates this book to him.

Claire Annesley, University of Sussex
Karen Beckwith, Case Western Reserve University
Susan Franceschet, University of Calgary
January 30, 2019

1

Explaining Gendered Patterns
of Cabinet Formation

Cabinets lie at the center of governing power. For politicians, appointment to cabinet may be the highpoint of a career, providing additional prestige and salary benefits, as well as the opportunity to set policy agendas and make important political decisions. In both presidential and parliamentary democracies, cabinet ministers enjoy considerable status and prestige, and are often more visible and well known than members of legislatures. Ministers are "visible, glamorous and important" (Blondel 1985, 3).

Ministers are also gendered. Examining cabinet appointments across time reveals that historically most ministers have been men, as have the heads of government who appointed them. In this book, we explore three questions: Why are more men than women appointed to cabinet? Why are women more likely to be appointed to cabinet in some countries than others? Why has women's presence in cabinet varied across time? Answering these questions reveals how the process of cabinet formation is gendered, providing men and women with different (and unequal) opportunities to be appointed ministers. In this book, we reveal the gendered dimensions of cabinet appointments through an in-depth analysis of seven countries: Australia, Canada, Chile, Germany, Spain, the United Kingdom, and the United States. We constructed a data set of ministerial appointments to post-election cabinets when a prime minister or president has the opportunity of forming a cabinet de novo. We track all cabinets formed from the point at which the first female minister was appointed in each country to the last post-election cabinet formed in each country before the end of 2016. Across all seven countries in this time frame, 127 cabinets were formed. Of these, 33 included only men as ministers, or 26.82 percent of all cabinets. Although a total of 2,229 ministerial appointments were made, of these, just 294 appointments went to women, or 13.19 percent of ministerial appointments. It is clear, though unsurprising, once women were included in cabinets, men have nonetheless predominated in cabinets in these seven countries for multiple decades.

Among our country cases, only Germany has consistently included at least one woman in post-election cabinets for more than 50 years.

These seven countries are useful cases for understanding women's presence in newly formed cabinets and, we argue, for understanding the gendered process of cabinet formation. We discuss our case justification in greater depth in Chapter 2. For now, while our data show that men are predominant in cabinet appointments within each of these countries, the data also reveal significant cross-national variation in women's representation in cabinets. For example, in terms of *timing*, women joined the ranks of ministers as early as 1929 in the United Kingdom and the 1930s in the United States and Spain. Elsewhere, women were entirely absent from cabinets until the late 1950s (Canada) and early 1960s (Germany).

Variation also appears in terms of the *magnitude* of women's cabinet presence. We categorize the magnitude of women's presence as an ordinal variable, ranging from very low (0 to 9.9 percent of cabinet), low (10 to 19.9 percent), medium (20 to 29.9 percent), high (30 percent or more), and parity (50 percent +/−1). In Australia, the United Kingdom, and the United States, women's presence in cabinet has remained in the low to medium category, while in Canada, Chile, Germany, and Spain, women's representation has reached high magnitude. More important, in this latter group of countries, parity has been achieved at least once in each country. These varying patterns challenge us to explain why more women are appointed to cabinet in some countries than in others.

Our cases also reveal important differences in the *persistence* of women's representation in cabinets. The appointment of the first female minister was not always a decisive turning point that marked women's subsequent cabinet inclusion. Even after the historic breakthrough of a first female minister, all-male cabinets continued to appear in all countries, with the exception of Germany.[1] As Table 1.1 shows, in countries such as the United Kingdom, whole decades passed between the appointment of the first woman to cabinet and subsequent appointments of female ministers. Our data also show more positive patterns of persistence. Once women's presence has increased beyond one female minister, especially since the 1980s, it has tended to do so in a continuous fashion. Increases in magnitude tend to be sustained, with minimal backsliding. We call this phenomenon the "concrete floor." The term

---

[1] Among our cases, only Germany has consistently included at least one woman in initial cabinets for more than 50 years (since 1961).

Table 1.1 First Female Ministers and Last All-Male Cabinets, by Country

Country	Year First Female Minister in Cabinet	Year Last All-Male Post-Election Cabinet	Years between Appointment of First Woman to Cabinet and Last All-Male Cabinet
Germany	1961	1957	+4
Canada	1957	1968	−10
Chile*	1952	1970	−18
Australia	1949	1993	−44
United States	1933	1981	−47
Spain*	1936	1986	−50
United Kingdom	1929	1987	−58

* Includes only democratically elected governments

"concrete floor" describes the minimum proportion or number of women for that ministerial team to be perceived as legitimate.

For each of our cases, we identify a point at which a selector (or selectors) increases, often significantly, the proportion of women in cabinet, unleashing a dynamic whereby subsequent selectors, regardless of party, perceive costs to violating the threshold set by their predecessors. We operationalize the "concrete floor" as a three-step process: (1) a selector *initiates* the appointment of women (in any magnitude), which (2) is *confirmed* at the same or higher magnitude by the subsequent selector, and (3) is *sustained* at the same or higher magnitude by a third selector. Each step in the process requires an election that brings in a new selector. We identify concrete floors in each of our country cases and explain how they emerge and how they function as mechanisms for continuity in women's representation. A final goal of our study is to explain why concrete floors vary across our countries.

Why Are More Men Than Women Appointed to Cabinet?

The existing scholarship on gender and cabinet ministers provides substantial insight into ministerial appointments. First, this research confirms that few ministers are women. The relative absence of women from cabinets has meant that gender scholars have focused more attention on women's representation in parliaments, where numbers grew significantly by the 1980s in much of the world. More recent gains in women's cabinet representation have prompted an expanding research agenda examining all aspects of women's involvement in cabinet, from gendered patterns of appointment and removal,[2] to gendered patterns of portfolio allocation (Barnes and O'Brien 2018; Escobar-Lemmon and Taylor-Robinson 2005), and gendered styles of policymaking (Atchison and Downs 2009; Atchison 2015; Escobar-Lemmon, Schwindt-Bayer, and Taylor-Robinson 2014).

Despite a rapidly expanding body of scholarship, there are two aspects of existing work that our book seeks to address. First, the findings of existing studies are mixed and therefore inconclusive when it comes to determining which factors account for larger proportions of women in cabinet. Second, along with scholars of ministerial recruitment, gender scholars have paid less attention to the *process* of cabinet appointment and more attention to outcomes, leaving us with gaps in knowledge about why fewer women than men become ministers.

Gender and politics scholars have employed supply and demand models, developed in research on legislative recruitment and its gendered consequences (e.g., Norris and Lovenduski 1995) to test four factors related to women's cabinet representation. In translating supply and demand models to cabinet, scholars operationalize supply factors as (1) the proportion of women in the legislature and (2) the type of political system (presidential or parliamentary). Demand factors include (3) party ideology and (4) the sex of the selector. The evidence that supply factors affect women's cabinet representation is mixed. While most studies find a positive correlation between the percentage of women in the legislature and the percentage of women in cabinet (Bauer and Okpotor 2013; Claveria 2014; Davis 1997; Krook and O'Brien 2012; Stockemer 2017), others find a relationship only in parliamentary but not presidential systems (Whitford, Wilkinson, and Ball 2007), and Bego, examining post-communist countries in Central and Eastern Europe, finds that larger percentages of women in parliament only predict the inclusion of at least one woman in cabinet (2014, 354). Adams, Scherpereel, and Jacobs (2016) examine women's legislative and cabinet representation

---

[2] The preponderance of research on gender and cabinets focuses on women's appointment to and, to a lesser extent, removal from ministerships. See Adams, Scherpereel, and Jacobs (2016); Bauer and Okpotor (2015); Bauer and Tremblay (2011); Bego (2014); Claveria (2015); Davis (1997); Escobar-Lemmon and Taylor-Robinson (2005, 2009, 2016); Krook and O'Brien (2012); Reyes-Housholder (2016); Reynolds (1999); Scherpereel, Adams, and Jacobs (2018); Siaroff (2000); Stockemer (2017); Whitford, Wilkinson, and Ball (2007).

in sub-Saharan Africa, finding a complex rather than straightforward relationship between women's parliamentary presence and the number of female ministers. The evidence with respect to system type and cabinet appointments is likewise inconclusive. Most studies find that women's cabinet presence is greater in non-parliamentary systems (Krook and O'Brien 2012) or countries with specialist recruitment norms, whereby ministers are selected for their policy expertise (Bauer and Okpotor 2013; Claveria 2014; Davis 1997), but a recent study of 194 countries finds that parliamentary systems have more women in cabinet than presidential systems (Stockemer 2017). Reynolds' (1999) comparative research involving 180 countries found no effect for political system type.

Findings about the impact of demand-side factors are likewise inconclusive. Most studies find that leftist selectors appoint more women (Claveria 2014; Krook and O'Brien 2012; Siaroff 2000), but Davis finds that party ideology has no effect (1997, 58), explaining that leftist leaders appoint more women to cabinet because there are more women in parliament when left parties are in government. She concludes that "ideology plays an indirect role . . . it does not appear to play a direct role in recruitment of women to cabinet office" (1997, 65). Bego's study of post-communist cases likewise finds no effect for party ideology (2014, 354–355). Studies of how selector sex affects women's representation point in different directions. Davis (1997) and Reyes-Housholder (2016) find that female selectors appoint more women to their cabinets, but other studies challenge such findings (Krook and O'Brien 2012). O'Brien and her coauthors (2015) find that female party leaders in parliamentary democracies include fewer women than do their male counterparts. In sum, despite significant efforts by gender scholars to determine the correlates of women's cabinet representation, the research findings are inconclusive.

Research into ministerial recruitment that does not focus on gender shares many similarities with studies of political elites more generally, focusing attention on *who* legislators and ministers are, rather than how they achieve their office. Studies of cabinet ministers emphasize their shared personal and political characteristics, including age, gender, years of parliamentary experience or former political experience, and, above all, party allegiance. Most studies use data on the social characteristics and political backgrounds of ministers to identify the common characteristics of ministers in specific countries or regions (Blondel and Thiebault 1991; Dowding and Dumont 2009, 2015; Escobar-Lemmon and Taylor-Robinson 2016; Vogel 2009).

Such studies confirm that men are vastly over-represented among ministers (Blondel 1985; Davis 1997).

Such studies tell us little about why the process of ministerial recruitment produces such skewed outcomes. Looking only at outcomes, that is, who ministers are, does not explain why some individuals are deemed qualified for ministerial office but others are not. The ministerial outcomes approach looks at ministers as an aggregate—appointments across time or across multiple countries, but this approach cannot take into account the fact that ministers are recruited as part of a discrete team. Ministers' individual experience or expertise matters not only for its own sake, but also because of what it contributes to that team. That means some qualified individuals might be ruled out because there is someone with a similar profile already in cabinet. Looking primarily at outcomes also fails to help us explain the gendered composition of cabinets. As early as 1985, Blondel expressed disappointment that, despite pressures from second wave feminism, few women had made it to the ranks of cabinet (1985, 30), and he remained pessimistic that the numbers of female ministers would increase.

Explaining why women are disadvantaged requires a focus on the process of cabinet appointments. While the ministerial recruitment literature has little to say about process, the government formation literature is deeply concerned with the procedural and temporal dimensions of forming cabinets, although few scholars working in this area focus on the gendered outcomes of government formation. Researchers have examined the process through which certain combinations of parties come together to form a government in relation to coalition building. Game theoretical studies of government formation such as Riker (1980) and Laver and Shepsle (1996) see coalition formation as a process strongly guided by preferences and strategic decisions made by rational actors for office-seeking or policy-seeking motives. For them, the focus is on how politicians as rational actors bargain and negotiate the process of government formation to secure their party in the new government. This model for the process of government formation is most explicitly concerned with the partisan identity of those who form government (Laver and Shepsle 1996, 57), wherein politicians are primarily viewed as agents of the party to which they belong (Laver and Shepsle 1996, 42). They are less interested in the selection of individual ministers once the partisan composition of government has been decided. Although these studies help us to understand general strategic calculations involved in cabinet formation, they do not explain the gendered nature of the process or the gendered outcomes.

While government formation studies tend to emphasize the strategic nature of the process, wherein party leaders and elites are rational actors seeking most the favorable outcome for their party, some scholars emphasize the rule-bound nature of this process. Strøm, Budge, and Laver challenge as "hardly realistic" (1994, 307) the premise of cabinet formation in coalition theory that treats political parties as if they are "unconstrained players in an institution-free world" (1994, 303). Instead, they argue that coalition formation is often "severely constrained by institutional arrangements and prior commitments" (1994, 303). For them, "government formation and mainte-nance are highly structured processes, and a variety of institutional features impinge on the choice set available to government *formateurs*" (1994, 305). The primary institutional constraints on coalition formation relate to the size or composition of the executive, rules of government investiture, and recog-nition rules (1994, 310–312).[3]

We find this recognition of the institutional context of the process of gov-ernment formation useful. Although constitutions are relatively silent on the formation of cabinet, the absence of written rules does not mean that the process of cabinet formation operates devoid of rules. While Strøm, Budge, and Laver (1994) focus on formal rules, albeit distinguishing between hard and soft constraints (309), other authors acknowledge the importance of in-formal rules. According to De Winter, "the process of government formation is governed by a restricted number of formal provisions and a wide variety of informal rules" (1995, 122). Similarly, Mershon's study of coalition for-mation acknowledges that, in the process of coalition bargaining, informal rules emerge alongside—and often at variance with—formal constitutional constraints. She argues, "politicians create informal rules to alter formal institutions that do not function to their benefit" (1994, 40). Politicians have incentives to invent informal rules.

Blondel (1985) also recognizes the importance of formal and informal rules in the selection of ministers. Rules are established "in order to give political advancement a more orderly outlook"; there must be "some recog-nition of the routes that should be followed to become a minister" (1985, 13). Blondel alludes to informal rules when he identifies various "profiles" of routes to ministerial office. These profiles "acquire the value of myths, in that they are felt to reinforce certain 'ideals' or 'principles' that political systems

---

[3] For discussion of country-specific rules of government formation, see Dowding and Dumont (2009); Rasch, Martin, and Cheibub (2015).

and its leaders attempt to extol" (1985, 14–15). Significantly for under-standing how gender functions in cabinet construction, Blondel recognizes how these profiles "also constitute many filters, which let some individuals come to the top while others are prevented from being selected" (1985, 15).

Drawing on the insights from existing scholarship, we investigate and ex-plain ministerial recruitment as a process, and, more important, a process in which gender, understood as ideas about men's and women's entitlement to political power, operates and shapes outcomes at each stage. The process of cabinet appointment begins with the results of an election and ends with the formal announcement of a cabinet by the president or prime minister.[4] We consider the entirety of the process to be strongly bound by rules, although, as we explain later, many of these rules are not codified in constitutions or statutes. Throughout the book, we identify all the sets of rules that determine the process of cabinet formation in seven democratic countries. We include rules that are codified and officially enforceable, as well as rules that are un-written yet routinely observed. Some of these rules are at the system level, and others are at the party level. We identify the components of these sets of rules that advantage men and inhibit women's access to ministerial office—in other words, rules that actively gender the construction of cabinets.

We further view ministerial recruitment as a process involving two sets of political actors: the selectors, including all actors with the authority to decide who will be invited to join the ministerial team; and the *ministrables*, defined as those political actors who are both eligible and qualified to serve in cab-inet as ministers. While these political actors are strongly rule-bound, they are nonetheless able to use their agency strategically to work with or around the rules to shape outcomes in ways that reinforce or challenge gender hierarchies. Explicating the rules of ministerial recruitment will help us an-swer our two other research questions.

Why Are Women More Likely to be Appointed to Cabinet in Some Countries Than in Others?

Existing studies, and our own data, tell us that more women are appointed to cabinets in some countries than others. But we do not yet fully know

---

[4] In this book, we do not include cabinet reshuffles or cabinets formed following a change in party leadership in the absence of an election.

why. Some studies offer rich detail on a series of individual countries, including detail about the presence of women, but they are not strictly comparative (Dowding and Dumont 2009, 2015). In the gender and politics literature, many studies are comparative, exploring variation in women's appointment to cabinet across countries. Some studies compare within a single region (Adams, Scherpereel, and Jacobs 2016; Bego 2014; Davis 1997; Bauer and Okpotor 2013; Escobar-Lemmon and Taylor-Robinson 2005, 2009). Most recently, Escobar-Lemmon and Taylor-Robinson's *Women in Presidential Cabinets* (2016) provides a comparative focus of the backgrounds, connections, and credentials of cabinet ministers in five presidential democracies in the Americas: Argentina, Chile, Colombia, Costa Rica, and the United States. Other studies offer a more global comparative perspective (Bauer and Tremblay 2011; Claveria 2014; Krook and O'Brien 2012; Reynolds 1999; Scherpereel, Adams, and Jacobs 2018; Siaroff 2000; and Whitford, Wilkinson, and Ball 2007). These studies have considerably expanded our knowledge about women's presence in ministerial office. But overall there is no single approach or consensus in findings, as scholars adopt different research designs, test different hypotheses, and operationalize differently the variables they believe to be relevant to explaining cross-national differences in women's cabinet presence.

As noted earlier, cross-national variation in women's cabinet presence is often attributed to differences in system type or modes of qualification. Researchers hypothesize, for example, that women are more likely to be recruited to cabinets in presidential systems because selectors are not limited to appointing from among members of parliaments (where there are always fewer women than men) when appointing ministers. According to Whitford et al. (2007, 564), "in a presidential system, the executive is less constrained in the appointments they make to cabinet positions and is free to place women in cabinet-level positions." Scholars who opt instead to distinguish generalist from specialist recruitment norms are looking at something rather different, namely, whether ministers are recruited primarily for their political skills and experience, or for their policy-specific expertise.

Some cabinet scholars, including Rebecca Davis, acknowledge the artificiality of the generalist versus specialist distinction, noting, "in every cabinet system at any given time, there is a mix of ministerial backgrounds" (1997, 38). Davis also notes that "[d]ifferentiation between generalist and specialist systems does not mean that specialization does not occur in generalist systems or that generalists to not serve in specialist systems" (1997, 38–39). Her study of women's presence in cabinet in 15 Western European countries uses the generalist–specialist variable, but she ranks rather than dichotomizes her cases. Other researchers have used system type (Siaroff 2000) or rules about incompatibility of holding a cabinet portfolio and sitting in parliament (Bauer and Okpotor 2015) as a proxy for distinguishing between generalist and specialist recruitment practices. Whether scholars use political system type of parliamentary versus presidential, or recruitment criterion of generalist versus specialist, both parliamentary and generalist recruiting methods limit the supply of women.

Our data set includes seven countries: two presidential democracies (Chile and the United States); two parliamentary democracies (Germany and Spain); and three Westminster parliamentary systems (Australia, Canada, and the United Kingdom). There is no clear cross-national pattern of women's cabinet inclusion in regard to political system type or recruitment criteria. Chile, with a presidential system, has had a parity cabinet, as have Germany and Spain, parliamentary systems, and Canada, with a Westminster system. In the US presidential system, rates of women's recruitment to cabinet have remained comparatively low, as they have in the Westminster systems of the United Kingdom and Australia. Clearly, there is much that we do not know. Explicating the rules of ministerial recruitment specific to each of these counties, and the parties that form governments, as well as how the rules are gendered, will give us a more nuanced explanation for cross-national patterns of women's presence in cabinets and for the gendered process of cabinet formation across countries.

Why Has Women's Presence in Cabinet Varied across Time?

Because many gender and politics studies are cross-sectional rather than longitudinal, increases in women's presence in cabinet have yet to be fully explained. Many longitudinal studies (Claveria 2014; Escobar-Lemmon and Taylor-Robinson 2005) begin their analysis in the 1980s or 1990s, when women's cabinet presence was becoming more common, but they do not seek to explain the long periods of time when women were absent from cabinet and when women's presence ranged between zero and one minister.

By identifying the rules of ministerial recruitment and how they are used and shaped by empowered and strategic actors, we hope not only to show what the rules are, but also to identify whether, when, and how they have changed over time and what impact rule changes have on women's cabinet presence. To understand how rules change, we draw insights from scholars who have been explicitly longitudinal in their approach. For example, Juan Rodríguez Teruel (2011a) has found that, over time, more ministers in Spain are being recruited from outside parliament and from regional political structures. Similarly, Kaiser and Fischer (2009) note the growing importance of regional political structures as a route into Germany's federal cabinet. Other studies demonstrate the growing power of presidents and prime ministers over time (e.g., Poguntke and Webb 2005). Although these studies do not deal with gender, they explain changes in rules of ministerial selection and qualification, which, in turn, may help to explain shifting patterns of women's recruitment.

Other studies address over-time variation in women's presence in cabinet (Claveria 2014; Davis 1997; Escobar-Lemmon and Taylor-Robinson 2005), finding that patterns of women's ministerial appointment are more volatile than those for parliamentary elections (e.g., Scherpereel, Adams, and Jacob 2018). Election outcomes rarely lead to the complete removal of all members of parliament in a single party; election loss is usually only partial for any parliamentary party.[5] Although an election loss may still leave a party with a degree of continuity of members in parliament, at the cabinet level an election loss means a complete change of ministerial personnel. The volatility of cabinets compared to parliaments means that conclusions about women's cabinet presence focusing on a single point in time are problematic, especially if system-level factors are being tested (Bauer and Okpotor 2013; Krook and O'Brien 2012; Reynolds 1999; Siaroff 2000; Whitford et al. 2007).

Scherpereel et al. (2018, 3) address volatility in women's cabinet presence, identifying differences as "backsliding" and "climbing." They define backsliding as "the difference in representation between $t-1$ and t if the change is negative; climbing is defined as the difference in representation between $t-1$ and t if the change is positive." The authors find differences between advances in women's legislative representation and women's cabinet presence, with "women's legislative representation . . . characterized by a

---

[5] A notable exception is the 1993 federal election in Canada. Prior to the election, the governing party, the Progressive Conservatives, held 156 seats. The party lost all but two seats in the election.

ratchet effect" and women's cabinet representation characterized by a "*see-saw effect*—an asymmetric process in which one year's representational gains erode in subsequent years" (2018, 1; emphasis in original).

In contrast to Scherpereel et al. (2018) we find little evidence of significant backsliding across time in women's inclusion in cabinets across our cases. Rather, we find that over time, gains in women's ministerial recruitment tend to be sustained across initial cabinets formed post-election. Once a prime minister or president appoints a woman (or some women) to cabinet, subsequent selectors in the same country tend to appoint at the same magnitude; some even increase the number of women included in cabinet. As noted earlier, we call this lack of volatility in numbers of women appointed to cabinet as the "concrete floor."

Data, Approach, and Main Contributions

The existing scholarship on ministerial recruitment equips us with the initial tools for explaining the patterns we see in our data: women are under-represented in cabinet; under-representation varies cross-nationally; and it changes over time. The following section sets out in more detail the patterns our data reveal, the approach we adopt to explain them, and the contribution we make to the scholarship on cabinets and executives.

The Patterns in the Data: Timing, Magnitude, and Persistence

We collected data on every post-election cabinet in seven countries, from the date of the appointment of the first female cabinet minister in each county to the end of 2016. By post-election cabinet, we mean the first cabinet appointed following a general election. The decision to focus only on post-election cabinets stems from our starting assumption that cabinets are not simply a collection of unrelated individuals; rather, a cabinet is a team made up of a collectivity of persons who bring different skills and talents to government. As a result, in constructing our data set, we focus on those ministers who are appointed to a cabinet together, as a team, at a one specific point in time, namely, following an election when a leader is forming the initial cabinet. When forming their initial cabinets, selectors are making and balancing numerous appointments, as many as 30 in some cases. Cabinet appointments made after the initial cabinet formation often involve considerations beyond the control of the prime minister or president and may involve factors that are unrelated to the politics of cabinet appointment, such as the death or resignation of a minister. Moreover, cabinet reshuffles normally involve only a handful of aspirant ministers; hence, competition for a small number of posts may be higher than is the case in formation of post-election cabinets.

Finally, for parliamentary systems, our data set includes only those cabinets formed by prime ministers following a general election. We are not counting those cases where new prime ministers emerge following the resignation of a prime minister or a party leadership contest. We exclude cabinets formed, for example, by Prime Minister Kim Campbell in Canada in 1993 or Prime Minister Theresa May in the United Kingdom in 2016. Both leaders assumed the prime ministership after winning party leadership contests. Neither leader was positioned to appoint a completely new cabinet, nor were they authorized to do so by the general electorate. When new prime ministers emerge via party leadership contests and subsequently win a general election, we include the cabinet formed after that election, such as the 2010 election of Australian prime minister Julia Gillard.

We count ministers rather than portfolios. For this study, we are more interested in the gendered inclusion of women in cabinet and less concerned with the distribution of cabinet responsibilities;[6] where a cabinet minister holds more than one portfolio, we count that minister, male or female, only once. We acknowledge that in parliamentary systems, prime ministers are also members of the cabinet; however, we do not include prime ministers in our count of cabinet members. Prime ministers achieve their position through a different procedure than ministers and are selected as party leaders by their party selectorate, authorized thereafter by success in a general election. Prime ministers are the selectors of ministers for their cabinet, but they do not select themselves.[7] We focus on the appointment process and on the selector separately, as an actor who works with the rules to select ministers rather than as a member of the cabinet.

---

[6] For recent research on the gendered distribution of cabinet responsibilities, see Barnes and O'Brien (2018); Escobar-Lemmon and Taylor-Robinson (2016).

[7] Thus, for example, we would categorize Thatcher's cabinets as having no women since, as selector, Thatcher is not counted among those selected.

For the purposes of this book, we count and compare the number of women appointed to each post-election cabinet and calculate the share of women in each cabinet as a percentage. Our data set contains the size of cabinet and number of women appointed following all democratic elections upon the appointment of the first female cabinet member. This means that the number of cabinets formed in each country varies according to (1) the date of the first female minister appointed, (2) the onset and the duration of democracy, and (3) how many elections have been held. We coded each post-election cabinet by the party allegiance of the main selector, as left, right, or center and by the selector's sex, either male or female.

An important goal of this book is to identify changing patterns in the recruitment of women to cabinet across time. Although most longitudinal studies begin their analysis in the 1980s or 1990s, when women's cabinet presence was becoming more common (Claveria 2014; Escobar-Lemmon and Taylor-Robinson 2005, 2016), we take a longer historical view of gendered appointments over time, including long periods of time when women were absent from cabinet and when women's presence ranged between zero and one minister. Our temporal frame of analysis begins with the appointment of the first female minister in each country (see Table 1.1). Women's first inclusion in cabinets ranges from as early as 1929 in the United Kingdom and 1933 in the United States to as recently as 1957 in Canada and 1961 in Germany. These dates are significant turning points in the composition of each country's cabinet, representing the first time the practice of appointing only men to cabinet is broken. It is important to note, however, that even after a woman was initially appointed to cabinet, all-male cabinets continued to appear regularly in many countries, and it took decades for women's inclusion to move beyond a single token female minister (see Table 1.1). To detect and explain patterns over time, we classify women's cabinet representation based on three dimensions: *timing*, *magnitude*, and *persistence*.

By *timing*, we are interested in how early or how late women's inclusion into cabinets beyond a token presence occurs. In other words, we want to know when selectors stop appointing cabinets with zero or one female minister. By *magnitude*, we mean the percentages and numbers of women and men in cabinet. We categorize the magnitude of women's cabinet presence as an ordinal variable, ranging from (1) very low (0 to 9.9 percent of cabinet), (2) low (10 to 19.9 percent), (3) medium (20 to

29.9 percent), to (4) high (30 percent or more) and (5) parity 50 percent +/−1 minister. We construct these categories from the research on women's parliamentary presence, where "the story of the story of critical mass" (Dahlerup 2006) identified 30 percent as an important turning point for women's political representation, although not necessarily one that would produce substantive changes in political outcomes. At the lower end, we categorize women's cabinet representation as "very low" if women constitute fewer than 10 percent of cabinet ministers (see Dahlerup and Leyenaar 2013). This category reflects the reality of many government teams worldwide, where only one woman sits in the cabinet. Given the comparatively small size of cabinets (e.g., 15–25 ministers), once two or more women are appointed to cabinet, most country cases fall into the "low" or "medium" magnitude categories. Finally, by *persistence*, we are interested in how much backsliding occurs, that is, once reaching a new magnitude of women's inclusion, say, moving from the category of "low" to the "medium" category, does a country regress to a lower magnitude?

We categorize cabinets both by the number of women and the percentage of women within each, across time. Because cabinets are small (the average size of a cabinet in our data set is 18) and the size of cabinet can vary within countries, the number of ministers is as important to note as the percentage. A small positive change in the number of women can lead to a large change in their percentage representation within a cabinet, and a reduction in the size of the cabinet can lead to an increase in the percentage of women, even if the number of women remains constant. Finally, given the small size of cabinets (e.g., relative to parliaments), cabinets of uneven numbers cannot produce pure parity cabinets, that is, those in which numbers of women and men in cabinet are equal. As a result, we define *parity* cabinets as those in which women (or men) constitute a range of 50 percent +/−1 minister. For example, in Germany, Chancellor Gerhard Schröder's 2002 cabinet included six female ministers in a 13-member cabinet (46 percent). Because cabinets often contain an odd number of ministers, a perfect 50 percent representation of women (or men) is not possible. The addition of one more woman in cabinet would have increased the presence of female ministers to 53 percent. By identifying gender parity cabinets as a range of 50 percent +/−1, we are able reasonably to classify gender parity cabinets of odd as well as even numbers of ministers. As a result, we include Schröder's 2002 cabinet as an example of a gender parity cabinet.

Our data reveal two gendered patterns in terms of timing, persistence, and magnitude. In one group of countries—Canada, Germany, Spain, and Chile—women's cabinet inclusion beyond a single female minister is early, persistent, and of relatively high magnitude. Among this group of countries, the era of cabinets with zero or one female minister ended decisively, without regressing and regardless of the party of the selector. The last German post-election cabinet where women's presence was lower than 10 percent was in 1983; in Canada it was in 1980, and in Spain it was in 1986. Chile, which did not have democratically elected governments in the 1980s, left behind the era of very few women in cabinet in 1990, which was the last time when women constituted less than 10 percent of ministers. These countries also demonstrate a consistently upward trajectory since surpassing the "very low" threshold, reaching the "high magnitude" category of at least 30 percent by 1998 in Germany, 2000 in Chile, 2004 in Spain, and 2008 in Canada. Notably, each of these countries has had at least two cabinets with more than 30 percent women and each has had at least one gender parity cabinet.

The second group of countries—Australia, the United Kingdom, and the United States—displays a different gendered pattern. Although the United Kingdom (1929) and the United States (1933) experienced the earliest inclusion of a woman in cabinet, the appointment of more than one woman in any subsequent cabinet occurred significantly later. The inclusion of women in cabinet has been more uneven, in terms of persistence, and, with the exception of the United Kingdom's cabinet formed in 2015, has not reached the "high" category in terms of magnitude. Australia, the United Kingdom, and the United States were also the last countries to leave the "very low" category, with women constituting less than 10 percent of cabinet ministers as recently as the 1990s. Australia continued to have cabinets where women constituted fewer than 10 percent of ministers into the 1990s and as recently as 2013; women were present at the lowest levels in post-election cabinets in the United Kingdom until 1997, and in the United States until 1993.

It is also worth noting that in both Australia and the United States, a pattern of including zero or just one female minister was not broken decisively at one point in time. The US case is one of slow startup, with several all-male post-election cabinets (from 1961 to 1977, and in 1981); only in 1977 and from 1993 to the present have post-election US cabinets included more than one woman. None of these three countries has had a gender parity cabinet.

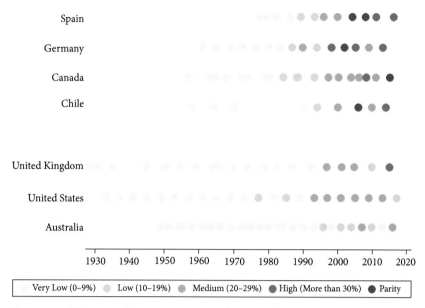

Figure 1.1. Women s cabinet appointments (magnitude percentage), across time by country.

These two patterns of women's inclusion in cabinet by timing, magnitude, and persistence are visually summarized in Figure 1.1.

Although our cases differ in terms of timing, magnitude, and persistence of women's inclusion in cabinets, the data also show at least one striking similarity: women's presence is increasing across all countries. Australia is an outlier in that it regressed to the "very low" magnitude category, dropping below 10 percent of women in cabinet in 1998 and 2013. Across all our other countries, every post-election cabinet since the early 1990s has included at least two women, and by the late 1990s, all countries (except Australia) have no post-election cabinets with fewer than three women. In fact, we find a clear pattern of moving with relative consistency from low to medium to high magnitude of women's presence in cabinet. There is no evidence of backsliding across more than one category (for example, from high back down to low). Likewise, although parity cabinets rarely follow each other in a consecutive fashion, especially when government changes hands, parity cabinets are likely to be followed by cabinets in which women are represented at the "high" or very close to high magnitude. Although the United States has yet to reach the "high" magnitude category, women's presence in post-election cabinets has ranged between three and four ministers for a period of more than 20 years (1993–2016). We are thus confronted with an important puzzle: Why do we see so little volatility in women's appointments to cabinet within each country given the structural potential for tremendous volatility?

Three Dimensions of Cabinet Appointments: Process, Actors, and Rules

To explain gendered patterns of ministerial recruitment cross-nationally and over time, we developed a model of cabinet appointment composed of three dimensions: (1) ministerial appointment is a dynamic *process* (2) involving two sets of *actors*, namely, selectors and ministrables, both of which are (3) governed by *rules* (many of which are unwritten). Explaining who becomes a minister requires that we shift the analytical focus away from the outcome and to the process instead. This process of ministerial recruitment starts with the announcement of election results, by which point the selector/s are known, and ends with the formal announcement of a cabinet. We propose that this process is strongly gendered, and throughout the book we illustrate the manifold ways that ideas and expectations about how men and women should behave structure the process and shape who is selected as minister. The cabinet formation process involves two sets of actors: those who have the authority to select ministers, whom we call selectors, and those who are eligible and are seeking to qualify for ministerial office, whom we call *ministrables*. We argue that the final construction of a cabinet can be explained by the actions of two sets of actors, by the interaction between them, and by the interaction of rules that prescribe, prohibit, and permit certain courses of action.[8] Moreover, we acknowledge that these actors themselves are gendered (Gains and Lowndes 2014). As men and women, they experience the gendered assumptions and expectations of other actors, and they themselves hold views about the appropriate roles of men and women in private and public life.

We also acknowledge that these actors are not merely behaving strategically to maximize benefits to themselves or their parties. Rather, we argue that the process of cabinet construction is very much rule-bound, despite the fact that most rules are unwritten. Formal (codified) and informal (unwritten) rules in political systems and political parties construct the institutional context within which ministers are selected. Rules empower and constrain the capacity of selectors to choose autonomously, and rules determine who is eligible and, crucially, qualified for ministerial office.

Finally, we show how these rules affect men and women differently. Following Gains and Lowndes (2014), we consider whether there are rules about gender, rules with gendered effects, and how gendered actors work with the rules of ministerial recruitment to produce specific outcomes. Although the process of cabinet appointment has few rules that are specifically about gender, we show that many of the rules that determine the process of ministerial recruitment have profoundly gendered effects. Specifically, we show how rules allocate power in ways that have historically prioritized men's appointment to ministerial office over women's. Our goal in the book is to identify the components of these rules that have functioned to advantage men and to inhibit women's access to ministerial office.

Change over time is an important dimension to this analysis. The last two decades have seen dramatic gains in women's appointment to cabinets across all countries, albeit at different magnitudes. Significantly, increases in

---

[8] Our definition of rules as *prescribing, prohibiting*, or *permitting* certain courses of action comes from Ostrom (1986) and is further developed in Chapter 2.

women's recruitment to cabinet have been sustained across all countries in our data set. For each country, we show when and how rules change, focusing on the crucial role played by agency, ambiguity and ideas (Mahoney and Thelen 2010). As we argue in Chapters 7, 10, and 11, ideational change across time that increases the numbers of women in cabinet, and that persists, can establish powerful informal practices. Agency, ambiguity, and ideas have changed informal rules that have shaped women's access to cabinet positions, for example, by expanding some of the qualifying criteria for becoming *ministrable*, to women's benefit, creating a concrete floor for women's cabinet inclusion.

Throughout the book, we show that patterns in cabinet appointment can be explained by (1) the rules about selection, which mostly empower presidents and prime ministers to choose their cabinet teams relatively unimpeded by other actors, (2) as well as rules about which individuals are eligible and qualified for a ministerial post. We find that rules about selection, eligibility, and qualifications are more consequential than political system type, party ideology, or sex of the selector. One of the strongest rules of cabinet appointment for most, although not all, of our cases is that selectors can choose ministers relatively autonomously, with little need to consult or negotiate with other political actors. Although we identify numerous rules about eligibility and qualifications that structure the pool of *ministrables*, we also find that the vast majority of these rules are non-codified. We argue that the intersection of rules about who selects and who can be selected explains how the process of cabinet formation is gendered and produces gendered outcomes, and we model this process in Chapter 2.

Because many of the rules about selection and qualifications are ambiguous and non-specific, they produce significant space for political agency. The degree of discretion enjoyed by most selectors helps to explain why deeply entrenched patterns can change rapidly and suddenly, namely, when specific selectors use their selection powers to increase the number of women in cabinet dramatically. Once a selector takes such a bold step, a new dynamic is unleashed, and the effects of a selector's political agency at an earlier point in time may become locked in. For each of our cases (except Australia), we can identify such a turning point, brought about by a particular selector, or set of selectors, who initiate a new concrete floor in terms of women's cabinet presence.

In cases where selectors use their political agency to take bold steps to increase the share of female ministers, they do so either out of personal conviction, because of pressure from feminists within their party, and/ or in response to changing ideas and representational rules about what a "balanced" cabinet looks like. Such ideas are often informed by changing notions of women's roles in society and politics. When an individual selector puts new ideas into practice, by setting a new threshold in terms of women's cabinet presence, the institutional context for subsequent selectors likewise changes, and new inclusionary base points are locked in. Once new standards of inclusion are set, subsequent presidents and prime ministers are held to account, we find, by other political actors—in particular, intraparty feminists—and by the media. It is now common, when a new cabinet is announced, for the media to note how many portfolios were given to women.

Ultimately, we have an optimistic story to tell. Across most of our cases, combinations of formal and informal rules intersect to create significant opportunities for political actors—namely, presidents and prime ministers acting as selectors, as well as feminists within parties—to bring about change. In Chapter 11, we show that instances of significant backsliding do not occur once political actors who enjoy discretion to select ministers put inclusionary norms with respect to gender into practice and set new concrete floors.

Our gendered institutionalist approach exposes the rules of ministerial recruitment in the seven advanced Western democracies countries in our study, but it also has broader applicability. This framework and method, we anticipate, can be used to identify the rules of selection and qualification for ministerial office in other regions and political systems, including countries with semi-presidential systems, and those with strong traditions of coalition government. The approach can also be used to expose the rules that determine the patterns of inclusion of other under-represented groups based on social class, race, ethnicity, sexual orientation, or gender identity. More broadly, our research provides a blueprint to guide scholars in how to analyze institutional settings that are largely devoid of formal rules, namely by specifying (1) the *number* of informal rules at play in an institutional setting; (2) whether rules *prescribe, prohibit,* or *permit*; (3) whether rules are *specific* or flexible; and (4) the degree of *institutionalization* of the rules.

Although we believe our model is generally applicable to all cases with governing cabinets, it is ultimately an empirical question whether the causal mechanisms producing concrete floors for women's inclusion exist in countries without democratic political systems. Although some authoritarian leaders have promoted women's rights as a way to garner political support (Donno and Kreft 2018), it is possible that the incentives for leaders to follow informal rules about what a representative or democratically legitimate cabinet team looks like do not exist in highly authoritarian contexts.[9] We hope that those studying women's representation in non-democracies see value in applying our model to identify the rules of ministerial recruitment.

Mapping the Book's Chapters

We begin in Chapter 2 by setting out our theoretical, conceptual, and methodological approaches for explaining gendered patterns of cabinet appointments. We employ a feminist institutionalist approach (see Kenny 2014; Mackay, Kenny, and Chappell 2010; Waylen 2014), emphasizing the significance of studying informal as well as formal rules, paying particular attention to how such rules create and maintain gendered hierarchies that advantage men in the cabinet appointment process; we also show how rules can change, emphasizing the importance of agency, ambiguity, and ideas; and we offer a model of the relationship among sets of rules to produce cabinets that include women. Chapter 2 also addresses the methodological implications of our feminist institutionalist approach and details our "qualitatively driven" approach (Mason 2006, 10) for analyzing qualitative data, including interviews, media data, and memoirs. Finally, we provide the justification for the selection of our cases, and present descriptions of the seven country cases.

The empirical chapters of the book expose the rules of ministerial recruitment and are structured as follows. First, in Chapters 3 through 7 we identify the rules of ministerial recruitment, explicating the variety and patterns of rules-in-use (Ostrom 2005, 20) in our seven country case studies. In Chapters 8 through 10, we demonstrate how these rules are gendered, explaining why rules of cabinet appointment produce different opportunities

---

[9] That said, it is notable that in 2013, Iran's president felt compelled to give in to widespread public criticism of his failure to appoint any women to his cabinet. Following sustained criticism on social media, President Rouhani appointed a woman to his cabinet and promised to promote more women to other government posts (Moghadam and Haghighatjoo 2016).

for men and women to be selected as ministers and how this varies across countries and over time.

In Chapter 3, we focus on who selects ministers, identifying all the rules that determine how empowered or constrained selectors are to choose their ministers. We show that in most cases, presidents and prime ministers are strongly empowered to choose their ministers, though in some cases selectors are constrained by having to share powers with co-selectors from other parties and within their own party organization. In Chapters 4 though 7, we turn our attention to the rules about how individuals who are in the eligibility pool for cabinet can demonstrate that they are also qualified to be selected as ministers. Challenging the idea that there are objective and universal qualifying criteria or "merit" that all individual ministers must display, Chapter 4 identifies three different types of qualifications that cabinets, as collectivities, must include: qualifications involving experiential criteria (political experience and policy expertise); affiliational criteria (membership in a selector's personal network of friendship, trust, and loyalty); and representational criteria (membership in a relevant political, territorial, or social group).

In Chapter 5, we focus more deeply on experiential criteria, demonstrating that in all cases *ministrables* qualify by demonstrating their political experience or policy expertise—and sometimes both. We argue, however, that such experiential criteria are applied post hoc and strategically as "merit" to justify a selector's choice of minister. We argue that qualification for appointment on the basis of policy expertise and/or political experience is insufficient to explain selection of ministers; if all ministrables meet some kind of experiential criteria, additional qualification criteria will be necessary to determine who is selected and who is not.

In Chapter 6, we identify the importance of affiliational criteria (membership in the selector's personal networks of friendship, trust, and loyalty) as a historically strong and enduring mechanism for determining who in the eligibility pool qualifies for cabinet. In Chapter 7, we show that ministers can qualify for cabinet by meeting representational criteria—membership in a relevant political, territorial, or socio-demographic group—that are deemed important to legitimize the cabinet.

In Chapters 8, 9, and 10, we turn our analysis explicitly to gender in order to demonstrate how the rules we identify in Chapters 3 through 7 distribute opportunities to male and female *ministrables* unevenly. We show that rules for the process of ministerial recruitment have traditionally been gendered to men's advantage, producing patterns of cabinets in which men are represented in significantly higher numbers than women. In the context of gendered rules, selector agency, feminist activism in the parties, and changing ideas about women's inclusion in politics have produced change across countries and over time.

In Chapter 8, we show how rules empowering and constraining selectors have gendered consequences for selectors and *ministrables*. The fact that, often, a single actor is empowered to select ministers means that the president or prime minister has the agency to choose to appoint women to cabinet. Indeed, we find that many commit to acting on that agency, evidenced by a pre-election pledge. Chapter 8 also examines whether the sex of the selector and increasing the number of selectors make a difference to the gender composition of ministerial teams.

Chapter 9 analyzes the gendered consequences of rules about qualification and investigates whether there are differences in the qualifications that male and female *ministrables* bring to a cabinet team. Although the type of qualifications of male and female ministers do not differ substantially, our data show that selectors employ experiential criteria strategically to justify their preferred appointments. Chapter 9 also addresses the gendered impact of selectors' ability to appoint ministers on affiliational grounds. Appointment on affiliational criteria, we argue, best explains the reproduction of male predominance in cabinets over time.

Chapter 10 addresses representational criteria. Across all seven country cases, the extension of gendered representational criteria to include women has become a strong predictor of women's inclusion in cabinet. The timing and strength of institutionalization of gender as a representational rule varies cross-nationally. Nevertheless, its presence is strong enough to shape a selector's choices of ministers, often reducing his capacity to appoint on affiliational grounds.

In Chapter 11, we bring the analysis of rules and gender presented in Chapters 3 through 10 together to answer our three research questions: Why are more men than women appointed to cabinet? Why are women more likely to be appointed to cabinet in some countries than others? Why has women's presence in cabinet varied across time? To do so, we explain how rules about selection and qualification have interacted to produce the specific outcomes in each country case and over time. We explicate in detail the establishment of the "concrete floor" in each country, identifying who initiated an increase in women's presence in cabinet and explaining the mechanisms through which the concrete floor has been sustained and maintained to become the new norm. We conclude with a discussion of the contribution and implications of our research for the practice of constructing cabinets, as well as for future executive and feminist scholarship in this field.

2

Institutionalist Approaches
to Cabinet Appointments

Concepts, Methods, and Data

Cabinet formation is a dynamic process, structured by an institutional environment made up of interacting sets of rules. The construction of a ministerial team results from processes of consultation and in some cases negotiation that begin with results from a general election and end with the formal announcement of a complete cabinet. This process can take days, weeks, or sometimes several months. What is perhaps most notable about this process is the relative absence of codified rules that determine how ministers are to be selected and the criteria that qualify individuals for a cabinet post. The lack of formal rules governing cabinet appointments does not mean, however, that the process is entirely ad hoc, allowing free rein to selectors to appoint to cabinet whomever they wish. Indeed, the process of ministerial recruitment is replete with rules, even if most of them are unwritten (De Winter 1995; Dogan 1989). The relative absence of codified rules has implications for scholars who want to understand the process, particularly for scholars who want to explain the gendered outcomes of cabinet appointments.

This chapter sets out our theoretical, conceptual, and methodological approaches for explaining gendered patterns of cabinet appointments. We combine feminist political science with the new institutionalism, an approach that some call "gendered institutionalism" and others call "feminist institutionalism" (Chappell and Waylen 2013; Krook and Mackay 2011; Mackay, Kenny, and Chappell 2010). Such an approach has become widespread in the gender and politics literature in recent years, and has been applied to a range of phenomena, including gender and candidate recruitment (Bjarnegård 2013; Kenney 2013; Krook 2009), women's legislative behavior (Franceschet 2011), gender and regime change (Waylen 2007), gender and social policy (Beyeler and Annesley 2010), and the core executive (Annesley and Gains 2010). We then offer our own conceptual framework for identifying the various types of rules that structure the process of cabinet appointments. Finally, we discuss the methods used to gather data and the challenges involved in studying processes that are almost entirely governed by unwritten rules and practices.

New Institutionalism, Feminist Political Science, and Cabinet Appointments

New institutionalist theories of politics conceive of rules as the building blocks of political life and thus as the basis of political institutions. Institutionalist scholars define institutions as "relatively stable collection[s] of rules . . . which guide behavior and stabilize expectations" (March and Olsen 2011, 480). For our purposes, there are two relevant features that distinguish "old" from "new" institutionalist scholarship. First, the "old" institutionalism focused primarily on codified rules, particularly those embodied in legal statutes and constitutions. Far less attention was paid to norms, ideas, and the informal practices that shape political outcomes. New institutionalists, in contrast, define institutions more broadly as "formal and informal procedures, routines, norms, and conventions embedded in the organizational structure of the polity or political economy" (Hall and Taylor 1996, 938). Such a definition includes rules that are codified in constitutions, laws, and internal party statutes, as well as rules and practices that are unwritten but just as powerful in shaping political action and determining political outcomes.

Second, the new institutionalism—particularly the strand of new institutionalism known as historical institutionalism—is deeply concerned with how rules and institutions create and reproduce power hierarchies (Hall and Taylor 1996; Thelen and Steinmo 1992). In this view, institutions are not neutral but distribute power, in part by determining who has access to decision-making arenas. As such, institutions are deeply implicated in the emergence and maintenance of power asymmetries. Both of these two features of the new institutionalism—namely, its focus on ideas and informal as well as formal rules, and its emphasis on how rules confer power and reproduce inequality—are crucial if we want to know why men have historically been advantaged in the process of cabinet appointment and how that process is gendered.

Our approach in this book is not derived from any single approach to institutionalism. Instead, we follow a "border-crossing" approach that draws from all variants of new institutionalism that we believe useful for explaining how the process of cabinet appointment produces unequal and variable gendered outcomes over time and cross-nationally. Following Thelen, our approach seeks to combine rational choice, historical, and sociological institutionalism in creative ways that "recognize and attempt to harness the strengths of each approach" (1999, 380). Two of our central starting points come from historical institutionalism. First, we view institutions as historical products that emerge from struggles over power and resources. Winners of those power struggles create institutions that reflect and protect their interests; hence the power relations that exist at the time of an institution's creation are ultimately reproduced through the rules, norms, and practices that comprise the institution (Hall and Taylor 1996; Thelen and Steinmo 1992). Second, we follow historical institutionalists in emphasizing the ideational aspects of institutions. According to Peter Hall (1986), ideas have crucial framing effects, making certain courses of action, particularly those that fit within an existing ideational frame, more likely than others. According to Sven Steinmo (2008, 131), focusing on ideas helps institutionalists to explain change: "institutional change comes about when powerful actors have the will and ability to change institutions in favor of new ideas."

We follow rational choice institutionalists by recognizing that, in addition to being embedded in institutional settings defined by formal and informal rules, selectors are also strategic actors guided by a relatively fixed set of preferences deriving from their role as chief executive. Key preferences of presidents and prime ministers include achieving their policy goals and ensuring governability and duration in office. Yet, we also agree with historical institutionalists that interests and preferences are not entirely independent from institutions (Steinmo 2008). Thelen and Steinmo note that even when political actors engage in strategic behavior, "we [still] need a historically based analysis to tell us what they are trying to maximize and why they emphasize certain goals over others" (1992, 9). Finally, we borrow from sociological institutionalists who view rules as establishing a "logic of appropriateness" through which actors seek to match their identities and situations to an appropriate course of action (March and Olsen 1989). Most important, however, we agree with March and Olsen that rules are never clear and straightforward, but rather "rich in conflict, contradiction, and ambiguity," (1989, 38; see also Mahoney and Thelen 2010). Other strands of institutionalism likewise recognize ambiguity in rules. Ostrom notes, "rules rarely prescribe one and only one action" (1986, 7). Even within an environment structured by rules, political actors nonetheless exercise agency when choosing how to comply with or ignore the sets of rules they confront. In some cases, political actors use this ambiguity to reinterpret rules and bring about different outcomes.

Long before the new institutionalism emerged in comparative politics, feminist scholars were focusing on informal rules and institutions, even if they did not necessarily use that language. Thus, in addition to the three variants of new institutionalism, we draw heavily on feminist political science, particularly those scholars seeking to reveal the persistent yet often hidden mechanisms that sustain gender inequality. As feminist scholars note, the very success of second-wave feminism in most of the world's democracies meant that formal rules, namely constitutions and legal statutes, were reformed in ways that eliminated explicit sex-based discrimination. Around the world, democratic countries outlawed discrimination based on sex, adopted equal opportunity laws and policies, and in some cases, amended constitutions to guarantee equality of opportunity. On the ground, however, especially in political institutions, the situation for women did not change very much. Men continued to be vastly over-represented among elected parliamentarians, and in all but a few cases, monopolized the most prestigious political offices of cabinet minister, president, and prime minister.

To explain the gap between formal rules that appear gender neutral and unequal outcomes in politics, feminist scholars turned to the unwritten yet deeply entrenched rules and practices that reproduce men's privileged position in politics and that marginalize women. In writing about the masculine codes of Westminster, for instance, Lovenduski writes, "Parliament is masculine. I mean this in the sense that it institutionalizes the norms of the men who founded it and for so many years inhabited it as a wholly male institution" (1995, 48). Likewise, Chappell identifies a "gendered logic of appropriateness" that defines "'acceptable' masculine and feminine forms of behavior, rules, and values for men and women within institutions" (2006, 226). The starting point for feminist institutionalists is that gender is constitutive of all social relations, serving "as a primary way of signifying (and naturalizing) relationships of power and hierarchy" (Mackay, Kenny, and Chappell 2010, 580). Essentially, that means all institutions are gendered in that their day-to-day practices reflect rules, norms, and values about masculinity and femininity.

Gains and Lowndes (2014, 527) provide more precise guidance for researchers to identify empirically how gender is embedded in and reproduced in institutions. According to the authors, researchers must consider four sets of variables: (1) rules about gender; (2) rules that are not explicitly about gender but have gendered effects; (3) gendered actors who work with the rules; and (4) gendered outcomes. Rules that are explicitly about gender include gender quotas or rules that restrict access to certain jobs or positions to members of one sex only. Most of the rules of interest to researchers, however, appear to be gender neutral, yet often rest on norms or ideas about gender and therefore affect men and women differently. For instance, "seemingly neutral rules about where and when meetings are held" affect women and men differently (Gains and Lowndes 2014, 528). Since women are more likely to have primary caring responsibilities, they are more likely to be disadvantaged by evening or late-night meetings. Women are doubly disadvantaged when such meetings take place at sites (like golf courses, dining clubs, or bars) where women's presence is less welcome. Likewise, informal rules about what makes a "good" leader or parliamentary candidate often include characteristics based on gendered stereotypes or expectations, such as a willingness to work excessively long hours, and behave in assertive and sometimes combative ways (Gains and Lowndes 2014, 528; see also Murray 2014).

Acknowledging that rules are followed (or not) and changed by actors means paying attention to who those actors are. Men and women may perceive of rules differently and may themselves face gendered opportunities and constraints when working with rules. For example, when working with rules that normally empower officials, a female official may perceive less autonomy and capacity than her male colleagues. Taking Gains and Lowndes' guidance seriously, we distinguish rules about gender (of which there are almost none) from rules with gendered effects (of which there are many). We also explore the gendered constraints and opportunities that rules pose, noting that the gender of the selector matters in mediating between rules and outcomes.

Conceptualizing Rules and Identifying Gendered Consequences

Institutions produce patterned behavior because they are made up of rules, norms, practices, and standard operating procedures that inform actors about what they should and should not do when confronted by particular situations. Unfortunately, institutionalist scholars lack a shared conceptual vocabulary for defining and identifying the most basic element of institutions, namely, rules. Some scholars, for example, March and Olsen (1989), use the terms "rules," "norms," and "practices" interchangeably, without identifying clear conceptual boundaries around different types of rules, such as whether they are codified or not. Other scholars, such as Lowndes and Roberts, distinguish "rules," which are formalized by being written down somewhere, from "practices," which refer to "the way we do things around here" (2013, 52). Helmke and Levitsky offer a binary distinction between formal and informal rules. While formal rules are codified, public, and "enforced through channels widely accepted as official," informal rules are "usually unwritten [and] created, communicated, and enforced outside of officially sanctioned channels" (2004, 727). An oft-heard complaint, however, is that concepts like informal rules, or even just institutions more generally, have been defined far too expansively, such that all behavioral regularities and patterned outcomes are said to be products of some kind of rule. Bo Rothstein notes that if institutions mean everything, they essentially mean nothing (cited in Lowndes and Roberts, 2013, 47). If the concept of rules is to be analytically useful, we must be able to identify when and where rules apply and when and where they do not.

Not all patterned behavior and regularized outcomes owe to the presence of rules. Mershon stresses the importance of separating rules from regularities: "Regularities are recurring outcomes of choice. Rules restrain options in the process of choice. Rules bring forth regularities, but outcomes can also occur without rules" (1994, 50). Even March and Olsen acknowledge that "behavior is driven by habit, emotion, coercion, and calculated expected utility, as well as interpretation of internalized rules and principles" (2011, 490).

A central task in this book is to understand how gendered regularized outcomes, such as the persistent construction of all-male or mostly male cabinets for much of the twentieth century, results from the interaction of different sets of rules, as employed by those constructing cabinets and those eligible and qualified to be cabinet members. To make sense of cabinet appointment as a rule-bound process, we adopt Ostrom's definition of rules as "prescriptions commonly known and used by a set of participants to order repetitive, interdependent relationships" (1986, 5). The most important element of Ostrom's definition is that rules identify which actions are "prescribed, prohibited, and permitted" (1986, 5). When confronted by a rule-governed situation, "individuals select actions from a *set of allowable actions* in light of the full set of incentives in the situation" (1986, 6, emphasis in original).

Ostrom's definition is useful for analyzing rules of cabinet appointments by drawing attention to the underlying mechanisms that produce patterned and predictable outcomes, whether these are cabinets with only men or cabinets that meet what we identified in Chapter 1 as a "concrete floor" for women's inclusion. As we argue in later chapters, a patterned outcome may owe to the presence of a rule or set of rules that prescribe a certain course of action, for example, appointing ministers from parliament or ensuring an appropriate degree of territorial representation among ministers. But other commonly observed practices, like appointing ministers on the basis of friendship or loyalty, do not result from rules that explicitly require such action, but rather from the absence of prohibitions about selecting one's friends as ministers. The appointment of trusted confidants still occurs within a rule-bound context: Even if the rules do not require selectors to appoint their trusted friends or allies, selectors not only are permitted to do so, but also may face strategic incentives to do so, for example, ensuring that cabinet secrets are not leaked, or that intra-party conflict remains confined to cabinet. Thus, we anticipate that these patterned outcomes occur because of these incentives *and* because the rules ultimately permit selectors to choose their ministers on the basis of personal affiliation.

In addition to identifying whether rules apply or not, we should also be able to identify what type of rule applies, and how rules are enforced. The conceptual framework we develop for this book helps us to identify and categorize different types of rules and rule enforcement governing cabinet appointments.

Formal and Informal Rules in Cabinet Appointment

In constructing a conceptual framework for identifying and distinguishing different types of rules and their enforcement mechanisms, we follow Ostrom's suggestion that rules operate on multiple levels of analysis and that situations are governed by "*configurations* of rules rather than single rules" (1986, 8, emphasis in original). Executive branch scholars who view cabinet formation as rule-governed likewise acknowledge the complex interplay among different types of rules. De Winter, for example, writes, "constitutional rules often do not reflect the way the [cabinet] formation process operates in practice" (1995, 122). Divergence occurs when informal (unwritten) rather than formal (written) rules provide stronger imperatives for political actors to follow (see also Bjarnegård and Kenny 2015). Researchers need a conceptual framework that captures not only whether rules are codified or not, but also the degree of prescriptiveness of informal rules.

Our conceptual framework includes both a binary distinction between formal and informal rules and a continuum along which both formal and informal rules can be placed to indicate how strongly or weakly institutionalized the rule is. Following Helmke and Levitsky (2004), we define formal rules as written rules that are communicated and enforced through public channels. Formal rules for cabinet appointments may derive from constitutions or legal statutes. Such system-level formal rules would apply to all selectors, regardless of party. But formal rules may also operate at the party level, in which case selectors from different parties face different formal rules. Informal rules, in contrast, are unwritten and thus more hidden from view. Political actors and insiders know what the informal rules are because they observe them (and likewise observe sanctions for non-compliance) and because other political actors communicate the unwritten rules. Informal rules are similar to formal rules in that they are enforced through sanctions or incentives, although sanctions for informal rule violations do not occur through official or publicly authorized channels. Breaches of formal rules are sanctioned by public officials whose authority is grounded in constitutions and legal statutes or, in the case of party-specific rules, in party statutes. Breaking informal rules also leads to sanctions, although such sanctions take different forms, ranging from criticism or disapproval that may be publicly (expressed in the media, for example) or privately voiced (expressed by political allies, aids, or advisors, outside of the public eye) to party revolts or the withholding of crucial political support. The presence of informal but powerful sanctions can be evidenced by responses from selectors, explaining why an informal rule has not been violated.[1]

Simply distinguishing formal from informal rules cannot tell us which rules actually matter, that is, which rules are more likely to be followed and

---

[1] See Barack Obama's defensive response to criticism of his second-term post-election cabinet appointments. Citing "attention to diversity," the *New York Times* noted, "Under fire for nominating a series of white men to top posts in recent days, President Obama vowed Monday that his second-term team would be diverse and urged critics not to 'rush to judgment.'" Peter Baker, "Obama Defends His Record on Diversity in Appointments," *New York Times*, January 14, 2013. See also Michael D. Shear, "Cabinet Diversity Poses a Question for Obama," *New York Times*, December 11, 2012.

which rules political actors can break without incurring a high cost. Formal rules are not necessarily more determinative than informal rules. De Winter, for example, notes that when forming coalition governments, some formal rules, especially those empowering heads of state, are consistently violated (1995, 123). To sort out which rules actually matter, we need some way of categorizing rules that captures how much they actually constrain or em-power political actors. Here, we follow Bjarnegård and Kenny (2015) in categorizing rules according to their degree of institutionalization. Formal and informal rules are concepts with clear boundaries; that is, a rule is not "more" formal or "less" formal, it simply is written (formalized) or it is not. In contrast, we can imagine institutionalization operating as a continuum, with both formal and informal rules being "more" or "less" institutionalized. Whether codified or not, rules are more institutionalized when they are rou-tinely observed, widely acknowledged, and when not complying would pro-duce sanctions that political actors want to avoid. Highly institutionalized rules are therefore strong prescriptive rules that are difficult to break. Less institutionalized rules are more subject to discretion, and more likely to be violated because the sanctions for non-compliance are weaker.

We can figure out if rules are more or less institutionalized by looking for incentives, sanctions, and enforcement mechanisms. By definition, in-formal rules cannot be legally enforced. Instead, informal rules are enforced politically or even socially. Sanctions for breaking informal rules may exact a very high cost, for example, refusal of other political actors to consent or cooperate, which can produce gridlock or political failures. As we show in later chapters, formal rules specifying the qualifications necessary for a cabinet appointment are entirely absent across all our case studies. Yet in-formal rules about what qualifies ministers abound. Such rules are enforced in various ways. In the United States, the Senate may withhold its consent to a president's cabinet nominations despite the absence of legally enforce-able qualifying criteria. In parliamentary democracies, even if members of parliament play no role in confirming a prime minister's choices of minis-ters, ongoing consent of parliament is needed for a government to remain in office. Such consent could in principle be withheld if a prime minister ap-pointed ministers perceived as lacking the requisite (albeit wholly informal) qualifications needed to serve in cabinet, or a governing party could opt to replace its leader.

Or, the cost may be disapproval or criticism that is publicly voiced by opponents, the media, or sometimes one's own co-partisans. Sanctions taking the form of publicly or privately voiced criticism are certainly weaker forms of rule enforcement, but they matter nonetheless. When assembling their cabinet teams, leaders know what kinds of past cabinet teams have provoked praise and which have provoked criticism. Later in the book, we offer evidence that selectors respond to such incentives and sanctions by appointing cabinet teams that meet, rather than violate, established informal rules about what a qualified ministerial team looks like. In sum, selectors face a complex array of informal rules, some of which are strongly institutionalized and others of which are only weakly institutionalized. We also show how and why these rules change over time.

When and How Do Rules Change?

A common criticism of new institutionalist theories of politics is that they are better at explaining stability than change (see Schmidt 2010, 2). Among the key conceptual contributions of institutionalism are things like path dependency and policy feedback, both of which imply that institutions contain mechanisms that ensure reproduction and limit the possibilities for change. Our goal in this book is to explain why the gendered cabinet appointment process, which remained stable for long periods of time, ultimately changed to include women. Two major changes are evident across our country cases. First, cabinets went from being entirely composed of men to including one or two women, and eventually, women's inclusion exceeded one or two token appointments, and cabinets regularly began to include women in proportions ranging between 10 and 30 percent.

Institutionalists identify four mechanisms for change (Thelen and Mahoney 2010): (1) the agency of individual actors; (2) windows of opportunity provided by the ambiguity and inconsistency inherent in rules; (3) contestation over power relations expressed in institutions; and (4) ideational change. We find evidence of all four mechanisms at work in our study, and, what is more, we consider all of them to be linked. Institutions confer agency in two ways. First, as outlined earlier, rules can be empowering. Rules identify what should be done and what ought not be done. Often, political actors expand their scope for action by following the precept that what is not prohibited by formal or informal rules is therefore permitted. Additionally, agency is enhanced because rules rarely provide actors a straightforward or clear-cut blueprint for action. The very fact that the rules governing cabinet appointments are largely informal creates more space for actors to invoke certain rules and disregard others, to seize on the ambiguity of rules and re-interpret or reimagine their meaning, and in so doing, to create new rules or change the meaning of existing rules. Institutionalists, in other words, understand rules as fundamentally messy and incoherent rather than straightforward.

Another possibility for change is built into institutionalist accounts that view rules as conferring power and thereby setting up possibilities for con-testation over power hierarchies. Historical institutionalists, in particular, view institutions as compromises rather than ideal solutions to collective action dilemmas. As compromises, institutions are subject to ongoing con-testation, particularly by those whose preferred political outcome was not achieved by the initial creation of an institution. Streeck and Thelen (2005) note that conceiving of institutions this way draws attention to the presence of both the "rule-makers" and the "rule-takers." The rule-makers must con-tinually work to maintain existing rules, practices, and arrangements, while those who are disadvantaged are engaged in challenging and contesting the rules. And because all rules—whether formal or informal—are "subject to interpretation, debate, and contestation," they ultimately "provide critical openings for creativity and agency" (Mahoney and Thelen 2010, 11). Change can thus come about through incomplete compliance or "rule reinterpreta-tion" (Capoccia 2016, 1099).

Finally, ideas matter greatly in setting up possibilities for change. Institutions reflect and reinforce different kinds of ideas. Rules reflect pro-cedural ideas about how things should be done or how decisions should be made. But institutions and rules also reflect substantive ideas, for example, which groups possess the appropriate characteristics to govern and what type of individuals deserve access to social citizenship rights like healthcare or income support. Such ideas are themselves subject to change, however, and such ideational change is often the motivating factor for actors to change the way things are done (Lieberman 2002). When it comes to gendering cab-inet appointments, we anticipate that changing ideas about women's political inclusion means that some selectors will act on the idea that an all-male cab-inet is problematic given advances in women's rights. Likewise, over time, the inclusion of only one or two token women is also likely to be seen as falling short of minimal democratic standards. Ideational change in civil so-ciety, however, will not have any real impact on cabinet appointments until ideas about gender equality are effectively transmitted to political actors empowered by rules to select ministers. Often, women in political parties play important roles in lobbying selectors on the right and the left to open up more space for women in cabinet. Their success is intricately linked to the ideational battles waged by women's movements to challenge men's dominance of political institutions, making women's inclusion in arenas of power a yardstick for public legitimation.

Ideas are a crucial part of the story of how rules change because, within institutions, empowered actors can bring about change when they respond to new ideas that challenge the status quo (Lieberman 2002). Often, new ideas will enter public discourse through the efforts of social movements, and as their ideas gain more traction, political actors put these ideas into practice when they share the same convictions, or because they believe that acting on such ideas is necessary for their actions and policies to be perceived as legitimate (Weldon 2011). To some extent, it does not matter whether political actors are responding to strategic incentives (that is, public support) or their own convictions. We anticipate that once new ideas, like gender balance, are pursued in political institutions, a new informal rule about inclusion will become established, and ideas about gender balance will therefore become part of a changed institutional landscape.

These mechanisms of agency, ambiguity, power, and ideas in the context of cabinet formations work together to shape processes that produce gendered patterns of ministerial appointments. The challenge is how to research and capture them, especially given the predominance of unwritten rules. In the following, we discuss the methods and data we use to identify the rules and processes of cabinet appointments, how they have changed, and the factors driving change. First, however, we discuss a model, developed inductively from the data presented in Chapter 1, to clarify how we understand the process of cabinet formation through the intersections of multiple formal and informal rules, varying in degrees of institutionalization, and where those intersections are gendered in process and produce gendered outcomes.

An Interactive and Rule-Based Model for Cabinet Appointments

We model the cabinet appointment process in Figure 2.1. The model involves two sets of rules that govern the process of cabinet formation: (1) a set of

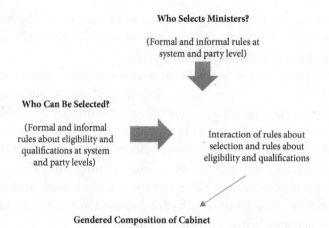

Figure 2.1. Interactive rule-based model of the cabinet appointment process.

formal and informal rules that condition presidents and prime ministers in their cabinet appointment powers (i.e., who selects ministers); and (2) a set of formal and informal rules that condition who can be selected, that is, those who are eligible and qualified for inclusion in cabinet. Both sets of rules vary in terms of their levels of institutionalization.

Formal rules, in both political system and party, can empower or constrain selectors in the process of cabinet formation. We anticipate that formal rules have gendered consequences, even as they appear on their face to be gender-neutral. In no country case are there explicitly gendered restrictions on, or advantages for, the selector in terms of formal rules, in regard to political system or party. This does not, however, mean that gender is absent in the process of cabinet construction, nor does it mean that formal rules have no gendered impact on cabinet appointments. Formal rules granting selectors autonomy to select their cabinet team permits them to appoint gender parity cabinets with little difficulty. Such rules do not guarantee the inclusion of women in cabinet, however. Indeed, the gendered impact of formal selector empowerment can work in many directions, resulting in the appointment of many women, or few women, or specific women. Again, this does not mean that cabinets therefore automatically produce some fixed number of women, but rather that formal rules empowering selectors are one point at which gender enters the process of cabinet formation. Few political parties have formal rules that constrain selector autonomy, although where such rules exist, their gendered

consequences are likewise variable.[2] In sum, formal rules—whether established by the political system or by a political party—are few and are a point
where the process of cabinet formation is gendered.

Informal rules vary across political system and within parties. Informal
rules that constrain the selector, like formal rules, are few but nonetheless
constitute a point where the process of cabinet formation is gendered. We
anticipate that selectors' powers in terms of cabinet formation will be shaped
primarily by the force of the informal rules of the specific political system
and the selector's party, and that these informal rules, even where they are
identified as gender-neutral, will contribute to the gendered process of cabinet formation. Such informal rules are discussed in Chapter 3; their gendered impacts are discussed in detail in Chapter 8.

We anticipate that the formal and informal rules determining who
selects ministers will interact with a second set of formal and informal rules
that condition who can be selected, that is, those who are eligible and are
perceived as qualified for inclusion in cabinet. It is not simply the empowerment of the selector or the interaction of the formal and informal rules that
construct the selector's powers; these formal and informal rules interact with
rules structuring the eligibility pool. We anticipate that the range of choices
available to the selector in terms of the eligible, qualified potential appointees
available for cabinet, structured by formal and informal rules, will also function to gender the cabinet-formation process. We find few formal rules
establishing cabinet eligibility across our cases; informal rules, however, are
plentiful in shaping both eligibility and perceptions of who is qualified to
serve in cabinet. These informal rules vary across our cases, applying both to
individual appointees (e.g., specific informal qualifications for justice ministers) *and* to the cabinet team as a collective whole. We anticipate that the
informal rules that qualify persons for appointment will be another major
point at which the process of cabinet formation is gendered. We discuss the
formal and informal rules that define the pool of potential cabinet appointees
in Chapters 5, 6, and 7, showing how they are gendered in Chapters 9 and 10.

Finally, rules determining who selects and who can be selected interact
in two gendered ways. First, they interact to gender the cabinet-formation
process (the interaction of rules about selection and rules about eligibility
and qualifications). How cabinets are constructed, in a context of selector

---

[2] In Chapter 3, we discuss party rules that constrain selectors in the UK Labour Party and the
Australian Labor Party.

empowerment and constraint, and of *ministrable* eligibility and qualification, is gendered *in process*. Second, as Figure 2.1 indicates, the results of this gendered process are also evidenced as gendered *outcomes*. These two sets of rules function on multiple levels and in multiple ways, varying according to the extent to which rules are institutionalized and in dynamic interaction across time, reflecting their operation in configuration, rather than as single rules (Ostrom, 1986, 8). In sum, we anticipate that gender will be evident in both the process and the outcome of cabinet formation. We discuss the model specifically in regard to process and outcome in each of our country cases, as well as to the model's applicability across all cases, in later chapters. In the following sections, we discuss our methodology, data collection, and how we operationalize the concepts used throughout the book.

Methods and Data

The biggest challenge in studying cabinet formation, as Dogan (1989) notes, is that so few of the rules for selecting ministers are written. What is more, much of what transpires when leaders are assembling their cabinet teams is entirely hidden from public view. Most politicians would likely prefer to keep it that way, since, as we show in our empirical chapters, some of the unwritten criteria for selecting ministers, particularly those related to personal friendship, trust, and loyalty, would not fare well under public scrutiny. The only way to reveal the rules about cabinet formation is to have political insiders share them with researchers (Dogan 1989; Siavelis 2014). Our main goal in this book is to determine whether certain configurations of rules produce predictable patterns of gendered cabinet appointments. To do so, we have to reveal rules that are normally hidden.[3]

To achieve our goals, we opted for a research design that follows what George and Bennett term a "structured focused comparison" (2005, 67). The study is "structured" to the extent that it is motivated by "general research questions that reflect the research objective and that these questions are asked of each case under study to guide and standardize data collection" (George and Bennett 2005, 67; see also Seawright and Gerring 2008). Data collection for our study involved both quantitative and qualitative strategies.

---

[3] Or, to use the phrase offered by Laurel Weldon at a workshop on institutional change (June 20–21, 2016, Manchester, UK), "to drag the rules into the field of scrutiny."

As we explained in Chapter 1, determining the gendered patterns of cabinet appointments required the collection of data on the number and percentage of women and men in all post-election cabinets, beginning with the appointment of the first female minister. We did so for all seven of our country case studies. Gathering data for the independent variables—namely, the rules governing selection, eligibility, and qualifying criteria for cabinets in each of the cases—involved using multiple qualitative methods to identify rules, whether formal or informal and less or more institutionalized (Mason 2006). We employed four data-collection strategies: (1) reviewing primary and secondary sources, (2) conducting elite and expert interviews, (3) compiling media data, and (4) reviewing published accounts of political insiders. With the qualitative data in hand, we could determine the rules about who selects ministers, what rules constrain or empower selectors, and how individuals qualify for cabinet in each of the country cases. To collect evidence on formal rules of cabinet formation and ministerial appointment, we sought documentary evidence of the written rules that shape ministerial recruitment and appointment in constitutions, laws, regulations, or policies at the political system and party levels. Our initial findings revealed a striking absence of formal rules in the process of cabinet recruitment.

Identifying informal rules was more challenging. We began by reviewing existing studies of politics, political institutions, and cabinets for each of our country cases. For the most part, we found few qualitative in-depth analyses of cabinet formation and very few studies that explored the informal rules of cabinet appointments.[4] Our main sources of evidence are interview data and media data, supplemented by biographies and memoirs from insiders, where they exist.

Data Collection

Interviews
We conducted interviews with political elites to ask about party- and country-specific processes of cabinet formation, in terms of the powers of presidents

---

[4] Some exceptions include Peter Siavelis' work on the informal dimensions of the executive branch in Chile (2009, 2013) and De Winter's work on the role of parliament in government formation (1995). Although there is substantial research on cabinet formation in cases of coalition governments (Amorim Neto 2006; Laver and Shepsle 1994; Mershon 1994), there is little research on the process of cabinet formation in countries where single-party governments are the norm.

and prime ministers, and the criteria that render individuals eligible and qualified for appointment to cabinet. Elite interviews were appropriate for collecting data on these processes because such interviews can "provide opportunities to learn about political actors and events in contexts one cannot observe and whose parameters may be difficult to infer" (Beckmann and Hall 2013, 207). Elite interviewing across parties and political systems of our country cases offered access to data that would otherwise have been impossible to collect and for which systematic records of the process are "virtually nonexistent" (Beckmann and Hall 2013, 208). We interviewed former ministers, political party elites, and country experts concerning the cabinet recruitment and appointment process and the context of rules within which it takes place. We also collected interview data concerning the parameters that establish eligibility and qualification criteria for *ministrables*.

We did not seek to interview ministers currently in office for this project. Interviewing former ministers and other political elites involved in the cabinet-formation process (including those not selected for cabinet) likely enabled us to collect more valuable data since those no longer in cabinet and those who were passed over for ministerial posts are freer than ministers currently serving to offer frank and reflective views than otherwise might have been the case.[5] Similarly, interviewees who were no longer (or had never been) ministers did not need to worry about their status or standing within a current government, and were not positioned to jeopardize their own position or to embarrass the government or cabinet.[6] Although we interviewed individuals, these were not our units of analysis. Our focus in these interviews of political elites involved not the elites themselves, but rather the process of ministerial recruitment in their parties and countries (see Lynch 2013, 38).

Between 2010 and 2016, we individually conducted 57 semi-structured interviews with various political insiders and experts in five of our seven country cases.[7] We used a common template for all interviews (see later discussion), and interviews were conducted in the native language of the

---

[5] See Aberbach and Rockman (2002, 675), and their claim that "the interviewees were frank in their answers, especially because our questions focused on general views and not information that might jeopardize the respondents' personal interests."

[6] See Bleich and Pekkanen (2013, 94), who write, "[I]nformation reported against one's interest is almost always more reliable than reports that serve to puff up a particular individual or group."

[7] Canada and the United States are the only two countries where we did not conduct interviews with political insiders. For both countries, however, we felt that we had a fairly rich secondary literature on which to draw.

interviewee. For details about the interview data set, see Appendix 1, List of Interviews.

Interview questions were open-ended and varied according to whether individuals were political insiders themselves or political experts. The main goal of the interviews was to find out "how things are done around here." We asked interviewees to describe all aspects of ministerial recruitment about which they had knowledge. We asked what happened when a leader was assembling a cabinet; for example, were they expected to seek input, or could they make decisions on their own? Who might they consult or seek advice from? We also had several questions about how individuals qualified for a cabinet post. Given how "hidden" many of the informal rules are, we often had to push interview subjects on their answers, getting them to reveal more about the less visible dimensions of cabinet formation. For instance, many interview respondents, and especially former ministers, often spoke about presidents and prime ministers needing to select "talented ministers" with demonstrated "leadership potential" or skill. Such comments, of course, are replete with assumptions about what talent and leadership actually mean in practice. We therefore asked numerous follow-up questions about what kind of talent selectors might be looking for, and what, in that context, is meant by things like "leadership" or "ability to manage complex issues." When interviewing ministers and former ministers, we also asked specific questions relating to the rules and practices within their own party, and their specific experiences and reflections on their own trajectory into cabinet.[8] Such open-ended, flexible questions, asked in conversation with our interview subjects, "have the virtue of allowing the subjects to tell the interviewer what's relevant and what's important rather than being restricted by the researcher's preconceived notions about what is important" (Berry 2002, 681).

Media Data

For each of our country cases, we compiled a data set of media stories for two specific instances of cabinet formation.[9] Each of the cases represents a post-election cabinet, including those where the selector was re-elected for a second term. For each instance of cabinet formation, we used Factiva to

---

[8] For example, we asked, "Why do you think you were appointed to cabinet?"

[9] We are grateful to the team of research assistants at the University of Manchester (Emmy Eklundh and Tomas Maltby), the University of Sussex (Adam Ahmet), the University of Calgary (Elizabeth Pando and Mariana Hipólito Ramos), and Case Western Reserve University (Olivia Ortega) who collected these data, and to grants from the Social Sciences and Humanities Research Council of Canada and the University of Manchester for providing funding for data collection.

Table 2.1 Newspapers, by Country and Election, Sourced for Media Data

Country	Year	Selector	Party (Left/Center/Right)	New Government	Newspapers
Australia	2010	Julia Gillard	Left	No	The Age; The
	2013	Tony Abbot	Right	Yes	Australian
Canada	2008	Stephen Harper	Right	No	Globe
	2015	Justin Trudeau	Center	Yes	& Mail; Ottawa Citizen
Chile	2006	Michelle Bachelet	Left	No	El Mercurio;
	2010	Sebastián Piñera	Right	Yes	La Nación
Germany	2002	Gerhard Schröder	Left	No	Frankfurter
	2005	Angela Merkel	Right	Yes	Allgemeine Zeitung; Süddeutsche Zeitung
Spain	2004	José Luis Rodríguez Zapatero	Left	Yes Yes	El País ABC
	2011	Mariano Rajoy	Right		
United Kingdom	2005	Tony Blair	Left	No	The Times;
	2010	David Cameron	Right	Yes	The Telegraph
United States	2004	George W. Bush	Right	No	New York
	2009	Barack Obama	Left	Yes	Times; Washington Post

search for newspaper articles from two major newspapers in each country. Where possible, we chose the two major national newspapers to capture the major and most detailed journalistic accounts of cabinet formation and ministerial selection. Table 2.1 identifies the newspapers for each of the seven countries. The media data include commentaries, editorials, and descriptive journalism. We were interested in gathering data on two distinct phases of media reporting: (1) the speculation phase, and (2) the reaction phase. We defined the speculation phase of cabinet formation as the period following the formal election results and the public announcement of the complete ministerial team, since "[m]edia scrutiny often starts even before an official nomination occurs" (Friedland 2015, 190).[10] The second period, the reaction

---

[10] In the case of Chile, however, the speculation phase begins slightly earlier for 2006. The first

phase, encompasses news stories about who was appointed to cabinet and why. Because most stories and columns appear in the first week following the announcement of the cabinet, and a smaller number thereafter, we collected all stories reacting to the entire cabinet or individual ministers for two weeks following the presentation of the whole cabinet. We searched stories in each newspaper, for each country, for evidence specific to cabinet posts, names of *ministrables*, appointment criteria, and other factors and mentions of relevance to cabinet construction.

Taken together, the media data constitute a rich source of primary material from which we were able to identify the informal rules surrounding the selection process, such as with whom selectors were consulting or seeking advice, as well as the qualifying criteria that made someone a *ministrable* and ultimately landed someone a seat at the cabinet table. During the speculation phase, journalists and columnists wrote about who was likely to be in cabinet and why, and during the reaction phase they wrote about who made it into cabinet (and why), and also importantly, who was left out of cabinet and why. Again, these data revealed a great deal about the unwritten rules about what qualifies someone to be a minister.

Insider Accounts: Memoirs and Autobiographies

Interview and media data were supplemented by published sources such as selectors' and ministers' autobiographies and other insider accounts. The accounts, often written by individuals after their political careers have ended, include frank behind-the-scene assessments of why they selected certain individuals for cabinet, why they did not select others, and the pressures they may have felt from other political actors, or from society in general when forming a cabinet. In some cases, multiple memoirs permitted us to triangulate reports about the process of cabinet appointments that were contentious, disputed, and/or involved competing (and occasionally self-serving and self-justifying) reports. Moreover, materials from memoirs and autobiographies allowed us to identify what was *not* being discussed and to show that absence of issues or concerns was not the result of missing data but accurately

round of the presidential election was December 15, 2005, but the electoral rules require the winner to have an absolute majority. Bachelet got the most votes, but did not win a majority, thus a run-off election between the top two vote getters took place on January 15. Speculation about cabinet appointments was well underway between the first and second round, so we began collecting media data on January 1, 2006.

reflected the reality of the process of cabinet appointments, both in terms of selection and who was considered *ministrable*.

Data Analysis

Our approach to analyzing and interpreting our data was entirely inductive. Once data collection was complete, we began a process of reading interview transcripts, media accounts, and memoirs, taking note of the key terms and phrases that repeatedly appeared. We read our data for mentions of informal rules about selection and qualification. We also looked for references to how strongly institutionalized rules are, for example, flagging evidence of sanctions when a particular course of action is not followed. Through this process we built up an understanding of the rules in use in each country case. In addition, as a research team, we discussed the data across the seven country cases and 14 instances of cabinet formation in detail, comparing notes and discussing categorization standards, and checking the data for reliability against other data sources. Taken together, our qualitative data helped us to identify the rules of cabinet appointments and their degree of institutionalization in each political system and, where relevant, within the major parties. The data also shed light on how rules have changed over time, and what sorts of factors have driven rule change.

Mentions of rules were not coded in quantitative terms. Instead, we discussed across the cases which narratives were apparent in and/or emerged from the data, what the pattern of evidence was, and how consistent narratives were across our data. We came to appreciate the narratives that emerged and used the ones that were consistent across data sources as a way of structuring and presenting our findings. For example, with regard to how empowered selectors are, the prominent narrative that came across was "ultimately it's his choice." We explore this further in Chapters 3 and 8. With regard to how individuals qualify for a spot in cabinet, we found that three sets of terms came up frequently. The first related to being "experienced," "capable," and "talented." We labeled these experiential criteria, and this concept informs our analysis in Chapters 5 and 9. The second set of terms that formed a dominant narrative in several of our cases revolved around "trust" and "loyalty." We developed the concept of affiliational criteria, which forms the basis of our analysis in Chapters 6 and 9. The third term that figured prominently in our data was "balance," referring to the need for a cabinet to accommodate appropriately a range of representational dimensions. We develop the concept of representational criteria, which forms the basis of our analysis in Chapters 7 and 10.

Advantages and Challenges of the Data

Our research is grounded in two original sets of data addressing the same research questions, and we scrutinize our interview data and our media data employing the same standards (see Lynch 2013, 37). The combination of these data sets increases the validity of the data, which is "best for . . . exploratory and in-depth work, but it makes coding and then analysis more difficult" (Aberbach and Rockman 2002, 674). Because we employ multiple country cases and multiple cabinet formations within each case, our data permit us to get both "breadth and depth" (Berry 2002, 680) in our analysis of the cabinet-formation process, the most appropriate approach for process-tracing research (Lynch 2013, 44). At the same time, we are able to focus on "the concrete and the particular" (Beckmann and Hall 2013, 198) in each case. Our interview data provide a richness of context that is crucial to understanding cabinet formation as a process. "[T]he inaccessibility of sources other than interviews [means] that whole areas of scholarship [are] impossible without them. . . . [S]ystematic records are virtually nonexistent for the many important activities that occur outside of official venues" (Beckmann and Hall 2013, 208). Substantial advantages accrue from our media data set. By employing media reporting from two national newspapers in each country case, we have comparability of data sources from the newspaper article evidence. These data are particularly important, given their comparability across countries and cabinets. Memoirs and autobiographies supplemented our data, also giving us candid elite perspectives that we could not access another way.

Securing the interview data presented the greatest challenges. Elite interviewing is data collection at the highest level. Access to actual ministers and to those who appoint them is difficult, given the demands of their positions and the requirements and uncertainties of their schedules. There are also potential high costs for the elite interviewee who, making a mistake or being overly frank in an interview, may face sanctions for participating in an interview. Interviewees operate within a political party context; comments about, for example, cabinet formation and cabinet coalition partners are fraught with issues of opposition, external and internal, making this kind of elite interviewing more challenging than other means of data collection. Moreover, such research is expensive, especially in comparative political research, requiring international travel in a context where one's interview subject may simply cancel a scheduled interview. As a result, we relied on interview data from interviews with former cabinet ministers no longer in government and sub-ministerial elites for data about elite behavior in the cabinet-formation process. We have no interview data for the United States or Canada; in all cases, and as explained earlier, we relied on evidence from country experts, media data, and secondary sources.

We recognize that in presenting qualitative data as examples of evidence concerning our research questions, we incur the risk of "selecting illustrative, theory-confirming pieces of interview data" (Lynch 2013, 38). To that end, we have been careful to select examples that are supported by the preponderance of the qualitative data sets for each country. We also identify where interview data conflict with or undermine claims in the media data. In addition, we examined the interview data across as well as within country, to understand the patterns of constraint and enabling of formal and informal rules empowering selectors and that qualify *ministrables*. We discussed these data and these cases extensively to identify dominant narratives of cabinet formation and of *ministrable* eligibility criteria, and to map where such narratives were consistent or conflicting across party, individual selectors, and political systems.

Country Cases and Case Selection

We selected seven established democracies as case studies: Australia, Canada, Chile, Germany, Spain, the United Kingdom, and the United States. When selecting our cases, the most important consideration was to ensure variation in system type. Given that so much of the existing literature focuses on the consequences of presidentialism versus parliamentarism or generalist versus specialist recruiting methods, we sought to ensure that our group of cases included countries from each category. Australia, Canada, and the United Kingdom are all examples of Westminster democracies where ministers are recruited from national parliaments and, according to scholars of ministerial recruitment, generalist political skills are believed to matter more than specialist policy expertise (Rhodes, Wanna, and Weller 2009).

Germany and Spain are parliamentary systems where some ministers are recruited from parliament, but others are appointed from regional political institutions or public administration. Ministers are often said to be specialists as well as generalists. Chile and the United States are presidential republics where ministers are recruited from outside of congress and are often said to be specialists.

Our country cases also vary across a range of factors that present opportunities for substantial analytical leverage. Our cases include variation in regard to the following: whether a country is a unitary or federal state, whether the country has had a female selector or a gender parity cabinet, and party affiliation of the selector. Four of the countries are federal political systems (Australia, Canada, Germany, and the US), two are unitary (Chile and the UK), and one is quasi-federal (Spain). Four of the countries (Australia, Chile, Germany, and the UK) have had female selectors, and four of the countries have had at least one instance of a gender parity cabinet (Canada, Chile, Germany, and Spain) (see Table 2.2). These differences and similarities

Table 2.2 Case Selection

Country	Political System	State Structure	Female Selector (number)	Governing Parties
Australia	Westminster parliamentary	Federal	Yes (1)	Labor Coalition (Liberals/ National)
Canada	Westminster parliamentary	Federal	No	Conservatives Liberals
Chile	Presidential	Unitary	Yes (1)	Christian Democratic Party, Socialist Party, National Renovation Party
Germany	Parliamentary	Federal	Yes (1)	Christian Democratic Union Social Democrats
Spain	Parliamentary	Quasi-federal	No	People's Party Spanish Socialist Workers Party
United Kingdom	Westminster parliamentary	Unitary	Yes (2)	Conservatives Labour
United States	Presidential	Federal	No	Democrats Republicans

provide analytical leverage for determining the extent to which intersections of formal and informal rules involving selector choice and *ministrable* eligibility are gendered in process and produce gendered outcomes. We also selected these seven countries rather than others with similar characteristics given that we, as researchers, have the requisite expert knowledge of the countries, as well as competence in terms of language skills to conduct interviews and read newspaper reports (Seawright and Gerring 2008, 295). For additional context, we provide brief overviews of the relevant features of the political systems in each country.

Australia

Australia is a constitutional monarchy with a Westminster-style parliamentary democracy, and a federal structure made up of six states and two territories. At the federal level, Australia has a bicameral parliament: Members of the 150-seat House of Representatives are elected through single-member plurality seats using preferential voting normally every three years, and members of the 76-seat Senate are elected for six-year terms using a system of proportional representation. Australia features two political party groupings, the Australian Labor Party (ALP) and the Coalition, which is a permanent arrangement between the right of center Liberal Party and the smaller National Party, and government formation alternates between the two, depending on election results. Governments are normally able to form majorities (although Prime Minister Julia Gillard (ALP) formed a minority government with support from independent MPs in 2010). As the prime minister and cabinet are not mentioned in the Australian constitution (Weller 2007), the roles and rules relating to those institutions are largely informal, albeit strongly institutionalized. The only formal rule written in the constitution is that ministers must be members of parliament, appointed from either chamber. A formal rule at party level for the ALP states that the caucus is empowered to select ministers. The size of the cabinet is not specified in the constitution and is normally determined by the prime minister. However, steps have been taken to reduce the size of cabinet. Menzies created an inner-outer cabinet structure in 1956 (abandoned only once by Whitlam, 1972–1975) and references are made in our 2013 media data to new restrictions on the size of cabinet for incoming Prime Minister Tony Abbott, though cabinet size increases again with his successor Malcolm Turnbull. Government turnover in Australia is comparatively high, with elections every three years and regular leadership challenges—referred to as "spills"—in between.

In 1902, white Australian women were the first worldwide to be granted the rights to vote and to stand in national elections (Sawer and Simms 1993), rights not extended to Aboriginal women for federal elections until 1962. However, the first women were not elected to either legislative institution until 1943, and while women have been consistently represented in the Senate since that date, their presence in the House of Representatives has only been ongoing since 1980. Women's representation in parliament has increased slowly and is higher in the Senate (39.5 percent in 2016) than in the House of Representatives (28.7 percent in 2016). While Moon and Fountain (1997) find that women are over-represented in state level cabinets compared with their parliamentary presence, at the federal level the representation of women as ministers has not kept pace with their growing parliamentary representation (Summers 2003, 213). The highest number of female ministers appointed in Australia is five, or 22.7 percent, in 2016, meaning that Australia has yet to form a gender parity cabinet. Julia Gillard's tenure as Australia's first female prime minster (2010–2013) laid bare the very gendered political culture that still exists within the main political parties, institutions, and the media in Australia (Gillard 2014; Johnson 2015).

Canada

Canada is a constitutional monarchy with a Westminster-style parliamentary democracy, and a federal structure made up of 10 provinces and three territories. At the federal level, Canada has a bicameral parliament: Members of the House of Commons are elected through single-member plurality districts with a maximum term of five years,[11] but members of the Senate are appointed by the governor-general on the recommendation of the prime minister and serve until the age of 75.[12] Canada has a multiparty system, but single-party governments are the norm; the only coalition government at the federal level was during World War I. Even if a party fails to win a majority, the practice is for the party with the most seats to govern as a minority government. Only two parties have ever held national office in the modern

---

[11] Currently, there are 338 members of the House of Commons.
[12] The Senate has 105 members.

era: the Conservatives and the Liberals. The third largest party in terms of electoral support is the New Democratic Party (NDP), and the other parties with seats in parliament include the Green Party and the Bloc Quebecois, a nationalist party that runs candidates exclusively in the province of Quebec. The two main federal parties, the Liberals and Conservatives, have been described as "catch-all" parties, rather than competing on clearly programmatic or ideological lines, but the Conservatives are considerably to the right of the more centrist Liberals. The NDP is a leftist party.

Like the British political system on which it is based, Canada's constitution makes few references to the cabinet or the prime minister. Most rules governing ministerial recruitment, cabinet formation, and the day-to-day functioning of cabinet are either conventions or informal rules. The size of the cabinet is not specified in the constitution, and the number of ministers has ranged from 12 (in the very early days of the country) to 38 (during the prime ministership of Brian Mulroney). By comparative standards, Canadian cabinets are large; the size of the Canadian cabinet is determined by the prime minister. Canada had its first gender parity cabinet, appointed by Prime Minister Justin Trudeau, in 2015.

Women were first granted suffrage at the provincial level, beginning with Manitoba, in 1916. Nationally, women did not win the right to vote until 1921, but even then, some groups of women, like Asian and indigenous women living on reserves, remained excluded. Asian Canadians were enfranchised after World War II, but under the terms of the *Indian Act*, indigenous people living on reserves were not entitled to vote until 1960. Even after extending suffrage, men continued to dominate electoral politics, federally and provincially. Although women's presence in elected office has grown in the past few decades, it remains low compared to other wealthy democracies (Thomas and Young, 2014). For the most part, Canadian political parties have not opened up much space for women. Party gatekeepers at the constituency level are frequently blamed for the small number of female candidates, particularly in safe or winnable districts (Thomas and Blodet 2013). At the national level, only the NDP (which has never formed government at the federal level) has a gender quota, and there is no realistic prospect for legislated gender quotas given the public's lack of support for any kind of affirmative action. Not surprisingly, women's parliamentary representation has yet to reach the 30 percent threshold. Indeed, the 2015 parliamentary elections returned the highest number of women to date: 88 female MPs, up from 60 in 2011. Although the increase appears sizable, in proportional terms, the gain is negligible, since the number of seats in parliament grew from 308 to 338. In percentage terms, therefore, women's presence grew by just one percent, from 25 to 26 percent.[13] No woman has ever won election as prime minister in Canada.

Chile

Chile is a unitary state with a presidential system, a directly elected president and bicameral congress (Chamber of Deputies and Senate). Chile's current constitution was adopted in 1980, in the midst of a highly repressive military dictatorship that governed the country from 1973 until 1990. Even after the return of democracy, Chile's political system is often described as "presidentialist," concentrating extensive legislative powers in the executive compared to the legislative branch (Siavelis 2000). Presidents are constitutionally prohibited from serving consecutive terms, and today serve four-year terms (decreased from six years). Chile's first and only female president, Michelle Bachelet, is the first post-transition president to win a second election. She governed from 2006 to 2010 and took office again in 2014 after winning the presidential elections of 2013.

Compared to neighboring countries in Latin America, Chile's political parties are strong, and the system overall is relatively stable. Parties are highly disciplined, relatively stable, and the party system is ideologically organized. Notably, electoral rules designed by the outgoing dictatorship encouraged parties to compete in two broad coalitions: the two-party coalition of the political right, the *Alianza*, included the center-right National Renovation (RN) and the deeply conservative Independent Democratic Union (UDI). In 2015 the coalition was renamed *Chile Vamos* (Let's Go Chile) and was joined by two smaller parties. The center-left coalition was known as the *Concertación* until 2013, when it changed its name to *Nueva Mayoría* (New Majority), and after winning the first set of post-dictatorship elections, has managed to win every presidential election except for 2010. Until 2013, it was composed of four parties: the large and centrist Christian Democratic Party (PDC), the more leftist Party for Democracy (PPD), the Socialist Party (PS), and the small centrist Social Democratic Radical Party (PSRD). By the 2013

[13] Erin Anderssen, "We Have a Record Number of Female MPs, but Hold the Applause," *Globe and Mail*, October 20, 2015.

elections, the newly named *Nueva Mayoría* grew to six parties, including two parties even further on the left. Maintaining coalition unity, especially for the *Concertación*, has been central to its political project, and as we show in sub-sequent chapters, practically all of the informal rules surrounding cabinet formation derive from the goal of maintaining coalition unity.

Women's movements played an important role in the pro-democracy movements that eventually led to the defeat of Augusto Pinochet's military government in a plebiscite in 1988. Women formed the backbone of the human rights movements that contributed to a growing legitimacy crisis for the military and to the neighborhood movements responding to the hardships created by the dictatorship's harsh economic policies (see Baldez 2002; Franceschet 2005). Yet the return of democracy did not open up many opportunities for women's representation in political institutions. Women won just 10 percent of seats in the first post-transition congress, and only one woman was included in cabinet (to head up the newly created National Women's Service). Even though women's cabinet representation reached 30 percent by 2000 and 50 percent by 2006 (one of our four cases with at least one gender parity cabinet), women's congressional representation continued to lag. Women won just 15.8 percent of seats in the 2013 elections. Women's legislative under-representation has improved, however. A new electoral rule passed in 2015 included a 40 percent quota provision. Women's representa-tion in the lower house grew from 15.8 percent in 2013 to 22.6 percent after the 2017 congressional elections.

Germany

The Federal Republic of Germany (FRG) is a parliamentary democracy founded by the Basic Law in 1949 and extended to include eastern German states in 1990. As a federal state, power is shared between the federal gov-ernment and the 16 German *Länder*. Legislative power is vested with the bicameral parliament comprising the 598-seat directly elected Bundestag and the Bundesrat, which is made up of representatives of the elected state governments. At the federal level, executive power lies with the chancellor, who is granted by the constitution sole responsibility for setting the direction of government policy. The chancellor is nominated by the largest party in the Bundestag and is appointed following a formal vote in the lower house. Postwar German politics was initially dominated by two main parties: the

Christian Democratic Union (CDU) and the Social Democratic Party of Germany (SPD), referred to as the *Volksparteien* or people's parties, but since 1990 they have lost ground to smaller parties. The German electoral system means that no single party gains a majority, and all postwar governments have been coalitions. The smaller liberal Free Democratic Party (FDP) traditionally acted as a pivot party, forming coalitions with parties of the left and right, and Alliance 90/The Greens formed a coalition with the SPD in 1998–2005. Grand Coalitions between the CDU and the SPD have also been formed, first in 1966–1969 and more recently under Chancellor Angela Merkel in 2005–2009 and in 2013. German coalition government is stable, mostly because coalition combinations are predictable, coalition agreements bind parties to a program of government, and votes of no confidence must be constructive. Cabinet size ranges from 13 to 22, and varies according to coalition and political considerations, for instance accommodating party factions or specific personalities (Conradt and Langenbacher 2013, 236).

Women's parliamentary representation in Germany is comparatively high, reaching 36.5 percent of the Bundestag in 2013, though falling back down to 30.7 percent in 2017. While West Germany is associated with traditional gender roles in the labor market, women's political presence was boosted as early as the 1980s by quota rules within the SPD and the Green Party. German unification in 1990 introduced to the FRG a nation of women raised on the principle of gender equality in public life. Germany has produced one parity cabinet, in 2009, and one female chancellor, Angela Merkel, who took office in 2005, and won re-election in 2009, 2013, and 2017.

Spain

Spain is a parliamentary monarchy whose political structure is governed by the constitution of 1978. The new constitution was adopted after the end of the dictatorship of General Francisco Franco, who led the country from 1939 until his death in 1975. Today, Spain has a quasi-federal political structure, composed of 17 autonomous communities, each with somewhat different and contested competencies and relationships to the central government. At the national level, Spain has a bicameral parliament: the lower house (Congress of Deputies) has 350 members, elected through proportional representation with closed party lists, and the upper house (Senate) has 266 members, some of whom are popularly elected, and others appointed by regional governments. The head of government, the prime minister (*presidente del gobierno*), is formally appointed by the monarch following an investiture vote in the Congress of Deputies. Prime ministers normally announce their cabinets within a week of an investiture vote, with cabinet size ranging from a high of 24 ministers to a low of 13 ministers. The structure and size of cabinet is determined by the prime minister, who is empowered to create and eliminate ministries (Real-Dato and Jerez-Mir 2009, 104).

Until very recently, Spain had a relatively stable "two-plus" party system, with two major parties, the conservative People's Party (PP) and the leftist Spanish Socialist Workers' Party (PSOE), holding more than 80 percent of seats in parliament since the return of democracy. Smaller regional parties also won seats, but until 2015, single-party governments were the norm, even in cases where no party has a majority of seats (Field 2016). The emergence of new parties and declining support for the PP and PSOE introduced uncertainty and instability into Spanish politics, and the general elections in 2015 failed to produce a government. A second set of elections held in 2016 produced another highly fragmented parliament, but a second investiture vote in October 2016 finally produced a government, led by Prime Minister Mariano Rajoy, who remained in power until 2018. Rajoy's government remained plagued by instability and was replaced by Pedro Sánchez (PSOE) after a no-confidence vote in 2018.

Women's political representation has been relatively high, crossing the 30 percent threshold in 2000, and reaching 39.1 percent in the 2015 parliamentary elections. Women have been active in both parties but have been more effective in securing party-level reforms in the PSOE, which first adopted a 25 percent internal gender quota in 1988, which was increased to 40 percent in 1997. Other leftist parties in Spain likewise use gender quotas, and by 2004, nine of the 12 parties with seats in the national Congress of Deputies had incorporated gender quotas into their party statutes (Verge 2012, 399). Even though the People's Party is rhetorically opposed to affirmative action, and has challenged the Equality Law in court, it has nonetheless felt compelled to incorporate women as candidates and cabinet ministers in order to compete electorally with the PSOE. Importantly, an Equality Law passed at the national level in 2008 requiring all political parties to ensure that no more than 60 percent of candidates are drawn from a single sex. As such, women's parliamentary representation in Spain is likely to remain high. Despite reaching high levels of parliamentary representation, Spain has never had a female prime minister; Spain has, however, had two gender parity cabinets, in 2004 and 2008.

The United Kingdom

The United Kingdom of Great Britain and Northern Ireland is a parliamentary constitutional monarchy. Though a unitary state, the United Kingdom has devolved some sovereign powers to Scotland, Wales, and Northern Ireland. The United Kingdom has a bicameral parliament. The House of Commons elects 650 members of parliament (MPs) through a first-past-the-post electoral system for a five-year term. The House of Lords is made up of around 800 members, most of whom are nominated as Life Peers; in 1999 the number of Hereditary Peers was reduced to 92. The prime minister as the head of government is formally appointed by the monarch (who is the symbolic head of state) and is by convention the leader of the party winning a majority of seats in the House of Commons. The prime minister appoints ministers to the cabinet, which in the postwar period typically includes between 17 and 23 ministers, predominantly from the House of Commons, but occasionally from the House of Lords. The number of cabinet posts is determined by the prime minister, but a de facto limit is set by the budget for ministerial salaries. The United Kingdom's party system is dominated by the Labour Party on the left and the Conservative Party on the right. Governments are normally single-party majority. However, in 2010 parliamentary electoral results failed to return a majority of seats to any single party; as a result, the Conservatives and Liberal Democrats formed the first coalition government since 1945 under Prime Minister David Cameron.

Despite universal suffrage being granted to all women in 1928, women's political representation in the United Kingdom has remained comparatively low, though the share of women in the House of Commons elected in 2017 reached 32.2 percent. Progress in the number of female MPs was initially made by the Labour Party through the introduction of All Women's Short Lists (AWSL), first used in the 1997 election, bringing women's presence up to 18.2 percent. The Conservatives have trailed behind in terms of women's parliamentary representation, having relied on softer mechanisms such as the "A List" of candidates drawn up by the party to boost diversity. The United Kingdom has never had a gender parity cabinet, but it has had two female prime ministers—Margaret Thatcher (1979–1990) and Theresa May (2016–2019)—both of whom are Conservative.

The United States

The United States is a federal political system where the national government shares sovereign powers with 50 individual state governments. A presidential system, the United States elects its president through the indirect mechanism of the Electoral College, and hence provides the president and members of the bicameral US Congress (the House of Representatives, with 435 voting members, and the 100-person Senate) with electoral independence from each other; neither the president nor the Congress can be removed from office by the other for electoral purposes or political reasons. The specific governing powers of the president and of the Congress are specified in the US constitution, ratified in 1789, which thereafter has been the major governing document of the United States. Cabinet size is relatively small, compared to other countries, with 15 cabinet departments in 2016. Cabinet positions are created by congressional legislation; presidents are not empowered to change the size of the US cabinet. Since the 1980s, "divided government"—where one political party controls the executive branch and the opposing party dominates in the legislature—has become increasingly common. Presidents serve four-year terms; Amendment XXII imposes presidential term limits of two full terms.

Two major political parties—the Democratic Party and the Republican Party—dominate the US party system. Parties are loosely organized, characterized as "catch-all" parties (Katz and Mair 1995), formed to capture minimum winning coalitions of voters in each election cycle. The relatively informal nature of each party is reflected in the lack of a formal party leader of the type that characterizes political parties in parliamentary systems; generally, an elected president is considered the leader of the party in power. In recent years, the two parties have become increasingly polarized around a wide range of political issues. The Democratic Party is generally considered the "left" party in the US party system; the Republicans constitute the "right-wing" party. No other political parties have effectively competed for congressional or presidential office in the post–World War II era. The US two-party system is shaped by the single-member plurality electoral system for Congress, and the majority electoral requirement of the Electoral College for the presidency.

All women were formally enfranchised at the federal level in 1920, with the ratification of the Nineteenth Amendment; only white women, however, had practical access to the ballot, with Jim Crow laws and other state-level restrictions effectively barring women of color from exercising voting rights until passage of the 1965 Voting Rights Act (Smooth 2011, 2006). The US electoral system and the nature of the presidential system have impeded women's access to Congress and the presidency. Among wealthy democracies, the United States has among the lowest representation of women in its national legislature, and a woman has never been elected president or vice president. In 2019, women constituted 25 percent of the US Senate, and 23.4 percent of members of the House (https://cawp.rutgers.edu/women-us-congress-2019), the "highest" levels of women's congressional representation in US history. Neither of the two major parties has gender quotas for candidate selection, although both have gender parity requirements for internal party organization. Women are similarly poorly represented in state legislative office (24.8 percent in 2017), and only five women were serving as governors of states. The United States has never had a female president; only in July 2016 did one of the two major parties nominate a woman as its presidential candidate. The electoral system and the closed nature of candidate selection are major barriers to women's access to elective office. Women have not fared much better in appointive office. Since 1993, women have been present in cabinet posts at only slightly higher levels than their congressional representation (approximately 20–25 percent), regardless of party. Five women have been appointed to key cabinet posts; three women have served as secretary of state, and two have been attorneys general. The United States has never had a gender parity cabinet.

Conclusion

This chapter has set out our theoretical and conceptual framework, offered a theoretical justification for our case studies, presented our model, and outlined the methods we used to collect and analyze our data. Our theoretical framework borrows from the various schools of institutionalism, combining insights about the importance of formal and informal rules in shaping politics with core arguments from feminist political science, namely that gender permeates all social and political relations and is an element of power hierarchies.

Formal and informal rules shape the powers of prime ministers and presidents to shape their cabinets. Cabinet construction is akin to putting together a puzzle: the individual cabinet ministers are not as important on their own as they are in how they fit with each other to constitute the governing team. Identifying rules that empower or constrain selectors in their ability to complete the puzzle of cabinet formation is complicated by the relative absence of written publicly identifiable rules at the system level and party level. Instead, many of the rules determining who selects ministers are unwritten, yet they powerfully shape the process of cabinet formation.

Formal rules are also sparse in regard to eligibility and qualification for cabinet appointments. Those who might constitute a cabinet eligibility pool face few formal conditions on qualifying for cabinet. Instead, informal rules have considerable power in gatekeeping for cabinet appointments. Even where one might anticipate formal rules identifying the credentials needed for certain posts, for example, a written requirement that justice ministers have legal training or that treasury ministers have economics degrees, such codified rules are absent. Instead, informal rules shape the qualifications of individuals for some appointments and the collective qualifications of cabinets for all appointments.

In the following chapter, we examine the formal and informal rules that shape the powers of prime ministers or presidents to select the ministers for their cabinets, identifying for each country how political system and party rules empower or constrain the selector to make the choice.

3

Who Selects Ministers?

Rules Empowering and Constraining Selectors

Constitutions tell us little about how ministers are selected. Some constitutions make no mention of cabinet at all, while others simply state that the president or head of state shall appoint a cabinet. To understand who is empowered to select ministers, we need to look beyond a country's constitution to the informal or unwritten rules governing who gets to select ministers. In this chapter, we explore both formal and informal rules at the political system level, as well as rules specific to political parties, to determine which actors select ministers and how empowered or constrained those selectors are when making cabinet appointments. In Chapter 8, we use our findings to explore the gendered consequences of rules about selection.

Existing scholarship exploring the rules surrounding cabinet formation offers us two main insights. First, there are few formal rules about the cabinet-appointment process (Dogan 1989); and second, informal rules are often more determinative than codified rules (de Winter 1995; Mershon 1994). These two insights support the conceptual framework outlined in the previous chapter, namely, that what matters is not whether a rule is formal or informal, but rather, whether or not a rule is institutionalized. Formal rules may be weakly institutionalized, in which case they do not really constrain or empower political actors at all since weakly institutionalized rules are seldom followed. Informal rules, on the other hand, may be strongly institutionalized, thereby actually affecting the behavior of political actors. For example, a "convention" is an unwritten but well-known, strong, highly institutionalized informal rule that has persisted across a long period of time and that includes sanctions for its violation. Conventions are common in Westminster systems without written constitutions or governing charters.

The main focus of much of the cabinet literature, however, is the formation of governments, rather than the selection of ministers. Most studies focus on countries where coalition governments are common, and the central research question is how cabinet posts are distributed across parties of the coalition, and which political actors participate in the process. For example, De Winter writes that, in countries with majoritarian electoral rules, government formation is relatively simple and straightforward. But even if forming governments is straightforward, the process of selecting ministers may not be so. In fact, different sets of rules apply to the process of selecting ministers. De Winter observes that normally, there is a single selector in single-party governments, while multiple selectors are always present in coalition governments (1995, 116–117). We find, however, that even in single-party governments, the rules about who selects ministers are not always straightforward.

This chapter focuses on the selection of ministers, exploring all the factors that affect whether selectors are empowered or constrained when assembling their ministerial teams, and how these have changed over time. As indicated in the preceding chapters, we define an empowered selector as one with the ability to choose ministers autonomously, as opposed to having to consult, negotiate, or take instructions from other political actors. We recognize that even when selectors are empowered by rules to select ministers autonomously, they may well discuss ministerial possibilities with advisors or close political allies. We distinguish between seeking advice and being compelled by rules to consult, negotiate, or share selection power with other political actors. We define constraints on selectors as anything requiring presidents or prime ministers to negotiate cabinet appointments with other political actors or to accept wholesale the ministerial selections of others.

Selectors may be empowered or constrained not only by rules, whether formal or informal, but also by the political context, namely, whether their position as party or government leader is secure or at risk due to an intraparty rivalry or party fragmentation. The rules granting leaders discretion to select ministers emerge principally from constitutions or constitutional conventions that give presidents and prime ministers sole authority to select (and remove) ministers and, in many cases, the power to determine the size of cabinet. Where constitutions make no mention of cabinets, as in Canada and the United Kingdom, strong conventions determine that the prime minister selects ministers, who are then formally appointed by the head of state. Selectors are further empowered by informal rules that proscribe certain behaviors on the part of other actors. For example, informal rules strongly discourage self-nomination, public campaigning for a cabinet post, or visibly competing against or opposing other *ministrables*. Ambitious politicians, recognizing the potential negative consequences of violating these informal rules, refrain from taking the initiative to deliver their résumés to a newly elected leader. Aspirant ministers also refrain from publicly campaigning for a cabinet post. Instead, politicians must await a leader's call inviting them to be a minister.[1] If the call does come, the invitation follows a lengthy process through which eligible *ministrables* have been vetted by a president's or prime minister's closest advisors, personal transition team, or the Whip's Office. In sum, in most cases, the formal appointment power of selectors is further underscored and reinforced by informal rules.

Although presidents and prime ministers are normally the central actors with the formal power to select ministers, their selection power is not always absolute. Formal and informal rules, some of which emerge at the party rather than system level, structure the cabinet appointment process in ways that constrain as well as empower selectors. Institutional features of the political system can also expand or delimit the discretion that selectors enjoy with respect to cabinet appointments. Some selectors are embedded within institutional environments structured by rules that constrain them in the cabinet-appointment process. In parliamentary systems, prime ministers (and their cabinets) must maintain the confidence of parliament or else face the threat of removal. In contrast, in presidential systems, an executive's authority to govern is constitutionally independent of the legislative branch. In principle, then, prime ministers are more constrained than presidents in assembling their cabinets since their tenure in office is dependent upon ongoing parliamentary support. Selectors' risk of removal (and thus the degree of constraints they face) depends also on party-specific rules. Where rules about party leadership increase the ease with which party leaders can be removed, prime ministers (who are also party leaders) are further constrained. Other factors empowering or constraining selectors emerge not from rules, but from contextual political factors like the size or scope of the electoral mandate, or the extent to which the party or coalition that the

---

[1] This informal rule was referenced in an early episode of the British television series *Yes Minister*, when an aspiring minister waits by the phone for a call from the new prime minister (Zussman 2013). For a real-life example, see Madeleine Albright's account of awaiting a phone call from President Bill Clinton concerning her possible selection as secretary of state (2003, 222–223).

selector leads is solidly behind the president or prime minister or is deeply divided and fractured.

Rules that are specific to the cabinet-appointment process may also constrain selectors. Selectors face the greatest constraint in the cabinet-appointment process when they lose discretion over some or all portfolios. This constraint emerges when electoral outcomes encourage the formation of coalition governments. In such cases, selectors must cede some discretion in appointing ministers to the leaders of their coalition partners. Selectors also lose discretion in parties where decisions over cabinet appointments are made by the parliamentary party or caucus rather than the selector. A similar, if weaker, type of constraint is imposed when the prime minister or president is required to consult with other party elites and to take their preferences into consideration.

The remainder of this chapter illustrates how selectors are empowered and constrained across our cases. In the first section, we identify rules that empower and constrain selectors when forming their cabinet. Our findings indicate that, despite constraints emerging in some situations, selectors in most of our cases are empowered to determine for themselves who will be on their ministerial teams. In the second part of the chapter, we categorize our country case studies, distinguishing countries by the extent to which the selector is empowered or constrained in forming a cabinet. We identify which rules are doing the work of empowering or constraining, namely, whether they derive from constitutional design or party rules. Finally, we identify whether and how political context factors can further empower or constrain leaders.

Empowering and Constraining: Factors Shaping Selector Discretion and Changes over Time

What rules empower or constrain selectors to choose their ministers? Constraints or empowering mechanisms may exist at the system level, thereby affecting all selectors, regardless of party. Such mechanisms may be properties of the political system generally, such as mechanisms for the removal of chief executives, or they may be rules (whether formal or informal) that apply specifically to cabinet appointments. In the following, we identify the main sources of empowerment and constraint that shape the procedural aspects of the cabinet-appointment process.

Formal and Informal Rules That Empower Selectors

A dominant formal rule in cabinet formation across all countries is that the chief executive selects ministers. This rule appears explicitly in many constitutions but, in some cases, it is a constitutional convention. In Chile, for instance, the constitution, as spelled out in Article 32.7, gives sole appointment authority to the president. In the United States, the president has the formal appointment power, although the Senate also has formal advisory and consent powers.[2] In the case of the United States, there are formal rules that empower the president and, by requiring consent of the Senate, constrain him.

In most parliamentary democracies, the formal rule is that the head of state appoints ministers, but does so on the recommendation of the head of government. For example, Article 64 (1) of the German Basic Law states, "federal ministers shall be appointed and dismissed by the federal President upon the proposal of the federal Chancellor." Spain's constitution requires that government ministers be "appointed and dismissed by the King at the President's proposal" (Section 100). Among our Westminster cases, constitutions do not explicitly spell out the role of prime ministers in cabinet formation, but convention determines that prime ministers select their cabinet members, who are then formally appointed by the head of state. Australia's constitution mentions that the "Governor General may appoint officers to administer departments of the state of the Commonwealth" (Chapter 2, paragraph 64). Canada's constitution makes no reference to cabinet ministers whatsoever. White notes the paradox: "[t]he central law-making body in the land is itself all but invisible in the statute books" (2005, 32–33). Despite the absence of formal rules empowering prime ministers in Australia, Canada, and the United Kingdom, strong constitutional conventions give selection powers exclusively to prime ministers. According to Kaufman, ministerial selection in the United Kingdom is the "prerogative of the prime minister" (1997, 4). A media report on the formation of the 2010 Australian cabinet noted that Prime Minister Gillard reserves the "ultimate right to determine who would form her new team,"[3] a statement supported by former minister Nicola

---

[2] The president "shall nominate, and by and with the advice and consent of the Senate, shall appoint ambassadors, other public ministers and consuls, judges of the Supreme Court, and all other officers of the United States, whose appointments are not herein otherwise provided for, and which shall be established by law" (US Constitution, Art. II, Sec. 2).

[3] "Gillard Asks MPs to Name Wish List," *The Australian*, September 10, 2010.

Roxon, who said "it's really up to the Prime Minister to work out where we can all be best used [. . .] And that's something that I will accept."[4] We know of no instances where prime ministers' formal authority to select ministers has been challenged.

The formal rules and conventions empowering chief executives to select ministers are reinforced by two strongly institutionalized informal rules. First, aspirant ministers cannot publicly self-nominate or lobby for a spot in cabinet. Second, other political actors cannot publicly interfere in the process of cabinet formation, whether by publicly advocating for a *ministrable* (although they may work privately to advance their preferred candidates) or by actively campaigning against someone. There is nothing akin to the process of securing a nomination for a parliamentary seat: there is no call for nominations; there is no formal application process; and there is no invitation to eligible candidates to apply. One awaits the call.

There are powerful sanctions if the rule prohibiting self-promotion is violated. Across all our cases, we find that it is highly detrimental to one's chances of becoming a minister to campaign or lobby openly for a ministerial post. In Australia in 2013, "[l]ikely candidates for the ministry all declined to comment yesterday, knowing it would cruel their chances of promotion."[5] Former UK prime minister John Major wrote that, in 1992, "Most of the newcomers wanted, and in some cases expected, to become ministers within months of arriving at Westminster. Four of the 1992 intake met the Chief Whip in 1993 to ask when they would be made ministers—unthinkable behavior in previous generations" (Major 2000, 347).

We find evidence that rules proscribing self-nomination are indeed enforced. For example, during an expert panel discussing cabinet appointments in Canada after the 2008 elections, a panelist noted that when former prime minister Jean Chretién was forming his cabinet, "there was somebody who leaked out that he was going to be appointed to cabinet and the rug was pulled out from under him right away. And that would happen with any government frankly if it did, because it's just so serious. It's a bad harbinger of what that minister is going to be like, frankly."[6] Similarly, a potential cabinet secretary in Barack Obama's first administration was criticized in the

[4] "Minister Resigns as PM Juggles New Portfolios," *The Australian*, September 9, 2010.
[5] "Libs 'Shocked' by Lack of Women in Cabinet," *The Australian*, September 13, 2013.
[6] Transcript of "The Globe Round Table," the *Globe and Mail's* weekly political podcast, October 29, 2008. http://www.theglobeandmail.com/news/politics/the-globe-round-table/article1064947/ ?page=all. Accessed March 30, 2016.

US press as having "a very obvious taste for a cabinet appointment in the new administration," and was not considered further for secretary of the interior.[7] In these two cases, the sanction for self-promotion was serious, with rule-breaking individuals ultimately passed over for cabinet appointment. In sum, the procedural rules for cabinet appointments are fundamentally distinct from those of elected offices: aspirants for elected office are frequently expected to self-nominate, and their selection proceeds through formally codified rules explicating how candidate selection should take place. No such process exists for cabinet appointments—a reality that, we argue, has the effect of further empowering selectors.

Nor can *ministrables* improve their chances by campaigning against likely opponents. Warren Christopher, head of US president Bill Clinton's transition team in 1992, recounts a political blunder made by Dave McCurdy, a potential appointee as secretary of defense:[8] "Once he knew he was under consideration for secretary of defense, Dave McCurdy made a bad move. To advance his candidacy, . . . McCurdy began circulating word that [likely competitor Les] Aspin's departure from the [House Armed Services] committee . . . would impair national security. When this suggestion reached the press and the source was identified, it was regarded as a hit below the belt" (173). In the end, Clinton nominated Aspin instead of McCurdy, further evidencing the sanction against ministerial aspirants who attempt to influence or interfere in the selection process.

Instead of applying or lobbying for the job of cabinet minister, aspiring politicians must wait for a call from the selector. What is more, when potential ministers do get the call, they must accept the post they are offered. In his autobiography, John Major "remembered the old adage: you don't negotiate with prime ministers, you say 'yes' or you say 'no' and take the consequences" (Major 2000, 112–113). Likewise, a former minister in the United Kingdom reported that when first offered a ministerial post she ideally wanted "time to consider," but an experienced colleague advised, "if you say that you won't get the post and they won't ask you again."[9]

A second informal rule prohibits other political actors from engaging in unsolicited attempts to influence the cabinet selection process. This rule is

---

[7] Felicity Barringer, "John A. Kitzhaber," *New York Times*, November 30, 2008; a charge repeated in Felicity Barringer, "Obama's Inner Circle: Members and Maybes: John A. Kitzhaber," *New York Times*, December 2, 2008.

[8] McCurdy was a member of the US House of Representatives (D-OK4), and a founding member of the Democratic Leadership Council.

[9] Interview, December 17, 2013, London.

evident in many of our cases, where interview respondents referenced the undisputed authority of the president or prime minister to select their ministers, and where political actors have made similar statements to the media. In Spain, the prime minister "does not have to consult, either formally or informally, with anyone."[10] According to political experts and insiders, prime ministers may seek advice from their closest confidants, but there are no expectations that other political actors be consulted during the process of cabinet formation. For example, even if a selector wanted recommendations for ministers from regional party leaders, the prime minister would always initiate the conversation; regional leaders would never lobby the selector or request that certain people be appointed.

The rule prohibiting interference with the autonomy of the selector is evident in Chile as well. After the election of Michelle Bachelet as president in 2006, some of the party leaders in her coalition worried that she might not respect existing informal rules about the proportional distribution of cabinet portfolios across the parties of the coalition; when speaking publicly, however, party leaders took care to reiterate her authority as sole selector. One party leader said to the press, "the parties can offer opinions [about who should be in cabinet], opinions are always welcome, but the person who decides is the president, in this case, Michelle Bachelet."[11] For the United States, newly elected presidents develop transition teams to manage the shift to the new administration elected in November from the previous administration concluding its term in January in the year following the election. During this extended period, presidents, regardless of political party, consult with valued advisors, close friends, loyal supporters, and family members. No rules prescribe, however, that a president consult major party leaders, including those in Congress. More important, the advice sought by a president is not binding; the president, ultimately makes his or her own decisions.

Finally, there are instances where selectors, even those fully empowered by formal rules, perceive even greater latitude to select autonomously, given the political context. Such a situation may emerge after a significant or decisive electoral victory, or when the selector is perceived as wielding uncontested power in her political party or coalition. Former Spanish prime minister José Luis Rodríguez Zapatero is a good example in both senses. In July 2000, he won his party's leadership decisively, leaving no strong rivals in the party,

[10] Interview with former minister, May 13, 2014, Madrid.
[11] Claudio Salinas, "Estilo Bachelet abre expectativas y dudas," El Mercurio, January 14, 2006.

and in 2004 he led the party to an unexpected electoral victory, ending eight years of the Socialists being in opposition. Zapatero's sweeping victory further empowered him to select ministers autonomously.

In sum, across our cases, rules generally empower chief executives to select ministers. Where formal rules exist, they are further reinforced by informal rules that ensure that selectors' autonomy is respected, and in some cases, by contextual political factors like the absence of strong party rivals. Nonetheless, we find that not all selectors are fully empowered to select cabinet ministers. Sometimes, chief executives must share selection powers with other political actors.

Constraining Factors: When Is Selector Discretion Constrained?

It is rare to find formal rules at the system level that constrain selectors. As noted previously, in the United States, the formal rule is that the president nominates cabinet secretaries, but an additional formal rule empowers the Senate to confirm these nominations. Nonetheless, the confirmation power has generally been acknowledged as secondary to the president's appointment power.[12] In practice the Senate appointment approval rate has been relatively high. Loomis (2001) reports that "Presidents Reagan, [George H. W.] Bush, and Clinton fared about the same in winning confirmation for their nominees. All three won approval of more than 95 percent of their appointees in their administrations' first two years," concluding that "[t]he great majority of presidential appointees to high-level executive positions win approval by the Senate, although the success rate hovers at about 80 percent once a president has initially constructed his administration." In regard to appointments of cabinet secretaries specifically, Gerhardt (2003: Table 5, lxi–lxiii) provides evidence that, among post–World War II presidents, the Senate rejected no cabinet nominees of Presidents Truman, Kennedy, Nixon, Ford, Reagan, Bill Clinton, or George W. Bush.[13] With the US exception of

---

[12] *Federalist Paper* #66 (405) underscores an intended, relatively limited role for the Senate: "It will be the office of the President to *nominate* and, with the advice and consent of the Senate, to *appoint*. There will, of course, be no exertion of *choice* on the part of the Senate . . . [The Senate] cannot themselves *choose*—they can only ratify or object the choice he may have made."

[13] The Senate rejected nominees of Presidents Eisenhower (Lewis L. Strauss, for Commerce) and George H. W. Bush (John Tower, for Defense). The Senate failed to report out of committee President Lyndon Johnson's nomination of Robert C. Wood, for Housing and Urban Development. President Clinton withdrew three nominees from consideration, and George W. Bush withdrew

formal Senate approval, in none of our cases are other branches or political actors formally empowered to confirm or reject a selector's ministerial picks.

Two other sets of rules constrain chief executives when selecting ministers. The first and strongest type of constraint is when the prime minister or president entirely loses discretion over some or all of her cabinet slots in the case of forming a coalition government. A second, weaker type of constraint on selector discretion is when a selector is required to consult with other party elites and must take their preferences into consideration.

Coalition Constraints

As is widely recognized in the literature, selectors commonly lose discretion over cabinet slots when electoral outcomes encourage the formation of coalition governments. When this happens, the primary selector must cede discretion to the leader(s) of the coalition partner(s). The need to form a coalition is principally a product of electoral outcomes. There are no formal rules that dictate whether coalitions or single-party minority governments emerge after an election. Rather, whether a coalition or a minority government emerges depends upon political calculations among multiple players (Amorim Neto 2006; Laver and Shepsle 2000). These calculations are shaped by strongly institutionalized informal rules that guide practice.

Coalitions occur in both presidential and parliamentary democracies, but given their institutional differences, forming a coalition has a greater effect on prime ministers' selection powers than on presidents. In parliamentary systems, where a successful no-confidence vote can topple a government, coalition governments are a common route to ensuring majority support in parliament. The other alternative is to form a minority government and rely on ad hoc support from smaller parties. In Canada and Spain, for example, parties have often governed alone in the absence of parliamentary majorities. In fact, minority governments have been common in Spain (Field 2016). In the United Kingdom and Australia, electoral rules normally produce majority governments, but hung parliaments occasionally occur. In

his nomination of Linda Chavez for secretary of labor (Gerhardt 2003: lxii–lxiii). It is worth noting that the confirmation process has taken increasingly longer to complete (Loomis 2001). President Obama did not have a complete cabinet three months into his presidency, "the longest [delay] in at least 20 years" (http://usatoday30.usatoday.com/news/washington/2009-04-19-cabinet_N.htm), in part because initial key appointees had to withdraw (e.g., Governor Bill Richardson, NM) or took themselves out of consideration (Senator Judd Gregg, R-NH).

these cases, the party with the most seats may choose to govern alone, as did the UK Labour Party after the 1974 general election and the Australian Labor Party after the 2013 election. Alternatively, they may choose to form a coalition, as did the UK Conservatives in 2010. In contrast, in Germany, coalition governments are common, even in the rare instance when a single party won a parliamentary majority. In 1957, Konrad Adenauer won an absolute majority in the federal parliament, yet he nonetheless invited the *Deutsche Partei* into cabinet. In Australia, the Liberal Party and the National Party govern as a permanent coalition.

In parliamentary systems, entering a formal coalition reduces prime ministers' discretion to choose ministers because of strong informal rules that prime ministers only select the ministers allocated to their party during the process of coalition negotiations. German chancellors have no say over the ministerial appointments of their coalition partner. A former German minister explained, "The Chancellor would never get involved in the choice of ministers from the . . . coalition. It is an unwritten rule that the coalition partner decides on its own ministers."[14] Similarly in the United Kingdom, after the Conservatives failed to win a majority in the 2010 elections, they entered a formal coalition with the Liberal Democrats, reducing Prime Minister David Cameron's discretion to select ministers. This was clearly referenced in the media data reporting on the formation of Cameron's coalition government: "Several leading Conservatives were moved, demoted or denied jobs altogether to make way for Lib Dems";[15] "David Cameron [. . .] had to disappoint a number of Conservative colleagues squeezed out because of the deal with the Liberal Democrats."[16]

Despite the coalition constraint on the German chancellor, she does retain some discretion. According to Fischer, she has "the right to reject ministerial nominees in extreme cases of political or personal incompatibility" (2011, 25, our translation). One example was cited—the so-called Edathy case—where incriminating evidence about an individual was passed on to the coalition partner to warn against this individual being appointed to cabinet.[17] German chancellors also have the discretion to keep out rivals.[18]

---

[14] Interview, October 29, 2014.

[15] "Five Lib Dems, a Big Beast and a Kitten-Heeled Home Secretary," *The Daily Telegraph*, May 13, 2010.

[16] "From Senior to Junior—Demoted Tories Lose Seats at the Top Table; Chris Grayling Loses the Home Secretary Prize as Coalition Reality Kicks In," *The Times*, May 12, 2010.

[17] Interview, September 23, 2014.

[18] Interview, September 23, 2014.

In a presidential democracy, such as Chile, coalitions do not significantly constrain the president's autonomy to select ministers. Although political parties join forces in formal and relatively permanent electoral coalitions, and there is a strong informal rule that cabinet posts are proportionally distributed among coalition parties,[19] the president does not share selection powers with the leaders of coalition parties (Dávila and Avendaño 2018, 94–95). Instead, the informal rule is for the coalition parties to give the president a list of names of those they would like to see in cabinet. But according to interviews with political insiders, the president is by no means bound by the parties' wishes. A former minister explained that presidents solicit recommendations from party presidents, but "that does not mean the president will abide strictly to those recommendations."[20] In sum, coalitions constrain selectors in parliamentary systems, where governments can fall if they do not maintain support from parliament, but not in presidential systems, where executive survival is independent of legislative support.

Party Constraints

A selectors' discretion can also be constrained by rules at the party level. The strongest constraint is when selectors lose the power of discretion entirely because they must hand over the selection of ministers to their parliamentary party or caucus. A weaker constraint is when selectors must consult with senior party officials before making ministerial appointments. Such rules vary by party.

Formal rules established within the Australian Labor Party and the UK Labour Party prescribe that prime ministers hand powers of ministerial selection over to the parliamentary party, empowering the parliamentary party to select ministers through a ballot. These party rules were introduced to secure a strong voice for the collective parliamentary party vis-à-vis executive leadership of the party (McHenry 1955; Punnett 1964; Rhodes et al. 2009). In the Australian Labor Party, the formal rule was agreed at the Labor interstate conference in 1906 (Weller 2007, 197). In the United Kingdom, the Standing

---

[19] The center and left have competed together since 1990, first in the four-party *Concertación* and, after 2013, in the six-party *Nueva Mayoría* (New Majority). The coalition on the right, with two parties, has operated under different names, first the *Alianza* and, later, the *Coalición por el Cambio*, or Coalition for Change.

[20] Interview, August 11, 2014, Santiago, Chile.

Orders of the Parliamentary Labour Party (PLP), established in 1906, empowered MPs to elect a "Parliamentary Committee" when the party is in opposition.[21] The elected Parliamentary Committee serves as the Cabinet when the party is first elected to office, but the prime minister has full discretion over ministerial appointments thereafter. Note that in both cases, once ministers are elected by the PLP or caucus, the prime minister then has full discretion to allocate portfolios (Rhodes et al. 2009, 105; Dowding and Lewis 2015, 47; Weller 2007).

These party rules in the UK Labour Party and the Australian Labor Party change the dynamics of ministerial recruitment. Rather than *ministrables* waiting patiently for the call from the prime minister, such party rules mean that aspiring ministers must "lobby hard" to secure strong support of the parliamentary party that elects the shadow cabinet (Ryan 1999a, 211).[22] It also means that there is little turnover in terms of who makes it onto the ministerial team. In his assessment of UK shadow cabinet elections from 1955 to 1963, Punnett (1964) found that there was little turnover on the lists, making it hard for newcomers to secure a place among shadow cabinet ministers. Moreover, there were "a lot of blocs in the PLP, Scots voting for Scots and so on."[23]

While these formal party rules act as a strong constraint on Labour prime ministers in the United Kingdom and Australia, we show later in this chapter that there are instances when these party formal rules appear less institutionalized, namely when context or agency come into play. Also, the formal party rule was changed in the United Kingdom in 2010, giving future Labour prime ministers full discretion to assemble a ministerial team.

In Germany, parties do not play a formal role in voting for the chancellor's ministerial nominations for cabinet. Yet selectors are constrained by the need to consult with party elites in the process of ministerial selection. The degree of consultation varies according to party.[24] Kaiser and Fischer (2009, 153 fn 4) explain that "[i]n the German case the effective selectorate in the ministerial appointment process is a small group consisting of parliamentary and party leaders, including the most influential leaders of the *Länder* party associations, the exception being the Free Democrats (FDP) where ministerial appointments are usually more formally decided upon in a joint meeting

---

[21] Interview with former PLP Chair, June 12, 2018.
[22] Interview with former minister, December 17, 2013.
[23] Ibid.
[24] Interview with expert on German politics, October 28, 2014.

of the parliamentary party and the party executive." An expert on German politics reinforced this view, explaining, "the practice [is that the Chancellor] needs to listen closely to his party in Berlin and across the Länder."[25] A former minister provided further nuance: "Most chancellors consult with the leadership of their parliamentary party because they need their support and confidence. And chancellors are also leaders of the main party of government. For that reason, the senior executive committee of the main party of government is involved."[26] Moreover, "[i]f the Kanzler is not party leader, then he will have to accept some ministerial nominees from the leader," as in the case of party leader Oskar Lafontaine and Chancellor Gerhard Schröder in 1998. The German chancellor, "[o]n the other hand does have the power to block: potential rivals don't get jobs. Friedrich Merz was not appointed by Angela Merkel."[27]

In sum, formal rules and conventions generally authorize a single selector of cabinet ministers, and in most cases, the effects of these rules are reinforced by informal rules that further empower selectors. The only exception among our cases is the United States, where formal consent of the Senate is required. In our other cases, constraints emerge from coalition government, or formal party rules requiring prime ministers to share selection power with the parliamentary party.

Consequences of Rules Empowering and Constraining Selectors across Our Cases

Taking into account the various combinations of formal and informal rules at the system levels and party levels, we see that among our cases, rules combine to empower selectors more often than they constrain them. Moreover, informal rules are more determinative than formal rules in both empowering and constraining selectors. Across all our cases, the only formal rules that effectively constrain selectors are at the party level, and, as discussed in the following, have either been discarded (UK) or are becoming less strongly institutionalized (Australia). Table 3.1 summarizes our findings, which this section discusses in detail. We begin by discussing

---

[25] Ibid.
[26] Interview, September 23, 2014.
[27] Interview, October 28, 2014.

Table 3.1 Combinations and Consequences of Formal and Informal Rules Shaping Selector Power to Form Cabinets, by Country

Country	Combination of Rules	Consequences of Rules
Chile	Constitution gives sole selection powers to presidents; informal rules support this arrangement. No party-specific rules constrain selectors.	Formal and informal rules combine to empower selectors in both Chile and Spain.
Spain	Constitution gives sole selection powers to prime ministers; informal rules support this arrangement. No party-specific rules constrain selectors.	
Canada	Prime ministers are empowered by constitutional conventions that give sole selection powers to prime ministers. No party-specific rules constrain selectors.	Formal rules are absent; informal rules empower selectors.
United Kingdom	Prime ministers are empowered by constitutional conventions that give sole selection powers to prime ministers. Party-specific rules have constrained some selectors.	Formal party rules previously constrained prime ministers from the UK Labour party and the ALP which empowered ministrables to lobby for ministerial office. Rule change and informal rules increasingly empower selectors from each party.
Australia	Prime ministers are empowered by constitutional conventions that give sole selection powers to prime ministers. Party-specific rules and permanent party coalitions have constrained some selectors.	
United States	Presidents formally empowered to nominate; Senate must consent to president's cabinet nominees. Informal rules prescribe deference to presidents. No party-specific rules constrain presidents.	Formal rules constrain, but informal rules empower selectors.
Germany	Chancellors formally empowered by Basic Law; informal rules and coalition conditions constrain selector autonomy.	Formal rules empower but informal rules constrain selectors.

cases where rules have always combined to empower selectors: Spain, Chile, Canada, and the United States. We then discuss the United Kingdom and Australia, where, over time, changes to party rules that constrain some selectors have led to more consistently empowered selectors across both of the main parties. We conclude our discussion with our sole case, Germany, where combinations of rules at both the system and party level serve to constrain all selectors.

Rules Have Always Empowered a Single
Selector: Spain, Chile, Canada, and the United States

The Spanish prime minister (known as *presidente de gobierno* or president of government) is one of the most strongly empowered selectors in our study. Formal and informal rules combine to consistently empower prime ministers. According to Bar (1988, 111), "The president of government is not really a Prime (first) Minister, as he is no longer a *primus inter pares* but a real President as his official title indicates. The cabinet revolves entirely around him—it is created, lives and dies with him and it acts under his direction and follows his political program." Interviews confirm that leaders are unconstrained by rules about consulting party elites or the parliamentary caucus. A former minister explained, "[the prime minister] does not have to consult, formally or informally, with anyone."[28] An academic expert said, "Decisions about cabinet ministers are very personalized in the president of government."[29] There are some differences across the two main parties, however. The Spanish Socialist Workers' Party (PSOE) has a federalized party structure; hence, a prime minister might consult with regional leaders to get recommendations for regional ministers. But the prime minister himself would always initiate such a consultation; regional leaders would never lobby the prime minister or request that certain people be appointed.[30] In contrast, the People's Party (PP) is highly centralized, and leaders rarely feel compelled to talk to anyone beyond their closest friends.[31] Media data from Zapatero's first election in 2004 and Rajoy's election in 2011 confirm that leaders do not share selection powers. Press reports from Zapatero's election note that the electoral outcome, in which he handily defeated Rajoy, gave him "free hands to choose" all of his ministers. That said, one reporter noted that the names of two members of his post-election cabinet were suggested to him, but that he alone selected all other ministers.[32]

In Chile, formal and informal rules likewise combine to empower presidents as the sole selectors of ministers. At the same time, informal rules

---

[28] Interview, May 13, 2014, Madrid.

[29] Interview, May 21, 2012, Madrid.

[30] Interview with former minister, May 13, 2014, Madrid.

[31] Interview, May 14, 2014, Madrid.

[32] The article says that two of the women in his initial cabinet, Elena Salgado (health) and Elena Espinoza (agriculture and fisheries) were appointed on the suggestion of Alfredo Pérez Rubalcaba and José Bono (respectively). Anabel Díez, "Zapatero garantizará por ley la paridad en los altos cargos de la Administración," *El País*, March 9, 2004.

appear to pull in two directions. On the one hand, Chile's constitution clearly empowers presidents. On the other hand, governments are always coalitions, and party leaders believe they have a role to play in recommending ministers to the president. Yet, our data indicate that while presidents receive recommendations, they ultimately decide for themselves who will be in their cabinet. Indeed, another institutionalized practice governing coalition politics is the principle of *suprapartidismo*, which requires presidents to promote the interests of the coalition rather than the individual parties within it. In practice, this implies a large degree of presidential autonomy in cabinet formation. Still, political parties try to exert some influence. After the 2006 election, a Socialist Party leader told the press, "the parties can offer their opinions, [these] have always been welcome."[33] Following the 2010 elections, won by the conservative coalition, one of the Independent Democratic Union (UDI) party leaders told the press that the party had delivered the new president a list of names of people they would like to see in cabinet.[34] Even though informal rules encourage presidents to communicate with party leaders, Piñera did not do so. A former senator describes the failure to meet with party presidents, "including the president of his own party," as having created a public scandal.[35]

With the exception of Piñera, all other presidents have followed informal rules about communicating with party leaders in the process of forming their cabinets. But it would be inaccurate to say that informal rules prescribe that presidents *negotiate* cabinet posts with party leaders. Presidents are not sharing or ceding selection powers to their coalition partners. Despite communication and parties submitting recommendations, our interview data and media data reinforce the conclusion that rules consistently empower selectors. A former minister said that the principle of *suprapartidismo* means that "there is no negotiation. The president decides."[36] Another said, "the president can designate alone. Absolutely alone."[37] The president's sole authority to select was also reinforced by Bachelet. When asked by a reporter about the status of the negotiations about cabinet ministers, the president

---

[33] Claudio Salinas, "Estilo Bachelet abre expectativas y dudas," *El Merucio*, January 14, 2006.
[34] Mónica Guerra and Pilar Molina, "UDI apuesta a ser partido eje del nuevo gobierno," *El Mercurio*, January 18, 2010.
[35] Interview, July 15, 2015, Santiago.
[36] Interview, January 8, 2013, Santiago.
[37] Interview, August 11, 2014.

responded, "I would suggest that nobody is negotiating because the truth is that the decisions are going to be taken by myself."[38]

Canadian prime ministers also wield tremendous power in the process of cabinet formation: there are neither formal nor informal rules to constrain them when selecting ministers. According to White, "long-established convention accords the first minister unquestioned authority to choose their ministers, the portfolios they hold, and whether they remain in cabinet" (2005, 31). David Zussman writes, "each prime minister has complete authority over building his or her own Cabinet" (2013, 86). Although there are numerous rules that constrain the pool of *ministrables* from which prime ministers can make cabinet appointments, as we explain in later chapters, Canadian leaders can make their choices without consulting their parties or ceding selection power to other actors. Neither the Liberals nor the Conservatives, the only two parties that have held national office, have rules requiring leaders to share ministerial selection with the parliamentary party. Nor must prime ministers consult other party elites. Because single-party governments are the norm, prime ministers do not cede selection powers to other parties.[39] Leaders may, of course, seek advice from their close political confidantes, but there is no requirement to consult with other party notables. Our media data from Stephen Harper's 2008 election and Justin Trudeau's 2015 election contain no mention of either prime minister engaging in consultations about cabinet formation with the party elite. In fact, the only reference to a prime minister seeking advice about cabinet formation effectively reinforces the idea that selectors decide for themselves. Shortly after the 2015 Canadian elections, a member of Justin Trudeau's transition team told the press that although he sought advice from his two closest advisors, Gerald Butts and Katie Telford, "[Trudeau] is the one who decides, it's not Gerry or Katie. He is the master of the decision-making process."[40] In sum, while formal rules are absent, informal rules consistently empower Canadian prime ministers to select ministers.

In the United States, the president, as the single selector, is formally empowered to nominate heads of cabinet departments (generally, secretaries of departments). However, this power is also formally constrained by the Senate's advisory and consent powers. Cabinet secretaries must win Senate

---

[38] Ibid.

[39] There has been only one case of a coalition government, during World War I (White 2005, 37), and none in recent history.

[40] Daniel Leblanc, "Cabinet to Be Smaller, More Diverse," *Globe and Mail*, November 2, 2015.

approval. Presidential nomination of cabinet secretaries and Senate confirmation of the nominees are formal rules that are also highly institutionalized, insofar as these rules are universally observed and widely acknowledged; lack of compliance would produce sanctions and, perhaps, a constitutional crisis.[41]

Nonetheless, in selecting cabinet secretaries, the president has substantial informal discretion, in terms of other participants and actual Senate behavior. There are no other formal nominators of US cabinet secretaries, beyond the president, and the Senate normally accedes to presidential wishes concerning cabinet appointments;[42] cabinet nominees "are usually confirmed within the first month or so of an administration" (Light 2015, 1509). Strong informal rules proscribe self-nomination, active campaigning, and unsolicited suggestions. These informal rules combine with the absence of any party rules requiring intra-party consultation[43] to give US presidents substantial discretion and autonomy in selecting cabinet secretaries. "Once a presidential nomination has been made, the presumption of confirmation—the likelihood or propensity of senatorial deference—generally provides a structural public impediment to its undoing" (Gerhardt 2003, 182). As a Republican senator said, reflecting on Barack Obama's first cabinet formation, "It's almost completely up to him."[44]

There is substantial evidence supporting strong presidential discretion in cabinet appointments. Incoming presidents form transition teams (even in advance of formal election results).[45] President Obama moved quickly to fill

[41] Indeed, it is hard to envision how a cabinet secretary would come into power in the absence of these rules.

[42] The pattern of Senate approval differs for presidential judicial appointments. "[C]onflicts between presidents and senators have intensified over federal appointments generally and with particular ferocity over judicial nominations. For six of Bill Clinton's eight years as president, Republican senators subjected his judicial nominees to unprecedented delays and obstruction in the hopes of barring the appointment of liberal activists to the federal bench. In the final year of Clinton's presidency, Republicans blocked final Senate action on forty-one pending judicial nominees to enable the next president to fill the positions instead" (Gerhardt 2003, xv).

[43] The absence of any formal—or even informal—rule that presidents confer with political party elites is evidenced by Obama's appointment of Janet Napolitano as secretary of homeland security, an appointment he announced without consulting with "members of the Senate homeland security panel" in advance ("Candidate for Homeland Security," New York Times, November 21, 2008, A16), including those in his own party and the Democratic chair of the panel.

[44] Jeff Zeleny, "Initial Steps by Obama Suggest a Bipartisan Flair," New York Times, November 24, 2008.

[45] Bill Clinton's transition team was in the planning stages by September 1992, and "ready to roll" in early November (Christopher 2001, 175). Barack Obama's transition team (as well as Senator John McCain's team) was consulting with the outgoing George W. Bush administration as early as the summer of 2008, with the Obama campaign identifying potential appointees for White House staff positions in May (Kumar 2009).

appointive positions in his first administration, "more quickly . . . than any newly elected president in modern history," naming "virtually the entire top echelon of his White House staff and nearly half of his cabinet."[46] Obama's appointments of Clinton and Holder were advanced with no informal consultation with Democratic Party elites or senators.

Second, presidents construct their own rules, criteria, and procedures for selection.[47] Past common practice of presidents had been to keep initial discussions with potential appointees private and to deny (or refuse to speak about) specific *ministrables*.[48] The ability of presidents to set their own terms and conditions for cabinet appointments, and to succeed in getting their nominees confirmed by a formally empowered Senate, is testament to the strength of informal rules empowering the selector. Moreover, in the United States, these informal rules that empower the selector are highly institutionalized. Senate deference to the president's cabinet selections is a long-standing practice in the United States, regardless of who is president and to which party he or she belongs.

It is worth noting that presidents do not always get to appoint whom they want. Presidents frequently "float" names, or specifically consult with senators, to ensure that their nominee faces no unanticipated roadblock.[49] Informal consultation in advance of cabinet nominations is a relatively common practice, insofar as it provides a president with information about likely opposition and potential barriers to nomination. Nonetheless, with cabinet appointments, presidents are not constrained by an informal rule requiring them to consult others or to be bound by their advice, and presidential nominees are almost always confirmed by the Senate.[50]

---

[46] Peter Baker and Helene Cooper, "Issues Pressing, Obama Fills Top Posts at a Sprint," *New York Times*, December 5, 2008.

[47] The criteria for qualifying as a *ministrable* are discussed in Chapter 4.

[48] Obama's transition team instead publicly identified at least two persons he intended to appoint to major cabinet posts. Hillary Clinton for secretary of state and Eric Holder for attorney general. "Clinton . . . was [Obama's] pick, period. Not a 'leading contender,' as often happens when a name leaks out or a trial balloon is purposely launched. . . . [O]n background, transition folks said it was a done deal for State" (Al Kamen, "A Democratic Cabinet with a Liberal Return Policy," *Washington Post*, November 20, 2008).

[49] For example, Obama's first choice for secretary of health and human services, Tom Daschle, withdrew his name from consideration "upon revealing that he had owed $128,000 in back taxes and paid it only after being selected. The White House used the time [between his withdrawal and the ultimate nomination of Kathleen Sebelius] not only to vet Ms. Sebelius, but also to make sure that the two Republican senators from Kansas [her home state], Sam Brownback and Pat Roberts, would not oppose her confirmation" (Kevin Sack, "For Obama Pick, a 2nd Chance to Move Ahead on Health Care," *New York Times*, March 2, 2009).

[50] This is not the case for federal judicial appointments, where judges "shall hold their Offices during good behavior" (US Constitution, Art. III, Sec. 1). Cabinet ministers, however, are removable, either by the president directly or by electoral defeat of the appointing president, and their terms of

Informal rules also concern those who would be ministers: there continues to be the prohibition against active campaigning or self-nominating. This informal rule is strong and recognized, and highly institutionalized, and it reinforces the formal nominating power of the president and his informal discretionary powers. Nonetheless, "[n]ominees are rarely passive figures in the selection process. It is quite common for potential nominees to wage campaigns to get themselves nominated or to have others wage such campaigns on their behalf" (Gerhardt 2003, 194). These campaigns are accompanied (and supported) by substantial media speculation about likely appointees, whose friends and supporters advocate for them, and insiders and transition team members acknowledge, off the record and sometimes on, those under consideration for appointment to specific positions. As Madeleine Albright writes in her memoir, *Madame Secretary* (2003, 215), "[c]abinet hopefuls are assigned the equivalent of a passive role in an old-fashioned courtship. It is considered inappropriate to brag, denigrate others, or openly display your interest. Subtlety is required. Campaigning is simply not done—or at least not admitted."[51]

The sanction for violating these informal rules is severe and straightforward: no nomination.[52] "Nominees have learned . . . that politicking on their own behalf (or against others interested in the same position) can backfire unless it is done with delicacy and tact. Some aspiring nominees have hurt, if not effectively killed, their chances for appointment by appearing to be too interested in self-promotion (as opposed to public service) or too covetous of the position (and the power that goes with it)" (Gerhardt 2003, 195). Reflecting on the process of her eventual nomination as secretary of state, Albright describes the "non-campaign" that took place, with "well-placed allies who gathered intelligence, provided suggestions, and put out

service are generally brief, making the cost of Senate confirmation relatively low. Average tenure of US cabinet ministers, from the Reagan to the Obama administrations, ranges from 3.6 to 4.8 years; average tenure of those appointed to specific cabinet posts ranges from 3.72 years (attorneys general, secretaries of education, health and human services, interior) to 2.39 years (commerce). See Phillip Bump, "Eric Holder and a Brief History of Cabinet Tenures," *Washington Post*, September 25, 2014.

[51] Some *ministrables* are active by removing themselves as potential appointees. See, e.g., John Brennan's request that he no longer be considered as a potential appointee to head the Central Intelligence Agency in the first Obama administration. Brennan "had been an early supporter of Obama, and many intelligence community insiders backed his candidacy," *Washington Post*, November 26, 2008. See also Colin Powell (1995, 602–603), where he declined to be considered for nomination as President Bill Clinton's secretary of state in 1994.

[52] See the earlier discussion in this chapter concerning Dave McCurdy's lost opportunity as a potential appointee for secretary of defense.

fires" (2003, 218).[53] The potential negative effects of campaigning in regard to the appointment process are reflected in media reports of the formation of Barack Obama's inaugural cabinet as well. Prohibitions on self-nomination, positive or negative politicking, and aggressive campaigning function as informal rules with serious sanctions. The president, with no obligation to consult with party members or members of Congress concerning his appointment preferences, was empowered with nearly full discretion to select. In the presence of a strong formal constraint on the president's discretion in selecting ministers, counteracting informal rules constrain the Senate, serving to empower the president in forming his cabinet.

Party Rules Constraining Some Selectors Have Declined over Time: United Kingdom and Australia

In the United Kingdom, at the system level, selecting ministers is the "prerogative of the Prime Minister" (Kaufman 1997, 4). The rule is as follows: prime ministers select cabinet ministers; *ministrables* await the call and are thankful when offered a cabinet spot. As Kaufman states, "If, for whatever reason, Downing Street one day telephones you and announces that the Prime Minister would like either to see you or speak to you, either seize the opportunity firmly, or reject it and do not afterwards complain" (Kaufman 1997, 8–9). The ritual associated with the rule of prime ministerial discretion is systematically documented by John Major in his autobiography, recounting his elevation through the government ranks (1981–1990), becoming prime minister and selector himself in 1990 (Major 2000).

Prime ministers in the United Kingdom are always leaders of their respective parties, and the office of prime minister confers a high degree of respect and deference on its holder. John Major describes how, as soon as he was announced party leader and therefore prime minister, a close ally of his "rushed up, seized my arm in delight, then dropped back as he realized I was no longer just another Cabinet minister" (Major 2000, 199). Governments

---

[53] Albright concludes that her nomination as secretary of state, over other potential candidates, was actually assisted by an attack against her, published in a story in the *Washington Post*. Denigrating Albright (who was then the US Ambassador to the United Nations) as a "second-tier" candidate, the story "galvanized [her] supporters and prompted requests by women's groups that the White House disavow it" (2003, 221), which they did.

also tend to be single-party, meaning that prime ministers do not have to re-linquish discretion to coalition partners.

Strong prime ministerial discretion in the United Kingdom does not mean that parties do not seek to influence the prime minister's decisions; various factions within the party do seek to shape ministerial nominations. In 1992, "[m]inisterial jobs were demanded by factions" (Major 2000, 347) and in 2010, "[r]ight-wing Tories have [. . .] demanded that MPs and peers from their faction [. . .] receive Cabinet positions."[54] Further, sitting or outgoing ministers may have the power to influence the prime minister's choice. According to John Major, Willie Whitelaw lobbied Thatcher for Major to be appointed Chief Whip, while Nigel Lawson "asked for me as chief sec-retary, and after a tussle he gained Willie's support and had his way" (Major 1999, 98). Later, Major lobbied Thatcher on who should replace him as for-eign secretary: "The offer of the chancellorship did put me in a position to argue for Douglas Hurd to succeed me at the Foreign Office" (Major 1999, 134). Finally, the Whip's Office offers the prime minister background infor-mation on potential ministers. John Major highlights this as particularly important. For him, the chief whip was particularly "crucial in advising the prime minister about the performance of ministers and backbenchers, which is vital in determining whether Members climb the parliamentary ladder to senior positions, slip from high office, or remain forever on the back benches waiting in hope" (Major 2000, 78).

As we have seen, in the Labour Party the Standing Orders of the PLP prescribed that prime ministers had no discretion over ministerial selection when the party was moving from opposition to government. The tradition-ally strong role of the PLP meant that a prime minister had to pay close at-tention to the wishes of the party when in government as well. An incoming prime minister was not obliged to adopt the PLP list wholesale (Punnett 1964), but Kaufman (1997) advises that the political costs of ignoring it would be high, a sentiment echoed in an interview with a former minister.[55] The evidence, however, points to a decline in the formal and informal role of the party in ministerial recruitment since 1997, when Tony Blair became prime minister.

Interviewees told us that in the past, Labour prime ministers "had to take account of the standing of the politician in the wider party and the

---

[54] "Fear of Backlash from the Right," *The Daily Telegraph*, May 12, 2010.
[55] Interview, December 17, 2013.

trade union movement and before 1994 most senior politicians were on the National Executive Committee (NEC), but not anymore. Also, before Blair it was the tradition that whoever topped the cabinet shadow elections could choose their own portfolio. This practice has also changed. Moreover, under Blair not everyone on the shadow cabinet made it into government."[56] Blair took less notice of the party and more notice of advisors such as Jonathan Powell and Sally Morgan.[57] The sense within the Labour Party is that "these days—since Blair—the prime minister is pretty free to choose his own ministers."[58]

In 2010 the Standing Orders of the PLP were changed. Following the report of a group commissioned to consider changing the rules, the practice of shadow cabinet elections was abolished: Labour MPs were "sick of all those bloody emails from lobbying MPs," and the 2010 intake had "no strong memory of shadow elections."[59] The Standing Orders now read: "When the Party is in Opposition the Shadow Cabinet, including the Chief Whip, shall be appointed by the Leader of the Opposition" (Labour Party 2016). This means that, since 2011, Labour Party leaders are as empowered as their Conservative counterparts to select their ministers autonomously.

In Australia, strongly institutionalized informal rules empower prime ministers at the system level, but formal party-level rules in the Labor Party create constraints, although these have been less strongly institutionalized in recent years. Selecting ministers is part of the "immense direct and indirect power that comes with being prime minister" (Gillard 2014, 25–26). The position of prime minister carries a high degree of respect and deference. While still a minister, Julia Gillard recalls, "because I was talking to the Australian Prime Minister, I expressed my views respectfully" (Gillard 2014, 13). In Australia, as in the United Kingdom, prime ministers select cabinets ministers; *ministrables* await the call, and they are "grateful" to the selector for what they are offered (Howard 2013, 119). According to former prime minister John Howard, "choosing a cabinet is the hardest people-oriented task that any prime minister has" (Howard 2013, 276).

Ministers are not able to choose their portfolios, except for deputy prime ministers, who traditionally get to choose theirs.[60] Other ministers have

---

[56] Interview with former minister, December 17, 2013.
[57] Ibid.
[58] Ibid.
[59] Ibid.
[60] Interview with former Australian minister, March 23, 2010.

been able to secure their ministerial positions when deals are made with the prime minister during party leadership contests. Foreign ministers under both Prime Ministers Howard and Gillard were former party leaders who demanded that portfolio when they handed over the leadership of the party to their successors. Howard told disposed leader Alexander Downer at the point of handover "that I would appoint him shadow Foreign Minister, with the expectation implied that he would be Foreign Minister if we won power" (Howard 2013, 247–248). Gillard, too, was obliged to take former leader and disposed Prime Minister Rudd as her foreign minister because, instead of doing the "decent thing and retiring at the 2010 election," Rudd sought to "sabotage the campaign" (Gillard 2014, 42–43). Gillard was "reluctant to give him the position of Foreign Minister, knowing he would try to refuse instruction from me" but she "had little choice: I had to stop what I considered to be the acts of treachery on his part" (2014, 43).

There are party-level constraints on selectors that are specific to the main Australian parties. All Liberal selectors experience a coalition constraint because they are required to hand over some discretion on some ministerial appointments to their coalition partner, the Nationals. This is a permanent coalition, so in that sense it is a predictable and expected arrangement. What varies is the number of cabinet slots the Nationals secure; that depends on election results. The Nationals also normally secure the position of deputy prime minister.

In the Australian Labor Party, the formal rule is that the caucus pre-selects ministers for the prime minister, thereby entirely removing his selection powers. That said, we find evidence that this rule has become less strongly institutionalized: the prime minister can exercise his agency, or an electoral context can strengthen the prime minister's authority. For example, in 1990 Prime Minister Bob Hawke sent the list back to the party faction and requested a "more balanced and representative selection" (Weller 2007, 198). Prime Ministers Kevin Rudd and Julia Gillard were granted full powers to make their ministerial picks as a reward for securing office. An Australian politician explained: "after the 2007 election, the prime minister because he'd won election—and we were very grateful for him having won that election—asked for and was granted the right to select the front bench."[61]

In sum, in Australia, system-level rules empower prime ministers in the process of appointing cabinet ministers, while party-level rules create some

---

[61] Interview with Australian politician, March 20, 2010.

constraints. Prime ministers may lose discretion over single cabinet spots as political deals are done, but overall, they can make the choices they wish. Liberal prime ministers hand over some discretion to their coalition partner, reducing the number of spots at their discretion. But this is a permanent and expected arrangement with which all Liberal prime ministers have to reckon. Labor prime ministers have historically had to accept caucus slates, but more recently they have, informally, been granted full discretion. While Liberal and Labor prime ministers generally enjoy strong powers of selector discretion, they are constrained in different ways. Liberal prime ministers always experience a coalition constraint, and Labor prime ministers need to take caucus preferences into account, unless their request for full discretion is granted by the party.

In the United Kingdom and Australia, formal party rules that have significantly constrained Labour prime ministers historically have now declined in force. The rule that the PLP selects ministers has been abandoned in the United Kingdom, and so we can say for sure that future Labour prime ministers will be fully empowered to select ministers. In Australia, the last two Labor prime ministers have been afforded full discretion, but this has been on an informal basis and granted on the basis of prime ministerial agency and electoral context. We expect that full empowerment for future Labor prime ministers will remain dependent on agency, electoral context, and interaction with the party caucus.

All Selectors Are Constrained: Germany

In Germany, formal rules clearly empower selectors, but such rules are weakly institutionalized. According to a former minister, "the chancellor can appoint who he or she wants. [. . .] the stronger he or she is, the stronger his or her own, personal influence" over ministerial appointments.[62] This authority derives from the formal rule that "federal ministers shall be appointed and dismissed by the federal President upon the proposal of the federal Chancellor" (Basic Law Article 64 (1)). Yet as Fischer (2011, 25) rightly points out, the legal foundations of the Basic Law are not a suitable way of identifying routes to ministerial office. Instead, the autonomy of the chancellor to select ministers is limited by numerous informal constraints

---

[62] Interview with former minister, September 23, 2014.

(Fischer 2011, 24–25). In Germany, informal rules that constrain selectors are more strongly institutionalized than are the formal rules that empower them. In fact, we find that the German chancellor's discretion to select her ministers is the most constrained of all our cases.

The first significant constraint is that German chancellors, without exception, need to form a coalition and therefore hand over discretion of some cabinet slots to their coalition partner. The number of ministerial posts granted to the junior coalition partner will depend on election results and the outcome of coalition negotiations. For many years, these coalition partnerships were regular and predictable, but since 1998 there have been new permutations. Chancellors have no discretion over a coalition partner's personnel decisions, though there is some latitude to reject ministerial nominees in extreme cases of political or personal incompatibility (Fischer 2011, 25) or if the chancellor's party is in possession of incriminating information about a coalition partner's ministerial nominee.[63] "In coalition governments, which all German governments are as a rule, it is common for there to be discussions between those conducting coalition negotiations about potential ministers. This could just mean preliminary information but might also mean something more specific [. . .]. In the last coalition negotiations the then home affairs minister announced that he had passed on incriminating information about someone to the coalition partner in order to warn against this person being included in government."[64]

The second significant constraint on the chancellor's discretion to select her ministers is the need to consult with and take recommendations from across the party. There is no formal requirement that the chancellor consults with the party or that a party convention gets to decide between ministerial nominations.[65] But the federal structure of the German political parties means that broad consultation is the practice. Also, chancellors are not always party leaders, and "if the chancellor is not party leader, then he will have to accept some ministerial nominees from the leader," as was the case with party leader Oskar Lafontaine and Chancellor Gerhard Schröder in 1998.[66]

Parties are the brokers of the process of ministerial recruitment: without the parties, nothing is possible. The selectorate for ministerial positions is the "high ranking politicians in the parties and parliamentary parties"

[63] Interview with country expert, October 28, 2014.
[64] Interview, September 23, 2014.
[65] Ibid.
[66] Interview, October 28, 2014.

(Fischer 2011, 33). According to one former minister, "most chancellors like to link the nomination of ministers with a public appearance at the Party Convention. That leads to a kind of collective approval by party delegates through applause."[67]

In sum, despite formal written rules granting the chancellor power to select minsters, their discretion is in practice significantly constrained by the need to form a coalition and the need to consult with high-ranking political figures in the party and parliament, including at regional level.

Conclusion: Informal Rules Do the Work

This chapter has explicated the rules that define the appointment powers of the selectors in our seven country cases. We have identified (1) a set of counties where formal and/or informal rules strongly empower a single selector (Spain, Chile, Canada, and the US); (2) countries where party rules constrain some selectors but have declined in force over time (Australia and UK); and (3) a country where selectors are always constrained (Germany). To our surprise, the degree of empowerment and constraint assigned by rules to the selector does not neatly map to type of political system. In our category of fully empowered single selectors, we find both presidential democracies (Chile and US) but also a parliamentary democracy (Spain) and a Westminster system (Canada). Nor do selector empowerment rules across our seven cases correspond clearly to whether the country tends to form coalition or single-party governments.

Overall, we find that knowing the formal rules does not reveal the extent to which selectors are empowered. There are, at the system level, no formal rules constraining the power of a president or prime minister to appoint his or her cabinet, with the one exception of the US Senate. The selector is formally fully empowered and has "the gift" of appointment. At the system level, informal rules are the primary determinants of how empowered a president or prime minister is to construct a cabinet. In the United States, the Senate rarely denies a president his cabinet choices, a practice that has the power of an informal rule. In Germany, although formally free to appoint whom she pleases, the chancellor is constrained by informal rules from doing so. Free to appoint whom they please on the basis of strongly institutionalized

---

[67] Interview, September 23, 2014.

informal rules at system level, Labor prime ministers in Australia and British Labour prime ministers have historically faced formal party rules that constrain their powers to appoint autonomously. Finally, selectors in Chile and Spain are always free to select ministers on their own, a power reinforced by informal rules that prohibit ceding selection powers or negotiating with other actors, and that could sanction actors who attempt to interfere with the appointment power of the president or prime minister.

Formal system rules appear to be less powerful in constraining—or in the case of Germany, in empowering—selectors than is the case for informal rules. This finding reveals that the degree of institutionalization of a rule matters as much as does whether a rule is codified or not. As noted in Chapter 2, selectors face sets of formal and informal rules in the process of forming their cabinet team. Formal rules exist, but highly institutionalized informal rules are very powerful. These informal rules—flexible and hidden, but well known to insiders—have powerful sanctions that the selector can employ or that can be employed against the selector. The formal rules of cabinet appointment, empowering (in Germany) or constraining (in the US) the selector, are adapted in use in response to informal rules that, in practice, weaken the formal rules, empowering US presidents through highly institutionalized informal rules of Senate deference to presidential preferences and constraining German chancellors by highly institutionalized informal rules of deference to party elites. How formal rules work in context is shaped by powerful, unwritten informal rules.

These findings are important for understanding the gendered consequences of rules empowering and constraining prime ministers and presidents in the process of selecting ministers, addressed in detail in Chapter 8. Drawing on the findings on gender and political recruitment, we expect that the higher the number of selectors, the greater the obstacles for women. We predict that countries in which single selectors are empowered to make ministerial appointments autonomously will have a higher share of women in cabinet.

It is worth noting for now that three of the four countries cases with fully empowered single selectors have reached high magnitudes of women's presence in cabinet and have produced at least one gender parity cabinet (Canada in 2015; Chile in 2006; and Spain in 2004 and 2008). Where (some) selectors have faced formal system rules or party rules constraining their autonomy in constructing a cabinet (Australia, UK, US), women's presence in cabinet has remained lower, and there has been no instance of a parity cabinet. That said, we identify a puzzle in Germany, where single selectors are formally empowered but consistently constrained by multiple strongly institutionalized informal rules that empower other selectors. Nevertheless, in Germany women's presence in cabinet is high and to date one government (Schröder, in 2002) has been a gender parity cabinet. This indicates the need to explore the other rules that interact with selector empowerment to shape the process of ministerial recruitment.

All presidents and prime ministers are faced with a second constraint. Regardless of how empowered they may be in terms of cabinet appointments, even if fully empowered to select ministers autonomously, they cannot appoint whomever they please. They must choose from among a subset of political elites, a subset that is also governed by rules establishing criteria about eligibility and qualifications. Some political systems have formal rules concerning ministerial eligibility, but no country has formalized the qualifications that ministers must possess for cabinet appointments. In the next chapter, we turn our attention to the rules establishing eligibility and defining qualifying criteria for cabinet appointment hopefuls.

4

Who Can Be a Minister?

Eligibility and Qualifying Criteria for Cabinet Appointment

Introduction: The Challenge of Identifying *Ministrables*

Presidents and prime ministers, regardless of how empowered in appointing their cabinet, cannot appoint whomever they please. Rather, selectors must choose ministers according to eligibility and qualification standards that define the subset of political elites who are *ministrable*. We define a *ministrable* as someone who is both eligible and qualified for ministerial office. Joining the ranks of cabinet is often the highest point in an individual's political career, and many elected officials aspire to a ministerial post. Cabinets, however, are small. This means that many politicians spend their entire career hoping for, but never achieving, appointment to a cabinet post.

Despite the importance of cabinet posts to individual political careers, scholars know little about why some politicians are ultimately rewarded and others are not. Three decades have passed since Blondel noted the scarcity of comparative research on cabinet ministers (1985, 8). Yet we still lack "systematic studies" of what selectors "regard as the most desirable competences for ministers" (Andeweg 2014, 533). Fleischer and Seyfried (2015, 503) likewise note the scarcity of studies that can explain why "certain ministrable candidates acquire a cabinet position and others do not."

One reason for the gap in knowledge is the absence of codified rules for selecting ministers. Constitutions are strikingly silent about eligibility and qualifications for cabinet appointment. Yet, as we argue in this book, the lack of formal rules about cabinet formation does not mean there are no rules. Even if many selectors can choose ministers on their own, without having to consult or negotiate with other political actors, as we established in Chapter 3, that does not mean that they can select whomever they wish. This chapter shows that there are indeed rules that establish criteria for eligibility and qualifications for cabinet, and that prime ministers and presidents choose ministers in a context governed by those rules. The previous chapter set out the powers of selectors in constructing their cabinets, and this chapter identifies the rules establishing eligibility and qualifications for those considered to be *ministrable*. Later in the book, we show that the criteria for ministerial selection and the degree to which selectors are empowered affect women's and men's opportunities to become ministers in different ways, thereby producing unequal gendered outcomes that vary over time and across countries.

Existing studies of cabinet appointments offer us some guidelines for determining what makes some individuals *ministrable* and others less so. Laver and Shepsle, for example, argue that competence matters greatly: "an aspiring politician must find some way to develop the *reputation for competence* needed to be considered ministrable" (2000, 14, emphasis in original). Other studies likewise highlight the policy knowledge and political experience needed for politicians to be considered *ministrable* (Escobar-Lemmon and Taylor-Robinson 2016; Fleisher and Seyfried 2015). On the other hand, Dowding and Dumont explain that prime ministers "sometimes choose ministers on the basis of personal loyalty" (2015). Studies of political appointment in the United States also note the importance of loyalty in presidential appointments (Borrelli 2010). Yet competence and loyalty are very different sorts of criteria. For the general public, competence as a qualifying criterion for cabinet appointment makes sense. The public expects ministers to be capable politicians and to have knowledge that is relevant to the department they will administer. Nonetheless, stories abound about ministers who are chosen not for their competence, but because of their close personal relationship with the leader who appointed them. What is more, the public often hears stories of talented politicians who are passed over in cabinet appointments because of political rivalry or some other factor that appears equally arbitrary. Former Canadian prime minister Jean Chretién notes this arbitrariness when reflecting on ministerial selection in his memoirs: "You spot one good person here and an equally good person in the riding next door, but because you don't have room for two people from the same region of the same province, one gets into cabinet and the other does not" (Chretién 2007, 23). Hence, as Blondel observes, there is a sense of chance and even arbitrariness to the process of cabinet appointment: "The ministerial career is viewed as a gamble, where the stakes are high, but failure is fairly routine" (1985, 13).

In this chapter, we argue that, despite appearances, ministerial selection is far from arbitrary, and that it is possible to identify a rule-governed set of qualifying criteria that move aspiring politicians into the pool of *ministrables*. We build on the existing literature on cabinet formation and ministerial recruitment, but challenge some of the underlying assumptions within those literatures. Specifically, we challenge a key assumption in the principal–agent approach to ministerial recruitment, namely, that principals (or selectors) are simply following strategic incentives rather than following rules. Second, we challenge the assumption that there are widely shared and easily observable indicators of "merit" that aspirant ministers must demonstrate.

Ministerial Recruitment and Selection Criteria

The vast literature on the social and political backgrounds of cabinet ministers shows that "ministers are likely to be drawn from among certain groups" (Blondel 1985, 15). Membership in these groups, therefore, can be considered a qualifying criterion for cabinet appointment. For instance, in some countries, one must serve many years as a member of parliament (MP) before being considered *ministrable* (de Winter 1991). Thus, one group from which ministers are drawn is the ranks of long-serving MPs in the governing party (or parties). Elsewhere, specialist policy expertise matters more than parliamentary skills (Andeweg 2014; Blondel and Thiebault 1988). A notable trend in recent years is the growing number of non-party and even non-political ministers appointed to cabinets (Costa Pinto, Cotta, and Tavares de Almeida 2018). Hence, other groups whose members often are appointed to cabinets include civil servants, business executives, and members of the military (Blondel 1985). Even if ministers share common professional and educational backgrounds, however, not all members of these groups are equally *ministrable*. What differentiates likely appointees from those with little chance of being offered a cabinet post?

Studies employing a principal-agent approach argue that selectors' decisions are motivated mainly by "reduc[ing] agency loss and ensur[ing] congruence between the agents' and the principal's policy preferences" (Fleischer and Seyfried 2015, 505; see also Martínez-Gallardo and Schleiter 2015). Such motivations can be used to derive a theoretically informed set of criteria to identify *ministrables*. Fleischer and Seyfried explain that certain characteristics (which can be understood as qualifying criteria) will improve a selector's confidence that agency loss will be minimal and that aspirant ministers share policy preferences with the selector. Such characteristics include the following: having held party office; having served in parliament (and particularly on parliamentary committees); and having previous policy experience, such as having served as a cabinet minister or having worked in government in a particular policy area (2015, 505–506). The policy positions of individuals with these profiles will be better known to selectors, increasing confidence about policy congruence and minimizing agency loss. In these studies, therefore, past political and policy experience are not so much demonstrations of merit or competence, but rather serve as information cues to selectors that allow them to strategically select ministers who will advance their political and policy goals. In this approach, qualifying criteria emerge from the strategic considerations of selectors, not from rules.

Although most studies employing a principal-agent approach examine parliamentary systems, research on cabinet formation in presidential systems likewise assumes that ministerial choices are guided by selectors' political calculations and strategy for securing policy objectives (Amorim Neto 2006; Martínez-Gallardo and Schleiter 2015). Escobar-Lemmon and Taylor-Robinson (2016) explain that cabinet ministers provide presidents with political capital resources (PCRs), and that ministers bring three distinct types of PCRs to cabinet: policy expertise, political experience, and client links to departments. Policy expertise matters because it provides ministers with credibility, which, in turn, "can signal competence and skill to constituents and to subordinates in the ministry" (Escobar-Lemmon and Taylor-Robinson 2016, 80). Political skills matter because ministers help presidents to obtain the support in congress needed to pass their legislative program and "to navigate political crisis" (103). Indicators of political skills include being a "political insider," which refers to those who have held previous cabinet posts, served as vice-ministers, or who have developed careers in national governments. Escobar-Lemmon and Taylor-Robinson also define political connections as indicators of political skills. Here, they determine whether the minister is linked to the president through friendship or having worked on the president's electoral campaign (107). But Escobar-Lemmon and Taylor-Robinson make an assumption that we challenge in this book, namely, that while things like political connections and loyalty are PCRs and political skills, they are not "qualifications." Escobar-Lemmon and Taylor-Robinson distinguish between political skills and qualifications, in testing whether "women and men with political connections are qualified for their post," using policy expertise as an indicator that a minister is so qualified

(104). Those with policy expertise are thus "qualified" to be included in cabinets in a way that those with political connections are not. We disagree, instead viewing personal relationships as a qualifying criterion commonly employed by selectors following strategic incentives.

In sum, the existing literature makes two assumptions that we challenge. First, scholars assume that selectors are guided primarily by strategic considerations rather than rules; and second, scholars take as a given that cabinet appointments are based on publicly observable traits that constitute merit, and that qualifications can be measured by looking at politicians' past political experience or their educational and professional backgrounds.

These assumptions miss three important factors. First, selectors are guided by rules that prescribe, prohibit, and permit the criteria that qualify individuals for cabinet consideration. Second, ministers are appointed as part of a team; thus what they contribute to that team matters as much as their individual attributes. Third, selectors may be guided by very different conceptions of "merit" than those held by the general public. Indeed, existing scholarship acknowledges that selectors are guided by strategic political considerations as well as rules about what characteristics need to be represented in a cabinet, while the public expects policy expertise and competence.

Recognizing these differences in criteria for being *ministrable* exposes a gap between the public's understanding of qualifying criteria for cabinet posts and the criteria actually applied by selectors. We address this gap and reveal some of the important hidden aspects of ministerial recruitment. More important, we think that viewing ministerial selection as occurring in a rule-governed context helps to identify a broader and more general set of criteria that apply across countries and types of political system. In brief, we challenge the idea that merit is constituted and identifiable exclusively by policy and political experience. Instead, we see political (and personal) connections as a subset of criteria that is highly relevant to selectors. Nonetheless, with Escobar-Lemmon and Taylor Robinson (2016), we also acknowledge the importance of social and demographic criteria, which, in many countries, take the form of strongly institutionalized unwritten rules about which groups must be represented in cabinet teams.

A Rule-Bound Framework for Identifying *Ministrables*

In Chapter 2, we outlined our conceptual framework for identifying the rules of cabinet appointments. Following Ostrom, we view rules as "prescribing, prohibiting, and permitting" certain actions (1986, 5). Viewing ministerial selection in this way does not mean rejecting entirely the principal-agent approach. We agree that strategic considerations matter. However, we think that a fuller account of the determinants of cabinet appointments requires us to place selectors' strategic considerations into a broader context defined by rules. In this framework, selectors continue to prefer ministers whom they can control and whose policy preferences will be in line with their own. Indeed, these are precisely the kinds of strategic goals that make personal connections to the selector so important. Selectors have good reasons for appointing long-time confidants and even friends to cabinet. Because there are no rules prohibiting selectors from appointing their friends, or others who have demonstrated loyalty, the rules permit selectors to use loyalty as a . criterion for appointment.

Additional rules may constrain selectors. That is, few selectors can staff their entire cabinet with loyalty as the sole criterion. As noted earlier, policy experience is key, not only because the public expects it, but also because for many portfolios, knowledge and expertise are critical to doing the job well. Finally, selectors' choices are also constrained by informal rules about which groups must be represented in cabinet. In some countries, party factions must be balanced, while in other countries, territorial representation is a central feature of cabinet formation. In the following, we explain our methodological strategies for identifying the rules that guide selectors in all of our cases.

Following the methodological framework elaborated in Chapter 2, we use interviews, media stories, and memoirs to reveal the rules about ministerial appointment that guide selectors in each country. Using an inductive method, we analyzed our media and interview data to figure out what criteria made an individual *ministrable*. For example, we asked former ministers why they believed they were appointed. We also asked experts and political insiders what the criteria for ministerial office were and what newly elected leaders must consider when selecting ministers. When analyzing our media data, we focused on what columnists and journalists wrote about who was likely to be appointed to a cabinet, who was "mentioned" as *ministrable*, paying particular attention to the justifications for why certain individuals were predicted as likely appointees. When the full slate of ministers was appointed and publicly announced, we paid close attention to how columnists and journalists described those individuals' qualifications for office. We gained additional insights on justifications for appointments from selectors' autobiographies and memoirs.

Despite the differences in political systems across our cases, there are substantial commonalities. For all of our cases, we noted the prevalence of political and policy experience as important qualifying criteria. But we also noticed frequent mentions of ministers qualifying because of personal relationships with leaders, providing crucial campaign support, and because they brought certain socio-demographic traits to a cabinet team, for instance, contributing to regional, gender, or ethnic diversity. Although the content and importance of these criteria varied, in every country a set of affiliational criteria and a set of representational criteria further delineated the boundaries of who is *ministrable* and who is not.

One way to visualize this is to imagine that each newly elected leader has a checklist of characteristics that must be present in the team. These characteristics apply to the collective cabinet, not to individual cabinet ministers. Some of the criteria take the form of prescriptive rules. For example, appointing ministers with policy expertise, especially for certain portfolios like justice or finance, is a strong prescriptive rule that is evidenced by its routine observation across our cases. Likewise, ensuring that cabinets include members with certain social or demographic backgrounds is a strongly institutionalized rule in many countries, even if it does not appear in that country's constitution or legal statutes. In contrast, appointing ministers based on personal connections is better conceptualized as being permissible under the rules, given the absence of prohibitions on using loyalty or past service as a criterion for selection.

In sum, in the rule-bound framework governing ministerial appointments, we see qualifying criteria as falling into three distinct categories: (1) experiential, (2) affiliational, and (3) representational. *Experiential* criteria encompass political skills and experience, as well as expertise in specific policy areas. *Affiliational* criteria refer to the personal relationship a *ministrable* has with the selector, a relationship that underpins the selector's ability to rely upon the *ministrable*'s personal (and political) loyalty and to trust him or her to be reliable, to keep promises, and to keep confidences. It is also a way for the selector to reward a *ministrable*'s past loyalty or to constrain a *ministrable*'s ability to disrupt and challenge the selector's authority. *Representational* criteria include politically relevant socio-demographic factors, such as those reflecting socioeconomic or other political cleavages; typical characteristics include region, race, religion, ethnicity, and gender, as well as party membership or internal party group or faction. Experiential and representational criteria are prescriptive rules, while the use of affiliational criteria is permitted by the rules.

These qualifying criteria govern selectors in all of our countries. Fully empowered selectors may construct cabinets, relatively unimpeded by rules requiring them to negotiate or consult with other political actors, yet they are still constrained by rules that render some persons *ministrable* and others both ineligible and unqualified. Significant variation appears, however, in terms of the relative strength of each of these sets of criteria, and what the subcategories within each are. In some countries, informal rules require that multiple criteria be taken into account, rendering many individuals *ministrable* and increasing their chances of inclusion in cabinet, as well as requiring selectors to engage in complex calculations when forming cabinets. In other countries, informal rules emphasize only a few criteria that the selector must consider. Whether criteria are extensive or minimal matters greatly because informal rules about criteria for inclusion in cabinet determine who is considered qualified for ministerial appointment (or not), as well as how much latitude selectors have in appointing some but not other *ministrables* to a cabinet.

Whether checklists are extensive or minimal, selectors are looking for the right mix of individuals to form teams that include all necessary experiential, affiliational, and representational criteria. Our data reveal how countries differ in terms of what qualities and characteristics are needed to build strong and legitimate teams. Because cabinets are teams that operate on high trust to do their work effectively, those who are part of personal networks linked to selectors and function as selectors' loyal allies and trusted friends constitute a substantial body of *ministrables*. The importance of affiliational linkages with the selector, as a criterion of potential cabinet appointment, is underscored by the occasional inclusion of the selector's past or potential rivals in the *ministrable* pool.[1] Because selectors need to balance a range of individual skills, experience, and connections, some individuals will be *ministrable* on some criteria but not on others. Some ministers will be chosen for their political skills in managing conflict or negotiating consensus, others for their

---

[1] See, for the United States, Barack Obama's appointment of Hillary Clinton, his primary election opponent in 2008, as secretary of state in his first cabinet.

ability to run complex government departments, and still others for their expertise in a specific policy area. We argue, moreover, that it is important to appreciate cabinets as sites of democratic representation, which creates public expectations that a cabinet should "look like the country." Thus, another criterion on which individuals may be included among the *ministrables* is their connection to the country's politically relevant demographic groups, ensuring resemblance between the cabinet and the society from which it is drawn. To reiterate, no single individual must embody all these characteristics; rather, the cabinet as a team meets the experiential, affiliational, and representational requirements of their country.

Qualifying for a Team Rather Than as Individuals

Conceptualizing cabinet recruitment as constructing a team, rather than appointing individuals, changes the way we approach the idea of qualifying for cabinet. The process of forming a cabinet is not about appointing the fifteen or thirty most qualified individuals in the country, as measured against some objective criteria. Rather, it involves putting together a team that balances the three different types of qualifying criteria—experiential, affiliational, and representational—we discussed earlier. This process of producing a balanced team is considered a complex art. As one former minister put it, forming a cabinet is "like a three dimensional chess game in which all pieces talk back."[2]

Understanding cabinet recruitment in collective rather than individual terms also allows us to explain why some eligible and qualified individuals make it into the team, while others do not. One individual might be included because they meet the requisite experiential, affiliational, and/or representational criteria, but a second individual with a similar profile might not be appointed because those pieces of the chess set have already been selected. For example, when German chancellor Angela Merkel was forming her first cabinet in 2005, a media source noted that "Clement and Steinbrück have a similar profile in the party. That speaks against their chances of both making it into cabinet."[3] Similarly, we find evidence that in earlier decades, when the norm was to include zero or one woman to cabinet, proposals to add

---

[2] Interview, December 17, 2013.
[3] "Grosse Koalition—Ende der wilden Tage," *Der Spiegel*, October 1, 2005.

additional women were resisted. In Canada in 1965, there was one woman serving in the cabinet. During the election campaign, a female member of parliament asked Prime Minister Pearson whether she might receive a cabinet post if elected. The prime minister is reported to have replied that, although she was qualified, he already had a woman serving in cabinet, and he was not planning to replace her (Tremblay and Stockemer 2013, 525).

Challenging the Concept of "Merit"

There is one further implication of our assumptions that there are multiple, overlapping criteria that qualify someone for cabinet and that cabinets need to combine and balance individuals with a range of qualifications. That implication is that there is no such thing as "merit," objectively defined. We return to this later, in Chapters 5 and 9, but for now suffice to say that we consider "merit" to be a flexible concept, applied retrospectively to the individual selected for a post. "Merit" for a spot in a cabinet can derive from a range of qualifications, including representational criteria. It is also, as we argue in Chapter 9, a rhetorical and political strategy to oppose and resist the inclusion of women in cabinets.

In Chapters 5 through 7 we excavate in more detail the rules in use for qualification for ministerial office in our seven countries. Before we do that, we want to set out clearly the difference between being *eligible* for cabinet appointment and being sufficiently *qualified* to be selected for the cabinet, and to stress the importance of not conflating these two stages. In the following section, we identify the formal and informal rules that establish eligibility for cabinet appointment. Like rules that empower or constrain selectors, formal rules are relatively few when it comes to determining who is eligible (or not) to be a member of cabinet.

Formal and Informal Rules Establishing Eligibility for Cabinet Appointment

Formal and informal rules determine who is eligible to be a minister, and these vary in terms of the strength of institutionalization. Westminster democracies are governed by rules that ministers are recruited from the ranks of parliament. Only Australia has actually codified this rule, however: the

Australian Constitution states that "no Minister of State shall hold office for a longer period than three months unless he is or becomes a senator or a member of the House of Representatives" (Commonwealth of Australia 2010, Ch. 2, Para 64). In the United Kingdom and Canada, the rule about recruiting ministers from parliament is not codified, but is a strongly institutionalized unwritten rule with force equivalent to a formal rule. As Parry and Maer (2012, 1) state, in the United Kingdom it is a "convention [. . .] that ministers must be members of either the House of Commons or House of Lords." Since membership in the House of Lords is now based primarily on selection rather than the hereditary principle, the prime minister's discretion is further enhanced, since he can proactively place favored ministerial candidates in the eligibility pool by appointing them to the House of Lords (Annesley 2015). For example, in 2008, Gordon Brown made former MP Peter Mandelson a Life Peer so that he could return to cabinet as business secretary (Eason 2011).

In Canada there are no codified rules requiring ministers to be drawn from parliament, but "convention does dictate that ministers without seats secure one as quickly as possible in either chamber" (Kerby 2015, 255–256). That said, prime ministers can and do appoint ministers who have not yet secured parliamentary seats. For example, Prime Minister Jean Chretién appointed three non-parliamentary ministers, but "all three sought and won election soon after being appointed to cabinet" (White 2005, 38). The force of this convention was evidenced in 1975 when Prime Minister Pierre Trudeau appointed a non-parliamentary minister, Pierre Juneau, who went on to lose the by-election intended to secure himself a seat. His failure to win a seat led to his immediate resignation from cabinet (White 2005, 39). In 2006, Stephen Harper likewise appointed a non-elected minister, Michael Fortier, to his cabinet. But instead of seeking a seat immediately through a by-election, Harper appointed Fortier to the Senate. The prime minister justified this move on the grounds that "we have to have a cabinet minister from Montreal," and the election did not return any Conservative MPs from that city.[4] Notably, during the 2008 election campaign, Harper promised that, if elected again, his cabinet would not include any non-elected ministers. In all three Westminster democracies there is clearly a strong informal rule to

---

[4] "Cabinet Includes Defector and Senator-to-Be," *CBC News,* February 6, 2006. http://www.cbc.ca/news/canada/cabinet-includes-defector-and-senator-to-be-1.627094 Accessed May 24, 2016.

appoint ministers with seats in the lower rather than the upper house. In Canada and the United Kingdom, ministerial appointments from the non-elected upper houses are limited, while in Australia, where the Senate is an elected body, an informal rule on eligibility requires balance between the lower and upper houses at a ratio of about 75:25 (Annesley 2015; Curtin 1997, 2010).

Other parliamentary systems have no formal rules about eligibility beyond citizenship and age requirements. Thus, while parliament remains an important eligibility pool for *ministrables*, prime ministers are permitted to recruit ministers from outside parliament. In Germany and Spain, most ministers are recruited from the lower house of parliament, yet several more are recruited from outside parliament, most commonly from regional government and party structures (Fischer 2011; Rodríguez Teruel 2011b). As noted earlier in the chapter, the selection of non-parliamentary ministers is a growing trend across Europe (Costa Pinto et al., 2018).

Presidential systems similarly have few formal rules that identify eligibility for cabinet office. Chile and the United States, the two presidential systems in our study, have formal rules that prohibit individuals from serving in both the legislative and executive branches simultaneously. For the United States, this requires presidents to be strategic about their nominations, since resignation by a member of Congress—either in the House or the Senate—who has been appointed to cabinet can shift the party balance in the chamber. Nonetheless, presidents do occasionally draw their department secretaries from Congress.[5] For both Chile and the United States, the eligibility pool for cabinet, therefore, essentially consists of all citizens, although presidents may be strategically constrained not to appoint *ministrables* currently serving in the national legislature. For Chile, this constraint is heightened, given that Chile, unlike many Latin American countries, does not elect *suplentes*, or alternates, to replace legislators appointed to cabinet.

---

[5] President Barack Obama considered senators (among them, the eventual secretary of state, New York senator Hillary Clinton, and Massachusetts senator John Kerry) for appointment to his initial cabinet, and at least two governors: Arizona governor Janet Napolitano, and Kansas governor Kathryn Sebelius. It was recognized at the time that Napolitano, if appointed as secretary of homeland security, would be replaced by the Arizona secretary of state, Republican Jan Brewer, and that Sebelius would be replaced by Kansas's sitting lieutenant governor, Republican Mark Parkinson. It was also seen as likely that the New York governor, Democrat David Paterson, would appoint a Democrat to fill Clinton's vacated Senate seat, which he did. See Chris Cillizza, "Obama Picks May Leave Big Holes; As Elected Officials Migrate, Democratic Seats Are Vulnerable," *Washington Post*, November 29, 2008.

In sum, with the exception of Australia, Canada, and the United Kingdom, where rules limit eligibility to parliament, the formal eligibility pools in each of our other cases are quite large. That said, eligibility pools are limited in scope by additional informal rules, described in the following, about party membership.

Party as a Strong Eligibility Rule

We find an inclusionary criterion for cabinet eligibility that is universal in our country case studies: eligibility for ministerial appointments is determined by membership in the governing party (or parties) of government. Indeed, party as an eligibility criterion is so strong across all cases that we consider it to be a strongly institutionalized informal rule. Prime ministers and presidents very occasionally select an independent or non-partisan cabinet member from outside their own party (or governing coalition), but appointment of opposition parties' members to cabinet is exceedingly rare. Moreover, there is evidence that violating the rule of selecting ministers from the ranks of one's own party may result in sanctions. For example, in the United Kingdom in 1997, newly elected Labour prime minister Tony Blair considered including Liberal Democrat members in his single-party cabinet, but he and the Liberal Democrat leader, Paddy Ashdown, decided "it would be premature; . . . despite our cavalier attitudes to our parties, we were both nervous about their respective reactions" (Blair 2011, 119).

In Canada, ministers are always parliamentarians from the governing party. There have been only three instances when the prime minister appointed MPs from outside the governing caucus. However, in all of these cases, MPs subsequently changed parties in order to join the cabinet (Gussow 2006). A controversial example followed Conservative leader Stephen Harper's first electoral victory in 2006. Harper only managed to win a minority of seats in the House of Commons, however, and his party failed to win any seats at all in three of the country's most important cities: Vancouver, Toronto, and Montreal. In order to ensure cabinet representation for Vancouver, Harper convinced David Emerson, who had been elected as a Liberal MP, to cross the floor and join the cabinet as a Conservative. Public outrage ensued, from other parties in parliament and from citizens in the Vancouver riding that Emerson represented. In March 2006, the parliament's

Ethics Commissioner issued a report that concluded that neither the prime minister nor the floor-crossing MP had broken any rules.[6]

In Spain, Germany, Chile and the United States, where ministers can be appointed from outside of the national legislature, appointments are still predominantly based on partisan criteria. In Germany, a former minister confirmed that appointing non-party people, while permitted, is rare "because otherwise the party would become rebellious. They would say, why are you taking them, we only have so many, why aren't you taking them from the party? Formally it's possible. But as a rule, it doesn't happen."[7] Another said, "if external people are appointed, the party and the parliamentary party would get frustrated because an external person and not them is being considered for office."[8] There are some rare cases where non-party people are appointed, and they even have a name: *Quereinsteiger* or *Seiteinsteiger*. However, according to Fischer (2011, 27) there is an empirically proven growing tendency since 1981 for German ministers to be party appointments rather than outsiders. The number of outsiders is strictly limited: "if someone really did come from right outside, then it could be one or two people and that's it. No more."[9]

In Spain, most ministers are party members. Even though non-parliamentary ministers are increasingly common, such ministers are rarely genuine "outsiders," and parties remain crucial (Rodríguez Teruel 2011b, 7). Nonetheless, compared to other western European countries, Spanish cabinets often include individuals who are non-partisans, but are appointed because of their skills or policy expertise (Rodríguez Teruel and Jerez Mir 2018, 140). But even when a minister is not a party member, that individual is likely to be a known ally or sympathizer of the governing party. For instance, a former minister appointed by Zapatero explained in an interview that although she was technically independent, and not a member of the Spanish Socialist Workers' Party (PSOE), she was nonetheless ideologically aligned with socialists, and had maintained informal links with the party.[10] Ultimately, most appointments are based on party because "the president of government cannot ignore the representation of the party"; the party must feel represented by the cabinet.[11]

---

[6] "No Rules Broken in Emerson Affair: Watchdog," http://www.cbc.ca/news/canada/no-rules-broken-in-emerson-affair-watchdog-1.587184. Accessed May 22, 2016.

[7] Interview with former minister, June 29, 2016.

[8] Interview with former minister, September 23, 2014.

[9] Interview with former minister, October 27, 2014.

[10] Interview, May 21, 2012, Madrid.

[11] Interview with former minister, May 6, 2014, Madrid.

In presidential systems, where the legislative and executive branches are constitutionally separate, party membership does not necessarily serve the same function in creating eligibility pools for cabinet inclusion. In a cross-national study of parliamentary, semi-presidential, and presidential regimes, Amorim Neto and Samuels found that non-partisan ministers are more likely in presidential systems (2010, 14). A study of Latin American presidential systems found that, on average, 40 percent of ministers are non-partisan (Martínez-Gallardo and Schleiter 2015, 232). That said, in the two presidential systems that are part of our study, party membership can be considered an important criterion in qualifying for a cabinet post. In the United States, it is clear that party allegiance is a dominant and primary means of qualifying as *ministrable*. Members of the party of the president predominate in cabinets, but "[h]aving *one* member of the other party in the 14 statutory Cabinet positions or the handful of Cabinet-rank slots—such as US trade representative or head of the Environmental Protection Agency—has been the norm."[12] In some cases, a cabinet secretary from a previous administration of the opposing party will continue in office in a newly elected government. For example, Norman Mineta served as President Bill Clinton's secretary of commerce until 2001, when he was nominated for secretary of transportation by newly elected President George W. Bush; Mineta was the only Democrat in the cabinet. In 2009, President George W. Bush's secretary of defense, Robert Gates, agreed to continue to head the Defense Department in newly elected President Barack Obama's initial cabinet, and served as defense secretary until July 2011.[13]

In the political context of the new administration, Obama was "serious about this bipartisan thing,"[14] and made attempts to include other Republicans in his initial cabinet.[15] Perhaps the most notable was Obama's consideration of Republican Senator Judd Gregg of New Hampshire for secretary of commerce. The Gregg case, however, reveals both the convention of appointing ministers from one's own party, and the sanctions that can be imposed for transgressing it. The pending nomination collapsed

[12] Al Kamen, "Bye, Partisanship?" *Washington Post*, November 7, 2008.

[13] Through the second George W. Bush administration, only four cabinet secretaries have ever served "in the cabinet of presidents of different parties." Matthew L. Wald, "Transportation Chief Quits, Citing 'Other Challenges,'" *New York Times*, June 24, 2006.

[14] Al Kamen, "Bye, Partisanship?" *Washington Post*, November 7, 2008.

[15] Transportation Secretary Ray LaHood, a former Illinois congressman, and Defense Secretary Robert Gates were the only two Republicans in Obama's initial cabinet.

after Gregg's last-minute, public about-face announcement that he was unwilling to serve in the cabinet. "The departure of Mr. Gregg [was] the latest setback to a White House that has struggled to fill several top positions and to fulfill Mr. Obama's pledge of building a bipartisan administration."[16] The failed Gregg nomination underscores the role of party in determining eligibility of potential cabinet members—a strong convention for US cabinet formation.

Party membership clearly matters in Chile, too. Presidents can and do appoint non-party ministers, but the overwhelming majority of ministers are party members, and the most strongly institutionalized rule in cabinet formation in Chile is the proportional distribution of portfolios across the coalition parties. Thus, being a member of a party that is part of the governing coalition is key to being in the eligibility pool. Presidents Bachelet and Piñera are outliers in terms of the number of independents they included in their cabinets. Bachelet's initial cabinet in 2006 included three non-party ministers (in a cabinet with 20 ministers) but in Piñera's first cabinet, party members were actually a minority among ministers. He appointed just eight (of 23) ministers from the two parties of the coalition. The remaining ministers were independents, and in an even sharper break with tradition, he appointed one minister, Jaime Ravinet, from the Christian Democratic party, one of the main parties of the opposition *Concertación* coalition.[17] Both presidents were sanctioned for violating the rule that ministers come from the governing parties. In both cases, political elites withheld support, leading both presidents to shuffle their cabinets and add ministers that conformed with rules. A political expert and columnist with experience working in government explained, "[Bachelet's] government began badly, with a lot of conflict, a lot of tension, and Bachelet ended up modifying her decisions and . . . appointing people to cabinet who were more representative of the parties in successive cabinet shuffles." Likewise, Piñera was compelled to shuffle his cabinet to bring in "people with weight in their respective parties."[18]

Even with party membership as key to eligibility, and even where, in the cases of the Westminster democracies, strongly institutionalized rules further restrict the size of eligibility pools, in most of our case studies, the

[16] Jeff Zeleny, "Gregg Ends Bid for Commerce Job," *New York Times*, February 13, 2009; https://www.nytimes.com/2009/02/13/us/politics/13gregg.html?searchResultPosition=2.
[17] "El primer gabinete de Piñera," *El Mercurio*, February 10, 2010.
[18] Interview, July 10, 2015, Santiago.

eligibility pool is actually quite large. Inclusion in the eligibility pool, however, is not an automatic ticket to a cabinet. In the course of the next three chapters, we explore in greater depth the rules that determine how those who are eligible for ministerial office actually qualify for inclusion in cabinets. Formal rules about how to move from the eligibility pool to a ministerial post are entirely absent, but that does not mean that selectors can pick whomever they wish. Even with eligibility requirements that give wide latitude to presidents and prime ministers in constructing cabinets, selectors must consider a variety of qualifying criteria, many of which take the form of rules, albeit informal ones.

Conclusion

The precise combinations of individual and collective characteristics that qualify eligible individuals for selection to cabinet vary considerably across our cases. We identify a few formal and informal rules that distinguish those who are *eligible* for appointment to cabinet. Then, from the large group of individuals formally eligible for appointment, we need to identify the rules that establish who is *qualified* and hence *ministrable*. Rules determining qualification are wholly informal. Three broad types of criteria emerged from our interviews, our media data, and autobiographies in all countries: (1) experiential criteria, (2) affiliational criteria, and (3) representational criteria. Although all of these criteria matter for all countries, our data nonetheless offer evidence that in some countries, certain criteria matter more than others. Using our interview and media data alongside secondary sources on ministerial recruitment and cabinet formation in each of our case studies, we can identify narratives in each of our countries about what types of qualifying criteria figure more prominently. Although we encounter some differences across our seven countries, there were nonetheless striking similarities in terms of the narratives about qualifications that appear in each country.

In Chapter 5, we explore the narratives about experiential criteria across our cases and then address affiliational and representational criteria in Chapters 6 and 7. Then, in Chapters 9 and 10, we assess the gendered consequences of rules about qualification. We anticipate, in line with assumptions in feminist institutionalist scholarship, that the informality of rules about qualification for ministerial office would be detrimental to women's chances of making the transition from *ministrable* to minister. Although this assumption is borne out to some extent in our findings, we also find evidence that empowered political actors use the ambiguity inherent in the informal rules of qualification to bring women into cabinet.

5

How to Qualify for Cabinet

Experiential Criteria

Introduction: What Kind of Experience Qualifies One for Cabinet?

Cabinets are the main sites for initiating and overseeing the implementation of national policy. Political leaders are expected to staff their cabinets with people who have the necessary political and policy experience for the posts. Indeed, our data are replete with references to presidents and prime ministers looking to fill their cabinets with experienced politicians and individuals with substantive expertise in a particular area. Terms like "capable," "talented," and "experienced" appear frequently throughout our interview and media data, leading us to identify experiential criteria as the first of three categories of qualifying criteria. Our data indicate that all ministers meet some experiential criterion. But what kind of experience qualifies someone to be a minister? As noted in Chapter 3, there is no formal application process, and no formal qualification requirements for the post of cabinet minister. Recall that according to Ostrom (1986), rules can prescribe, prohibit, or permit certain courses of action. Prescriptive rules about experience are non-specific and flexible. All ministers have some kind of qualification, whether political experience or policy-relevant professional or educational backgrounds. Yet we find no evidence of specific prescriptive rules, whether formal or informal, about what form that experience should take. Instead, we find that a range of possible experience is permitted as a pathway to ministerial office. We also find few formal prohibitions concerning experience. [1]

---

[1] To give a rare example of a prohibition: generals in the US military cannot move directly into the secretary of defense position, without congressional exemption. See 10 U.S. Code § 113 (a): "There is a Secretary of Defense, who is the head of the Department of Defense, appointed from civilian life by the President, by and with the advice and consent of the Senate. A person may not be appointed as Secretary of Defense within seven years after relief from active duty as a commissioned officer of a regular component of an armed force."

Existing scholarship identifies political experience through previous cabinet or parliamentary service, holding or having held party office, or demonstrating talent or skill in political management or communication (Blondel 1985, 1991; Dowding and Dumont 2009). Scholars identify policy experience through educational credentials, professional experience, or client links (Escobar-Lemmon and Taylor-Robinson 2016; Fischer and Kaiser 2009, 27–32; Kam and Indridson 2009, 44–47). Much of the comparative research on ministers has sought to categorize ministers according to their backgrounds, but has been guided by different questions than those explored here.

Jean Blondel's earliest work on cabinet ministers introduced several terms to describe ministers' backgrounds: "Generalists," "amateurs," or "representatives" are ministers with extensive political experience, usually accumulated in parliament, but little policy expertise or knowledge directly related to their ministerial portfolio. On the other hand, "specialists" or "managers" are terms to describe non-parliamentary ministers, that is, ministers appointed from outside the ranks of parliament. Such ministers normally have technical policy expertise, sometimes acquired through careers in public administration, relevant to their portfolios (Blondel 1985, 1991; see also Blondel and Thiébault 1988). The distinction between generalist and specialist ministers interested researchers who wanted to know the consequences of having mainly specialist or generalist ministers in cabinet. Researchers of Western European cabinets, for example, wanted to know how the presence of specialists, amateurs, managers, or representatives affected how cabinets functioned, how they deliberated and made decisions, and, above all, whether being a generalist or specialist affected how long a minister stayed in cabinet (Blondel and Thiébault 1991).

While scholars acknowledged the analytical utility of the distinction, they also discovered its limited use in empirical research. Blondel and Thiébault conclude that, rather than finding a clear dichotomy among ministers who are amateurs or generalists versus ministers with specialist or policy expertise, "cabinet ministers in all Western European countries are probably more often experts—or at least part experts—than is usually believed" (1991, 120). Likewise, in his study of the backgrounds of ministers around the world, Blondel (1985) found multiple routes to cabinet, and that even where a single path was common, that is, where parliamentary routes were dominant among ministers, exceptions could still be found. More recent work likewise urges caution, noting that distinguishing between "politicians" and "outsiders" is challenging, "since these categories are not always mutually exclusive" (Costa Pinto et al. 2018, 6).

Research on presidential cabinets likewise sought to categorize ministers, distinguishing mainly between insiders and outsiders and partisan versus technocratic ministers. These scholars, too, were primarily concerned with things like cabinet stability and ministerial turnover (Camerlo and Martínez-Gallardo 2017). Essentially, scholars were more interested in how ministerial backgrounds affected cabinet functioning or the career trajectories of ministers than in identifying a set of qualifications necessary to be appointed to cabinet. Researchers were particularly interested in how the party backgrounds of ministers affected the tenure of ministers and, more important, whether cabinets were more prone to reshuffles when more non-partisan ministers are present.

In this chapter, we draw on our qualitative data to reveal multiple routes to qualifying for cabinet on experiential grounds. Significantly, system type does not determine which path ministers take. Cabinets in presidential, parliamentary, and Westminster systems include ministers with political experience, as well as ministers with extensive policy experience. Indeed, the central finding of this chapter is that all ministers meet some experiential criterion, and that many ministers meet multiple criteria, that is, having political experience, policy expertise, and educational or professional backgrounds relevant to their portfolio. Throughout this chapter, we draw on secondary sources and interview data to determine general trends in each country, while using our media data to provide concrete illustrations of how all cabinets, regardless of country or system type, include ministers with multiple experiential qualifications. As discussed in Chapter 2, our media data include news stories from two elections for each country.[2] For this chapter's analysis, we carefully read through each story to find references to ministers' backgrounds and qualifications related to the portfolio they were assigned. In some cases, ministers' qualifications appear in media stories speculating about who would be appointed. Here, journalists reference a *ministrable*'s experience or credentials as a way of justifying why that individual is likely to be appointed. In other cases, qualifications and credentials are discussed after the makeup of cabinet is known, in which case journalists are either describing who the ministers are, for instance their political,

---

[2] See Table 2.1 in Chapter 2 for the elections and newspapers included in the database.

professional, and educational backgrounds, or they are explicitly connecting an individual's background to his or her appointment.

Based on our reading of the data, as well as the categories that other cabinet scholars use, we distinguish among three categories of qualifications:

(1) *Political experience*: This category includes references to ministers' political backgrounds, namely, whether and how long they served in parliament, whether they held other elected or appointed offices at the local, regional, or national levels, which parliamentary committees they served on, and whether they held previous posts as minister. This category includes individuals' roles in party leadership, namely, whether they currently or previously held party office. We also include positions in government below the post of minister.

(2) *Policy expertise*: Here, we looked for indicators that a minister's knowledge or expertise was related or relevant to his or her portfolio, and therefore may have served as a reason for selection. In many cases, policy expertise is indicated through previous cabinet experience or government service in that portfolio. But it can also be gained through work in the private sector, for example, in business, academia, or culture, sport, or the arts.

(3) *Educational credentials*:[3] To identify the importance of educational background (and not simply level of education), we employ three criteria: (i) references to educational attainment (e.g., degrees held), (ii) relevance of degree to cabinet post, and (iii) links to highly prestigious institutions (e.g., Cambridge, Oxford, Harvard, Yale).

We count a minister as meeting any one of the three types of experiential criteria whenever a media story or opinion piece mentions a particular type of experience, expertise, or educational credential. We make no inferences about whether an individual was appointed to cabinet because a certain type of experience or credential was mentioned. Instead, we were simply interested in whether certain experience, credentials, or expertise were mentioned by journalists and political pundits. It is also worth noting that even if our media data make no mention of political or policy experience for

---

[3] We rely solely on our media data here, departing from existing scholarship that looks at a variety of sources to find full information about ministerial backgrounds. We are not concerned with whether ministers have university degrees, but instead, whether their educational backgrounds are mentioned by journalists and columnists when discussing their appointment.

a specific minister, we do not infer that the minister does not have policy-relevant expertise or that he or she lacks any political experience. We address the question of experiential criteria in terms of what presidents and prime ministers consider important in selecting ministers and in terms of how the media understand the importance of political experience, policy expertise, and educational background in shaping the eligibility pool of potential cabinet appointees. With respect to educational credentials, we do not consider any specific degree as important in and of itself, but rather consider how educational background is publicly understood and employed—or not employed—as an explicit criterion for selecting ministers.

We also recognize that the three categories sometimes overlap in practice. For instance, serving as a former minister or shadowing a cabinet post while in opposition indicates both political experience and policy expertise. Thus, where ministers are appointed to the same (or clearly related) post that they had previously held, and when it is mentioned in a media story, we count that minister as having both policy and political qualifications. Similarly, holding a law degree or a medical degree may be taken as an educational credential while also providing policy-relevant expertise for serving as justice or health minister, respectively. That experiential qualifying criteria may overlap makes it difficult to say with any certainty which qualifications matter the most in cabinet appointment. Indeed, our central finding is that there is no consistent pattern of difference across cases. Instead, we find striking similarities. Political system type does not determine whether ministers have primarily political experience or policy expertise. As a result, we conclude that across all cabinets, regardless of system type, political experience, policy expertise, and educational credentials can all serve as routes to ministerial office.

Our media data contain ample evidence of the multiple pathways to cabinet. Nonetheless, for most cases, political experience appears to be mentioned in media discussion more frequently than policy expertise or educational backgrounds (see Table 5.1). There are 264 ministers in the 14 cabinets we examine in this chapter. Political experience is mentioned by the media for 73 percent of those ministers; policy experience is mentioned for 50 percent of ministers; and educational backgrounds are mentioned for 23 percent of ministers. We must be cautious in interpreting these figures, however. Fewer media mentions of educational backgrounds does not mean that education is irrelevant and that selectors could fill their cabinets with

Table 5.1 Ministers' Experiential Qualifying Criteria: Media Mention by Country and Selector

Country	Selector (Year Cabinet Appointed)	New or Returning Government	Total Number of Ministers	Type of Qualifying Experience		
				Political Experience N (%)	Policy Expertise N (%)	Educational Credential N (%)
Chile						
	Bachelet (2006)	New	20	14 (70.0)	9 (45.0)	12 (60.0)
	Piñera (2010)	New	23	6 (26.1)	8 (34.8)	12 (52.2)
United States						
	Bush (2005)	Returning	15	14 (93.3)	11 (73.3)	6 (40.0)
	Obama (2009)	New	15	14 (93.3)	12 (80.0)	8 (53.3)
Germany						
	Schröder (1998)	Returning	13	7 (53.4)	2 (15.4)	0 (0)
	Merkel (2005)	New	14	14 (100.0)	9 (64.3)	0 (0)
Spain						
	Zapatero (2004)	New	16	14 (87.5)	9 (56.3)	8 (50.0)
	Rajoy (2011)	New	13	13 (100.0)	8 (61.5)	2 (15.4)
Australia						
	Gillard (2010)	Returning	18	15 (83.3)	5 (27.8)	1 (5.6)
	Abbott (2013)	New	18	18 (100.0)	14 (77.8)	0 (0)
Canada						
	Harper (2008)	Returning	26	25 (96.1)	16 (61.5)	0 (0)
	Trudeau (2015)	New	30	15 (50.0)	16 (53.3)	7 (23.3)

(Continued)

Table 5.1 Continued

Country	Selector (Year Cabinet Appointed)	New or Returning Government	Total Number of Ministers	Type of Qualifying Experience		
				Political Experience N (%)	Policy Expertise N (%)	Educational Credential N (%)
United Kingdom	Blair (2005)	Returning	22	8 (36.3)	0 (0)	0 (0)
	Cameron (2010)	New	21	16 (76.2)	13 (61.9)	6 (28.6)
All cabinets			264	193 (73.1)	132 (50.0)	62 (23.5)

Sources: Media data.
Note: Ministers' experiential criteria are dichotomized as any media mention / no media mention.

ministers with no university education. The lack of attention to educational backgrounds more likely indicates the ubiquity of university education among the political elite. Being highly educated is not in and of itself sufficient to move someone from the eligibility pool to cabinet.

Precisely because all ministers meet some indicator for experience, we cannot say that experiential criteria are determinative of ministerial appointments. Instead, we argue that experiential criteria allow selectors to justify all cabinet appointments post hoc, in public terms, although such public justification may not necessarily reflect the selectors' reasons for making the appointment. As discussed in Chapter 4, there are three types of qualifying criteria. Selectors may appoint ministers on the basis of political and policy experience, but selectors are also permitted and also have strategic incentives to appoint trusted allies, whose selection they cannot publicly justify on the basis of affiliational criteria. Moreover, selectors may also be required to appoint according to relevant representational criteria, but, again, given public expectations that ministers be selected for their experience and skills, they face potential criticism for justifying ministerial appointments solely on representational grounds. Our research makes clear that while not every minister is selected primarily on the basis of experiential criteria, presidents and prime ministers will emphasize ministers' policy knowledge or political experience as the justification for their appointments. Likewise, media commentary emphasizes ministers' political, policy, and educational backgrounds when speculating about or reacting to cabinet appointments.

Multiple Routes to Ministerial Office

Experiential criteria are flexible. Precisely because there are no strong prescriptive rules that spell out qualifying criteria for appointment, selectors are permitted to define ministers' qualifications in a variety of ways. More important, because cabinets are teams, selectors are also looking to balance different types of backgrounds. Our findings illustrate both the flexibility of experiential criteria and the likelihood of cabinets containing individuals with varying types of backgrounds and experience. In this section, we provide evidence that there is no single route to cabinet office. Instead, across all of cases, regardless of system type, we find a mix of ministers meeting various types of experiential criteria. Indeed, some ministers meet all three types of experiential criteria, while others meet just one. Most important, we find no strong evidence that system type determines what kind of experiential criteria ministers are likely to have. In presidential systems like Chile and the United States, countries conventionally classified as having specialist recruitment rules, we find several ministers with political experience, as well as many with policy expertise. In parliamentary systems like Germany and Spain, sometimes classified as having specialist recruitment rules, we likewise find that political skill and experience appear equally important. Finally, our data show that in the Westminster systems of Australia, Canada, and the United Kingdom, normally classified as using generalist criteria, where ministers qualify based on their political experience, we find that many ministers also have policy expertise related to their cabinet post. Our findings thus mirror those in Blondel's classic 1985 study, namely, that there are multiple routes to ministerial office, even within a single country.

The fact that political system type does not predict whether ministers qualify based on policy expertise or political experience has important consequences for women's appointment. Gender scholars have assumed that when political experience is prioritized over policy expertise, then women are likely to be under-represented (Bauer and Okpotor 2013; Davis 1997). Our data indicate that political experience is prized across all types of political systems, and in Chapter 9, we reveal the gendered consequences of experiential criteria, showing how some experiential criteria pose obstacles to women's cabinet appointments.

Experiential Criteria in Presidential Systems: Chile and the United States

Although Chile is a presidential democracy, our evidence indicates that ministers do not qualify for cabinet solely on the basis of policy expertise; most ministers have political backgrounds. Finance ministers, at least in the last decades, tend to have PhDs in economics, but our data show that political experience matters greatly, particularly for cabinet posts that are more political than technical. The most important cabinet committee in Chile is the Political Committee, composed of three posts: minister of interior, government spokesperson (SEGOB), and secretary general of the presidency (SEGPRES). A former minister explained that "political influence" was necessary to qualify for one of these posts. When pressed about what it meant to have political influence, the former minister replied: "It means having influence in the parties, having a good network of connections," which, he explained, is more likely among people who have held leadership positions before, like a party president, senator, or former minister.[4] Other interviewees likewise explained that while technical or policy expertise may matter for social or economic portfolios, for the political portfolios ministers needed to have political skills, for example, the president must know that the person is able to manage conflict.[5]

Our media data for the initial cabinets of Michelle Bachelet (2006) and Sebastián Piñera (2010) support this chapter's central argument. Several ministers have both political experience and policy relevant expertise. Among President Bachelet's 20 ministers, two were former ministers and an additional seven held previous posts in government, but below the rank of minister. Ministers like Viviane Blanlot (appointed to the defense portfolio), Paulina Veloso (minister of the presidency), Clarisa Hardy (minister of planning), and Laura Albornoz (national women's service) all held several posts in government prior to their appointment to cabinet. Several ministers have educational credentials that are described by journalists as being relevant to their portfolio. For example, despite having no experience in politics and not being a member of any of the governing parties, finance minister Andrés Velasco's educational and professional credentials were repeatedly

---

[4] Interview, August 6, 2014, Santiago, Chile.
[5] Interview, August 11, 2014, Santiago, Chile.

mentioned by journalists and political pundits. Velasco earned a PhD in economics at Columbia University and later taught economics at Harvard. The educational credentials of other ministers were mentioned in media reports as well, particularly when degrees were earned at prestigious US universities or at one of the two leading universities in Chile, the Catholic University and the University of Chile, both located in Santiago.

Notably, Bachelet departed from the practices of previous *Concertación* presidents by not using leadership or influence in the coalition parties as a central qualifying criterion. Still, one of the most important cabinet posts was awarded to someone with extensive political experience: Andrés Zaldívar, appointed as interior minister, was a well-known political figure, having held cabinet posts in previous governments and having spent 16 years as a senator. The other minister with extensive political experience was Alejandro Foxley, appointed as the minister of foreign affairs. He was the former president of the Christian Democratic Party, and a former finance minister. Yet only two of her ministers, Osvaldo Andrade (appointed to labor) and Martín Zilic (minister of education) held party office at the time of appointment in the Socialist and Christian Democratic parties, respectively. Among Bachelet's 20-person cabinet, 14 ministers have some type of political experience, ranging from holding government posts at the national or regional levels, to holding party office or serving as previous minister. Nine of the 20 ministers have policy-relevant expertise, acquired either through their previous government posts or through their educational and professional backgrounds. The media made reference to educational backgrounds for 12 of Bachelet's 20 ministers (see Table 5.1).

President Piñera's initial cabinet differed from all previous post-transition cabinets primarily because it was the first time since the dictatorship that a leader from the political right took office. Unsurprisingly, few of Piñera's cabinet ministers had political experience since the parties of the right had been shut out of government for 20 years. Like Bachelet, Piñera departed from past presidents in not appointing individuals with lengthy trajectories of political leadership in the parties or congress. Only one minister had served in congress, namely, José Antonio Galilea Vidaurre, appointed to the agriculture portfolio. Just six ministers of Piñera's 23-member cabinet had some kind of political experience, ranging from campaign advisor to former presidential candidate. In the media data, educational or professional backgrounds, particularly in law, economics, or business, were the most frequently mentioned type of experiential background.

In the United States, "the Constitution specifies nothing about the qualifications nominees must or should have in order to be nominated or confirmed, leaving the responsibility to the president and the Senate to work out between themselves the requisite qualifications for various offices" (Gerhardt 2003, 180). With a cabinet of only 15 persons, US presidents must accommodate a variety of informal rules concerning the criteria for cabinet appointment. Several of the criteria for a *ministrable*'s inclusion in cabinet overlap and reinforce each other. For example, policy expertise is usually acquired through several years in a career that requires—or develops—political talents and skill, locating two criteria in a single individual and hence satisfying both criteria for cabinet appointment. Generally, policy expertise is a major criterion for appointment as cabinet secretary (although this varies by department); political skill is an important criterion, but often is identified more through its violation than its exercise. Even policy competency is difficult to define; as Gerhardt (2003, 190) observes, "this is the most difficult ground on which to object to [or to support] a nomination, because no consensus exists on the appropriate qualifications for most confirmable positions. . . . [A] credible case can be made for the competence of almost any nominee."[6]

Substantive policy experience is more important for some cabinet positions than others. For many of our cases, formal legal training and experience are crucial requirements for consideration for justice ministers, including the US attorney general.[7] Similarly, secretaries of the treasury are likely to be economists, to have extensive experience in corporations and/or banking, and/or to have served as CEO of a major corporation. Finally, the Department of Homeland Security (DHS) is seen as requiring a high level of policy and political expertise: heading the DHS requires "skills [and] . . . experience to run the sprawling, chaotic Department . . . , to manage its more than 180,000 employees, or to establish priorities for the 22 agencies under

---

[6] See also Gerhardt (2003, 211).

[7] In the early years of the Republic, lawyers gained entry to the bar by apprenticing with a law firm or by studying law independently; attending a formal law school was not necessary for admission to the bar. All the post–World War II attorneys general held formal degrees from schools of law. From 1961 to the present, all of the past 20 US attorneys general have held law degrees, almost exclusively from private prestigious law schools. These include, from most recent, Harvard (Lynch), Columbia (Holder), Yale (Mukasey), Harvard (Gonzales), Chicago (Ashcroft), Harvard (Reno), George Washington University (Barr), Pittsburgh* (Thornburgh), UC-Berkeley* (Meese), Harvard (Smith), Maryland* (Civiletti), Mercer (Bell), Chicago (Levi), Ohio State* (Saxbe), Harvard (Richardson), Harvard (Kleindienst), Fordham (Mitchell), Chicago (Clark), Yale (Katzenbach), and Virginia* (Kennedy). Asterisks mark the non-private institutions.

its purview. . . . Whoever is . . . proposed for this unusually demanding Cabinet position should . . . be . . . an unusually gifted, even visionary manager."[8] Similarly, the Department of Defense and the Department of Veterans' Affairs, elevated to cabinet status in 1989, have specific experiential requirements for qualifying for appointment as secretary: being a veteran of the armed forces is crucial. In sum, experiential criteria vary in content and strength across presidents and US cabinet departments.

Media reports concerning the initial cabinet of Barack Obama's first administration reflected this emphasis on experience and expertise.[9] "[T]he list [of potential nominees was] also notable for the number of people who have experience in the field to which they will be assigned. . . . There's a lot of street-level knowledge in this Cabinet. . . ."[10] President Obama was quoted as stating, "What we are going to do [in terms of cabinet selection] is combine experience with fresh thinking." Of the 15 appointments to his first cabinet in 2009, 14 clearly had the relevant political experience or policy expertise that qualified them for appointment. Appointees for the four major cabinet posts—state, treasury, defense, and justice—were clearly qualified for their positions. Hillary Clinton was a two-term senator from New York, who had served for six years on the Senate Armed Services Committee. Robert Gates, former defense secretary in the second George W. Bush administration, continued in that post as Obama's first secretary of defense.[11] Timothy Geithner had been under secretary of the treasury before his appointment as treasury secretary. Eric Holder, like the attorneys general who preceded him, held a law degree from a prestigious Ivy League university, and had served in various capacities in the US Department of Justice, including as deputy attorney general.

The media data provide evidence that reporters and pundits discussed experiential criteria in their assessments of Obama's first cabinet appointments and emphasized the merit of his choices. Examples of assessments of Obama's

[8] "Who's Next at DHS?" *Washington Post*, January 10, 2005. It is worth noting that "gifted" and "visionary," although presumably measures of "merit," are not operationalized and there is no clear measure, especially at the appointment stage, of what gifted and visionary mean in this context.

[9] As discussed further in Chapter 6 concerning affiliational criteria, media reports and evaluations of the initial cabinet of President George W. Bush's second term were generally silent on issues of experience and policy expertise, in part because many of the members of the new cabinet were holdovers from Bush's first term.

[10] Alec MacGillis, "For Obama Cabinet, a Team of Moderates," *Washington Post*, December 20, 2008.

[11] It is worth noting that Gates is, in some ways, the most educated among those appointed to the top four cabinet posts, holding three degrees, including the terminal PhD in history.

cabinet nominees, from the *New York Times* and the *Washington Post*, indicate both the importance of experiential criteria and the extent to which cabinet appointees were assessed on experiential grounds, both policy and political. The *Washington Post* observed that "[t]he best thing the new administration has going for it . . . is the amount of executive branch experience it has to call on," summarizing Obama's choices as "an all-star cabinet with . . . picks [that] thus far are experienced, capable, smart and pragmatic. . . . A common thread among most of these selections is a deep understanding of the legislative process and congressional players."[12]

The media also noted the importance of other selection criteria for cabinet appointments, but nonetheless equated merit most strongly with experiential criteria: "No one can look at any of these selections and think that gender or race was the driving factor in the selection."[13] President Obama justified his cabinet selections primarily on experiential grounds, even as he recognized the importance of representational criteria for nominating cabinet secretaries: " 'I think people are going to say this is one of the most diverse cabinets and White House staff of all time,' Mr. Obama said. '*But more importantly*, they're going to say these are all people of outstanding qualifications and excellence.' "[14]

Experiential Criteria in Parliamentary Systems: Germany and Spain

Germany and Spain are parliamentary democracies in which ministers can be appointed from within or from outside parliament. We find evidence of multiple pathways to cabinet in both countries, with ministers possessing both political experience and policy expertise.

In Germany, both policy experience—referred to as *Fachkompetenz*—and political skills are relevant in the process of determining which actors in the eligibility pool are appropriately qualified and therefore *ministrable*. Political

[12] "Editorial: The Cabinet So Far," *Washington Post*, November 22, 2008. See also David E. Sanger, "The Candidate of Change Chooses Experience," *New York Times*, November 22, 2008: "Mr. Obama continues a place a premium on deep experience." This was seconded in a *Washington Post* article by Alec MacGillis, "For Obama Cabinet, a Team of Moderates," December 20, 2008: "[T]he list is also notable for the number of people who have experience in the field to which they will be assigned. . . . They're smart, they're well-educated, they're the upper crust. . . . It reflects a team-oriented approach."

[13] "Editorial: The Cabinet So Far," *Washington Post*, November 22, 2008.

[14] Peter Baker, "Long Road Behind Him, Richardson Gets a Post," *New York Times*, December 4, 2008, emphasis added.

skills are important qualifying criteria because, as a former minister explains, "a minister has to be able to direct a ministry and get on top of a wide range of topics in a short space of time. What is more, a minister has to have political skill—good, open communication with voters and the parliamentary party. The ability to compromise and representative skills are hugely important."[15] Another former minister said, "What you need is a great capacity to understand political situations, know how to prioritize things, if you are active in a range of activities across a constituency you need to be able to handle and work on a range of topics. So, a lot of things come together. And so, you think, do I think they are up for that, do they have the necessary steadfastness to work calmly and carefully on difficult situations? ... You need to show you can organize politically, that you can work through problems."[16]

In Germany, ministers accumulate political experience predominantly through the positions they hold within parliament and their party. Kaiser and Fischer (2009, 149) find the "main recruitment pool was the parliamentary group of the governing parties," more specifically that "most ministers come from the standing committee of their parliamentary group, i.e. they have been in a leadership position there." However, over the years, political experience accumulated in regional governments has been increasingly important (Fischer 2011, 27).

The importance of the Bundestag and the party as a political training ground for ministers was confirmed in interviews. Ministers are "established respected people who have played a role in the party,"[17] and former ministers describe their own political experience when explaining how they qualified for ministerial office. For example, one former minster shared that "I was in the executive committee of the party and deputy chair of the parliamentary party."[18] Another explained, "I was for a long time an MP (MdB), then I was in the [name of Bundesland] state parliament, I was deputy leader of the parliamentary party there."[19] Another former minister reported having "held a number of high level leadership positions in the party and parliamentary party over a number of decades"[20]

Ministers also describe the importance of policy expertise or *Fachkompetenz*. For instance, one former minister explains that "for the

---

[15] Interview with former minister, October 22, 2014.
[16] Interview with former minister, October 29, 2014.
[17] Ibid.
[18] Ibid.
[19] Interview with former minister, October 27, 2014.
[20] Interview with former minister, September 23, 2014.

main part *Fachkompetenz* is important."[21] Ministers report that "competence or connection with a topic is part of the equation" of demonstrating experience that qualifies you as *ministrable*.[22] Aspirant ministers need to be able to "work through an issue and make a name for their competence on that issue [. . .] you have to work on a topic or two and the selector needs to know, she can do it. Don't just jump around different subjects. That gets you nowhere."[23] Ministers are clear that they are not referring to any formal qualifications or professional background required to master a portfolio. It is only "with the minister for justice that you would unlikely take someone who has not had a legal training."[24]

Our media data for Gerhard Schröder's 2002 cabinet and Angela Merkel's 2005 cabinet reflect the importance of both political skills and policy expertise for the recruitment of ministers. Chancellor Schröder's 2002 cabinet is characterized by considerable continuity from the previous SPD-Green Coalition, with nine of 13 ministers continuing in their previous portfolio. This cabinet is defined as being rich in "the capacity to be pragmatic and drive things through."[25] New cabinet picks are characterized by their political experience: for the backing they have from the public or their particular region, the political experience they have accumulated in various offices, or their links in the parliamentary party. One new minister—Renate Schmidt—is noted for her *Fachkompetenz*: the newspaper reports that she "had in recent years made a name for herself as a committed expert in family policy," which is relevant to her portfolio as minister for family, senior citizens, women, and youth.[26] In an interview, when her political skills were questioned, she retorted that "it has never been said of me that I am not assertive."[27] The incoming minister for justice, Brigitte Zypries, emphasized her experiential criteria by saying, "In my career as a public servant I have taken every step from senior civil servant to undersecretary of state."[28]

In the media data on Chancellor Angela Merkel's 2005 cabinet, all 14 ministers are noted for their political skills, accrued either in previous ministerial posts, or in party or parliamentary roles at national or regional levels. Fewer

---

21   Interview with former minister, October 22, 2014.
22   Interview with former minister, October 27, 2014.
23   Interview with former minister, October 29, 2014.
24   Ibid.
25   "Mit einem Kabinett der erfahrenen Männer," *Der Spiegel*, October 21, 2002.
26   "Außerdem in dieser Ausgabe Rot-Grün erwartet vier schwierige Jahre," *Süddeutsche Zeitung*, October 17, 2002.
27   "Aus allen Wolken gefallen," *Süddeutsche Zeitung*, October 17, 2002.
28   "Keine Unterabteilung Schilys," *Süddeutsche Zeitung*, October 31, 2002.

comments and references are made relating policy expertise, with fewer than half of ministers noted for their *Fachkompetenz*. About Peer Steinbrück, minister of finance, one report says: "the economist has a steep career as a civil servant behind him"; Horst Seehofer, minister of consumer protection, nutrition, and agriculture, is referred to as "an expert in social affairs"; and Franz Josef Jung, minister of defense, "served in the Bundeswehr." In most cases, however, media reports simply note policy expertise when a minister is returning to a portfolio: "Now [Wolfgang Schäuble] becomes Minster for Home Affairs for the second time" and "Zypries has been Minister for Justice since October 2002."[29]

The media make little reference to the educational credentials of ministers. If a minister's background is relevant to the portfolio—Minister of Finance Peer Steinbrück is an economist by training—then it may be mentioned, but the data contain no reference to level of education, or to schools or universities attended. We attribute this to Germany's more egalitarian education system and generally, to the lower salience of class in structuring access to politics, when compared to the United Kingdom, Chile, or the United States.

In Spain, too, most cabinet ministers have political experience, but many also have policy expertise, sometimes gained through political or government careers, and sometimes gained through education or professional backgrounds. According to interviews with former ministers and party insiders, holding party office is an important way to qualify for a ministerial spot. A former minister explained, "The most logical thing is for an important part of the government to come from the party directive. That is very common."[30] Another former minister noted, "normally [the prime minister] wants to have a political section [in cabinet] and later you . . . can add in people with more technical and professional profiles."[31] Our media data indicate that both Zapatero and Rajoy included several ministers from their parties' executive. In fact, in Rajoy's government "the whole nucleus of the national directive of the PP . . . is entering the government."[32] The only exception was González Pons, who was not appointed to cabinet. In Zapatero's cabinet, 14 of 16 ministers had political experience, some in regional

[29] "Das Kabinett der großen Koalition," *Süddeutsche Zeitung*, November 22, 2005.
[30] Interview, May 6, 2014.
[31] Interview, May 13, 2014, Madrid.
[32] Joaquín Ferrandis, "Margallo se convierte en la esperanza de Fabra en el Gobierno tras no entrar Pons," *El País*, December 22, 2011.

governments and others at the national level. In Rajoy's cabinet, each of the 13 ministers had political experience. But in both governments, most ministers also had policy expertise relevant to their portfolio (see Table 5.1).

Our media data for Zapatero's election make repeated reference to Zapatero's wish to appoint ministers who are "experienced politicians" alongside people with "proven professional capacity" or expertise.[33] In using such terms, the prime minister was indicating that both political experience and policy expertise mattered, and these experiential criteria are evident in the way the media describe the appointments. For instance, Miguel Angel Moratinos, appointed to the foreign affairs portfolio, is described as having extensive international experience and being a talented diplomat.[34] Pedro Solbes, appointed to the finance portfolio, is described as a "political heavyweight" with a solid reputation in finance.[35] He had served as agriculture and then finance minister in the González government. Carmen Calvo was appointed to the culture portfolio, the same post she had previously held in the regional government of Andalusia. Magdalena Alvarez was appointed minister of public works, after serving several years in an economic post in the Andalusian government. She is described as having "profound knowledge of budgets and financing."[36] The minister for education, María Jesús Sansegundo, a former university professor, was likewise described as highly knowledgeable about the education sector and education financing.[37] Several journalists and political observers referenced the educational backgrounds of ministers, particularly when ministers held doctorates in fields related to their portfolio.

Rajoy's cabinet ministers all had extensive political backgrounds. Indeed, several had served as minister in the Aznar government. Others were regional ministers or long-term deputies. But policy expertise clearly mattered, too. The foreign affairs minister, José García Margallo, had served as member of the European parliament (MEP) and was described as having extensive experience in matters related to the European Union, something that would matter greatly to the foreign affairs post. Rajoy's finance minister, Cristobol Montoro, held a PhD in economics, but had also held the finance post in

[33] Anabel Díez, "Zapatero garantizará por ley la paridad en los altos cargos de la Administración," *El País*, March 9, 2004.

[34] Peru Egurbide, "Un gran diplomático por vocación y talante," *El País*, April 1, 2004.

[35] "El arte de decidir sin molestar," *El País*, April 1, 2004.

[36] "Negociadora contundente," *El País*, April 1, 2004.

[37] José Luis Barbería, "No suenan aires de celebración en la sede central del socialismo español," *El País*, March 21, 2004.

Aznar's government. One journalist noted that in the 13-member cabinet, there were seven law degrees and four economics degrees.[38]

Experiential Criteria in Westminster Systems: Australia, Canada, and the United Kingdom

The parliamentary route to cabinet is most strongly associated with Westminster systems where there are strong rules that ministers hold seats in parliament and qualifying experience is said to be political or generalist. Our data show that political experience is an important route to ministerial office in Australia, Canada, and the United Kingdom. Yet there are important differences across the three countries: in the United Kingdom, on average, ministers served 12.2 years in parliament, and "fewer than 10 percent of ministers arrived at cabinet within five years of the first election" (White 2005, 39). In Canada, in contrast, higher rates of parliamentary turnover mean "staggering proportions of ministers take up their duties having had little or no legislative experience" (White 2005, 39).

Westminster democracies also have strong traditions of forming shadow cabinets, which set up ministerial opportunities by preparing potential government ministers politically and substantively for their respective portfolios. In the United Kingdom and Australia, shadow ministers take the lead in holding government ministers to account in parliamentary debates, but in shadowing a portfolio, they also build up substantial expertise and knowledge in the policy area. In both Australia and the United Kingdom, selection to shadow cabinets strongly predicts selection to cabinet when elections produce a change in government.

The importance of serving in shadow cabinets is evident in our media data. In Australia, ahead of the 2013 election of Tony Abbott, the opposition leader, stated explicitly that "[a]ll of my frontbenchers can expect to be doing the same job in government as they are now"[39] to give voters confidence that they had policy expertise to get the job done well. Likewise, in the United Kingdom, newspaper commentaries following the 2010 election note how "the most senior members of Mr Cameron's Conservative team got the

---

[38] Carlos E. Cué, "Un gobierno de amigos y fieles," *El País*, December 22, 2011.
[39] "Loss Would Leave Just One Woman Standing," *The Australian*, September 12, 2013.

jobs they prepared for in opposition"[40] and that "only four members of the Cabinet are completely new to their briefs."[41]

Turning specifically to Australia, political experience is extremely important to qualify as a *ministrable*, and ministerial opportunities are regularly set up in the shadow cabinet. According to one former minister, ministerial appointments might be attributed to having put in a good campaign performance as a shadow minister, time served on the political stage, and having developed some good policies that helped secure the party's election.[42] In our media data for Julia Gillard's 2010 cabinet and Tony Abbott's 2013 cabinet, political experience is frequently referenced, and policy experience less so. The media note political experience for 15 of the 18 ministers appointed to Gillard's cabinet. Ministers are, for instance, noted for being a "capable and accomplished politician," for having "experience and the ability to lead," as someone who "understands Realpolitik," is "seen as fixer," or as "someone who truly gets under Tony Abbott's skin, always a useful asset for a minister."[43]

In contrast, just five of Gillard's ministers are discussed in terms of their policy expertise, although more are returning to a portfolio for which they have previous experience. The most notable example referenced is Craig Emerson, appointed minister of trade: "He has taught the subject at university and was a senior economic adviser to Labor's greatest prime minister at securing trade competitiveness for this nation, Bob Hawke. Emerson has a theoretical and practical understanding of the trade portfolio." Emerson's education qualifications are also referenced: he "has a PhD in economics."[44]

With Tony Abbott's 2013 cabinet, media reports focused on Abbott appointing an "experienced" cabinet because it is a continuation of his shadow cabinet: "Tony Abbott largely left his shadow cabinet intact when naming his first ministry yesterday. . . . At his press conference yesterday, Abbott declared his new-look frontbench was 'one of the most experienced incoming ministries in our history.'"[45] The media data emphasize both political and policy expertise, for example noting that "15 of those in the inner sanctum were ministers in the previous Coalition government, while the

---

[40] "Five Lib Dems, a Big Beast and a Kitten-Heeled Home Secretary," *Telegraph*, May 13, 2010.

[41] "Cameron Has Resisted a New Leader's Biggest Pitfall: Fiddling Around," *The Times*, May 14, 2010.

[42] Interview with former minister, March 20, 2010.

[43] "Christian Kerr's Potted Guide to Our Top Pollies," *The Australian*, September 25, 2010.

[44] "Why Rudd Is the Wrong Person in the Wrong Job," *The Australian*, September 22, 2010.

[45] "A Few Gaps in Abbott's Team," *The Australian*, September 17, 2013.

remaining four members have been settled in their general portfolio areas for many years."[46]

Reference is made to policy experience, for example by referencing how ministers have grown into their portfolios: Julie Bishop "has steadily mastered the area" of foreign affairs.[47] In other cases, policy experience is used as a justification for why a weak minister is being kept on: there are doubts about David Johnston's clout within cabinet and media profile, but he is "widely recognised as having a detailed knowledge of defence issues, especially hardware"[48]; and Joe Hockey "[w]ill keep treasurer's job despite lacklustre campaign."[49] But at the same time, the discussion in the media data is about whether these really are the most experienced ministers, or whether they are only there because of previous selection for shadow cabinet. Media commentators referenced the need to get rid of "dead wood" and promote genuine talent or on "merit."[50]

In Canada, ministers are more likely to be politically experienced when a government is re-elected. For example, when Prime Minister Stephen Harper's government was re-elected in 2008, all but one of the ministers he appointed had extensive political experience, with 11 of his 26 ministers staying in the same portfolio they held in his first government. Other ministers were shuffled around, and some had previously been secretaries of state (not full cabinet ministers). Only Lisa Raitt, appointed minister of natural resources, entirely lacked political experience. In Harper's cabinet, most of the policy expertise came from having served in the portfolio or having served in related posts. For example, Health Minister Leona Aglukkaq had served as a minister in the territorial government of Nunavut, where she had developed a public health strategy. Because Harper's was a returning government, and so many of the ministers he appointed were already in government, the media tended to talk about ministers' political backgrounds, making no reference to the educational backgrounds of ministers.

Justin Trudeau's government differed from Harper's because the Liberal Party had been out of office for several years and did not even form the official opposition party during the previous Harper government. Only six of Trudeau's 30 ministers had federal cabinet experience, but three had

---

[46] "A Stable Team That Looks Ready for Government," *The Australian*, September 17, 2013.

[47] "Close Relations between PM and Foreign Minister Will Help Abroad," *The Australian*, September 12, 2013.

[48] "Johnston Fights Off Portfolio Challenge Defence," *The Australian*, September 14, 2013.

[49] "Trusted Team to Govern Team Abbott the Likely Line-Up," *The Australian*, September 9, 2013.

[50] "Lycra or Not, Abbott Has a Mandate," *The Australian*, September 12, 2013.

experience in provincial or territorial governments. Others had served as members of parliament or in provincial legislatures. Ministers lacking in political experience are described in the press as having policy-relevant expertise. For instance, Jean-Yves Duclos, the minister for families, children, and social development, was an academic with extensive expertise in inequality, the elderly, and taxation. He is described as "an expert on the impact of public policies on the poor."[51] The minister for the status of women, Patricia Hajdu is described as having served "on the frontlines when it comes to helping the vulnerable."[52] The minister for science, Kirsty Duncan is described as "an academic with wide experience in the science of nutrition and climate change."[53] Chrystia Freeland, a well-known financial journalist, was given the post of international trade, and Bill Morneau, a political newcomer but former chair of an economic think tank and former CEO of a private pension fund, was given the finance portfolio. In sum, 15 of 30 ministers have some political experience, while 16 of 30 ministers have policy expertise, sometimes based on political roles or service and sometimes based on education or professional backgrounds.

In the United Kingdom, previous political experience is an important qualifying criterion for ministerial appointment, and service in the shadow cabinet sets up opportunities to ministerial office. A former minister informed us that "the shadow cabinet is an important stepping stone to ministerial office, but it is not a guarantee that you will get in."[54] Equally, policy experience can be important for those in the eligibility pool to demonstrate that they are *ministrable*. As former minister Kaufman puts it, "It pays also to achieve a reputation for having a competent grasp of a subject" (1997, 5). This does not mean that ministers need formal qualifications in their subject, except for the position of Lord Chancellor since "being a barrister, and preferably a QC, also helps, since every Prime Minister has to find suitable candidates for Lord Chancellor and for four English and Scottish law officers" (Kaufman 1997, 8). As Riddell, Gruhn, and Carolan (2011, 29) note, "The Lord Chancellor was statutorily required to be a lawyer until 2005, but since then—when the Lord Chancellor and Justice secretary has been able to sit in the Commons, and does not have to be a lawyer—the three occupants of the post have still all been barristers."

[51] "Fresh Faces, Heavy Files," *Globe and Mail*. November 5, 2015.
[52] Ibid.
[53] "Meet the Liberal Cabinet," *Ottawa Citizen*, November 5, 2015.
[54] Interview with former minister, December 17, 2013.

In our media data for Tony Blair's 2005 cabinet and David Cameron's 2010 cabinet, the political experience of appointed ministers is referenced more frequently than policy expertise. The cabinet appointed in 2005 was Blair's third, and many ministerial appointments were to people with existing cabinet positions and experience. For the new ministerial appointments made, the media only discuss political experience: David Blunkett, who returned to government as secretary of state for work and pensions following a scandal, is described as "a talented administrator" and praised for his commitment to political campaigning;[55] Patricia Hewitt, appointed secretary of state for Health, is said to know nothing "about the intricacies of medicine" but "[h]er real skill is in helping bedding in significant changes";[56] and David Miliband's "rapid ascent" to minister of communities and local government is attributed to "his largely assured judgment."[57]

The experiential criteria cited in the media about ministers appointed to David Cameron's new 2010 cabinet are predominantly political: 16 of 21 ministers have political experience attributed to them in media reports. When discussing the Chancellor of the Exchequer George Osborne, one report states, "The chancellor's main skill, they say, lies in politics rather than economics."[58] Theresa May's key attributes for being selected for the Home Office—a high-profile portfolio she had not previously shadowed—were political: previous service as Conservative Party Chairman, "an unflagging, pitch-perfect performance during the campaign,"[59] and "refusing to be tribal and keeping out of trouble."[60]

Policy experience and educational criteria are also extensively referenced for Cameron's ministers. Of the 21 ministers appointed, 12 have policy experience attributed to them in our media data, either because of previous ministerial experience, because they have been shadowing the portfolio for some time, or because of policy expertise accrued outside of politics. For example, David Laws, "did well in the City— he worked for JP Morgan—and is

[55] "Changing Places; A Complex Cabinet Reshuffle with Intriguing Implications," *The Times*, May 9, 2005.

[56] "Professionals Muse on the Destiny of Ministers; Issue of the Week; The Future," *The Times*, May 17, 2005.

[57] Helen Rumbelow, "Blair Shapes His Legacy with March of the Modernisers; Cabinet Reshuffle; Election 2005," *The Times*, May 7, 2005.

[58] John Arlidge, "The New Establishment; With the New Government Comes a New Elite," *The Sunday Times*, May 23, 2010.

[59] Cristina Odone, "Theresa May Is Hated by Dinosaurs on the Left and Right. Good for Her," *The Telegraph Online*, May 13, 2010.

[60] Andrew Porter and Robert Winnett, "Minister in Kitten Heels Who Wants to Be Tough, Not Nasty; Interview," *The Daily Telegraph*, May 15, 2010.

now chief secretary to the Treasury [. . .] 'Osborne has nothing approaching David's ability when it comes to understanding the economy and the markets,' says a Laws fan."[61]

A strong theme for Cameron's 2010 cabinet is educational background. The media reference David Laws' "double first in economics from Cambridge"[62] and David Cameron, William Hague, Chris Huhne, Jeremy Hunt, and Philip Hammond, Danny Alexander's politics, philosophy, and economics (PPE) degrees. More significant than specific qualification, however, are references to the elite nature of the educational backgrounds of ministers. According to media data, Cameron "crammed his shadow cabinet with Etonians"[63] and "one sixth of MPs in the new parliament went to Oxford, with five members of the cabinet attending the same college (Magdalen)."[64] Another article asks, "When was the last time these four great offices of state were held by Oxford graduates?"—prime minister (Cameron, Brasenose), chancellor of the exchequer (Osborne, Magdalen), foreign secretary (Hague, Magdalen), home secretary (May, St Hugh's).[65] Discussing educational backgrounds in this way implies that such backgrounds serve less as indicators of policy expertise and more as indicators of membership in an elite political network, a theme developed further in Chapter 6.

In sum, across all political systems, we find that experiential criteria are important factors in cabinet appointments and in the justification of those appointments. We do not find, however, that experiential criteria take the form of specific or strongly institutionalized prescriptive rules. In the absence of specificity on the type of background a minister must have, the rules permit selectors to employ a range of experiential criteria. Hence, we cannot conclude that an individual minister was appointed to cabinet solely or even primarily on experiential grounds, of political experience or policy expertise. We cannot be confident that selectors' claims of appointing on the basis of experiential criteria are the actual grounds on which presidents appoint, since most appointees meet multiple criteria. Moreover, cabinets are collective constructions, and selectors, regardless of political system or political party, form cabinets to create a collective governing whole; hence, a

[61] Arlidge, "The New Establishment," *The Sunday Times*, May 23, 2010.

[62] Arlidge, The New Establishment," *The Sunday Times*, May 23, 2010.

[63] Clive Aslet, "The Prime Minister Factory; Eton Produced 19 PMs before David Cameron," *The Daily Telegraph*, May 15, 2010.

[64] India Lenon, "Judging by the New Parliament, PPE is the Path to Power," *The Telegraph Online*, May 17, 2010.

[65] Damian Thompson, "The Oxford Cabinet," *The Daily Telegraph*, May 13, 2010.

variety of criteria combine in the cabinet-formation process. Experiential criteria are important, but they do not necessarily take the form of strong prescriptive rules.

Conclusion: The Strategic Importance of Experiential Criteria and Merit

Policy expertise and political experience are precisely what the public and the media associate with "merit." Presidents and prime ministers reinforce this view when they make public pronouncements about their cabinet picks, remarking that they have chosen the most talented, politically skilled, and experienced individuals. If the press points out that a long-time friend of the prime minister received a plum post, the prime minister will vigorously defend the appointment by highlighting his friend's political skills or policy acumen. Journalists and political pundits likewise reinforce the association between experiential criteria and merit, by highlighting the political background, policy skills, and educational credentials of ministers. While our evidence clearly supports the idea that ministers are likely to be highly credentialed and talented individuals, we suggest that the concept of "merit" is unhelpful at best, and profoundly misleading at worst. Instead, claims of merit serve as strategic devices that allow selectors to justify cabinet appointments regardless of the primary reasons for making them. Critics use arguments about merit as a strategy to undermine the qualifications of appointees. In such cases, invoking "merit" is a political strategy and not a substantive claim about the suitability of a minister for cabinet.

Of course, we are not implying that political experience and policy expertise are unimportant in qualifying for appointment to cabinet posts. That prime ministers and presidents appoint cabinet ministers with political and policy experience relevant to their appointment, and that such appointments are justified in experiential terms, are evident from our data. Experiential criteria for cabinet appointment are explicitly present in all our cases, regardless of political system. Moreover, the media recognize and privilege experiential criteria in assessing appointments (and potential appointments) of cabinet ministers. Such expertise and experience, however, do not confirm that experiential criteria were dispositive in the appointments of these cabinet secretaries. As discussed in the next two chapters, affiliational and representational criteria are also important factors shaping the qualifications of *ministrables.* As a result, we cannot conclude that experience as "merit" is the most important component of qualifying for cabinet appointment. Claims of "merit" for qualifying for cabinet appointments do not reflect clear appointment standards, but rather are deployed strategically to justify the appointments. The elasticity of "merit" as a qualifying criterion encompasses a wide and disparate range of justifications for appointments to cabinet; as we have shown for several country cases, nearly every cabinet appointment is justified by the selector on the basis of "merit," regardless of political system, whether a government was returning or newly elected, specific cabinet posts, or party of the selector. In the next two chapters, we show that meeting experiential criteria is just one of the ways that *ministrables* qualify for cabinet, and that affiliational and representational criteria appear to hold more explanatory value.

We evaluate the gendered implications of experiential criteria for qualification to cabinet in Chapter 9. Much of the scholarship on gender and cabinets assumes that women are more likely to be appointed for their policy experience and that it is harder for them to be appointed on the basis of their political skills. Our finding from this chapter—that all experiential criteria matter in all cases—somewhat neutralizes this assumption that women do not have the requisite qualifications because, in practice, female *ministrables* could benefit from the flexibility of qualifying criteria. Instead, the assumption that we take forward in Chapter 9 is that women's experiential qualifications are either not seen by selectors, or are strategically ignored in order to appoint men on "merit" instead.

6

How to Qualify for Cabinet
Affiliational Criteria

Introduction: The importance of trust and loyalty

Next to prime ministers or presidents, ministers are among the most visible faces of government. Ministers must promote and defend the government's agenda and are often the key figures associated with particular legislative initiatives. Unlike parliaments, which do much of their work in the public eye and produce a written record of their deliberations, cabinet work is hidden from view, and discussions, deliberation, and disagreements are carefully kept under wraps. Because cabinet is a collective body, ministers are expected to speak with one voice, and any disagreement can only be voiced away from public hearing. Revealing cabinet discussions through leaks is taboo. For all these reasons, selectors have real incentives to appoint those they can trust.

The importance of trust means that affiliational criteria—namely, membership in a selector's personal network of trust and loyalty—is an important qualifying criterion for cabinet. Affiliational criteria fall into the category of personal networks, but the networks themselves construct relationships based on trust and loyalty. Trustworthiness "is relational; it involves an individual making herself vulnerable to another individual, group, or institution that has the capacity to do her harm or to betray her. Trust is seldom unconditional; it is given to specific individuals or institutions over specific domains. . . . When we call someone trustworthy, we often mean . . . competence in the domain over which trust is being given. The trustworthy will not betray the trust as a consequence of ineptitude" (Levi and Stoker 2000, 476). By loyalty, we mean that the individual will not betray a trust relationship through bad faith and will work to maintain trust across time. As a result, personal networks that define cabinet eligibility pools are established on the basis of relationships between and among individuals, persist across time, and serve as mutual resources for those involved.

Unlike experiential or representational criteria, however, rules do not *require* selectors to employ affiliational criteria when choosing their ministers. Instead, following Ostrom's framework in which rules prescribe, prohibit, or permit, the use of affiliational criteria is permitted by rules about cabinet appointments. More important, there are two powerful incentives for presidents and prime ministers to appoint their closest allies and most trusted friends to cabinet. One incentive is strategic: according to principal–agent theory, appointing individuals about whom selectors know little can lead to future problems when selectors (principals) cannot control or predict the behavior of agents (ministers) (Dowding and Dumont 2015). A second incentive is psychological, namely, the emotional benefits of surrounding oneself with people one trusts and knows well. According to former Canadian prime minister Jean Chretién, "All leaders need what's termed a 'Roman guard' around them—people who have been there from the start, who believe in them, and who can therefore create a zone of comfort and security" (2007, 25). Taken together, strategic and psychological incentives mean that cabinets have tended to be fairly homogeneous, filled with people from similar social, professional, and political networks.

Incentives to select trusted friends and allies make affiliational criteria an important set of qualifying criteria. Indeed, affiliational criteria are raised consistently in our interview and media data, as well as in autobiographies. Our data reveal that affiliational criteria for cabinet appointments are relevant across all of our country cases. What is more, when we analyzed media reports of specific instances of cabinet formation, we were able to identify how many ministerial appointments were attributed to affiliational criteria (see Table 6.1). Our data show variation in terms of how common it is for selectors to have affiliational links with those whom they appoint as ministers. In Spain and the United States, for instance, the overwhelming majority of ministers have some kind of affiliational link with the person who selected them.[1] Leaders in these countries enjoy substantial latitude to select ministers from their personal networks. Although it is rare for selectors to justify their ministerial picks on the basis of close friendships, the fact that so many ministers have affiliational links to selectors indicates that selectors

---

[1] Escobar-Lemmon and Taylor-Robinson (2016, 54) find that in the United States, presidents "also put much emphasis on selecting cabinet secretaries who will be loyal to the president and to the president's policy agenda." They cite Edwards (2001, 82): "the White House places a premium on reliability and trust" in selecting cabinet appointees (Escobar-Lemmon and Taylor-Robinson 2016, 104).

Table 6.1 Three Patterns of Affiliational Qualification for Cabinet (New Governments Only)

Affiliational Qualification	Country	Selector (Year)	Total Number of Ministers	Ministers with Affiliational Links N (%)
Consistent[a]	Australia	Abbott (2013)	18	17 (94.4)
	Spain	Zapatero (2004)	16	13 (81.3)
		Rajoy (2011)	13	10 (76.9)
	United Kingdom	Cameron* (2010)	22	15 (68.2)
	United States	Obama (2009)	15	10 (66.7)
	Chile	Bachelet* (2006)	20	12 (60.0)
Occasional[b]	Chile	Piñera* (2010)	23	8 (34.8)
	Germany	Merkel* (2005)	14	3 (21.4)
Rare[c]	Canada	Trudeau (2015)	30	3 (10.0)

*Coalition government.

[a] More than half of all appointees have an affiliational relationship with the selector.

[b] Between 20 and 50 percent of appointees have an affiliational relationship with the selector.

[c] Fewer than 20 percent of appointees have affiliational relationships with the selector.

in these countries routinely use trust and loyalty as qualifying criteria for ministerial appointment. In the United Kingdom and Australia, there is also strong evidence that affiliational criteria account for a high number of ministerial appointments because selectors face few constraints in their choices of recruiting ministers, except when ministerial selection is made by the parliamentary party or caucus. In addition, both countries have strong traditions of appointing shadow cabinets. We find evidence that shadow cabinets serve as a mechanism for establishing relations of trust and loyalty prior to cabinet formation.

In Chile and Germany, affiliational criteria matter, but the complex nature of forming and managing governing coalitions means that leaders in these two countries face more constraints when selecting individuals from their personal networks. The media data from Bachelet's cabinet mention affiliational links for about half of the ministers, although interviews with political experts and political elites routinely mentioned the importance of personal connections in the appointment process. For Piñera's initial cabinets, the media mention affiliational links for fewer than half of the ministers appointed; in Germany just three of 14 ministers had close affiliational links to Chancellor Angela Merkel. In Canada, we find very few affiliational links between selectors and ministers. This is not because this practice is in any way prohibited, but rather because informal rules about representational criteria, which we discuss in Chapter 7, are strong and numerous, leaving less space for appointing ministers on the basis of affiliational criteria.

It is important to note that the degree to which selectors are empowered or constrained in recruiting ministers does not predict the prevalence of affiliational criteria. In Spain and Canada, for example, there are no constraints on prime ministers' ability to select ministers autonomously. In Spain, prime ministers are permitted to—and do—appoint their close allies to cabinet. But in Canada, the myriad representational criteria mean that empowered prime ministers cannot fill their cabinet with friends and allies (see Chapter 7). In Canada, representational prescriptions constrain ministerial appointments on affiliational grounds. Affiliational criteria therefore are not decisive for qualification to the Canadian cabinet.

Affiliational criteria also capture the qualification routes of *ministrables* who are not friends, but potential competitors who may nonetheless be included in the trust and loyalty network of *ministrables* through cabinet membership and party discipline, to ensure the survival of government. Cabinets in parliamentary systems are governed by norms of ministerial responsibility, meaning that ministers cannot speak publicly against government members or the government's policy direction. As such, some selectors might appoint rivals to cabinet as a way to prevent them from publicly speaking or maneuvering against the selector. Recruiting former leadership rivals to cabinet is common in Canada. In 1993, Canadian prime minister Jean Chretién appointed his former leadership rival Paul Martin to cabinet. In 2010, Australian prime minister Julia Gillard appointed former leader Kevid Rudd, whom she ousted, as minister for foreign affairs. Such a practice may be more common in parliamentary systems, where prime ministers face the threat of removal by parliament (or by their party), than in presidential systems, where presidents remain in office whether or not they have support from Congress.

Affiliational criteria vary in the means by which the selector and *ministrables* are linked. From our data, we identify five affiliational categories and the functions they appear to serve. Although not all selectors are linked to their cabinet appointees in the same way, across all our cases, selectors have affiliations with some of their ministers on the basis of the following five criteria:

(1) personal friendship;
(2) selector's personal political or party network;
(3) political service or campaign support to the selector;
(4) shared personal connection through university; and/or
(5) party competitor or rival of the selector.[2]

Personal friendship implies a one-to-one, long-standing personal relationship with the selector. Personal friendship is evidenced by explicit claims of such connections in the media, and by claims of the selector himself or herself. For example, UK chancellor George Osborne is described as "a friend of [Prime Minister David] Cameron and godfather to the Camerons' son."[3] We distinguish *political or party networks* as membership in an inner circle of confidants or allies on which the selector relies. The basis for such membership is, for example, having worked together in government or in parliament, or within a party or a coalition of parties. In Spain, for example, five ministers in Rajoy's cabinet are described as "high-level functionaries like [Rajoy] from his generation and having much political experience. But above all, all are friends."[4] In this case, political networks also serve as a site where friendship is forged.

Political service or campaign support for the selector is evidenced by *ministrables'* defense of or support for the selector and his or her leadership. It can also be demonstrated through campaign work, campaign contributions, and/or campaign endorsement. For example, in Spain, "Rajoy has rewarded

---

[2] We differ here, with some overlap, with the classifications employed by Escobar-Lemmon and Taylor Robinson (2016, 207), who use three variables as indicators of *ministrables'* political connection to the president: connected to the president, friend of the president, and member of a political family. They found that while women appointed to cabinet were more likely than their male counterparts to have political connections, "women with political connections typically also have policy expertise" (2016, 125).

[3] John Arlidge, "The New Establishment; With the New Government Comes a New Elite," *Sunday Times*, May 23, 2010.

[4] Carlos E. Cué, "Un Gobierno de amigos y fieles," *El País*, December 22, 2011. Note that, as in this case, political networks also serve as a site where friendship networks are forged.

only those who supported him in his crisis of leadership following his [electoral] defeat in 2008."[5] In Chile, Cristián Larroulet, minister for the secretariat of the presidency, "won the confidence" of Chilean president Sebastian Piñera during the 2009–2010 campaign, when they worked together closely.[6] Additionally, political support for the selector can be demonstrated through a *ministrable*'s prior service in cabinets or shadow cabinets, a common path to a ministerial appointment in Australia and the United Kingdom.

Ministrables also have affiliational connections to the selector through *shared university connection*; school and university, apart from personal friendships, often signal shared, reliable connections of power and support. Prime Minister David Cameron is, "along with [his chancellor of the exchequer George] Osborne, a former member of the Bullingdon Club, the elitist Oxford University drinking and dining clique."[7] Similarly, US president Barack Obama and his first attorney general, Eric Holder, share law degrees from Harvard University, although they did not overlap during their time at Harvard. Their common law school experience quickly solidified their connection when they met at a dinner party in 2004.[8]

Party competitors or rivals of the selector also become *ministables* on affiliational grounds. In such cases, the *ministrable* benefits from a selector's desire to create or to strengthen affiliation in order to capture *ministrable* loyalty and to control behavior. An excellent example comes from the UK case, following the Conservative Party leadership contest that brought John Major into office as prime minister:

> There was a question, too, over what to do with Michael Heseltine [Major's opponent]. He had hoped to go to the Department of Trade and Industry. He had won substantial support in the leadership contest, and his appointment to a senior position was right in principle and necessary in practice. He would also be a huge asset in winning the election. . . . Michael [Heseltine] and I did not really know one another. We had never worked. or socialized together. As rivals in the recent leadership elections, we were still reserved with one another and uncertain how our relationship would work. . . . I gradually came to recognize . . . that when the chips were down

[5] Ibid.
[6] "Piñera promote gobierno de unidad nacional y prepara gabinete para el fines de enero," *El Mercurio*, January 28, 2010.
[7] *Sunday Times*, May 23, 2010.
[8] Eric Lichtblau and John M. Broder, "Holder Seen as Obama Choice for Justice Post," *New York Times*, November 18, 2008.

he is absolutely loyal, and 100 percent supportive. . . . As Deputy Prime Minister, he never failed me. (Major 2000, 208)

In contrast, Canadian prime minister John Diefenbaker appointed rivals to cabinet but reflected later that it was a mistake. In his memoirs, he writes, "I believed—wrongly—that in cabinet, their plotting would cease" (1976, 36).

Each of the affiliational links outlined in the preceding serves to ensure that a *ministrable* can be trusted to keep confidences, to adhere to the government's program and policies, and to continue to be loyal to the prime minister or president during the term of service. We anticipate that several of the affiliational components will be mutually reinforcing, strengthening the selector's confidence in the cabinet's trustworthiness and loyalty. Given the importance of trust and loyalty in cabinet, affiliational criteria will always matter greatly to selectors. Yet selectors must balance affiliational criteria with experiential and representational criteria. Our country cases display significant variation in terms of how many ministers have affiliational links to selectors. In the following, we draw on our media data for all cases in which a new government took office, looking for evidence of affiliational links between selectors and ministers. We did not consider cabinet appointments for selectors who won re-election because in such cases, links with the president or prime minister have already been forged in the first cabinet.[9] Instead, we wanted to know whether and how selectors forming new governments, often moving from opposition to government, choose potential ministers from networks of trust and loyalty.

There is significant variation across countries in the range of ministers who had affiliational links with their selectors; this is particularly true for newly elected prime ministers with shadow cabinet members and single-party (non-coalition) governments. Australian prime minister Tony Abbott had prior personal affiliations with nearly all of his ministers (94.44%); Canadian prime minister Justin Trudeau had affiliational connections with only three of the 30 persons he appointed to cabinet (see Table 6.1).

We find three patterns of affiliational criteria in our data: (1) strong and *consistent* affiliational linkages, with more than half of cabinet appointees meeting at least one of the affiliational relationships; (2) *occasional* affiliational

[9] For example, in George W. Bush's 2004 cabinet and in Stephen Harper's 2008 cabinet, several ministers were carried over from the previous government. Similar relationships are also formed by ministers in shadow cabinets. See our brief discussion earlier in this chapter.

linkages (between 20 and 50 percent); and (3) *rare* affiliational links (fewer than a fifth of all appointees). The first group of countries—where affiliation is a strong and consistent qualification for appointment to cabinet—includes Spain, the United States, the United Kingdom, and Australia. In these countries, the majority of ministers meet at least one affiliational criterion, a consistent pattern across these four cases. For Chile and Germany, the pattern is less consistent. For these cases, we find some evidence of affiliational links, but the use of affiliational criteria appears less frequently and more intermittently, with many ministers having no publicly identifiable affiliational links to the selector. Finally, Canada is an outlier case, where very few ministers have affiliational links with selectors at the time of their appointment.

Strong and Consistent Affiliational Linkages: Australia, Spain, the United Kingdom, and the United States

In Australia, affiliational criteria, such as personal friendship networks and connections of trust and loyalty to the selector, are important qualifying criteria for ministers. In his autobiography *Lazarus Rising*, Prime Minister John Howard makes numerous references to the importance of trust and loyalty in ministerial appointments. For example, in 1996 Alexander Downing qualified as Howard's foreign minister as a result of a deal in 1995 whereby Downing agreed to a leadership transition without a ballot. Howard writes, "I have never forgotten that gesture to the Liberal Party and to me, and repaid it as best I could with years of collegiality, support and loyalty as we worked together as Prime Minister and Foreign Minister for almost twelve years" (Howard 2013, 247–248). About Robert Hill, whom he appointed minister for the environment, Howard writes, "The trust between the two of us was an important ingredient in the remarkable cohesion of the party during our years in government" (Howard 2013, 259).

Affiliational links to the selector are also regularly referenced in media data. When Julia Gillard appointed her cabinet following the 2010 election, part of Defence Minister Stephen Smith's qualification was that he "understands the importance of loyalty."[10] For Tony Abbott's 2013 cabinet, our media data identify affiliation links to six of his 18 ministers. Minister for Foreign Affairs Julie Bishop, for example, is described as "close to" or "a close

[10] "CHRISTIAN KERR'S Potted guide to our top pollies" *The Australian*, September 25, 2010.

friend" of Abbott, one of his "core of four." Other ministers are described as "close," a "safe pair of hands"; another three are part of Abbott's "core of four."[11] Two members had affiliational links through shared elite schooling.

More broadly, Abbott's 2013 ministerial appointments are explicit continuations of his shadow cabinet. Abbott made a pre-election pledge that his shadow team would continue in government, and he delivered on this: 17 of 18 of his ministerial appointments previously served on his shadow cabinet. Media reports note how Abbott's ministerial selection was very much about rewarding loyalty and previous service, rather than meeting experiential criteria. One report said, "Abbott is not about to change direction and start dumping loyal frontbenchers who have helped project the sense of a united Team Abbott."[12] Another noted that "Abbott's aim is to reward hard work, focus, determination and achievement,"[13] meaning that, as another story notes, "some frontbenchers are set to survive purely through previous selection rather than ability. . . . Among these were names such as . . . defence shadow David Johnston."[14]

In Australia there is also evidence of political enemies being brought into cabinet to build affiliation and bind them to cabinet collective responsibility. For example, Kevin Rudd qualified for the post of foreign minister in Julia Gillard's 2010 cabinet despite their extremely low trust relationship after she disposed him as leader earlier that year. According to Gillard, ahead of the election she had been obliged to "guarantee he would be Foreign Minister if the government was re-elected [. . .] to stop what I considered to be the acts of treachery on his part" (Gillard 2014, 43). A media report confirmed this, noting,

The only thing right about Rudd's appointment as foreign minister is that it avoids his having a dummy spit and forcing a by-election in his Queensland electorate, which could bring down the minority Gillard government. (Perhaps an added benefit is that he will be overseas a lot—plenty of his colleagues worry he will be a constant source of cabinet leaks).[15]

---

[11] " 'Grown-up' Tactics Trump Negativity," *The Australian*, September 9, 2013.

[12] Dennis Shanahan, "Caution to the fore as loyalty is rewarded," *The Australian*, September 17, 2013.

[13] Janet Albrechtsen, "The Unheralded Heroine at the Coalition's Herart," *The Australian*, September 25, 2013.

[14] "Abbott Told to Drop Also-Rans from Team," *The Age*, September 11, 2013.

[15] "Why Rudd Is the Wrong Person for the Job," *The Australian*, September 22, 2010.

The point is that selectors sometimes bring political enemies into the high trust environment of cabinet to avoid certain problems such as the collapse of government or leaks to the media. The occasional case of a minister qualifying for cabinet on the basis of being not just outside a selector's personal network but hostile to it underscores the importance of affiliational criteria.

In Spain, affiliational criteria are key for cabinet appointments as well. Interviews with former ministers support the idea that leaders select ministers in whom they have confidence. Often that trust has been built through previous political relationships.[16] The media data provide overwhelming support for the importance of trust and loyalty as key criteria for both Zapatero's and Rajoy's cabinets. For example, most of the media speculation about who would be in Zapatero's first cabinet included people described as being close to the party leader or who had demonstrated "extraordinary loyalty." This was particularly true for Jesus Caldera, who was frequently described as being Zapatero's "right hand."[17] José Bono, appointed minister of public security, had competed for the PSOE leadership against Zapatero, but is described as having demonstrated loyalty to Zapatero and having maintained a very close relationship to him.[18] José Antonio Alonso is described as a childhood friend and former university classmate of Zapatero's.[19] Likewise, 10 of the 16 members of Zapatero's initial cabinet came from the advisory committee that he put together in the lead-up to the election.[20]

Media reports speculating about who would be in Prime Minister Rajoy's cabinet likewise focused on trust and loyalty. Most of the individuals expected to be in cabinet are described as having been with him during "the difficult years in opposition."[21] Ana Pastor, for example, is described as "so linked to the leader of the PP that she has been in almost all of his trusted teams," while Cristóbol Montoro is described as hailing from the "initial clan."[22] After his cabinet was publicly announced, a reporter commented, "Rajoy has surrounded himself with a team of the greatest trust, composed of loyal people in the party, longtime friends, and other leaders that helped him when his leadership was in danger."[23] Soraya Saénz de Santamaría was

[16] Interviews, May 29a, 2012; May 29b, 2012; and May 6, 2014, Madrid, Spain.
[17] "El brazo derecho," *El País*, March 21, 2004.
[18] "Zapatero quiso siempre a su lado al presidente de Castilla-La Mancha," *El País*, March 18, 2004.
[19] "Magistrado progresista y amigo de Zapatero," *El País*, April 1, 2004.
[20] "Gobierno paritario," *El País*, April 1, 2004.
[21] Fernando Garea, "Ministrables sin cartera," *El País*, November 21, 2011.
[22] Ibid.
[23] "El presidente Rajoy leyó ayer, en una comparencia sin preguntas," *El País*, December 22, 2011.

appointed minister of the presidency and government spokesperson, essentially serving as Rajoy's right hand. She is repeatedly described as having demonstrated immense loyalty to Rajoy and even as Rajoy's "political creation."[24] A journalist commented that only people who supported Rajoy during his leadership crisis in 2008 were promoted to cabinet. He went on to say, "the PP leader has surrounded himself with people with whom he has spoken almost daily over the last 30 years, true intimates, something that is rare in politics."[25]

In the cases of both Zapatero and Rajoy, political networks of trust and loyalty were forged during years where the party was in opposition: Both leaders came to national power after eight years in opposition, and many of the individuals they appointed to their initial cabinets were described in the press as having demonstrated loyalty to their party leaders as MPs on the opposition benches.

Affiliational criteria are critical in the United Kingdom as well. In *How to Be a Minister* (1997, 3), former Labour MP Sir Gerald Kaufman notes, "genuine loyalty [...] is [...] a rightly valued quality which is properly rewarded." Kaufman notes that "being Parliamentary Private Secretary to the leader, whether in government or Opposition, is itself almost a guarantee of office" (Kaufman 1997, 6). Our own data from the United Kingdom are replete with reference to ministers qualifying through affiliational links, by being in the prime minister's high trust networks or for being rewarded for loyalty to the prime minister and service in the shadow cabinet. As one former minister put it: ministerial office is a reward for being "loyal and discrete."[26]

Firsthand practitioner accounts report qualifying criteria based on affiliation. Prime Minister John Major justifies his 1990 ministerial picks in his autobiography as follows: Ken Baker, "loyal Chairman of the party," Chris Patten, "an old friend with whom I could work easily," and Ian Lang, "a close ally" (Major 2000, 208). Major justified the appointment of John Patten to his 1992 cabinet simply as a "fellow Blue Chip Club member"; the Blue Chip Club is a Conservative dining club in the House of Commons "which is determined to monopolize the allocation of higher office" (Clark 2010). What is stunning here is no further justification for Patten's cabinet appointment was offered: he was a fellow member of an exclusive dining club. At no point

---

[24] Carlos E. Cué, "Soraya Saénz de Santamaría, Vicepresidenta, Ministra de presidencia, y portavoz de gobierno, Una política imprevista que ascendió a la sombra del líder," *El País*, December 22, 2011.

[25] Carlos E. Cué, "Un Gobierno de amigos y fieles," *El País*, December 22, 2011.

[26] Interview, December 17, 2013.

were questions about the "merit" of the appointment raised. Patten qualified by being in the same elite high-trust network as John Major.

Media data from David Cameron's 2010 coalition cabinet further highlight the importance of affiliational links in determining ministerial selection. Eight of Cameron's 22 ministerial picks are explained by the media through affiliational criteria. For example, "Mr Cameron has kept his closest colleagues in the key positions. Michael Gove is Education Secretary, George Osborne Chancellor, and William Hague Foreign Secretary."[27] The appointment of George Osborne as Chancellor of the Exchequer is not justified on the basis of any formal qualification in economics or finance (he had none), but because Osborne was "David Cameron's closest ally and has been Shadow Chancellor since 2005, as well as having overseen the general election campaign."[28] He is described as the prime minister's "closest ally [...] who had co-ordinated the campaign,"[29] a "close colleague of David Cameron"[30] and "a friend of Cameron and godfather to the Camerons' son Elwen."[31]

Cameron's ministerial appointments are also explained in terms of membership in a tight inner circle. Osborne is "part of his London set" and Michael Gove is "another member of David Cameron's North Kensington set,"[32] "Cameron crammed his shadow cabinet with Etonians,"[33] and Cameron is, "along with Osborne, a former member of the Bullingdon club, the elitist Oxford University drinking and dining clique."[34] Media accounts note that 13 of the cabinet went to fee-paying schools and 15 went to Oxford or Cambridge.[35] The significance here is not the formal qualification, but the elite status of the high-trust networks established at elite schools and Oxbridge: "The new elite is divided up into distinct groups and tribes. [...] They are linked by background, friendship and family ties—but most of all by class."[36]

[27] *Daily Telegraph*, May 13, 2010.
[28] "Clegg May Get Key Portfolio to Go with Role as Deputy," *The Times*, May 12, 2010.
[29] "Power Play; As the UK Election Result Became Clear, the Secret Meetings Began," *Sunday Times*, May 16, 2010.
[30] Andrew Porter, "Ministers Begin Work with a 5pc Pay Cut," *Daily Telegraph*, May 14, 2010.
[31] Arlidge, "The New Establishment," *Sunday Times*, May 23, 2010.
[32] Andrew Porter, "Ministers Begin Work with a 5pc Pay Cut," *Daily Telegraph*, May 14, 2010.
[33] Clive Aslet, "The Prime Minister Factory; Eton Produced 19 PMs before David Cameron," *Daily Telegraph*, May 15, 2010.
[34] Arlidge, "The New Establishment," *Sunday Times*, May 23, 2010.
[35] "Heart of the Partnership's Power," *Sunday Times*, May 16, 2010.
[36] Arlidge, The New Establishment," *Sunday Times*, May 23, 2010.

Loyalty and service demonstrated in shadow cabinet is also strong in the United Kingdom. In Cameron's 2010 cabinet, only three of his 18 ministerial picks had not previously served in the Conservative shadow cabinet.

In the United States, affiliational criteria are also important in positioning potential cabinet appointees. As Gerhardt (2003, 201) points out,

> Most nominees have a close personal or professional relationship with the president or those responsible for advising the president on the nominations he should make. . . . Moreover, nominees . . . must satisfy certain criteria. Such criteria are crucial for ensuring the appointment of people who are likely to repay political debt, yield political dividends to the president who selected them, or implement the constitutional and political ideals of greatest importance to the president.

Those who are eventually appointed to cabinet qualify in part because they are within the selector's personal networks.[37] Although the formal rules for eligibility for cabinet are silent on the personal and political affiliations of *ministrables* with the selector, affiliational criteria are strong determinants of qualifications for appointment to cabinet in the United States. Presidents are often criticized for appearing to employ affiliational criteria in the appointment process; nonetheless, all presidents have used these criteria to identify likely cabinet appointees. Incoming presidents are most likely to face criticism for appointing persons from their personal networks to cabinet posts if the president is considered outside the Washington beltway. Bill Clinton, former governor of Arkansas, faced considerable criticism for appointing his Arkansan friends to a wide range of positions in his first administration; Gerhardt (2003, 206) reported that "President Clinton brought more than 175 friends from Arkansas to join his administration."[38] In 2008, incoming

---

[37] Gerhardt (2003, 207, 208) claims that "every president has done it" and that "virtually every president has . . . appointed an even greater number of friends or allies who have proven to be more than up to the tasks they were appointed to handle." Those within a president's personal network also advise on cabinet appointments and in initial administrations, constitute major actors in a president's transition team. See Carol D. Leonnig, "Obama's Team Rankles the Right; To Some Conservatives, Advisers Are Alarmingly Liberal," *Washington Post*, January 2, 2009.

[38] Gerhardt (2003, 206) adds, "the vast majority of these people discharged their official duties with great skill and professionalism and without any hint of scandal." Clinton was famous for his FOB contingent: Friends of Bill. See Frank Lockwood, "Bill Clinton Touches Home Base, Arkansans Catch up in Philadelphia," *Arkansas Online*, July 28, 2016 (http://www.arkansasonline.com/).

President Barack Obama "announce[d] decisions about his Cabinet secretaries from Chicago rather than inside the Beltway."[39]

Affiliational criteria were important for qualifying for cabinet appointment in the first Obama administration (2009–2013). In several cases, Obama appointed those whom he knew from his various personal and political networks. Among the most *ministrable* in Obama's first cabinet were those meeting at least one of the following affiliational criteria: (1) longstanding friendship and/or collegial relationship with Obama in Chicago, at Harvard, or through another personal network; (2) membership in the endorsement network for Obama's presidential campaign; and (3) intraparty support network, including intra-party competition. Several of those appointed to cabinet positions met these affiliational criteria—but not all. Long-standing friendships were also the basis of qualification for Obama's inner circle of advisers and consultants in the Oval Office and on the White House staff; it is worth noting that such individuals are political appointees whose appointments do not require Senate consent and hence do not require justification on policy expertise or representational grounds.

As Borrelli explains in *The President's Cabinet* (2002, 142, 144), the *New York Times* has offered a series of articles reflecting on those who might be appointed to cabinet; specific speculation articles were available for the George W. Bush and Barack Obama administrations and serve as the basis for assessing affiliational connection of the president to his potential cabinet nominees. Of the 15 persons appointed to cabinet in the first Obama administration, half had campaign links and were early endorsers of his candidacy for president. These included Kathleen Sebelius, Obama's eventual choice for secretary of health and human services, who was an early endorser of his campaign and "campaigned on his behalf."[40] Janet Napolitano, appointed to lead the Department of Homeland Security, had been "heavily courted" by Obama during his presidential campaign; despite her close ties to Hillary Clinton, Napolitano nonetheless endorsed Obama early in his campaign, helping him to do well in the Arizona primary election.[41] Another example is Eric Holder, attorney general in Obama's first cabinet, who reflected other affiliational qualifications necessary for his appointment. Holder received

[39] Michael D. Shear, "Obama Team Moves to Keep Its Distance from Lobbyists," *Washington Post*, November 12, 2008.

[40] Steven Greenhouse, "Kathleen Sebelius," *New York Times*, December 5, 2008.

[41] Randal C. Archibold, "Janet Napolitano," *New York Times*, November 12, 2008. http://politics.nytimes.com/election-guide/2008/results/states/AZ.html

his bachelor's and law degrees from Columbia University, Obama's alma mater. They had met through mutual friends and "immediately clicked" at a dinner party. Holder is quoted as saying, "Loyalty is something I value an awful lot. And so my decision to support Barack was not necessarily a difficult one. . . . My inclination would be support Senator Clinton, but I was overwhelmed by Barack."[42] Shaun Donovan, appointed as Obama's first secretary of housing and urban development, worked on Obama's presidential campaign, "[taking] a leave of absence from his job in New York . . . to campaign for Mr. Obama."[43] Arne Duncan, eventual secretary of education, was linked to Obama through a long-standing friendship initiated by Michelle Obama's brother, a friendship that turned on playing pick-up basketball and was reinforced by Duncan's and Obama's degrees from Harvard.[44]

Perhaps the strongest evidence of the importance of affiliational criteria in positioning individuals for cabinet appointments comes from the appointment of Robert Gates as secretary of defense in two presidential cabinets. Appointed as defense secretary by President George W. Bush in 2006, Gates continued in that post at the request of President Barack Obama in 2008, serving through 2011. Gates remains "the only Secretary of Defense in U.S. history to be asked to remain in that office by a newly elected President,"[45] and the only one who served as defense secretary for presidents of two different political parties. Gates "knew neither man when [he] began working for them, and they did not know [him]" (Gates 2014, ix).[46] Before his first meeting with President George W. Bush to discuss the defense position, Gates "had never had a conversation with the president. [He] had played no role in the 2000 campaign and was never asked to do so" (Gates 2014, 6). In the absence of any affiliational connection, however, such connection was established immediately and specifically in Gates' first meeting with President-elect Obama. Gates reports saying to Obama, " 'I want you to know that . . . you would never need worry about my working a separate or different agenda. . . . Should you decide on a different [policy] path, I would either support you or leave. I would not be disloyal' " (Gates 2014, 272).

In sum, these examples show the importance of affiliational criteria as a route to cabinet. In Spain, the United States, Australia, and the United

---

42 David Johnston, "Candidates for Obama's Inner Circle," *New York Times*, November 12, 2008.
43 "Shaun Donovan," *New York Times*, December 13, 2008.
44 Sam Dillon, "Candidates for Obama's Inner Circle," *New York Times*, November 24, 2008.
45 http://www.defense.gov/About-DoD/Biographies/Biography-View/Article/602797.
46 Robert M. Gates, *Duty: Memoirs of a Secretary at War* (New York: Vintage Books, 2014, ix).

Kingdom, affiliational links are not the only criteria that establish qualification for *ministrables*, but their prevalence indicates that they are nonetheless important in establishing the ministerial selection pool and the likelihood of being appointed to cabinet. Selectors can apply affiliational criteria for cabinet eligibility because of the "absence of any consensus on the credential required for certain offices [that] makes it easy for many of these [appointed on affiliation grounds] to fill them" (Gerhardt 2003, 209). Moreover, the strength of affiliational criteria for qualifying for cabinet is present not only for those cases where opposition parties construct shadow cabinets (Australia and the UK), but in a parliamentary system (Spain) and in a presidential system (the US). The strength of affiliational criteria for cabinet appointments underscores the importance of conceptualizing rules as not merely prescribing or prohibiting, but also *permitting*.

Occasional Affiliational Links: Chile and Germany

Affiliational criteria matter in Chile, yet many ministers are appointed in the absence of personal relationships to the president. The first two presidents following the 1990 transition to democracy—namely, President Aylwin and President Frei—were able to appoint their closest political allies to their cabinets (Dávila 2011; Siavelis 2009). In both cases, lengthy relationships of loyalty had been forged in the long years of political struggle against the Pinochet dictatorship. Notably, however, President Lagos (2000–2006) was unable to appoint his most trusted allies to his cabinet. Instead, he selected ministers more in keeping with the coalition parties' wishes, placing his closest political allies in what became known as the "Second Floor." According to reporters, "Because Lagos had to make concessions to the party in his first cabinet, he was obliged to form a 'kitchen cabinet' " in which he placed his most trusted political advisors.[47] Located on the second floor of La Moneda, the headquarters of the Chilean presidency, the "Second Floor" was widely known as the real site of power and influence during the Lagos years (Fernández and Rivera 2013; Siavelis 2009, 2014). This underscores the importance of trust and loyalty in the executive branch. Personal relationships with the president mattered enormously during Lagos' government, and

---

[47] Mariela Herrera and Rocío Montes, "La primera prueba de Michelle," *El Mercurio*, January 29, 2006.

because the president perceived impediments to putting his most trusted allies in cabinet, the balance of power between cabinet and the president's advisory network (the "Second Floor") shifted during the six years that Lagos was president.

President Bachelet and President Piñera, on the other hand, both appointed some ministers from inside their personal networks, but many ministers were appointed without such links. President Bachelet is often described as someone who is closed and distrustful, and for that reason, only appoints ministers with whom she has had some kind of personal or past working relationship.[48] In an interview, a political expert explains that Bachelet did not appoint ministers that the parties wanted, but instead, "appointed people from her closest teams, people who [sic] she trusted."[49] After Bachelet's 2006 election, much of the speculation about who would be in cabinet mentioned people who had worked on her campaign, or had worked closely with her when she served as health and defense minister in Lagos' government. Other journalists noted the think tank Expansiva as an important site for building political networks. According to one journalist, "the main party represented in the government is precisely the one that is not registered: Expansiva."[50] Four individuals appointed to Bachelet's initial cabinet had links to the think tank. Olivares et al. (2014) also note the importance of think tanks as a recruiting ground for ministers for the Bachelet and Piñera governments. Participation in a think tank may indicate policy expertise, but even more important, serves as a crucial site where political networks and policy knowledge overlap.

Reporters noted that, because of her electoral success, Bachelet could be more independent from the parties than Lagos. Hence, "her closest advisers will be the ministers, and it will not be necessary to have a 'Second Floor.' "[51] Just over half (12 of 20) of the ministers in Bachelet's initial cabinet have publicly identifiable links to the president. But far fewer ministers have affiliational links to President Sebastián Piñera, although some clearly have important links. The individual appointed to one of the top political posts, SEGPRES,[52] was Cristián Larroulet, described as someone who had "won

[48] This point was made repeatedly in conversations with political experts in Chile.

[49] Interiew, July 10, 2015, Santiago, Chile.

[50] Rocío Montes Rojas and Pamela Aravena Bolívar, "El paso más atrevido de Michelle Bachelet," *El Mercurio*, February 5, 2006.

[51] Mariela Herrera and Rocío Montes, "La primera prueba de Michelle," *El Mercurio*, January 29, 2006.

[52] Ministerio Secretaria de la Presidencia de Chile, one of the three posts on the political committee.

the confidence" of the president during the electoral campaign, and the interior ministry was awarded to Rodrigo Hinspeter, described as Piñera's closest ally, whom he had known for more than 20 years.[53] As with Bachelet, think tanks served as an important site for building political networks. In Piñera's case, it was the conservative think tanks Liberty and Development Institute (Instituto de Libertad y Desarrollo) and the Jaime Guzmán Foundation that served as sites for recruiting ministers.

In Germany, ministerial appointments are "to some extent about rewarding past loyalty."[54] In the Christian Democratic Union (CDU), a pact was forged among leading members of the party to secure dominant political positions. The *Andenpakt* (Andes Pact)—so-called because it was made on an overnight plane from Caracas to Santiago in 1979—created a "powerful network of patronage" within the CDU. The network created "a deep feeling of belonging. Because of the high level of trust, members spoke honestly with each other."[55] According to one media report, "[o]ver the years, new members joined and secured important party positions, including state prime ministers Roland Koch [. . .], Christian Wulff, [. . .] and Peter Müller,"[56] though the pact was not particularly successful at securing ministerial posts for members at federal level. Chancellors have also been known to appoint close allies from their own particular region (*Land*) which can lead to over-representation of their region in cabinet: both Kohl and Schröder did this.[57] But the scope to appoint several ministers on affiliational grounds is constrained by three factors that combine to reduce the number of slots for close allies that are available to selectors: the chancellor's limited powers of selection, coalition government requirements, and strong representational criteria.

Despite these constraints, in 2005 Chancellor Angela Merkel was able to appoint three of her close allies to the five cabinet spots allocated to her party. According to our media data, Merkel preferred "to rely on the absolute loyalty of a small trusted group."[58] Among her ministers were Ursula von der Leyen, "a loyal supporter,"[59] Annette Schavan, who is consistently referred to as one

[53] "Piñera promote gobierno de unidad nacional y prepara gabinet para el fines de enero," *El Mercurio*, January 18, 2010.

[54] Interview with country expert, October 28, 2014.

[55] R. Neukirch and C. Schult, "Der Männerbund," *Der Spiegel*, June 30, 2003, pp. 38–46.

[56] Ibid. p. 38.

[57] Interview with country expert, October 28, 2014.

[58] "Lohn der Treue," *Süddeutsche Zeitung*, October 17, 2005.

[59] Ibid.

of one of Merkel's closest confidants,[60] and Dr. Wolfgang Schäuble, who is described as "always loyal to Merkel."[61] Given the limited number of slots, Merkel's other close allies had to settle for non-cabinet positions. Thomas de Maizière, a "political confidant" of hers since unification, was appointed minister to head up her chancellor's office,[62] and Volker Kauder, "a close confidant," became chair of the CDU/CSU parliamentary group in the Bundestag, "and important conduit between the Chancellery and the Bundestag."[63] Note that a chancellor can veto appointments of disloyal *ministrables*, and Merkel, for example, did not consider including Friedrich Merz, a leadership challenger, in her cabinet. She was, however, obliged to include Franz Josef Jung, a close ally of Roland Koch, prime minister of the Land Hesse, a powerful region for her party.[64]

Given this limited scope of appointing on affiliational criteria, aspirant ministers find that having a power base (*Hausmacht*) within a party can be more important than loyalty to the selector in securing ministerial office. As one former minister put it:

> I have to have some kind of group that backs me. It can be a wing of the party, that lets the Chancellor know, if you do something to her, then we'll be at your throat. Or it could be a *Land* association or the SPD women's group. They will support me when the going gets tough. My *Land* association was my backing. Your power base will go to the barricades when something unjust happens to this person.[65]

Such power bases are important in qualifying for ministerial positions because "in each party—and it's exactly the same in the CDU as the SPD—there are groups that say she would perform well in cabinet, and he says, 'aha, she has that background and that background.' And if [the Chancellor] doesn't know then he has people who know that for him."[66]

[60] "Die Zähmung der Tiger," *Der Spiegel*, October 17, 2005; "Rau folgt Schavan als Minister," *Süddeutsche Zeitung*, September 28, 2005; "Das Kabinett der großen Koalition," *Süddeutsche Zeitung*, November 22, 2005.

[61] "Das Kabinett der großen Koalition," *Süddeutsche Zeitung*, November 22, 2005.

[62] Ibid.

[63] "Zwei Frauen unter Männern," *Süddeutsche Zeitung*, October 11, 2005.

[64] "Die Zähmung der Tiger," *Der Spiegel*, October 17, 2005; "Eifersüchtiges Wachen über den eigenen Vorteil," *Süddeutsche Zeitung*, October 12, 2005.

[65] Interview with former minster, October 27, 2016.

[66] Ibid.

In some countries, appointing ministers on affiliational grounds may be enhanced or constrained by institutional or contextual factors. Forming a coalition reduces the number of ministerial slots to which a selector can appoint her allies, as is the case in Germany, for instance. Alternatively, a high level of electoral success may render irrelevant—or less constraining— any conventional limits to appointing ministers on affiliational criteria, opening up opportunities for the selector to appoint allies, as we have seen with Michelle Bachelet in Chile. Overall it seems that, because selectors are permitted to appoint allies, they will do so, unless there are constraints. If they cannot appoint their allies to cabinet, it seems they appoint them to another high-trust office.

Rare Affiliational Links: Canada

Very few ministers qualify for cabinet primarily on the basis of trust and loyalty in Canada. As we discuss in the next chapter, the most important criteria for appointment to cabinet in Canada concern territorial representation. Because rules about regional representation are so extensive, and because the House of Commons is the primary eligibility pool, fewer cabinet spots are available for prime ministers to fill with their political friends and allies. A Canadian prime minister who does not have friends who qualify for appointment to cabinet in each province, or in Toronto and Montreal, will not be able to employ affiliational criteria in appointing ministers from those provinces or cities. Instead, many of the prime minister's closest political confidants and advisors are brought into the Prime Minister's Office.

The media data for both the 2008 and 2015 elections contain very few references to ministers qualifying on the basis of friendship, personal networks, trust, or loyalty, to the prime minister. After Harper's 2008 election win, columnists and journalists talked about the prime minister wanting to keep "trusted veterans" in key portfolios;[67] in this case, however, Harper was forming his second consecutive government, and the reference to trusted veterans includes people who were already in cabinet. After the Liberal Party's victory in 2015, only three of the 30 ministers appointed by Prime Minister

---

[67] Daniel Leblanc and Jane Taber, "Harper to Project Competence with New Cabinet; Trusted Veterans to Remain, Though Newly Conservative Ridings Are Expected to Be Rewarded When PM Unveils His Team Next Week," *Globe and Mail*, October 24, 2008.

Justin Trudeau were described in the media as coming from his inner circle. During the media speculation period, before cabinet was announced, newly elected Montreal MP Mélanie Joly was described as a "shoo-in" because she had "headed the Quebec advisory committee for Mr. Trudeau's leadership campaign."[68] After the cabinet was announced, she was described as a "friend of Mr. Trudeau."[69] The only other minister described in this way was Dominic Leblanc, identified as having been selected not only for his parliamentary experience, but because he "is a trusted friend of Trudeau."[70] In sum, the strong requirements of regional representational criteria limit the impact of affiliational criteria for qualifying for appointment to cabinet in Canada.

Conclusion: Affiliational Qualifying Criteria Matter in All Cabinets

It is clear from our data that one significant way to qualify for a cabinet post is to meet affiliational criteria. In the absence of rules that prohibit the appointment of ministers on affiliational grounds, selectors will do so as long as no competing rules constrain them. We find no evidence of sanctions for selectors who choose ministers on affiliational grounds. On the contrary, there are strong strategic incentives for selectors to appoint people they can trust and who are loyal; doing so helps reduce conflict and improve efficiency. That said, selectors do not justify ministerial appointments overtly on affiliational grounds. At the time of appointment, no selector will claim that a minister is appointed because he or she is a close friend or ally, though the selector may later admit to such behavior in a memoir. Nevertheless, media data offer excellent insight into the appointment of close allies to ministerial posts. The repeated media mentions, across six of our seven cases, of personal friendship, membership in personal political networks, political service or campaign support, shared personal connection through university, and/or rivalry provide strong evidence that affiliational criteria are important considerations for appointment to cabinet. Such media mentions were reinforced by our interview data. When asked about how to qualify as a minister in their country more generally, interview subjects, including former

---

[68] "Much to Consider for Cabinet," *Globe and Mail* editorial, October 21, 2015.
[69] Affan Chowdry, Tun Tanh Ha, and Sean Fine, "Fresh Faces, Heavy Files," *Globe and Mail*, November 5, 2015.
[70] "Meet the Liberal Cabinet," *Ottawa Citizen*, November 5, 2015.

ministers, frequently mentioned trust and loyalty as key factors in making an eligible politician fully *ministrable*.

Although present in all cases, affiliational criteria for ministerial recruitment are not uniformly strong across our study. This is not because the age-old tradition of rewarding loyal friends and allies is permitted in some countries but not others, but rather because the capacity to appoint on affiliational grounds depends on the degree of institutionalization of qualifying rules with more prescriptive force, particularly those establishing representational criteria. As we show in Chapter 7, Canada and Germany have strong rules about regional representation in cabinet. In such cases, there are simply fewer spots in cabinet to which selectors can appoint friends and political allies, unless of course those allies also meet representational criteria.

Overall, affiliational criteria, the original basis for qualifying for cabinet, have remained strong and resilient over time. In some countries the expansion of representational criteria to include gender requires selectors to either include women in their political networks, or to find women who qualify on experiential grounds. Our data make clear, however, that there is still substantial scope for ministers to qualify for cabinet on affiliational grounds. Later in the book (Chapter 9), we explore the gendered consequences of rules permitting selectors to appoint friends and allies to the highest political office. Although we predict that affiliational criteria will serve as an obstacle to women's inclusion in cabinets, we find that it is not quite as straightforward as that. Instead, we find evidence that some selectors—male and female— have more diverse affiliational networks, permitting women as well as men to qualify on affiliational grounds.

7

How to Qualify for Cabinet

Representational Criteria

Introduction: The Importance of Cabinets That "Look like" the Country

Cabinet ministers are always expected to have political skills, experience, and/or some level of policy expertise, yet they are not merely political managers or administrators. Cabinet ministers also play important representative functions. The inclusion of individuals from politically relevant socio-demographic groups sends a powerful symbolic message about the importance of that group to the government and to the polity more generally. This chapter shows that across all of our country cases, representational criteria constitute an important set of qualifications for *ministrables*. Stated another way, membership in a politically relevant socio-demographic group is one of the ways to qualify for cabinet. Representational criteria, however, have a very different quality when compared to affiliational criteria. Recall that with affiliational criteria, the absence of clear, formal rules about how to qualify for ministerial office *permits* selectors to appoint friends and allies to cabinet. Representational criteria have a difference force. Where they exist, they *prescribe* what choices selectors are required to make in order that the cabinet is perceived to be representative and legitimate. Experiential criteria are also prescriptive, although two things distinguish them from representational criteria. First, selectors will almost always publicly invoke an individual's experiential qualifications rather than their representativeness to justify an appointment. Although selectors may privately say, "I really need a woman for this post," once an individual has been appointed, the appointment will be justified on the grounds of political skill or policy knowledge. Journalists, columnists, and political experts, however, are far more likely to acknowledge the importance of representational criteria in qualifying individual ministers for a cabinet spot. Second, while experiential criteria are flexible and non-specific, representational criteria are more precise, requiring cabinets to meet specific socio-demographic characteristics, like region, race, or gender.

Although precise and prescriptive, we find a range of representational criteria emerging from our data, and we organize these criteria into three categories: political, territorial, and social.[1]

(1) Political: *Party or party faction*. Ensuring that all parties in a coalition government are included in cabinet is crucial. In some cases where there are internal party factions, we find that including members from different wings of the party is frequently a key consideration when appointing ministers.[2]

(2) Territorial: *Region or geography*. This includes representation of provinces or states in federal systems, but it may also mean ensuring representation from both large urban centers and rural areas, or politically, economically, or electorally important regions in the country.

(3) Social: *Race, ethnicity, language, religion, or sex*. Entirely homogenous nation-states are historically rare. Most countries, and certainly all the countries in our study, are characterized by some degree of ethnic, religious, linguistic, and racial diversity. Whether the representation of an ethnic or religious minority counts an informal rule for cabinet formation varies significantly by country. Sex or gender counts as an inclusionary rule in all our cases, although the timing and magnitude of the rule vary. Historically, women were entirely absent from cabinets but, over time, all-male cabinets disappeared, with the last one appearing in our data set more than two decades ago, in 1993 in Australia. Appointing not only men but also some women is thus becoming a clear representational criterion across the board. What varies is how strong the inclusionary rule is, and how many women are needed to satisfy the informal rule. We have developed the concept of the "concrete floor" to capture the minimal base point for women's inclusion in cabinet.

Using these three categories of representational criteria, the remainder of this chapter identifies which ones are present, and how strongly

---

[1] Note that other categories that we might expect to find based on theories of democracy and representation were not present. For example, we found no evidence in our data of an inclusionary rule based on social class or trade union membership.

[2] See Peter Riddel, Zoe Gruhn, and Liz Carolan, *Challenge of Being a Minister* (2011, 39).

institutionalized they are, in each of our seven country cases (for a summary, see Table 7.1). To preview our findings briefly, we find that representational criteria vary in terms of content, number, and strength. Notably, with few exceptions, the use of these criteria in cabinet formation do not differ across parties within a country. With respect to variation across countries, the first thing to note is that the politically relevant socio-demographic groups that must be included in cabinet tend to reflect a country's political and social cleavages—though class is notably absent. Second, in some countries, the checklist of representational criteria for identifying *ministables* is extensive, while in other countries it is fairly minimal. Finally, some representational criteria are crucial for cabinet formation, and those in the eligibility pool who reflect required characteristics may be more *ministrable*—and hence more qualified for appointment—than others. Among our country case studies, there are two countries with multiple representational criteria that are strongly institutionalized and consistently observed by all selectors: Canada and Germany. In each of the other cases, representational criteria matter, but there are fewer categories, and they are either not as strongly institutionalized or discretion can be exercised by empowered actors regarding whether and how they are observed. Finally, we find some representational criteria that must be reflected in cabinet; these are strongly institutionalized criteria. Notably, we find that, today, gender is a representational category across all our country cases. Where "appoint only men" had historically been permitted

Table 7.1 Representational Qualifying Criteria, by Country

Country	Sex	Region Territory	Race/ Ethnicity	Party/ party Faction	Language	Religion	Chamber of Parliament
Australia	√	√		√*			√
Canada	√	√	√		√		
Chile	√			√			
Germany	√	√		√		√*	
Spain	√	√*					
United Kingdom	√	√	√				
United States	√		√				
Total	7	5	3	3	1	1	1

*Varies by party

in cabinet formation, we find that today, women's inclusion, albeit in different magnitudes, is a strong prescriptive rule across all of our countries.

We know that representational criteria are prescriptive in force because we find evidence of enforcement mechanisms and sanctions. Enforcement comes predominantly from political parties, but we also find evidence of the media holding selectors to account for whether or not they meet established representational criteria. We find no evidence of enforcement through mechanisms such as international norms, or cross-national pressure from other countries.

Political Representational Criteria

Rules about political representation refer to party membership in cases of coalition governments, membership in a party faction, and balance between chambers of parliament. The need to distribute cabinet posts according to party and party faction structures the selector's subsequent strategic decisions. Among our cases, Chile and Germany are the only countries where coalition governments are common. In Australia, only one of the two main governing parties typically forms a coalition, but this is a permanent arrangement whereby the Liberal Party always forms a coalition with the Nationals. In the United Kingdom, there has been just one example of coalition government in the postwar period, namely, the 2010 coalition of the Conservatives and Liberal Democrats.

In Chile, where all post-transition governments have been coalitions, and parties compete as electoral coalitions rather than individual parties, the single most important rule for cabinet appointment is that ministerial posts be proportionately distributed across the parties forming the coalition. This rule applies to coalitions on the center-left (the *Concertación* until 2013, renamed the *Nueva Mayoría*) and the center-right coalition (*Alianza*). David Altman explains that "the general rule for postauthoritarian presidents was to appoint cabinets proportional to the relative power of the coalition's constituent parties" (2008, 262). This formula is known as the *cuoteo*. Peter Siavelis (2006) identifies the *cuoteo* as critical to the success of the center-left coalition that governed Chile for all but four years between 1990 and 2017. Likewise, Mireya Dávila's (2011) study of *Concertación* cabinets from President Alywin to the first Bachelet government shows that the practice of dividing portfolios among the parties in rough proportion to their popular support, reflected in each party's share of congressional seats, has been remarkably constant over time.

The importance of the *cuoteo* was confirmed in every single interview conducted in Chile and is referenced repeatedly throughout the media data. Former ministers and political experts explained that the most important consideration when forming a cabinet is the equilibrium among the parties.[3] Notably, the proportionality rule applies within cabinet as well, and not simply to the cabinet as a whole. For example, a former minister explained that the three political posts that make up the Political Committee—the minister of interior, the secretary general of the presidency (SEGPRES), and the secretary general of the government (SEGOB)—must be distributed to individuals from different political parties.[4] Another deeply entrenched informal rule is that vice-ministers and ministers come from different parties. An academic expert further explained that the parties themselves contain multiple currents and that achieving equilibrium in cabinet formation is "also about constructing a *cuoteo* or balance of the internal tendencies of the parties. That is more complicated."[5]

In Germany, where all governments are coalitions, ministries are shared between coalition parties. The allocation of ministries to coalition partners is agreed during coalition negotiations conducted by the parties, and formally published in the coalition agreement. Formally, the discussion of personnel must await the publication of the coalition agreement, but political insiders told us that, in practice, discussion of individuals is often interwoven into the process of allocating portfolios to parties. For example, Chancellor Gerhard Schröder wanted to get rid of a particular person deemed to be the SPD expert in a certain portfolio. To fix the problem, the SPD allowed that portfolio to go to the coalition partner during negotiations.[6] In addition, German selectors need to achieve a balance within their own parties. As one minister put it, "there's also the question of where these people are positioned in the party. Are they on the left wing or more on the right wing or more in the middle?"[7]

---

[3] Interviews: January 8, 2013; January 15a, 2013; January 15b, 2013; January 10, 2013; August 6, 2014; August 11, 2013; August 13, 2013; and August 19, 2014, Santiago.

[4] Interview, January 8, 2013, Santiago.

[5] Interview, August 13, 2014. This sentiment was repeated in other interviews, too: January 15b, 2013, and August 11, 2014, Santiago.

[6] Interview with former minister, June 30, 2016.

[7] Interview with former minister, October 27, 2014.

For the Greens "there is quota between the Realos and the Left wing of the party."[8]

In Australia there is an additional dimension to political representation. Prime ministers are expected to recruit a representational balance of ministers from the upper and lower house (Annesley 2015). As a rule, between two-thirds and three-quarters of Australian ministers are recruited from the lower House of Representatives and the rest from the Senate (Curtin 1997, 2010). Moreover, certain ministerial appointments—prime minister, treasurer, and minister for foreign affairs—are informally reserved for members of the House of Representatives (Curtin 2010).[9] This informal rule means that senators with certain ministerial aspirations "have had to relinquish their Senate position and seek election to the lower house" (Curtin 2010, 401).

Territory as a Representational Criterion

It would be fair to assume that territorial criteria would matter the most in federal rather than unitary political systems. Our data only partly support this expectation, however. Our country cases include four federal states (Australia, Canada, Germany, and the United States), one quasi-federal state (Spain), and two unitary ones (Chile and the UK). While geographic and regional criteria matter enormously in Canada, and a lot in Germany and Spain, they are less consequential in Australia, and do not matter at all in the United States. Regional representation has always been an important criterion in the United Kingdom with regard to Scotland, Wales, and Northern Ireland, but, unsurprisingly, regional representation is not at all important in Chile, by far the most centralized political system in our study.

In Canada, the "representational imperative" for cabinet appointments is paramount. According to White, "all regions as well as all important ethnic, cultural, and linguistic groups, and various other politically salient groups (such as women and certain occupations) should be represented in cabinet by ministers sharing their sociodemographic characteristics" (2005, 25). The idea that cabinet is a critical site of representation has long roots in Canada's political history. In 1867, Canada's first prime minister, John A. Macdonald, used

---

[8] Interview with former minister, June 30, 2016. Realos are members of the pragmatic, as opposed to the radical, wing of the German Green movement.

[9] Interview with former minister, March 20, 2010.

cabinet formation as a tool to unify "the disparate regions and cultural groups" out of which the country was created (White, 2005, 41). Although we have an-alytically separated the categories for territorial representation, linguistic, re-ligious, and ethnic representation, these categories often overlap in practice. One of Canada's largest provinces, Quebec, is predominantly French-speaking and historically Catholic, although today mostly secular. Most important, the province has long perceived itself as culturally distinct from the rest of Canada.

Territorial representation in Canadian cabinets is expressed in the strongly institutionalized rule that each province be represented by a minister in cab-inet, and that the larger provinces receive multiple ministers. Moreover, "[t]he largest cities—Vancouver, Toronto, and Montreal—must have several ministers; [and] significant regions in larger provinces, such as Northern Ontario, must be accommodated as well" (White 2005, 41). Prime ministers will appoint non-elected individuals to cabinet to ensure regional represen-tation and, in rare instances, even convince MPs from the opposition party to cross the floor to the governing party, as Prime Minister Harper did when he needed a minister to represent Vancouver (as described in Chapter 4).

The representational imperative means that the primary way of qualifying for cabinet in Canada is to represent a geographic constituency that appears on the selector's checklist. The primacy of territorial representation is clear in how former prime ministers describe their process for forming cabinets. Conservative prime minister John Diefenbaker (1957–1963) noted the com-plexity of territory and religion as representational criteria: "Every province must be represented. There must be a Catholic from Ontario and a Protestant from Quebec" (1976, 31). Religion, however, is no longer a criterion, al-though province and language remain paramount. In his memoirs, Jean Chretién wrote, "First, I listed all the provinces, then I put down the names of the leading contenders from each" (Chretién 2007, 23).

Our media data from 2008 and 2015 provide further evidence of how strongly institutionalized the rule of territorial representation is. Columnists and reporters repeatedly reference individuals being selected for cabinet based on which province or city they represent. In some cases, representa-tional criteria clearly trump other criteria. In 2008, there was speculation about whether Conservative MP Scott Reid, described as a "smart guy," would get a post in cabinet, but a political expert quoted in the story correctly predicted that Reid would be passed over because he did not bring the right demographic to the table: "Everybody knows he is smart and hardworking and competent, but the issue is the need to compose a cabinet with political balance and symbolism."[10] Although editorialists frequently rail against it, calling on prime ministers to select ministers based on the skills or talents they bring rather than which city or province were elected in, or which language they speak, criteria based on regional and linguistic representation nonetheless remain the most important way to qualify for cabinet in Canada.

In Germany, *Proporz* is the term used to describe the strong tradition of balancing numerous representational criteria in public office, including cabinets. For Fischer (2011, 28), *Proporz* refers to "balancing party faction, regional origins, religious orientation (with declining importance) and gender (with growing importance)." Dausend confirms the significance of representational balance:

> [V]oters hope for ministers who are selected for their competence and character. Instead they are always confronted with the political reality that is the holy trinity of *Proporz*: region, gender and party faction. In the process of choosing ministers for cabinet, capabilities and performance are less important than where ministers come from, whether they are men or women, or where they are positioned in the party. (2013, 160 author translation)[11]

Within the "holy trinity" of *Proporz*, region is consistently important. One former minister told us, "there are clear expectations in every government relating to a range of criteria, including [. . .] region of origin,"[12] while another said, "it's important that *Länder* are adequately represented."[13] Given the large number of *Länder* (16 since 1990), the comparatively small size of cabinet, and the fact that posts are shared among coalition partners, there is no expectation that each *Land* is represented in cabinet. Rather "if you only have six ministries and there are 16 states, then you try to even it out with other positions, such as junior ministerial positions or deputy chair of parliamentary party."[14] Instead, there is a strong expectation that *Länder* be adequately represented in cabinet in proportion to their population size and strength in the party. Notably, there are some differences across the two main parties. For example, in the SPD, "[n]o Chancellor can afford not to pay

[10] Doug Fisher, "'Smart Guy' a Cabinet Candidate; Many Believe Scott Reid Has What It Takes," *Ottawa Citizen*, October 29, 2008.

[11] http://pdf.zeit.de/2013/46/kabinettsbildung-ministerienverteilung.pdf.

[12] Interview with former minister, September 23, 2014.

[13] Interview with former minister, October 27, 2014.

[14] Interview with former minister, October 29, 2014.

enough attention to North Rhine-Westphalia,"[15] while "the CDU pays close attention to its strong regional associations."[16] For all parties of government, it is important that there is ministerial representation from the five eastern *Länder* as well as the 11 western states: "you must make sure that one comes from the east";[17] "there isn't an east-west quota but you probably need one from the east."[18]

Spain is a quasi-federal state where territorial representation in cabinet matters. Unlike Canada, where each province is expected to have a minister, rules about territorial representation in Spain are far less demanding. Like Germany, the regional categories on prime ministers' representative checklists vary considerably by party. The PSOE and PP have different internal structures, and this difference shapes the degree to which regional representation must be reflected in cabinet. The PSOE has a federalized structure, and regional party bosses (*barones*) play an important role in the party. Certain regions—Andalusia, Catalonia, and the Basque Country—have historically been important electorally for the PSOE, and PSOE prime ministers will ensure that those regions have cabinet representation.[19] The PP, in contrast, has a far more centralized structure, making regional representation less important. That said, media commentary following the announcement of both Zapatero's and Rajoy's cabinets was full of references to ministers as meeting the Valencian quota or the Catalan or Andalusian quota, implying that even if territorial representation is not a strong convention (as in Canada, for instance), there are nonetheless public expectations that cabinets include ministers from the country's main regions.

The United Kingdom is traditionally a unitary state. Despite this, "there are informal quotas including representation of the regions, which are taken quite seriously."[20] Most significantly, there is a strong rule about ensuring representation of Scotland and Wales in cabinet, and this is achieved through the secretary of state for Scotland and the secretary of state for Wales. Both posts are reserved for Scots and Welsh MPs. Thus, according to Kaufman (1997, 7–8), "[b]eing Welsh or Scots is also a help [. . .] because of the need to fill numerous positions at the Welsh and Scottish Offices." This rule presents

---

[15] Interview with former minister, October 27, 2014.
[16] Interview with former minister, September 23, 2014.
[17] Interview with former minister, October 27, 2014.
[18] Interview with former minister, June 30, 2016.
[19] Interviews with former ministers and political experts, June 22, 2011; May 28, 2012; May 29, 2012; May 13, 2014.
[20] Interview with former minister, December 17, 2013.

particularly favorable conditions for aspirant Conservatives in Scotland, as there are so few elected Conservatives there. In Labour there are historically "so many Scots and Welsh MPs that they have to take their chance with the rest, though naturally receiving preference for the Welsh and Scottish Office posts" (Kaufman 1997, 8). A former Labour minister recalled that once "when a vacancy arose on the Labour shadow cabinet, someone was proposed, but the reaction was 'But he's another Scot'!"[21] Beyond Scotland and Wales, there is a secretary of state for Northern Ireland, though this post is not reserved for an MP from that community, and it is important to ensure a spread of ministers across the regions within England, too.[22]

Australia is a federal state, and region is included in the checklist of representational criteria, although achieving regional representation is far less onerous than it is in Canada. Lacking the linguistic cleavage that has so profoundly shaped Canadian federalism, "the politics of place exist to a lesser extent in Australia" (Rhodes, Wanna, and Weller 2009, 110). According to Weller, "Each state requires some representation and there is likely to be some balance between the larger states. It may be possible to ignore Tasmania for a time, but not the others. Placating state interests does not mean that every state will be represented in cabinet, but one minister at least will be in the ministry" (2007, 199). Weller also identifies some variation across parties (2007, 198–199), noting that this rule applies particularly to Liberal–National Coalition governments, while Labor governments are more concerned about balancing national party factions. States are also rewarded with additional ministerial positions if they are instrumental in getting a government elected. The importance of representational criteria is reflected in our media data. Following the 2013 election, it was noted that "Mr Abbott faces a difficult task balancing competing considerations in designing his line-up to ensure adequate representation in the ministry by state of origin, gender, membership of the upper or lower house and party—as between the Liberal and Nationals parties."[23] Former minister Kay Patterson "acknowledged that Mr Abbott had to ensure a fair balance between states as well as between the lower and upper houses."[24] Another article bemoaned the way that "quality performers [were] overlooked for promotion during the life cycle of the

---

[21] Ibid.
[22] Interview with former minister, June 7, 2016.
[23] "Abbott Told to Drop Also-Rans from Team," *The Age*, September 11, 2013.
[24] "Libs 'shocked' by Lack of Women in Cabinet," *The Australian*, September 13, 2013.

Labor government, for base reasons such as factional deal-making, petty gripes or balancing state representation."[25]

In sum, territory as a representational criterion matters to varying degrees in Australia, Canada, Germany, Spain, and the United Kingdom. The only two countries where we could find no evidence of territorial criteria as informal qualification for cabinet appointments are Chile and the United States. For both cases, our interview and media data contain no reference to presidents needing to consider region or territory when selecting ministers.

Social Characteristics as Representational Criteria: Religion, Ethnicity, Race, and Gender

Social characteristics such as religion, ethnicity, race, and gender are embodied in the individual, physically or spiritually. Few countries today are homogenous in terms of religion, race, or ethnicity, and none of our country cases is ethnically homogenous. Four of our cases—Australia, Chile, Canada, and the United States—are white settler societies, and in each, indigenous populations have organized around historical grievances based on mistreatment by colonial authorities and subsequent abuse from independent rulers. In one of our cases, namely the United States, politics and society continue to be marked by the legacies of slavery and persistent patterns of inequality based on race. All of the countries in our study, including Chile, have become destinations for migration, particularly in the twentieth and twenty-first centuries. While all of our country cases are marked by religious, ethnic, and racial diversity, the degree to which these identities matter for cabinet appointments varies significantly.

Ethnicity, Race, and Religion as Representational Criteria

In the United States, race and ethnicity have become increasingly important in electoral politics. As the racial balance has shifted nationally,[26] race as a

---

[25] "Only a Competent Team Can Spur Labor Renewal," *The Australian*, September 14, 2013.
[26] See "New Census Bureau Report Analyzes U.S. Population Projections," US Bureau of the Census, March 3, 2015; http://www.census.gov/newsroom/press-releases/2015/cb15-tps16.html.

representational criterion for inclusion in the US ministerial eligibility pool has diversified. Four US states are now "majority minority" states, where non-white citizens outnumber whites: California, Hawaii, New Mexico, and Texas. As the United States has become more racially and ethnically diverse, multiple races and ethnicities require cabinet representation, and hence new groups are encompassed in new representational criteria. In regard to race (and ethnicity) generally, Barack Obama appointed 10 persons of color to cabinet posts across his two administrations, including a record number of Asian Americans—Steven Chu (energy, 2009–2013); Gary Locke (commerce, 2009–2011); and Eric Shinseki (veterans affairs, 2009–2014)— who served concurrently in his first cabinet. He also appointed three cabinet members of Hispanic descent, as well as four African Americans, two of whom, Eric Holder and Loretta Lynch, he appointed as attorney general. George W. Bush also appointed six persons of color as cabinet members in his second term. Across both terms, nine persons of color served in Bush's two administrations; among these were four African Americans, two Asian Americans, and three Latinos. The numbers of persons of color appointed to cabinet has been relatively constant since the Clinton administrations. President Clinton appointed 11 persons of color to cabinet posts from 1993 to 2001; seven of these appointees were African Americans, nearly twice the number appointed to cabinets by Presidents Bush and Obama. Clinton also appointed three Latinos and one Asian American as department secretaries. Beyond the numbers of non-white cabinet members appointed by the past three two-term US presidents, media data speculation about likely cabinet ministers who were not white often mentioned the race or ethnicity of the *ministrables*.[27]

In Canada, ethnicity has always been an important cleavage, and one relevant for cabinet representation, but its meaning has significantly changed over the years. In the earlier part of the twentieth century, religion was politically salient and ethnic representation meant ensuring a balance among "English, French, Irish, and Scots" (White 2005). More recently, inclusionary

[27] The *New York Times* noted that Condoleezza Rice's "appointment as secretary of state would be a first for a black woman" (Glenn Kessler and Thomas E. Ricks, "Rice's NSC Tenure Complicates New Post," *New York Times*, November 16, 2004); and Secretary of Education Rod Paige as "a son of segregation in Mississippi who rose to become the first black secretary of education" (Diana Jean Schemo, "Secretary of Education Will Leave Bush Cabinet," *New York Times*, November 13, 2004. Norman Mineta, secretary of transportation, was noted as "an American citizen of Japanese descent [who had] been sent to an internment camp along with his family during World War II" and as "the first Asian-American cabinet secretary" (Matthew L. Wald, "Transportation Chief Quits, Citing 'Other Challenges,'" *New York Times*, June 24, 2006).

norms around ethnic diversity have changed to mean the inclusion of visible minorities from the country's largest immigrant communities and Canada's First Nations. It is worth noting, however, that indigenous Canadians and racialized minorities have only recently found representation in cabinet. Conservative prime minister Joe Clark appointed the first Black member of cabinet in his short-lived 1979 government. It was not until the Liberal government of Jean Chretién that two other large immigrant groups in Canada were represented in cabinet: Rey Pagtakhan was the country's first Filipino-Canadian in cabinet and Raymond Chan was the first Chinese-Canadian minister. Chretién also appointed Hedy Fry (of Trinidadian ancestry) to cabinet. Although Chretién appointed many "firsts," Conservative prime minister Stephen Harper continued to appoint racialized minorities to cabinet, particularly those from Canada's largest immigrant communities, including Bev Oda, Michael Chong, and Tim Uppal. More significant, Harper was the first prime minister to appoint two indigenous Canadians to cabinet: Leona Aglukkaq and Peter Penashue. Yet even by 2005, "the appointment of a minister from a visible minority community is still sufficiently unusual as to render it newsworthy" (White 2005, 36).

No cabinet has been as ethnically diverse as Justin Trudeau's. His 30-member cabinet included five ministers from racialized minority groups[28] and two indigenous Canadians.[29] In addition to appointing Canada's first gender-parity cabinet, Trudeau was likewise the first to include such a large number of racialized minority ministers. Applause and praise for diversity in terms of gender and ethnicity were frequent themes in our media data, and also attracted global media attention. It is likely that even if future prime ministers fall short of the large number of visible minority ministers that Trudeau appointed, a new bar in terms of ethnic inclusion has been set, and public expectations about what diversity means in practice have shifted.

In Germany, religion used to be an important component of *Proporz*, but is declining in significance as a representational criterion (Fischer 2011, 28). Ministers acknowledge the significance of religion, flagging, however, that it varies by party and is declining in significance. According to a former minister, "the CDU pays close attention to balancing religious denominations."[30]

[28] These ministers are: Navdeep Bains, Harjit Sajian, Amarheet Sohi, Maryam Monsef (the first Muslim in cabinet), and Bardish Chagger.

[29] The two indigenous ministers in Trudeau's initial cabinet were Jody Wilson-Raybould and Hunter Tootoo.

[30] Interview, September 23, 2014.

In the CDU, "there had to be a few Protestants because it was overwhelming Catholic," whereas "in the SPD that was never a significant issue. I mean, once someone who is Catholic might have had a harder time in the SPD but I'm [retired now] and I cannot remember a time when that mattered."[31] Despite Germany's increasingly ethnically diverse population, with some 3 million people of Turkish origin living in Germany, such ethnicity is not mentioned in interviews or media data as part of the representational checklist for ministerial recruitment. Further, no German citizens of Turkish origin have ever been selected to the ranks of cabinet at the federal level.

Although the United Kingdom has a sizable minority ethnic population, comprising predominantly Commonwealth citizens from the Caribbean and Southeast Asia, it was not until 2002 that a Black or Asian minister was appointed to cabinet. Paul Boateng became the United Kingdom's first Black cabinet minister when Prime Minister Tony Blair appointed him as chief secretary to the treasury, followed by Baroness Amos as secretary of state for international development in 2003, the first Black woman to sit in cabinet. Conservative prime minister David Cameron appointed Baroness Warsi, the Conservative Party chairman, to his 2010 cabinet as minister without portfolio, the first female Muslim to attend Cabinet, and then Sajid Javid as secretary of state for culture, media and sport from 2014 to 2015 and later secretary of state for business, innovation and skills and president of the Board of Trade from 2015 to 2016. Javid served as secretary of state for communities and local government and then home secretary under Prime Minister Theresa May. May also appointed Priti Patel as secretary of state for international development to her cabinet in 2016.

While ethnicity as a representational criterion was not mentioned by ministers in interviews, the ethnicity of Black and Asian ministers is discussed in media reports. Our media data from 2010 clearly reference Baroness Warsi's status as the "[f]irst Muslim woman to be selected as Tory candidate and sit in Cabinet,"[32] noting how she "posed in Downing Street in traditional dress after the coalition Cabinet's historic first meeting [. . .] Lady Warsi's pink shalwar kameez was in sharp contrast to the dark suits sported by most of the other, predominantly male, Cabinet members."[33] One commentator described

---

[31] Interview with former minister, October 27, 2014.

[32] "Timeline Ministers Make Their Presence Felt; Cameron at No 10," *The Daily Telegraph*, May 15, 2010; "In the Pink: Britain's First Female Muslim Cabinet Minister Brightens up Downing St," *Daily Telegraph*, May 14, 2010.

[33] "In the Pink: Britain's First Female Muslim Cabinet Minister Brightens up Downing St," *Daily Telegraph*, May 14, 2010.

Baroness Warsi as "a double whammy, being not only female, which is mar-velous, but Muslim as well, which is thrilling."[34] It is worth noting that, since Paul Boateng's appointment in 2002, there has been at least one minister from a visible minority appointed to every UK cabinet, indicating perhaps the establishment of a new concrete floor in terms of ethnicity.

Race and ethnicity are clearly important representational criteria in two of our country cases: Canada and the United States; and ethnicity is emerging as a criterion in the United Kingdom. In all three cases, the appointment of an all-white cabinet would surely be criticized in the media and would be viewed as unrepresentative. Religion is declining in significance in Germany. In Australia, Chile, and Spain, none of our interviews or media data referenced race, religion, or ethnicity as relevant representational criteria.

Gender as a Representational Criterion

Gender is referenced repeatedly in interviews and media data across all our cases as a representational criterion. The importance of gender as an inclu-sionary norm—for women as well as men—has been promoted by women in the political parties, especially by feminists in leftist parties, but also by the broader women's movement. In some countries, mobilization around the need for women's presence in politics led to the adoption of formal party quotas or to informal party commitments of active recruitment of female candidates for elections. In some cases, new norms around gender have been established by selectors who break with past practice of appointing mostly men to include unprecedented numbers of women in cabinet. Some are motivated by feminist principles, for example, Canadian prime minister Justin Trudeau, who often proclaimed himself a feminist, while others, like former UK prime minister David Cameron, recognized an electoral advan-tage to being inclusive.

In Germany, a strong norm about gender representation in cabinet devel-oped in the 1980s, and gender is confirmed as one of the three components in *Proporz* (Dausend 2013). Indeed, for Fischer (2011, 28), gender as part of *Proporz* is growing in importance, evidenced by the fact that there has not been an all-male cabinet since 1957. The origins of this norm can be found

---

[34] "It's Okay to Like Both Shoes and Politics; The Debate over the Lack of Female MPs Is Missing the Point," *Daily Telegraph*, May 15, 2010.

in the German Social Democratic Party (SPD), where a formal party rule, dating from the mid-1980s, requires "at least 40 percent of each gender in boards and lists" (Party Statutes, Article 11 [2][35]). Importantly, when the SPD was able to form a government in 1998, gendered actors working with the rules interpreted the 40 percent rule as applying to cabinet spots as well. The German Green Party also introduced an internal party quota in the 1980s, which applies to cabinet appointments as well. According to a former minister, "There has been a rule in the Greens since the 1980s—we were the pioneers—that lists should have equal numbers of men and women and should start with a woman."[36] The CDU has a weaker, more discretionary provision—a *Kannbestimmung*—that it *should* be 30 percent. In 2009, when the CDU formed a coalition with the liberal Free Democratic Party, which does not have a party rule on gender, women's inclusion in cabinet dipped to 26.6 percent. Despite this drop, women's cabinet presence was still comparatively high compared, for example, to the Australian case. This confirms a more widely accepted inclusionary gender norm across all German parties.

Gender is a key representational category on prime ministers' checklists in Spain as well, with most of the pressure for women's inclusion coming from women in the parties, particularly in the PSOE (Verge 2007, 2012). Although the last all-male post-election cabinet was formed by a socialist prime minister, Felipe González, in 1986, the PSOE was also the first to adopt an internal gender quota of 25 percent in 1988, increasing it to 40 percent by 1997 (Verge 2012). When Zapatero appointed a gender parity cabinet in 2004, it was viewed as a natural extension of parity norms already accepted in the PSOE. Although the conservative People's Party (PP) has strenuously rejected the idea of gender quotas, it has nonetheless sought to improve women's representation. Indeed, for the PP, appointing women to cabinet, and nominating women for election to parliament, serves as a way to signify the party's status as a modern conservative party, challenging any lingering ideas about the party's links to the Franco regime. As such, when the PP won national office in 1996, after four consecutive socialist governments, José Maria Aznar's first cabinet contained what was at the time a historically high number of women (26.6 percent). In sum, gender, including women, is clearly an important category on the representational checklist in both of Spain's main parties.

---

[35] http://www.quotaproject.org/uid/countryview.cfm?CountryCode=DE#sources.
[36] Interview with former minister, June 30, 2016.

In the United States, there has not been an all-male cabinet since 1981.[37] The major increase in numbers of women in the US cabinet came after the 1992 election of President Bill Clinton. Clinton had campaigned in the context of the "Year of the Woman," when numbers of female congressional candidates increased dramatically, resulting in record numbers of women elected to the US House.[38] With high levels of attention to women's political representation, and with pressure from women organized in the Coalition for Women's Appointments (Borrelli 2002, 71), Clinton made a campaign promise to appoint a cabinet "that looks like America" (Borrelli 2002, 218; Christopher 2001, 163),[39] a promise thereafter modified to be "more like America than previous administrations" (Christopher 2001, 163). The transition team for Clinton's initial cabinet "ask[ed] for every cabinet position whether there were qualified women or members of minority groups who could be added to our list" (Christopher 2001, 163). Warren Christopher, who led the transition team, described the construction of Clinton's first cabinet (2001, 167):

The symbolic and exemplary value of seeking a cabinet that "looked like America" outweighed whatever transient problems we encountered. . . . [We] showed that qualified appointees could be found among women and minority groups that had been seriously underrepresented in the past. Not only were the people chosen by the president equipped to do their jobs, they performed another vital service for the administration and the country: they were role models, inspiring and encouraging the next generation.

The emphasis on two major representational criteria—race and sex—in US cabinet appointments continued in George W. Bush's and in Barack

---

[37] President Ronald Reagan's post-election cabinet, appointed in 1981, had no female department secretaries, but by 1983, Reagan had appointed Elizabeth Dole as secretary of transportation. Every post-election cabinet thereafter included at least one female cabinet minister, including Reagan's second administration.

[38] In the 1992 elections, the percentage of women elected to the House surpassed 10 percent for the first time in history, as was true as well for Democratic women in the House. Since 1992, women's House representation increased, without exception, in every succeeding congressional election until 2016. In 2016, 84 women were elected to the House, the same as the number elected in 2014. In 2018, 102 women were elected to the House (23.4%).

[39] Clinton's goal of constructing a cabinet that included representational criteria so that "the cabinet would be responsive to the concerns of all Americans . . . continued into the George W. Bush administration; it may have become a permanent characteristic of the nomination coverage" (Borrelli 2002, 218).

Obama's cabinets. Bush's first cabinet, with three female department secretaries, and his second, with four female cabinet members, perfectly matched Clinton's record; moreover, six women ultimately served in the two Bush administrations, one more than had been the case in the preceding Clinton cabinets. The pattern was reversed in Obama's two administrations, with four women appointed to Obama's first cabinet but only three in the second; Obama nonetheless appointed more women across his eight years in office than any previous president—eight, enough in total to staff a gender parity cabinet.

Examining race and sex together shows that "cabinet representation for women is primarily cabinet representation for white women" continues to be the case (Borrelli 2002, 218).[40] George W. Bush's record of appointing women of color improved in his second administration (2005–2009), with two women of color among the six women appointed to his cabinets: Elaine Chao (labor) and Condoleezza Rice (state). Bush's second initial cabinet is the only presidential cabinet in which two women of color served simultaneously in the entirety of US history. By this very modest measure, President Obama's record of appointing women, and women of color, is disappointing. In his first cabinet, only one of Obama's four initial appointees was a woman of color (Hilda Solis, labor), and at the conclusion of his two-term presidency, Obama had appointed only two women of color to his cabinets: Solis (2009–2013), and, near the end of his second term, Loretta Lynch (justice, since 2015); they did not serve concurrently.

The attention in the media to the categories of race and sex underscores their importance in representational terms.[41] Moreover, activist groups have been highly attentive to their own representation in cabinet and were often critical of presidents for not doing enough in representational terms in their cabinet nominations.[42] Advocacy organizations have been crucial actors in

[40] Note that Borrelli's work analyzes cabinet appointments only through George W. Bush's initial first-term cabinet (2001–2005).

[41] Representation of women within a US cabinet was also taken seriously by Obama's 2012 presidential election opponent, former Massachusetts governor Mitt Romney, in the presidential debates. Romney reportedly "worked with Mass GAP to find the best-qualified women for top positions in Massachusetts government. The efforts resulted in Massachusetts having the most women in top positions in the entire country" (Michael Wines, "As Governor, Romney's Eagerness to Hire Women Faded," New York Times, October 17, 2012).

[42] "The President and Women," New York Times, May 9, 2004; and Mark Leibovich, "Man's World at the White House? No Harm, No Foul, Aides Say," New York Times, October 24, 2009; Peter Wallsten and Anne E. Kornblut, "Frictions over Women's Role in Obama's White House Was Intense," Washington Post, September 20, 2011; Olga Belogolova, "Jarrett Confirms Tensions over Role of Women in Obama White House," National Journal, September 20, 2011. See also Annie Lowrey, "Obama's Remade Inner Circle Has an All-Male Look, So Far," New York Times, January 8,

putting inclusionary norms for racial minorities and women on the public agenda, making cabinets with insufficient representation of women and minorities difficult to legitimize.

In Canada, according to White, "no [prime] minister would even contemplate an all-male cabinet" (2005, 41). Indeed, among our country cases, Canada, along with Germany, was among the first to leave behind the practice of appointing all-male initial cabinets. The last post-election cabinet to include no women was assembled by Liberal prime minister Pierre Trudeau in 1968. Trudeau won three more federal elections and appointed one woman to each of those cabinets. But a turning point came with Conservative prime minister Brian Mulroney's election, when he appointed four women, setting a new threshold for women's inclusion in cabinet. Since 1984, women's representation has expanded with relative persistency, reaching the 30 percent threshold in 2008 and gender parity in 2015. Although subsequent parity cabinets are by no means guaranteed, it is clear that sex is an important representational criterion for cabinet appointment in Canada.

In Chile, the last all-male cabinet to be assembled by a democratically elected president appeared in 1970. With the return of democracy in 1990, women's movements, and women in the political parties, especially those in the *Concertación*, have actively promoted the idea that sex is a critical representational category for cabinets, and have worked hard to lobby presidents to appoint women. All cabinets since 1991 have included at least one woman, and beginning in 1994, the number of women in cabinet has expanded with relative persistence, reaching parity by 2006 (although not remaining at that level). Clearly, sex is an important representational criterion in Chile.

In the United Kingdom, gender as a representational rule has emerged, albeit gradually and unevenly across the parties. The last all-male post-election cabinet was formed as late as 1987. The Labour Party drove changing expectations about women's presence in cabinet from the late 1970s, through feminist campaigning within the party.[43] Changes to the Parliamentary Labour Party's (PLP) Standing Orders, which govern the process of shadow cabinet elections, were made to the secure the appointment of more women (Annesley 2015). First, the size of the shadow cabinet was increased from 12 in 1979 to 15 in 1982, 18 in 1992, and 19 in 1995, to create more openings for

2013; and Annie Lowrey, "In Obama's High-Level Appointments, The Scales Still Tip Toward Men," *New York Times*, August 26, 2013.

[43] Interview with Labour MP, June 7, 2016.

women.[44] Then new voting rules were introduced: for the 1992 shadow cabinet election the top three women would be included in the shadow cabinet, even if they were not among the top 18 based on votes alone; from 1993 to 1996 MPs were required to vote for four women with the sanction that ballot papers would be void if four were not selected. Further reforms were initiated after Labour returned to opposition in 2010: shadow cabinet elections then required PLP members to vote for six women in the ballot for it to be valid so that the share of women in the shadow cabinet would reach 31.5 percent, equal to their representation in the House of Commons. In 2011, the practice of shadow cabinet elections was abolished and then Labour leader Ed Miliband explicitly committed to 50 percent female representation in ministerial office, an improvement on the 31.5 percent that was achieved through quota rules. Miliband's successor, Jeremy Corbyn, continued the commitment to a parity shadow cabinet, sustained through pressure from Labour feminists.[45]

In the Conservative Party, Prime Minister John Major appointed an all-male cabinet when he succeeded Margaret Thatcher in 1990, but he then appointed two women to his 1992 post-election cabinet. By the time the Conservative Party was next in government, in 2010, expectations about gender and cabinet had changed significantly. Indeed, in 2008, party leader David Cameron made an overt pledge that, if elected, one-third of his government would be women by the end of the first term in office.[46] Notably, Cameron did not make this pledge in response to any feminist pressure within the Conservative Party,[47] but rather as part of his pitch to change the image of the Conservative Party (Childs and Webb 2011) and to compete with Labour for female voters (Annesley and Gains 2014). When elected in 2010, Cameron managed to appoint one-third women among the ranks of Tory ministers, but none was appointed by the Liberal Democrats, meaning that the share of women in cabinet overall fell from 25 percent in 2005 to 18 percent.

Australia is the real outlier among our seven cases, as there is no strong evidence of any change in the representational qualifying norm of gender: being male. The last all-male cabinet was appointed as late as 1993. Since then, there have been two post-election cabinets with just one woman: in 1998 and

---

[44] Interview with former Labour minister, December 17, 2013.
[45] Interview with Labour MP, June 7, 2016.
[46] "Cameron Vow on Women Ministers," *The Guardian*, March 2, 2008.
[47] Interview with former minister, June 7, 2016.

2013. This is not to say that gender is absent from the selector's checklist. Our media data include reference to how a new prime minister must assure "adequate representation in the ministry by state of origin, gender, membership of the upper or lower house, and party—as between the Liberal and Nationals parties."[48] We also find evidence of how gender as a representational rule varies by party. While the Liberal Party "appoints and promotes on merit, not gender. That's what women are looking for recognition of their talents, not of their chromosomes,"[49] an Australian Labor Party politician explained, "we absolutely appoint on merit as well but we are missing out on half the population if we don't give proper regard to their merit."[50]

In sum, gender is an important category on the representational checklists for all selectors, though to a lesser extent in Australia. What varies across our cases, as we have seen, is the timing of the emergence of gender as a category on the checklist, how many female ministers are needed to satisfy the inclusionary rule, whether representational rules on the checklist are considered to be competing or complementary, and how strongly selectors perceive the rule. In four of our countries—Canada, Chile, Germany, and Spain—cabinets are expected to include a relatively high magnitude of women. Each of these countries has had multiple post-election cabinets with more than 30 percent female ministers, and no instances of backsliding to low magnitudes of women in cabinet. In the United Kingdom and the United States, public expectations about including women are evident. US presidents and UK prime ministers have clearly been responding to the pull of inclusionary norms in their parties and countries, although they have not yet included women in cabinet at the high levels seen in Canada, Chile, Germany, or Spain. Australia is the outlier, where a much weaker inclusionary norm is evident across both major parties. In all seven countries, however, qualifying for cabinet by being male is no longer the representational criterion; all-male cabinets are no longer acceptable.

Representational Criteria Matter in All Countries

Representational criteria play a critical role in setting up ministerial opportunities for individuals. Cabinets are collectives, not merely

---

[48] "Abbott Told to Drop Also-Rans from Team," *The Age*, September 11, 2013.
[49] Liberal minister Julie Bishop, cited in *The Australian Magazine*, September 28, 2013.
[50] Interview, March 23, 2010.

disparate or unrelated individuals who are individually selected to manage or administer government departments. As collectives, cabinets must embody the representational categories that are deemed politically relevant in a particular country. The role of representational criteria is to solidify the legitimacy of the cabinet. Representational categories, however, vary in both content and strength across our case studies, with the consequence that they shape who may be more or less *ministrable* in each country.

We find that regional representation is a consistently prescribed criterion, appearing in five of our cases: Australia, Canada, Germany, Spain, and the United Kingdom (see Table 7.1). Although region appears on selectors' checklists in all these countries, it is only in Canada where satisfying the representational imperative is truly demanding, with a complex set of prescriptive rules requiring cabinet representation for each province, as well as urban-rural diversity. Even though populations are becoming increasingly diverse in all of our case studies, race and ethnicity only appear as qualifying criteria in three of our countries: Canada, the United Kingdom, and the United States. Party or party faction appears in three of our countries, namely those in which coalition governments are common: Chile, Germany, and Australia.

Gender is the only representational category that appears across all countries (see Table 7.1). In all cases, gender includes women as qualified for cabinet, yet the magnitude of women's inclusion varies significantly. The number or proportion of women deemed sufficient to satisfy representational rules ranges from more than 30 percent in countries like Germany and Spain, to just one or two women in Australia.

In those countries where feminist advocates in political parties have successfully achieved rule changes in their parties, like the German Greens, the German Social Democrats, and the Spanish Socialist Worker's Party, gender quotas at the party level have been applied to the sphere of cabinet, requiring women's cabinet representation to mirror as closely as possible the floor set by the party quota. Likewise, women in the UK Labour Party secured rule changes to ensure that gender would be a representational criterion for shadow cabinet elections, which set up ministerial opportunities. In all cases, the media has played a role in articulating shifting public expectations about women's inclusion in arenas of power, making cabinets composed exclusively of men appear democratically illegitimate. Parties and the media also play important roles in enforcing rules about representation and sanctioning deviations from the rule, primarily through public criticism.

A final important point: we find that representation criteria for qualifying for cabinet are the most strongly prescriptive of the three types of qualifying criteria that we identify in this book. Where they exist, our data show that selectors consistently observe them in order to ensure the legitimacy of their cabinet. Representational criteria, therefore, serve as important filters in moving individuals from the eligibility pool into the pool of qualified candidates. This finding leads to certain expectations about the gendered consequence of representational criteria that we assess in Chapter 10. We expect that women's presence in cabinet will be higher where gender is more firmly established as a representational criterion. We also expected that it would be hard to add gender to the selector's representational checklist in cases where numerous rules about representation already apply. But, as we show in Chapter 10, that assumption was not borne out in our data.

Conclusion: How to Qualify as a Minister

Over the course of the last four chapters—Chapters 4 through 7—we have excavated and described all of the rules establishing eligibility and qualifying criteria for ministerial office. From our data we identified three qualifying criteria: experiential, affiliational, and representational. Few individual cabinet appointees will meet all three categories of qualifying criteria,[51] and not all ministers in a cabinet qualify for appointment in the same way. As collective entities, cabinets need to secure a balance of individuals who, when viewed collectively, meet the full range of these criteria. We found that all three types of criteria matter in all seven of our case study countries and that a country's constitutional design—whether parliamentary or presidential, federal or unitary—does not predict what type of qualifying criteria move individuals from the eligibility pool to a spot in cabinet.

Our findings confirm that the rules governing how to qualify for cabinet are entirely informal, and therefore not legally enforceable. That said, we

---

[51] For example, in his first cabinet, US president Barack Obama's treasury secretary nominee, Timothy Geithner, met no representational or affiliational criteria for appointment; in contrast, Hillary Clinton, nominee for secretary of state, met all three: she was in Obama's affiliational network, met a representational criterion (sex), and, like Geithner, had substantial policy expertise (as well as political experience).

identify some unwritten rules as more strongly institutionalized than others. Using Ostrom's classification whereby rules prescribe, prohibit, or permit, we showed that experiential and representational criteria are prescribed, while affiliational criteria are permitted. Looking closely at our media data, we found that all ministers had political or policy experience. But we also found that experiential criteria are not the decisive factor that determines which *ministrables*, from the range of eligible and talented individuals, are selected and which are not. Rather, they serve as a minimum threshold for qualification. All *ministrables* must demonstrate experience, but there is flexibility with regard to whether their experience is political or policy related. Put another way, experiential criteria are prescribed, but they are not specific.

Our data have led us to conclude that it is affiliational and representational criteria that serve as the main filters determining which eligible individuals get elevated to ministerial office. Put another way, rules about affiliation and representation are the informal rules for qualification that structure or guide selectors' behavior and choices as they assemble their cabinets. But the two sets of criteria function somewhat differently: affiliational criteria are permitted, while representational criteria are prescribed, and, indeed, are the most strongly prescriptive rules for cabinet appointment. Rules about qualifying for cabinet do not prohibit selectors from appointing their trusted friends and loyal allies, and there are important strategic reasons why selectors use affiliation as a qualifying criterion. Historically, and in many cases today, membership in a selector's personal or political network remains an important route to qualify for ministerial office.

A selector's capacity to appoint friends and allies is constrained, however, if representational criteria, which are prescriptive in force, are strong and numerous. In those circumstances, selectors have fewer spots available to appoint their friends or allies to cabinet, even though they are permitted to do so. In these cases, the prescriptive nature of representational criteria take priority over the permissive nature of affiliational criteria. Even when faced with strategic incentives to appoint friends and allies, selectors operate within a rule-bound framework. But because all rules about qualification are informal, selectors are able to behave strategically in appointing ministers who meet various representational criteria to the cabinet.

Our identification of the factors that make some individuals more *ministrable* than others makes clear that discussion of "merit"—rarely defined—is unhelpful at best in discussing cabinet appointments. Claims of merit (or lack of merit) are often political claims, issued post hoc, to justify inclusion of a specific minister or to limit access to others. Merit, as conventionally understood, does not determine appointment of cabinet ministers. An advisor to Canadian prime minister Justin Trudeau said that a cabinet appointment "is never a pure and simple meritocracy."[52] Instead, our evidence indicates that representational criteria serve as the most prescriptive of all three sets of criteria, and therefore serve as a primary filter for determining which individuals move from the eligibility pool into cabinet. In discussing cabinet formation during his years as prime minister, former Canadian prime minister John Diefenbaker wrote about the complex representational rules in Canada, concluding, "thus, A and B may be selected, whereas C and D, who are better qualified, may be left aside" (Diefenbaker 1976, 31). No specific, fixed, constant criteria of merit exist; rather, combinations of qualifying criteria determine the likelihood that some individuals will be selected while others are passed over.

We have concluded each of the previous four chapters by identifying our assumptions about the potential gendered consequences of the informal rules about qualification for cabinet. For example, we anticipated that the informal nature of rules about qualification for ministerial office would be detrimental to women's chances of making the transition from *ministrable* to minister. In many respects, this assumption is borne out in our findings, but we also find evidence that political actors are able to exploit the ambiguity inherent in the informal rules of qualification to bring women into cabinet. For example, we have shown that experiential criteria are flexible and nonspecific. We find no evidence that women are more likely to be appointed for their policy experience rather than their political skills. The fact that all *ministrables* need some kind of experience to secure their inclusion into cabinet leads us to wonder whether women's lower representation in cabinet over the decades has been because experiential qualifications are either not "seen" by selectors or are strategically ignored in order to appoint men on "merit" instead.

Regarding gender and affiliational criteria, we assume that women's presence in cabinet will be low in cases where affiliational criteria remain strong over time, though, as our analysis in Chapter 9 shows, it is not quite as straightforward as that. Where gender has been established as representational criterion, we anticipate that the percentage of women included in cabinet will be relatively high. Although we had expected to find that countries

---

[52] Bob Hepburn, *Toronto Start*, November 1, 2015.

with multiple representational rules would make it difficult to add gender to the checklist of criteria, the evidence shows otherwise (see Chapter 10). Before we turn to the gendered consequences of rules about qualification in Chapters 9 and 10, we first assess the gendered consequences of rules about selection in the next chapter.

8

The Gendered Consequences of Rules about Selection

Rules are not neutral. A core insight of institutionalist theories of politics is that rules confer power, advantaging some actors while disadvantaging others (Thelen and Steinmo 1992). Feminist institutionalists have revealed the myriad ways in which rules are created by those with power (historically men), and as a result, tend to reproduce the power relations that existed at the time of their creation. This chapter identifies the gendered consequences of rules that empower and constrain selectors when assembling their cabinets. In Chapter 3, we showed that rules about selection tend to give presidents and prime ministers considerable discretion to assemble their cabinet teams without interference from other political actors. In some of our cases, namely, Canada, Chile, Spain, and the United States, formal and informal rules consistently combine to empower a single selector to choose ministers. In other cases, however, rules constrain selectors by requiring them to share selection power with other actors, or by the threat of removal.

In this chapter, we use insights from research on gender and political recruitment to show how the rules empowering and constraining selectors affect men and women differently. We organize the chapter around two key insights derived from the existing literature on candidate selection and feminist institutionalism:

(1) Who selects, and where and how selection occurs, matter greatly and have gendered consequences (Hinojosa 2012; Norris and Lovenduski 1995).
(2) Selectors are themselves gendered actors (Bjarnegård 2013; Gains and Lowndes 2014; Tremblay and Pelletier 2001).

Research on gender and legislative candidate selection finds that "who selects and how" affect the opportunities and obstacles for women to be selected as parliamentary candidates (Norris and Lovenduski 1993). Women face fewer obstacles when (1) recruitment is centralized in the hands of national party directorates, and (2) recruitment and selection processes are exclusive rather than inclusive. According to Hinojosa, inclusive processes like primaries create an important gendered obstacle, namely, the need to self-nominate (2012, 44). In the absence of a single selector or internal selectorate, potential candidates must self-nominate and, moreover, must face a larger group of selectors among voters in the party primary electorate. Considering extensive research showing that women are less inclined to throw their hat into the ring (see Fox and Lawless 2004; Pruysers and Blais 2017), it is not surprising that women are more likely to emerge as candidates in parties where recruitment is more exclusive, in other words, when there are fewer and known selectors (Hinojosa 2012, 44, 112).

The gendered problem of self-nomination does not exist at the level of cabinet, however. As we showed in Chapter 3, one of the strongest informal rules governing cabinet appointments is that aspirant ministers cannot publicly self-nominate or lobby for a spot in cabinet. Moreover, other political actors cannot visibly interfere in the process of cabinet formation, whether by publicly advocating for someone else's appointment (although they may work privately to advance their preferred candidates) or by actively campaigning against someone. Indeed, cabinet formation is marked by the complete absence of formal, codified processes for recruiting ministers. As a rule, there is nothing akin to the process of securing a nomination for a parliamentary seat: there is no call for nominations; there is no formal application process; and there is no invitation to eligible candidates to apply. Aspirant ministers, whether men or women, must simply await the call from the selector.[1]

Another gendered obstacle frequently found in the gender and recruitment literature emerges when candidate selection occurs at the local level. Here, the need for female aspirants to navigate male-dominated local power monopolies serves as a gendered obstacle (Bjarnegård 2013; Culhane 2017). Hinojosa (2012, 112) finds that local power monopolies hurt women's chances of securing nominations when candidate selection occurs at the local level; when candidate selection is more centralized at the national level, however, more women are selected. Ministerial recruitment, in contrast, is generally centralized in the hands of a single selector, namely, the president or prime minister.

---

[1] The exception, as we have shown, is in the UK Labour and Australian Labor parties, where aspirant ministers have, at times, been required to self-nominate to be considered for cabinet elections.

We use these broad insights to show that rules about ministerial recruitment have important, although sometimes contradictory, gendered consequences. In the first section, we argue that the insights from research into candidate recruitment help us understand the gendered consequences of rules governing presidents and prime ministers in forming cabinets. Yet ministerial recruitment differs in at least one critical way from candidate selection, namely, that there are relatively few *formal* rules about how ministers are to be selected. To these insights, we emphasize an additional difference: few persons (and usually only one) are authorized to appoint cabinet ministers. Unlike electoral gatekeepers—who include party elites, party selection committees, and, ultimately, voters—in most cases, a single actor constructs the cabinet and appoints ministers. We demonstrate that, taken together, the formal and informal rules about who selects ministers combine to provide selectors with significant space to exercise political agency. Rules that empower selectors create gendered opportunities because selectors may use their agency to continue long-standing practices of selecting mostly men for cabinet. Or selectors can use this agency to increase the number of women in cabinet. We illustrate these contrasting outcomes with the examples of two leaders who formed parity cabinets (Canadian prime minister Justin Trudeau and Spanish prime minister José Luis Rodríguez Zapatero) and another leader, Australian prime minister Tony Abbott, who selected only one woman for his cabinet.

Our second section explores the gendered consequences of selection rules that constrain prime ministers and presidents as sole selectors by increasing the number of selectors. Although existing research on gender and political recruitment would lead us to expect that increasing the number of selectors disadvantages women, our findings differ. In some cases, co-selectors are equally or more inclined to appoint women than the primary selector. Also, because rules about who can select interact with rules about who can be selected, we find that in countries that have established relatively high magnitudes of women's inclusion, rules empowering multiple selectors do not disadvantage women. All selectors are bound by rules establishing gender as a representational criterion; where such rules exist, all those involved comply. We refer to this as the concrete floor; and we show how concrete floors emerge in all of our cases in Chapter 11.

In the third section of the chapter, we focus on selectors as gendered actors. Our analysis shows that a selector's sex or his or her commitment to gender equality does not directly predict whether there will be many or few women in cabinet. Both male and female selectors who are committed to increasing women's representation in politics have used their agency to appoint women to cabinet. But there are also instances where even committed selectors are unable to do so. We contrast two cases of female (and feminist) selectors—Michelle Bachelet and Julia Gillard—to test the assumption that female selectors are more likely to appoint female ministers. We focus on the institutional context, investigating how the sex and gender of Bachelet and Gillard intersect with the rules about selector discretion to produce different outcomes.

Formal and Informal Rules and the Gendered Consequences of Political Agency

The starting point of Norris and Lovenduski's process-based model of political recruitment is that candidate selection is "an *interactive process* in which both selectors and aspirants affected outcomes that were organized in several sets of institutions" (Lovenduski 2016, 518, emphasis in original). Even though many political parties have codified rules to select candidates, researchers of recruitment and selection agree that informal rules are usually more determinative than formal party statutes (Bjarnegård and Kenny 2015; Culhane 2017; Piscopo 2016). Likewise, as the previous chapters of this book have shown, informal rules are more plentiful, and often more consequential, than formal rules when it comes to cabinet appointments.

Does it matter in terms of gender whether recruitment is governed by formal or informal rules? Research suggests that it does (Chappell and Waylen 2013; Waylen 2017). The absence of clear, codified rules governing political life, and particularly the recruitment and selection of individuals for political office, makes equality-enhancing reforms more difficult. Around the world, feminists in political parties and civil society have mobilized in pursuit of formal institutional change, such as the adoption of gender quotas, to improve women's access to political office. Gender scholars have noted, however, that such formal rules may be insufficient to bring about gender equality, since informal rules are "sticky," and practices that entrench men's dominance in candidate selection often persist despite formal rule changes (Johnson 2016; Mackay 2014). Moreover, informal but deeply entrenched practices are more difficult to change since there is no clear target for advocacy efforts. In contrast, we find that when it comes to cabinet formation, informal rules are not necessarily disadvantageous to women. Instead, the informal rules governing cabinet appointment create significant space for selectors' political agency, which can be advantageous to women, particularly when political actors are motivated to pursue equality.

Although our data set contains more than one hundred post-election cabinets spanning the years 1933–2016, only five of the cabinets formed had gender parity (and two of them were in Spain). In the following, we discuss two instances where selectors used the extensive powers granted to them to produce favorable outcomes for women: Spanish prime minister Zapatero's first parity cabinet in 2004 and Canadian prime minister Justin Trudeau's parity cabinet in 2015. We find that these two leaders highlighted their commitments to gender equality during their electoral campaigns and made promises about including an equal number of men and women in their cabinets. We also outline one case where a selector, namely, Australian prime minister Tony Abbott, used his political agency in a way that reinforced the status quo to men's advantage. In Australia, Abbott's post-election cabinet in 2013 contained just one woman, representing a backward step, since all post-election cabinets in the previous 10 years had included at least two female ministers, and one cabinet had four.

These three selectors—Zapatero, Trudeau, and Abbott—are good examples of empowered selectors in parliamentary democracies. One is from a left-wing party (Zapatero), one is from a center party (Trudeau), and one is from a right-wing party (Abbott). All three prime ministers were unconstrained in their selection powers; two used their power to appoint gender parity cabinets, but one (Abbott) appointed fewer women to cabinet than had his predecessor, evidencing how rules that empower selectors can be a double-edged sword. Political actors may use their agency to ignore changing ideas about gender and act in ways that reproduce men's advantages in accessing cabinet. Our analysis makes clear that this is not simply a left-right story about party ideology. Although only selectors from left or center parties appointed parity cabinets, we find significant evidence that selectors on the right have initiated significant increases in the representation of women in cabinets. For instance, our data includes four prime ministers from right parties who increased the representation of women to historically high categories of magnitude in their countries. These include Canada's Brian Mulroney, who, in 1984, increased the proportion of women in cabinet from 3.7 to 14.81 percent, and Stephen Harper, who increased women's cabinet representation from 23 to 30.77 percent in 2008; Prime

Minister José María Aznar of Spain, who increased the proportion of women from 17.6 to 26.6 percent in 1996; and the UK Conservative prime minister David Cameron, who appointed women to 33.3 percent of his cabinet in 2015, an increase from 18.8 percent in his 2010 cabinet.

Political Agency and Gender Parity Cabinets: Spain

When the PSOE won Spain's general elections in 2004, the new prime minister, José Luis Rodríguez Zapatero, appointed eight men and eight women to his post-election cabinet. Upon winning a second term in 2008, he appointed nine women and eight men. As discussed in Chapter 3, Spain's prime ministers enjoy high levels of discretion when assembling their cabinets. A former minister explained that when selecting ministers, the prime minister "does not have to consult, either formally or informally, with anyone."[2] Zapatero's discretion in cabinet selection was enhanced further by his decisive victory in the 2000 PSOE leadership contest; he had few ties and owed few debts to the previous generation of party notables (Encarnación 2009; Field 2009). Zapatero's unexpected and decisive victory in the 2004 general election ended eight years of conservative rule, further strengthening his power as sole selector.

Zapatero's progressive views were well known and formed the basis of the party's 2004 electoral campaign. Since becoming party leader, one of Zapatero's main goals was to mobilize segments of the population, particularly social movements and young people, who had been growing progressively disengaged from politics. Zapatero made frequent appeals to feminists, the LGBTQ movement, human rights activists, and to environmentalists; during the electoral campaign, he explicitly described himself as a feminist (Encarnación 2009, 118). According to a former minister, when he won the leadership of the PSOE, "[Zapatero] immediately began to incorporate more women into front lines of party leadership."[3] Women likewise made up a sizable proportion of Zapatero's key advisory committee during the electoral campaign, and many of these women were later appointed to his cabinet. In addition to Zapatero's promise to appoint an equal number of men and women to his cabinet if elected, equality issues figured prominently in the

---

[2] Interview with former minister, May 13, 2014, Madrid.
[3] Interview, May 21, 2012. Madrid.

overall campaign. For example, Zapatero advocated for a new gender-based violence law and for an equality law to increase the number of women elected and appointed in all political institutions.

Zapatero's predecessor, Prime Minister José María Aznar, had already appointed more women to cabinet than the previous socialist government of Felipe González (1982–1996). Zapatero's appointment of a gender parity cabinet more than doubled the percentage of female ministers. Prior to Zapatero's election, Spain had not yet surpassed the 30 percent threshold of women's cabinet inclusion.

The formation of a gender parity cabinet was possible not only because of Zapatero's political agency as the selector. Such agency was undergirded by norms about gender equality that first emerged in the PSOE. As a result of feminist mobilizing in the party, the PSOE had adopted an internal gender quota in 1993. A precedent of a gender parity cabinet had already been set at the regional level, when Manuel Chávez's PSOE government in Andalusia included an equal number of male and female ministers. While Zapatero's decision to appoint a parity cabinet was entirely consistent with his own principled commitment to gender equality, his commitment also found expression and prior support within the broader party (Franceschet and Thomas 2015). In sum, Zapatero represents a clear example of a selector who used his power of discretion to (1) issue a promise of a gender parity cabinet, and (2) act on formal party rules applicable to legislative candidacies (in terms of gender quotas) and on informal norms that feminists in the PSOE and in civil society had been developing for decades, namely, that gender balance in politics is a central principle of democracy.

Political Agency and Gender Parity Cabinets: Canada

Like their Spanish counterparts, Canadian prime ministers wield considerable power in the process of cabinet formation. Neither formal nor informal rules constrain their autonomy when selecting ministers. Canadian leaders can make their choices without consulting their parties or ceding selection power to other actors. Neither the Liberals nor the Conservatives, the only two parties that have held national office, have rules requiring leaders to share ministerial selection with the parliamentary party. Nor must prime ministers consult other party elites. Because single-party governments are the norm, prime ministers do not cede selection powers to other parties.

David Zussman writes, "each prime minister has complete authority over building his or her own Cabinet" (2013, 86).

Conservative prime minister Brian Mulroney was the first Canadian leader who substantially increased the number of female ministers, appointing four women to his post-election cabinet in 1984, quadrupling the number of women in cabinet.[4] Women's inclusion in Canadian cabinets continued to grow throughout the 1990s, and, by 2008, another prime minister from the Conservative Party, Steven Harper, appointed women to 30 percent of cabinet posts, a record high at that point in Canadian history. This record was surpassed when Liberal prime minister Justin Trudeau assembled the country's first gender parity cabinet at the federal level. In early November 2015, Canada garnered international attention when, during the press conference that followed the cabinet swearing-in ceremony, a reporter asked Trudeau why gender parity was such an important goal for his cabinet. The prime minister replied: "Because it's 2015." The comment made global headlines and went viral on social media. Canadians, however, were less surprised by Trudeau's gender parity cabinet since a commitment to gender balance in government had been a key part of his campaign platform. Canadians had also seen three previous examples of gender parity cabinets, albeit at the provincial, not federal, level. Quebec premier Jean Charest formed two consecutive gender parity cabinets, in 2007 and 2008, and Alberta premier Rachel Notley formed a gender parity cabinet in 2015. Quebec's example may have played a role in Trudeau's motivations to have a parity cabinet, since Charest's government was a Liberal government and some of the individuals playing roles in Trudeau's 2015 election campaign had been involved with Quebec's Liberal government.

The Liberal Party's 2015 campaign platform had promised "Government appointments that look like Canada," and that a "Liberal cabinet will have an equal number of women and men."[5] In an interview more than one month before the election, a skeptical reporter asked Trudeau about his promise of gender parity. The reporter wondered how it would be possible to have an equal number of male and female ministers, given that the Liberal Party would clearly not have an equal number of men and women in their parliamentary caucus; just 30 percent of Liberal candidates were women. Trudeau

---

[4] Mulroney's predecessor, Pierre Trudeau, had just one woman in his 1980 initial cabinet, and no Canadian prime minister had ever included more than one woman in his cabinet.

[5] Liberal Party, *Real Change: A Fair and Open Government* (2015, 12).

reinforced his promise of gender parity, saying, "I look forward to showing that women are needed in positions of power. And I certainly hope that, after people see how effective a cabinet with gender balance in it is, we're going to draw even more women into politics in subsequent elections."[6]

Aside from a small number of media columnists who lamented that quotas would undermine the principle of merit, there was remarkably little public criticism of Trudeau's promise of a parity cabinet, and instead, much public praise.[7] During the election campaign, the governing Conservatives paid almost no attention to Trudeau's promise for a gender parity cabinet, instead focusing their criticism on his policy issues or his lack of experience for the demanding role of prime minister. We take the relative absence of public criticism of Trudeau's promises, and later, of his delivery, of a gender-balanced cabinet as evidence that progressive ideas about women's place in politics and society were already widely accepted in Canada, and that openly and publicly criticizing gender parity in cabinet would risk exposing an individual candidate, or a political party, as clinging to outdated ideas about gender roles. As was the case with Zapatero and the PSOE, Trudeau and the Liberal Party leveraged an improved, gendered political opportunity context, unconstrained by formal or informal rules of cabinet selection. As an empowered selector, Trudeau used his considerable discretionary powers to build on inclusionary norms gaining strength in society and examples of gender parity in two Canadian provinces, Alberta and Quebec, to promise and deliver a cabinet with an equal number of female and male ministers.

Political Agency to Exclude Women from Cabinets: Australia

Rules that empower selectors allow them to promise gender parity cabinets; such rules also permit selectors to exclude women from cabinet. Political actors may use their agency to ignore previous practice, to valorize criteria other than gender, or to re-gender cabinets to male advantage. The case of Australian prime minister Tony Abbott and the formation of his right-wing

---

[6] Cormac McSweeney, "Q & A: Toe-to-Toe with Justin Trudeau on His Latest Promises," *Maclean's*, September 9, 2015.

[7] Kate Heartfield, "The Feminist Cabinet-Maker: Why Trudeau's Half-Female Cabinet Could Be Much More Than Symbolic," *Ottawa Citizen*, October 31, 2015; Shari Graydon, "Gender Parity Is More Than Good Optics," *Globe and Mail*, November 4, 2015; David McLaughlin, "Cabinet-Making Tips for the Novice PM," *Globe and Mail*, October 27, 2015.

Liberal Party's post-election cabinet in 2013 show how empowered selectors can act to exclude women from cabinet.

Although Abbott's three predecessors appointed between two and four women to their post-election cabinets, Abbott appointed just one woman to his 18-member cabinet following the general election in September 2013. Before the election, Abbott had said his main priority was to maintain the stability of the team that he created while his party was in opposition. In February 2013, and again throughout the year, he promised, "All of my frontbenchers can expect to be doing the same job in government as they are now."[8] At the time, Abbott's shadow cabinet included three women: Julie Bishop, Sophie Mirabella, and Concetta Fierravanti-Wells. Ultimately, only Bishop was included in Abbott's post-election cabinet, keeping her foreign affairs portfolio. Fierravanti-Wells was excluded, despite the pre-election promise, because of Abbott's "displeasure at [her] performance."[9] Mirabella failed to retain her parliamentary seat of Indi in rural Victoria, and thus could not be included in the new cabinet. In his 18-member post-election cabinet, Abbott included only one woman.

Australian prime ministers have considerable powers to select ministers. Indeed, the only real constraint on Liberal prime ministers in Australia is their need to form coalitions with the National Party. This is a permanent and predictable coalition arrangement, however, and one for which the Liberal Party leader always plans. There is no evidence that this coalitional arrangement has constrained previous Liberal Party leaders from including women in cabinet. Note that Abbott's Liberal Party predecessor, Prime Minister John Howard, appointed multiple women to three of his four post-election cabinets. In 2004, he appointed three—more women than had ever been the case in Australian history. In 2013, Abbott was operating in a context where a higher level of representation of women in cabinet had already been achieved. Since 1996, with only one exception, previous Australian prime ministers had consistently appointed at least two women. As well as the precedent set by his Liberal counterpart, Labor prime ministers Kevin Rudd and Julia Gillard subsequently appointed four and three women to their 2007 and 2010 cabinets, respectively. As one media report put it, "Abbott's new ministry reveals he is not afraid to stare down the zeitgeist on gender equality."[10]

---

8 "Loss Would Leave Just One Woman Standing," *The Australian*, September 12, 2013.

9 "Shorten Likely Labor Leader," *The Age*, September 10, 2013.

10 Janet Albrechtsen "The Unheralded Heroine at the Coalition's Heart," *The Australian*, September 25, 2013.

As in the cases of Zapatero and Trudeau, women in the Liberal Party had mobilized to encourage the inclusion of women in cabinet. In 2013, Abbott faced general pressure to improve women's cabinet presence, and some of this pressure came from within his own party. "Senior Liberals said the prime minister elect should use the reshuffle to promote women into cabinet."[11] When Abbott failed to include more than one woman in his cabinet, he was publicly criticized. For example, Ruth Medd, head of Women on Boards, said, "It's a very nonsense argument but people get away with saying we select on merit. You define merit in your own image."[12]

Abbott clearly did not share these views about the importance of women's representation in politics. Instead, he made a promise to keep women's representation in cabinet contingent on their prior inclusion in his shadow cabinet; he subsequently removed one of them from consideration, post-election (Fierravanti-Wells); and he appointed Ian MacFarlane to replace shadow minister Sophie Mirabella, as minister for innovation, industry, science and research. Abbott did not respond to the structural autonomy he enjoyed as the empowered selector of cabinet ministers by improving (or even maintaining) the record of appointing women to cabinet in Australia. As selector, Abbott used his considerable discretionary powers (1) to campaign on a promise to continue with members of his shadow cabinet in government, if elected; (2) to appoint fewer women to cabinet than had been the case in the four preceding Australian governments; (3) to include only one woman in cabinet, in the context of developing civil society norms that militated for improved political representation of women; and (4) regardless of the political practice, in both major parties, to include at least two women in cabinet, independent of cabinet size. As an unconstrained, autonomous selector, Abbott—unlike Zapatero and Trudeau—used his discretion to construct a cabinet with fewer, rather than more women than had been the case for previous Australian governments. Unlike Zapatero and Trudeau, Abbott did not align himself with feminist values. Recall that Julia Gillard's 2012 "Misogyny and Sexism" parliamentary speech was directed at Abbott as leader of the opposition. In it, Gillard repeated sexist statements Abbott

---

[11] "Libs 'Shocked' by Lack of Women in Cabinet," *The Australian*, September 13, 2013.
[12] Cited in *The Australian*, September 27, 2013.

had made throughout his political career, including the occasion when he asked if it were true that if "men have more power generally speaking than women, is that a bad thing?"[13]

The Gendered Consequences of Empowered Selectors

The contrasting examples of Zapatero, Trudeau, and Abbott demonstrate the importance of political agency in institutional contexts dominated by informal rules. In all three cases, prime ministers Zapatero, Trudeau, and Abbott were fully empowered to make their ministerial selection. In each country, party feminists and equality advocates had succeeded in putting new ideas about the value of women's presence in politics on the public agenda. In the case of Spain, these ideas were put in practice in the form of a gender quota in the PSOE. In Spain and Canada, the prime ministers both responded by appointing gender parity cabinets and, in each case, there was much public support for these historic moves. In Australia, the informal rules permitted Abbott, as selector, to appoint just one woman, ignoring expectations about women's presence and prioritizing an alternative informal rule about the continuation of shadow cabinet. He faced sanction in the form of criticism from within his party and the media more broadly.[14]

Selectors do not operate in isolation from rules about qualification. Prescriptive representational rules about gender set expectations about what a legitimate cabinet should look like, and a concrete floor in each country defines the established level of women's representation. Women's representation in cabinet had already reached the 30 percent magnitude threshold in Canada, and in Spain, Zapatero's predecessors had appointed cabinets with 20 and 26 percent women's representation. In Australia, the bar was much lower, with the highest magnitude ever reached at 18.75 percent. Empowered selectors have agency, but they also respond to the cues of other informal rules.

---

[13] Transcript of Julia Gillard's speech, *The Sydney Morning Herald*, October 10, 2012, http://www.smh.com.au/federal-politics/political-news/transcript-of-julia-gillards-speech-20121009-27c36.html.

[14] Note that Abbott holds the Australian record for the shortest tenure of a Liberal Party prime minister, serving from September 2013 to September 2015, at which point he was replaced as Liberal Party leader by Malcolm Turnbull.

The Gendered Consequences of Constraints on Selectors: Coalitions and Political Parties

There are three circumstances in which presidents or prime ministers share selection powers with other political actors. First, in parliamentary systems, entering a formal coalition requires an otherwise autonomous selector to share ministerial selection powers. Coalition government reduces the chief executive's discretion to choose ministers: a strong informal rule in coalition governments is that prime ministers only have discretion to select the ministers allocated to their party during the process of coalition negotiations. Second, in some political parties, there are rules that empower the caucus or parliamentary party to choose ministers. In such cases, prime ministers cannot necessarily choose the individuals who will be cabinet ministers, but they can allocate ministerial portfolios. Third, some political parties have informal rules that require selectors to consult with other political actors within their party.

Each of these circumstances has the effect of increasing the number of selectors. Following the gender and candidate selection literature, we anticipated that fewer selectors would lead to more favorable outcomes for women than would be the case where multiple selectors are involved. We anticipated that three gendered mechanisms would be in play. First, in the case of coalition constraint, the primary selector has discretion over fewer spots in cabinet, which would, in turn, increase the competition for these positions. We anticipated that the combination of high competition and a tradition of male dominance would disadvantage women in cabinet appointments. Second, because coalitions increase the number of persons involved in the selection process, the inclusion of women in cabinet would require more political actors to be committed to ideas about gender equality or to be persuaded that gender equality is a legitimate and important goal; with a large number of participants involved in the selection process, uncertainty about participant commitment to gender parity increases. Third, and similarly, where selection is directed by multiple members of a party caucus, the larger number of participants should decrease the likelihood of women being appointed as cabinet ministers.

Among our cases, we find no clear pattern of the impact of centralization and larger numbers of selectors on women's inclusion in cabinets. The unanticipated UK Conservative–Liberal Democrat coalition in 2010 likely reduced the number of women that a single-party Conservative cabinet might have produced; party rules restricting sole selector powers in the Australian Labor and UK Labour parties may have had the same effect. Germany, however, the country in which selectors consistently experience multiple constraints, has strong gender equality in cabinet. German coalition cabinets feature a higher share of women than single-party governments in Australia and the United Kingdom. Clearly, it is not just about the number of selectors.

Gendered Consequences of Coalition Constraints: The United Kingdom and Germany

The 2010 UK election failed to deliver a parliamentary majority to the Conservative Party, led by David Cameron. Rather than forming a minority government, Cameron opted to form a coalition with the Liberal Democrats. In so doing, Cameron had to share the task of ministerial recruitment with Nick Clegg, the leader of the Liberal Democrats. The result of negotiations, Cameron had discretion over 17 spots in cabinet; his Liberal Democrat coalition partner had five.

Prior to the election, Cameron sought to improve his party's standing with women voters by promising to appoint women to one-third of government posts. Post-election and in coalition, Cameron selected five women for his 17 cabinet slots (or 29.41 percent), thereby coming very close to meeting his pre-election commitment. Cameron's coalition partner, Nick Clegg, failed to appoint any women, producing a cabinet where women held just 18.8 percent of all posts, falling far short of Cameron's one-third pledge. Media reports noted how Cameron's situation had "been made worse by the Liberal Democrats, the supposed mould-breakers of politics, who didn't select a single woman to take up one of their five cabinet seats."[15] A junior minister appointed to the Liberal Democrat team, Lynne Featherstone, was said to lament "the 'male and pale' line-up" of the coalition government.[16]

Germany offers an interesting contrast. The German Basic Law formally empowers the chancellor to select ministers. In practice,

[15] "The Election's Biggest Loser Is Us, Ladies," *The Sunday Times*, May 16, 2010.
[16] "Counting the Cabinet," *The Times*, May 15, 2010.

however, all German chancellors have had to share selection powers. Since Germany's electoral system does not produce parliamentary majorities, coalition government has been the result. In these cases, the chancellor has no say over ministerial appointments of the coalition partner. A former German minister explained, "The Chancellor would never get involved in the choice of ministers from the . . . coalition. It is an unwritten rule that the coalition partner decides on its own ministers."[17] In coalition, German governments have nonetheless produced impressive levels of women's cabinet representation. Germany was the first country among our cases to cross the 30 percent threshold, under the chancellorship of Gerhard Schröder in 1998. Since then, a clear and consistent pattern has emerged. In four post-election cabinets, at least 30 percent of cabinet posts were given to women: two Social Democrat (SPD)–Green coalitions led by Schröder (1998, 2002), and two Christian Democrat (CDU)–SPD grand coalitions led by Merkel (2005, 2013). In only one instance was women's presence in a post-election cabinet lower than 30 percent: the CDU–Free Democrat (FPD) coalition led by Merkel in 2009. Even in this case, the decline was marginal, with women appointed to 26.6 percent of cabinet posts.

Increasing the number of selectors does not automatically or consistently reduce the number of women in cabinet. Co-selectors in the form of coalition partners who are equally committed to gender equality can use their political agency to include women among their cabinet picks. For example, Germany's Green Party, as junior partners in coalition with the SPD in 1998 and 2002, ensured that their ministerial nominations took gender equality into account. Similarly, in the Merkel-led Grand Coalitions formed in 2005 and 2013, the SPD as co-selector nominated three women among its allocation of eight portfolios in 2005 (or 37.5 percent) and three of six in 2013 (or 50 percent). In contrast, in 2009, when the CDU formed a coalition with the Liberal FDP—"a party that opposed quotas"[18]—the junior partner nominated just one woman among its allocated five cabinet posts (or 20 percent). In Germany, there is a strong norm of women's representation across all parties that might form a governing coalition, with the exception of the FDP.

---

[17] Interview, October 29, 2014.
[18] Interview with former minister, October 29, 2014.

Gendered Consequences of Party Selectorates: The United Kingdom, Australia, and Germany

As the gender and candidate selection literature has documented, party selectorates operate as additional barriers to women seeking access to political office (Kenny 2013). The UK Labour Party, built on strong male working class and trade unionist traditions, traditionally prioritized class over gender (Lovecy 2007), and could be expected to impede a single selector's attempt to construct a cabinet that included relatively large numbers of women. In Australia, the Labor Party (ALP) caucus features a cleavage between the party's right, influenced by Catholic social teaching, and its left, influenced by traditional labor-market protectionist beliefs (Kent 2009, 145; Sawer 2013, 108); such a cleavage, combined with the role of the party in selection of ministers, similarly could be expected to constrict the ministerial possibilities for women. Nonetheless, our cases show that, in these parties, increasing the number of selectors does not predict that a cabinet therefore will include fewer women.

In Australia and the United Kingdom, some prime ministers lose discretion over ministerial appointments because formal party rules require them to hand the selection of ministers over to the parliamentary party. As Chapter 3 explained, these rules were introduced by the UK Labour Party and the Australian Labor Party to secure a strong voice for the collective parliamentary party vis-à-vis executive leadership of the party. In the United Kingdom, the Parliamentary Labour Party (PLP), when in opposition, had the power to elect shadow ministers who subsequently would become members of the cabinet after a successful general election. The practice of shadow cabinet elections in the PLP took place annually until 2010, when the formal rules were changed to empower the party leader as sole selector. In Australia, caucus elections take place when the party is in government, although there are instances when prime ministers can exercise agency to amend a list or, following strong electoral results, choose ministers themselves. Rules empowering parliamentary parties over prime ministers may be declining in force, but their existence has over time had a strong impact in terms of the gendered composition of cabinets in the United Kingdom and Australia.

The rules in the UK Labour and Australian Labor parties increase the size of the selectorate and thereby change the dynamics of ministerial recruitment. Rather than *ministrables* waiting patiently for the call from the prime minister, these party rules mean that aspiring ministers must "lobby hard" to secure strong support of the parliamentary party that elects the shadow cabinet (Ryan 1999a, 211).[19] In his analysis of UK shadow cabinet elections from 1955 to 1963, Punnett (1964) found that there was little turnover on the lists, making it hard for newcomers to secure a place among shadow cabinet ministers. This was reinforced by the fact that there were "a lot of blocs in the PLP, Scots voting for Scots and so on."[20] Both situations present the gendered obstacles identified in Hinojosa's study of candidate selection (2012): the need to self-nominate and lobby for a cabinet spot and the need to navigate male-dominated power monopolies.

Australian Labor Party (ALP) caucus elections have been identified as one of the biggest hurdles to women in executive office (Ryan 1999a), in part due to the strong masculinist factions within the party (Summers 2003). The first female ALP minister, Susan Ryan, appointed in 1983, wrote, "factional party power stymied more women than parliament" (Ryan 1999a, 138). None of the five post-election Labor governments appointed 1983–1993 included more than one female minister. More women are selected only when ALP prime ministers manage to assert their authority over the rules of caucus selection. Following successful elections, prime ministers Kevin Rudd and Julia Gillard were permitted to bypass the formal rule and to make their own ministerial appointments as a "reward" for returning the party to government.[21] In 2007 Rudd appointed four women to cabinet (or 20 percent) and was, according to an Australian Labor Party politician, "very good at appointing women to key portfolios."[22] In 2010, Gillard used her selection power to appoint three women (or 15.79 percent). When Labor moved back into opposition in 2013, caucus selection rules were reinstated, and were again criticized by women in the party. The former speaker of the House of Representatives, Anna Burke, depicted faction leaders as "faceless men" who were "firmly in control" of the ministerial selection process, to the detriment of women who hoped for a "meritorious selection."[23]

In the United Kingdom, rules empowering the Parliamentary Labour Party (PLP) to elect ministers to shadow cabinets (and thus to cabinet, if the party moves from opposition to government) were judged detrimental to

---

[19] Interview with former minister, December 17, 2013.
[20] Ibid.
[21] Interview with former minister, March 23, 2010.
[22] Interview with Australian Labor Party politician, March 20, 2010.
[23] David Crowe, "Fraction too much faction in Labor 'cabal'," *The Australian*, October 14, 2013. See also Dowding and Lewis 2015, 47.

women's representation (Harman 2017, 132). Feminist campaigning within the party, backed by supportive male party leaders such as Neil Kinnock, led to a series of formal rule changes to PLP shadow cabinet elections that ultimately improved the gender imbalance. Initially, the power of selection was retained by the PLP, but the size of the shadow cabinet was increased from 12 in 1979 to 15 in 1982, 18 in 1992, and 19 in 1995, to create more openings for women.[24] The new voting rules for the 1992 shadow cabinet election specified that the three women getting the highest number of votes would be included in the shadow cabinet, even if they were not among the top 18 candidates, based on votes alone. Between 1993 and 1996, MPs were required to vote for at least four women, with the sanction that ballot papers would otherwise be invalidated.

These formal rule changes were controversial within the Labour Party and were strongly resisted by incumbent men through tactics of hostility, ridicule, and sabotage. Harman (2017, 133–134) recalls how the new rules to promote women in the shadow cabinet were referred to derogatorily as the "Assisted Places Scheme"[25] within the PLP and the "Tarts' Charter" in the House of Commons bars. She describes how opponents who now "had to put up with the new scheme" made sure that those who had advocated the reforms were not beneficiaries of it, but rather "felt the full force of backlash" (2017, 134). Opponents of the new rules tried to sabotage the scheme by "dumping" votes on women (2017, 134). Harman explains,

> Opponents of the new scheme hatched a plan to "dump" their votes on the most "useless" women, in the hope that, if the votes could be spread out thinly, no woman would win enough to be elected. Some MPs actually wanted a "useless" woman to be elected, thinking that, then, the whole scheme could be discredited and abandoned. (2017, 134).

Despite resistance and sabotage, the rule change was effective. By the time Labour was elected to government in 1997, there were five women in the elected shadow cabinet. These five women were selected by the PLP and were not Blair's ministerial picks.[26] This example of rule change in the Parliamentary Labour Party demonstrates the effectiveness of addressing

---

[24] Interview with former UK minister, December 17, 2013.
[25] "A derogatory reference to the highly unpopular (with Labour MPs) government scheme to pay for low-income children to go to private school" (Harman 2017, 134).
[26] Interview with former advisor, July 11, 2016.

gender inequalities in institutional sites that interact with cabinets. This is another example of how constraints on selector discretion need not be detrimental to women's ministerial representation. If party feminists are able to secure formal rule changes, this can ensure the selection of women.

The German case also shows how increasing the number of selectors need not be detrimental to women's presence in cabinet. Although parties in Germany do not play a formal role in voting for the chancellor's ministerial nominations for cabinet, there are strong informal rules requiring chancellors to consult with party elites in the process of ministerial selection. The degree of consultation varies according to party.[27] Kaiser and Fischer (2009, 153 fn 4) explain that "[i]n the German case the effective selectorate in the ministerial appointment process is a small group consisting of parliamentary and party leaders, including the most influential leaders of the *Länder* party associations, the exception being the Free Democrats (FDP) where ministerial appointments are usually more formally decided upon in a joint meeting of the parliamentary party and the party executive."

Again, despite increasing the size of the effective selectorate, Germany has been a front runner in terms of gender equality in cabinet, consistently delivering cabinets with strong representation of women. Here, the process of party consultation functions to help chancellors identify qualified women from across the party, and across the regions. In the process of consultation, the chancellor's advisors will scan for potential ministers. When asked about how she was selected for ministerial office, one former minister said, "the chancellor, then Schröder, most probably with Walter Steinmeyer, the minster for the chancellor's office, [. . .] they got together and thought it through and probably thought, let's ask [name of female minister]."[28] This process of consultation also allows groups within the party to lobby for ministers from among their members. One such group is the *Arbeitsgemeinschaft Sozialdemokratisher Frauen*.[29] A former minister explained: "In each party—and it's exactly the same in the CDU as the SPD—there are groups that say—for example the Jusos say we want a young face, it's clear what the ASF wants; [. . .] it could be the *Mittelstand* in the CDU. It's not that they sit on Merkel or Schröder's lap and say 'you must, you must,' but he knows. And if he doesn't know, then he has people who know that for him. And those people say, 'she

[27] Interview with expert on German executive politics, October 28, 2014.
[28] Interview with former minister, October 29, 2014.
[29] Association of Social Democratic Women.

would perform well in cabinet,' and he says, 'aha, she has this background and that background.'"[30] In Germany, the process of consultation, and the inclusion of gender as a consideration, combine to produce cabinets that include women, even in a context where several persons are involved in the identification and selection of ministers.

In sum, we expected that increasing the number of selectors would lead to poor outcomes in terms of gender parity in cabinet. Contrary to our prediction, this was not consistently the case. What makes the difference across these cases is the variation in the gendered standpoints of the co-selectors. Where co-selectors—whether in an individual or a party—are committed to gender equality, then the outcome need not be detrimental. In the United Kingdom and Australia, the parties that were preventing selectors from reaching higher outcomes themselves had masculinist gendered cultures that disadvantaged female *ministrables* and disadvantaged the sole female selector herself.

Selectors as Gendered Actors Working with Rules about Ministerial Recruitment

Feminist political scientists have shown that women holding executive power are assigned different gendered attributes than male selectors, in terms of their competence, authority, and motivations (Duerst-Lahti and Kelly 1996; Murray 2010). All selectors, men and women, are expected to conform to the gender norms associated with their sex, what Chappell (2005) calls the "gendered logic of appropriateness." Gains and Lowndes (2014) acknowledge that those working with rules are themselves gendered actors. The offices of president and prime minister are replete with masculinist assumptions about power, leaving male and female selectors differently empowered in practice (Duerst-Lahti and Kelly 1996). Although it might be expected that a female president or prime minister would appoint more women to cabinet than her male counterparts might select, we find that a selector's sex is not a good predictor of whether there will be many or few women in cabinet. We have five female selectors in our seven country cases,[31] one of whom, Michelle

---

[30] Interview with former minister, October 27, 2014.
[31] Margaret Thatcher, United Kingdom, 1979–1990; Angela Merkel, Germany, 2005–; Michelle Bachelet, Chile, 2006–2010 and 2014–2018; Julia Gillard, Australia, 2010–2013; and Theresa May, United Kingdom, 2015–2019.

Bachelet, appointed a parity cabinet, and another, Margaret Thatcher, who appointed no women to any of her three post-election cabinets. We argue that female selectors' propensity to appoint other women to cabinet is not attributable to their sex, and not even the degree of their commitment to gender equality. Rather, the institutional context plays an important role in determining whether female selectors appoint women to their cabinets.

The contrasting cases of Chilean president Michelle Bachelet and Australian prime minister Julia Gillard show the centrality of institutional context and how it intersects with the selectors' sex and gender. Each woman was the first woman to hold executive office in her country; both served as leaders in the second decade of the twenty-first century. Although we recognize that both male and female selectors are gendered actors, in this section, we offer these two illustrations of women operating in political environments saturated by gendered ideas about leadership, and we outline how rules empowering selectors intersect with the selectors' own gender and the broader institutional context to produce varying gendered outcomes.

Julia Gillard, Australia's first female prime minister and leader of the Australian Labor Party (ALP), formed a cabinet following the general election in 2010. She appointed three women to cabinet, fewer than her predecessor, Kevin Rudd, who had appointed four (20 percent), including Gillard herself. Having successfully led tricky negotiations with one Green and two Independent MPs to allow the Australian Labor Party to form a minority government, Gillard had permission to form her own government independently, rather than accepting a slate from the ALP caucus. The media speculated that "within the Labor Party Gillard will enjoy enhanced authority; it is her skill, discipline and will-to-power that has kept Labor in office and saved the party and herself from a historic humiliation."[32] Nevertheless, Gillard chose to consult with her party on ministerial appointments—"it is understood Ms Gillard is consulting more than Mr Rudd on her ministerial line-up"[33]—but "Ms Gillard reserv[ed] the ultimate right to determine who would form her new team."[34] Gillard's discretionary selection powers were confirmed by the incumbent health minister Nicola Roxon, who stated that while she would be eager to continue in her present portfolio, "ultimately . . . it's really up to the

[32] "Recipe for Uncertain Government," *The Australian*, September 8, 2010.
[33] "Gillard Asks MPs to Name Wish List," *The Australian*, September 10, 2010.
[34] Ibid.

Prime Minister to work out where we can all be best used [. . .] And that's something that I will accept."[35]

In practice, Gillard was not afforded the full authority that derived from her position as prime minister and as a leader who negotiated her party's return to government. We argue that her ability to exercise the power conferred by formal and informal rules on ministerial selection was limited by her gender. A feminist, Gillard later became known for calling out "sexism and misogyny" in Australian politics in 2012. Yet, at the start of her term as prime minister in 2010, Gillard "tried to behave so carefully as prime minister to try to minimize the gender card being used against her" (Johnson 2015, 306). Her gender was a contentious public issue, and she was under constant scrutiny as a woman. She was the first prime minister who was "not a man in suit"; she came to power through an inner party coup that was deemed "unusually bloodthirsty for a woman" (Johnson 2015, 303), transgressing the expected behavior of women. Much attention was paid to the fact that she was not married, and does not have children.

Gillard reflected in her autobiography *My Story* that on becoming prime minister she decided she "would not campaign on being the first woman. It was so obvious that it did not need constant reference" (Gillard 2014, 113). She emphasizes the ways her discretion and authority as prime minister, and her ability to use that discretion to promote gender equality, were constrained by both sex and gender (Gillard 2014). She writes, "as Australia's first female prime minister, I came to see the outlines of the bars of [my gender prison]. But of all the experiences I had as prime minister, gender is the hardest to explain, to catch, to quantify" (2014, 98). "Gender 'doesn't explain everything' about my prime ministership, 'it doesn't explain nothing; it explains some things'" (2014, 98). As Gillard concluded, "by the end of my prime ministership, political commentators were recognizing that I had faced more abuse because I was the first woman" (2014, 113). Gillard's perception is that her gender meant that she received less deference than had conventionally been shown to male prime ministers (2014, 97–114). She describes operating in "an environment in which it became unremarkable to treat me with less respect than is normally accorded a prime minister" (2014, 82). Referring to her treatment by the media, the opposition, and, despite having returned her party to government, other members of her own party, Gillard speculated

---

[35] "Minister Resigns as PM Juggles New Portfolios," *The Australian*, September 9, 2010.

that her gender explained the "calculated disrespect" (2014, 97) directed toward her.

Rather than bowing out of politics at the 2010 election, Kevin Rudd, former Labor Party leader and Gillard's predecessor as prime minister, impinged on Gillard's power of selector discretion by insisting on being made foreign secretary. Instead of doing the "decent thing and retiring at the 2010 election," Rudd sought to "sabotage the campaign" (Gillard 2014, 42–43). Gillard was "reluctant to give him the position of Foreign Minister, knowing he would try to refuse instruction from me" but she "had little choice: I had to stop what I considered to be the acts of treachery on his part" (2014, 43). From Gillard's perspective, Rudd embarked on a "remorseless pursuit of a return to the leadership" (2014, 90) and another former ally, Martin Ferguson, switched allegiances to support Rudd, a man he had "long despised" (2014, 80). This was a move that Gillard believed to be "fuelled by a deep resentment of my advancement in politics to a status above his own" (2014, 83).

Julia Gillard's power to act in feminist ways was also constrained by the institutional context in which she acted. Australian politics is characterized by regular elections, high party-leadership turnover, and precarious, short-term governments, making it harder to sustain governments across time and weakening the position of party leaders and prime ministers. The Australian Labor Party is strongly divided along factional lines, which define governments, cabinet formation, and leadership contests; in addition, the gendered culture of the party is not welcoming to women. Although Gillard had carefully negotiated the formation of an Australian Labor Party–led minority government, this success, rather than empowering her within her party, put her in a more precarious political situation.

Ultimately, the political context in which Gillard formed her post-election cabinet limited her ability to act on feminist principles and to use her discretion as prime minister to break dramatically with past practice by appointing a greater proportion of women to cabinet. When it came to ministerial selection, Gillard was constrained in her capacity to act on her commitment to gender equality; she felt that she had to play down this commitment and could not act as a feminist in the same way that a male selector could. Gillard is an example of a gender equality advocate whose powers of selector discretion were constrained by limitations common to all Australian Labor Party prime ministers and intensified by her gender and status as a woman. As she asked in *My Story* (2014, 98), "Is that why less respect flows—because the gender roles just do not seem quite right?"

When Michelle Bachelet became Chile's first female president in 2006, she kept her campaign promise to appoint a gender parity cabinet. Her post-election cabinet included 10 women and ten men. Chile's constitution gives sole appointment authority to presidents, and strong informal rules likewise proscribe other actors from infringing on this discretion. Although Chilean presidents always head coalition rather than single-party governments, the separation of executive and legislative powers gives presidents more secure power to select cabinets than is the case for prime ministers in parliamentary systems. There are strong informal rules in Chile that coalition parties be proportionally represented in cabinet (an informal rule known as the *cuoteo*), but the president, not the coalition partners, selects all ministers. According to a former minister, "there is no negotiation. The president decides."[36] Another said, "the president can designate alone. Absolutely alone."[37]

During the 2005 election campaign, Bachelet explicitly promised gender equality in cabinet, a promise that some political elites viewed with concern. They worried that male party elites with long-established trajectories in leadership positions would be passed over for cabinet posts in favor of women, many of whom were not well known politically. In Chile, however, as in Canada and Spain, overt public criticisms of Bachelet's promises about gender parity were relatively muted. At the level of public discourse, politicians from across the party spectrum agreed that Chile's poor showing in terms of electing women to congress and, compared to other Latin American countries, lower rates of women's labor force participation, were problematic. As a result, party leaders did not openly criticize Bachelet's promises about gender parity.

Gender played out in several interesting ways when Bachelet formed her post-election cabinet in 2006. First, gendered perceptions about Bachelet in her role as president (and therefore selector of ministers) produced concerns among party elites about her lack of communication over the two-week period during which she was assembling her cabinet. Although formal and informal procedural rules about selection empower presidents to make the ultimate decision about appointments, there are nonetheless competing informal rules that encourage communication between party leaders and the president, and some degree of input from party leaders is expected. In the week before Bachelet announced her cabinet, the media reported concerns among party

---

[36] Interview, January 8, 2013, Santiago.
[37] Interview, August 11, 2014.

leaders that the president was too "distant" and that party leaders were being left out of the process.[38] In an interview, a former party president, using clearly gendered language, said: "With presidents Aylwin, Frei, and Lagos, the process [of cabinet formation] was very political. It was discussed a lot with the parties. With Michelle Bachelet, it was [different], as if she were a queen, as if one could not pressure her too much, couldn't ask her for too much."[39]

Perceptions about Bachelet's "distance" and aloofness are highly gendered, since Bachelet did not belong to the "old boys' networks" within the parties. Chile's party elite is strikingly homogenous: it is composed mainly of men, and men from a similar class background, all of whom attended a small handful of elite private schools, attended the same university, and live in the same neighborhoods in Santiago (Joignant, Perello, and Torres 2014). Bachelet's gender, and the fact that it placed her outside of elite party networks, thus contributed to party leaders' perceptions that she was not conforming to established practices with respect to cabinet formation.

During the 2005 election campaign and in her first year as president, Michelle Bachelet was often subject to political rhetoric that questioned her competence and leadership skills through a gendered lens (Thomas 2011). One of her critics coined the term *cariñocracia*, from the Spanish word "caring" (*cariño*), to imply that Bachelet's popularity with citizens was linked to voters' (gendered) perceptions about her empathy rather than her leadership skills (Franceschet and Thomas 2015).

Second, the institutional context for cabinet formation in Chile provided some protection to Bachelet in her appointment of a gender parity cabinet. In Chile's presidential system, the separation of powers means that presidents are not dependent on parties or on support from the legislative branch; they cannot be removed from office for mere political reasons. Presidents are thereby more institutionally empowered to take some risks than are prime ministers. In this context, Bachelet took the modest risk of appointing equal numbers of women and men to cabinet posts.

Third, the institutional context gave support to Bachelet's principled commitments to gender equality. She frequently spoke about the importance of bringing more women into politics, a call that resonated with concerns about sexism in Chilean society, particularly among women (Thomas 2011).

---

[38] M. Garrido and F. Torreabla, "Formación de gabinete entra en recta final," *El Mercurio*, January 21, 2006.
[39] Interview, August 18, 2014, Santiago.

Indeed, although Bachelet followed procedural rules and asked party leaders for their recommendations for cabinet, she reminded leaders of her intention to have gender balance in cabinet. She explicitly "asked the parties for lists with names of men and women. She demanded that there be women and men on the lists."[40] In addition to appointing an equal number of women and men to cabinet, Bachelet substantially increased the number of women in key positions throughout government.

Finally, Bachelet was well positioned to appoint a gender parity cabinet by the actions of the previous president in constructing his cabinet. Bachelet's immediate predecessor, Socialist president Ricardo Lagos, had appointed a record number of five women to cabinet (29.4 percent). Bachelet took the further step of appointing a gender parity cabinet. These factors—gender-based criticism by the established party elite, public support for improving women's political representation, institutional protection against removal from office, and a prior positive example of an increase in the number of female cabinet ministers—empowered Bachelet to make a promise about a gender parity cabinet, a promise she was able to keep.

Selectors as Gendered Actors

Bachelet and Gillard—both feminists—used their political agency as selectors very differently. Bachelet formed Chile's first gender parity cabinet, while Gillard appointed women to just 15 percent of her cabinet posts. The contrasting cases of Michelle Bachelet and Julia Gillard reveal the importance of the selector's own gender as mediated by the institutional and political context. In Chile, political party elites were skeptical rather than hostile to the president's gender equality commitments, and the public was broadly supportive of Bachelet's promises of political renovation and inclusion; moreover, Bachelet was more institutionally secure and freer to take risks in cabinet formation. The political climate in Australia was far less propitious for using cabinet formation to make a statement about the importance of gender equality. Gillard's party, the opposition, and the media were actively hostile to her as prime minister and as a woman—hostility that constrained her range and choice of action. Gillard made no promise to appoint women to cabinet, and she did not assert herself as a woman holding public office.

---

[40] Interview with former minister, August 11, 2014, Santiago.

Furthermore, in a Westminster parliamentary democracy, Gillard was more constrained by the relative ease with which her parliamentary party could remove her as prime minister.[41] Gillard came into office having deposed her preceding party leader and sitting prime minister, Kevin Rudd, and, within a short period of time, had to form a government and lead the Australian Labor Party into a national election. Like her predecessor, Gillard was precariously positioned, easily removable as a result of institutional and party rules and lacking a Labor majority in the Australian parliament.

These two cases underscore the importance of system rules that empower and constrain selectors. Despite facing some hostility and sexist attacks, Bachelet had sufficient support in civil society and sufficient institutional security to promise a gender parity cabinet. Gillard, lacking such support in her own party, and institutionally insecure in her tenure as prime minister, made no promises about women's political representation in her cabinet and, indeed, felt she had to efface herself as a woman in the context of her campaign. In a context of unsupportive public opinion and sexist hostility, institutional security may embolden a female selector to include women in her cabinet; in the absence of such security, the combination of hostility and misogyny limits opportunities for feminist assertion of gender parity, even by a prime minister.

Ultimately, in both cases, the sex of the selector had major political meaning and consequences for cabinet formation. For Gillard, structurally unprotected from potential removal as party leader, being a woman in the Australian electoral and party context of 2010–2013 was a disability. Bachelet, institutionally guaranteed a four-year (non-renewable) term as president, could withstand personal attacks against her as a woman. In sum, what it means to be a woman as the selector of cabinets depends upon the gendered meanings of sex and politics in the selector's party and political systems; variation in these meanings can be politically empowered by the institutional arrangements that secure the selector's discretion.

Conclusion: The Gendered Impact of Cabinet Selection Rules

Political recruitment is gendered in process and outcome. In terms of process, those who are doing the recruiting are gendered actors, working with

---

[41] Gillard faced two leadership challenges within her party, in 2012 (which she won) and in 2013 (which she lost).

rules that are saturated by ideas and norms about the appropriate roles and behavior of women and men. Gendered processes, not surprisingly, produce gendered outcomes: historically, men have been over-represented as the single selectors of cabinet ministers,[42] and men have been over-represented among ministers selected for cabinet. The data for our seven country cases, however, show that male selectors have been increasingly willing to appoint women to cabinet, with men's dominance among cabinet ministers declining fairly significantly in Germany, Spain, Canada, and Chile, and slowly waning in the United Kingdom and the United States.

Feminist scholars of candidate selection encourage a closer examination of the procedural dimensions of political recruitment, in order to see how gender operates in the different stages of legislative recruitment and selection. One of the most significant gendered barriers to women in legislative recruitment does not apply to ministerial recruitment, namely, the problem of self-nomination. A strong informal rule for cabinet selection is that aspirants do not lobby or actively seek an appointment.[43] Moreover, the selection of legislative candidates involves multiple selectors; in contrast, there are few selectors who function as veto players in appointing cabinet ministers, and usually only one: the president or prime minister. Hence, two important gendered obstacles particular to legislative candidate selection are absent in the process of selecting cabinet ministers.

Other gendered barriers found by scholars of women and candidate selection, namely, rules that are informal rather than formal, are magnified in ministerial recruitment compared to legislative recruitment. Comparative studies of gender and legislative recruitment find that women are disadvantaged when processes are governed by informal rather than formal rules. For candidate selection, there is considerable variation, both cross-nationally and within countries, in terms of how formalized (that is, where selection is governed by codified and publicly available rules) the process for recruiting and selecting candidates is. There is little variation in the process of cabinet formation across countries, given that no countries have formal rules spelled out in constitutions to structure the process of ministerial recruitment. Most

---

[42] Among our seven country cases, only Australia, Canada, Chile, Germany, and the United Kingdom have ever had a woman as prime minister or president, and only the United Kingdom has had more than one ($n = 2$).

[43] Of course, there are some exceptions that prove the rule. In some cases of contested leadership or negotiating support for leadership bids, political competitors (or even rivals) may make deals where support for a leadership bid is traded for a future cabinet spot. These are fairly rare exceptions.

constitutions say little beyond indicating that the president or prime minister shall select cabinet ministers.

Informal rules and, in some cases, formal party rules that increase the number of selectors do not predict gendered outcomes in cabinet. In other words, cabinets with many women or few women cannot be directly tied to rules about who selects ministers and whether there is a single selector or multiple co-selectors. Instead, rules about who selects ministers matter because they determine how much space for political agency actors enjoy. In the countries we examined, most selectors enjoy considerable autonomy to form their cabinets without consulting or negotiating with other actors.[44] Selectors share power with other actors only in Germany, where coalition governments are routine, and informal party rules require chancellors to consult with the party leadership, and in the Australian Labor and UK Labour parties, where the parliamentary party has historically played a key role. Elsewhere, prime ministers and presidents enjoy undisputed and sole authority to choose their team.

Rules that empower selectors have important gendered consequences, insofar as selectors are empowered to select women and/or men as cabinet ministers; in every case, the sex balance among the members of the cabinet will be gendered by the preferences of the prime minister or president authorized to appoint them. More specifically, selectors with their own commitments to gender equality can use their agency to achieve favorable outcomes for women. Selectors like Justin Trudeau, Michelle Bachelet, and José Luis Rodríguez Zapatero used their selection powers to increase women's presence in cabinet, sending strong signals to the political class and to society about the importance of gender equality at the highest level of government. As we note, however, selectors may also use their agency to gender their cabinets to advantage men by disregarding public (and party) pressure to improve women's representation, as did Australian prime minister Tony Abbott.

In *Political Recruitment*, Norris and Lovenduski (1995) conceptualize political recruitment as an interactive process through which those who select and those who are selected are linked. Such a dynamic applies to cabinet as well. Rules that confer political agency on selectors permit them to establish

---

[44] Even in the United States, where the Senate must confirm presidential cabinet nominees, the Senate generally confirms presidential preferences and has no specific selection powers of its own.

new criteria—such as women's inclusion in cabinet in greater numbers—that subsequently develop into new rules about who can be selected.

This interactive dimension of cabinet formation establishes a country's concrete floor, from which selectors use their agency to increase the number of women in cabinet, creating new expectations about women's inclusion that take hold as informal rules, thus affecting future processes of cabinet appointment. Concrete floors are evident in all our countries, albeit at different levels. The concept is helpful because it evidences the interactive and dynamic components of the selector's appointment authority and helps to explain why, across all our cases, and despite changes in the party of government, we see very little reduction in women's cabinet presence. When the numbers of women in a country's cabinet decrease, from one government to the next, such decline is relatively minimal and short-lived. In sum, rules about selection matter because they create space for political agency; how actors use their power can create newly gendered informal rules that become locked in as concrete floors, leading to sustained levels of women's inclusion in cabinet.

9

The Gendered Consequences of Qualifying Criteria

How do rules about qualifying for cabinet appointment affect men and women differently? As discussed in Chapters 4 through 7, qualifying criteria take three forms. Experiential criteria include previous political experience, policy expertise relevant to a portfolio, and educational background. Affiliational criteria refer to membership in the selector's personal network as a friend, political ally, or contemporary who evidences loyalty and trust. Finally, representational criteria are membership(s) in political, territorial, or social groups that appear on the selector's "representational checklist." Applying Ostrom's framework (1986) to these three types of qualifying criteria, with rules either prescribing, prohibiting, or permitting, we find that while affiliational criteria are permitted, experiential and representational criteria are the most prescriptive. Chapter 5 showed that all *ministrables* must meet experiential criteria, although the experience or credentials that ministers must possess are non-specific and flexible, thereby allowing selectors considerable latitude in their application. Chapter 6 showed that rules do not prohibit selectors from appointing their trusted friends and allies; hence, in practice, rules permit presidents and prime ministers to apply affiliational criteria to filter the pool of potential *ministrables*. It is only with representational criteria that rules are strongly prescriptive and unambiguous, requiring selectors to appoint individuals with the specific territorial, social, or party identities that are on the selector's representational checklist.

This chapter outlines the ways in which the ambiguity and flexibility of qualifying criteria create different opportunities for men and women to be selected for cabinet. As argued in Chapter 5, political experience and policy expertise are flexible and elastic standards, allowing selectors to justify any of their cabinet appointments post hoc on the basis of experiential criteria. Such justifications are employed by selectors both to exclude and include women among their cabinet appointments. In more recent years, the degree to which affiliational criteria are automatically disadvantageous to women depends on who the selector is and the degree of homogeneity of the selector's network, that is, whether the network includes women as well as men. The gendered nature of representational criteria historically was clear but invisible: selectors were permitted to form all-male cabinets in the absence of a representational criterion prescribing women's inclusion. More recently, representational criteria are gendered to women's advantage where informal rules about gender entrench "concrete floors" in terms of the minimum number or proportion of women believed necessary for a cabinet to be perceived as legitimate.[1] Such concrete floors are established when selectors and feminists in political parties work to make "women" a politically relevant demographic group, requiring inclusion in cabinet, and empowering selectors to use their agency to set new rules about appointing women to cabinet. In the following, we describe the gendered consequences of experiential and affiliational qualifying criteria; in Chapter 10, we consider representational criteria and their gendered consequences.

Experiential Criteria through a Gendered Lens

Feminist scholars have extensively documented the myriad ways that political institutions reinforce male dominance and make it difficult for women to access and exercise power (Duerst-Lahti and Kelly 1995; Lovenduski 1998, 2005; Young 1998). It is worth remembering that men created the rules and organizing principles of political institutions at a time when women were formally denied political rights. Historically, ideas about women's "difference" and particularly their caretaking obligations in the family served as justifications for denying women the right to vote or stand for office. Even though first- and second-wave feminist movements successfully challenged these ideas, their historical legacy continues to resonate. "Men in organizations were good at setting rules of the game that ensured that the qualifications of men were better valued and led more reliably to power and rewards" (Lovenduski 1998, 347). Decades after the legal changes that enfranchised women and removed formal barriers to their participation,

---

[1] To reiterate, we define "concrete floor" of women's inclusion in cabinet, constructed as a three - step process, where (1) a selector initiates the appointment of women (in any magnitude or by any party), which (2) is thereafter confirmed (at the same magnitude or higher) by the subsequent new government, (3) a magnitude below which no future cabinet regresses. We discuss this concept and its relationship to representational criteria in the concluding chapter.

the rules structuring political institutions remain "symbolically interpreted from the standpoint of men" (Acker 1992, 567). Gender scholars examining candidate recruitment, legislative committee membership, legislator behavior, and party leadership selection find that men's dominance, masculinist standards, and preference for other men in leadership positions are defining features of political life (Beckwith 2015; Bjarnegård 2013; Hinojosa 2012; Franceschet and Piscopo 2014; Murray 2014; Schwindt-Bayer 2010; Verge and Claveria, 2016).

Men's historical dominance in politics affects how the public and political gatekeepers alike evaluate political aspirants against seemingly objective criteria like skills, talent, and experience. Gender scholars have examined how party candidate recruiters use criteria like service to the party or having a local profile in ways that favor men and make it difficult for women to demonstrate to selectors that they are qualified (Culhane 2017; Hinojosa 2012). Rainbow Murray explains, "the difficulty for 'outsiders' in demonstrating their capacity to be effective representatives is exacerbated if the criteria for proving merit are derived from the dominant 'insider' group" (2013, 522). The central problem for women is that so many of the qualities associated with effectiveness in politics are qualities that men are naturally assumed to possess, such as assertiveness, competitiveness, and objectivity. In contrast, social constructions of femininity mean that women struggle to be perceived as capable and steady leaders (Duerst-Lahti and Kelly 1995).

Similar gendered dynamics are at play in the cabinet-appointment process. When selectors look for ministers with demonstrated political skills or political experience, the gendered division of labor in politics and the scarcity of women in highly visible and prestigious positions make it harder for women to meet the qualifying criteria. One of the questions we asked in our interviews with political insiders was what the criteria were for being appointed to cabinet in their country. Their answers, along with journalists' and columnists' accounts in our media data, and evidence from former ministers' and selectors' memoirs and autobiographies, reveal how experiential criteria, especially political qualifications, are gendered in ways that advantage men.

Consequences of Experiential Criteria in Practice

The gendered consequences of needing political, policy, or educational experiential qualifying criteria are evident in all our country cases. From our data we identify four ways they affect women; three are gendered to the detriment of women's inclusion in cabinet, and one is gendered to women's advantage. First, women face gendered obstacles to accumulating the requisite political, policy, or educational experience to be perceived as qualified for cabinet. Second, women's experience, though present, is not "seen" by the selector or selectors who are in charge of determining ministerial appointments. Third, the flexibility inherent in experiential criteria is deployed strategically to keep women out—for example, by calling into question a woman's "merit" or downgrading her experience for a particular post. Fourth, the informal and flexible nature of experiential criteria creates an opportunity to employ such criteria to find and recruit women into cabinet.

Gendered Obstacles to Women's Accumulation of Qualifying Experience

Chapter 5 showed that across our seven countries all ministers qualify for a post in cabinet by demonstrating political experience, policy expertise, or relevant educational criteria. Experiential criteria that emphasize specific credentials to demonstrate policy-relevant experience or knowledge create both opportunities and obstacles for women's appointment. Women may be structurally disadvantaged by portfolio-specific qualifying criteria for posts like finance, defense, or veteran's affairs. Tables 9.1 and 9.2 offer evidence of men's dominance of the most high-profile posts in most countries' cabinets, namely, finance, justice, foreign affairs, and defense. Gender segregation in economics and the corporate sector means that women are far less likely than men to qualify for a finance post if the criteria involve having a PhD in economics or experience in the banking

Table 9.1 High-Status Cabinet Portfolios Held by Women, by Country, 1929–2016

Portfolio	Australia	Canada	Chile	Germany	Spain	United Kingdom	United States
Finance/Treasury	No	No	No	No	No	No	No
Defense	Yes	Yes	Yes	Yes	Yes	No	No
Foreign Affairs	Yes	Yes	Yes	No	Yes	Yes	Yes
Justice	Yes	Yes	Yes	Yes	Yes	Yes	Yes

Table 9.2 Number of Times a Female Minister Has Held a High-Profile Portfolio, All Countries (through 2016)

Country	Portfolio			
	Finance/Treasury	Defense	Foreign Affairs	Justice
Australia	0	1	1	1
Canada	0	1	2	3
Chile	0	2	1	3
Germany	0	1	0	3
Spain	0	1	2	1
United Kingdom	0	0	1	1
United States	0	0	3	2
Total	0	6	10	14

or corporate sector.[2] If a military background is a requirement for being appointed a defense minister or veteran's affairs minister, then women are likewise disadvantaged, since fewer women will have garnered the experience and expertise necessary for inclusion in the eligibility pool for such posts.[3] Notably, women's advancement in the legal profession has eliminated gendered obstacles to their appointment as justice minister or attorney general. The justice portfolio is the only high-level post that has been held by a woman across all of our country cases (see Table 9.1). It is also the portfolio to which the greatest number of women have been appointed. As shown in Table 9.2, 14 women across our seven cases have served as justice minister or attorney general.

In the United States, neither the Department of Defense nor Veterans Affairs has been led by a woman. As expected, selection for these posts is not governed by formal rules setting out explicit criteria detailing the necessary experience and expertise that *ministrables* for these positions must possess. For Veterans Affairs, at least two factors have been crucial for appointment as secretary: (1) the political experience of serving in the military (and hence

---

[2] The campaigns for gender quotas for corporate boards, in Germany, Norway, and in other countries, where successful, should serve in part to degender the male advantage in access to Treasury ministerships. See "The Spread of Gender Quotas for Company Boards," *The Economist*, March 25, 2014. (http://www.economist.com/blogs/economist-explains/2014/03/economist-explains-14).

[3] See Tiffany Barnes and Diana O'Brien (2018) for a global study of the appointment of women to defense portfolios. They find that women are more likely to be selected as defense ministers in countries where perceptions of women's roles in politics are being transformed.

being a veteran of the armed forces), and (2) an academic degree from one of the prestigious US service academies. These criteria on their face do not discriminate against women, but they are gendered to women's disadvantage as potential candidates for secretary. The historical exclusion, until relatively recently, of women from all components of military service, and from admission to the military service academies have made women ineligible for appointment on the grounds of these seemingly neutral and informal appointment criteria.[4] Appointment as defense secretary similarly rests on apparently neutral but gendered experiential criteria. The eight secretaries of defense appointed by the three most recent two-term presidents share similar experience and achievements.[5] If their shared profiles—election to Congress, military service, and advanced degrees—represent the experiential criteria necessary for inclusion in the defense secretary eligibility pool, these are standards that women are still hard-pressed to meet.

Among our seven country cases, only the United States and the United Kingdom did not have a female defense minister during our period of study. In contrast, women have been appointed to the defense portfolio in Australia, Canada, Chile, Germany, and Spain. As of 2016, only Chile, however, had done so more than once. Of the remaining high-status posts, foreign affairs and justice appear to be less consistently gendered to women's disadvantage: in the United States, three women have held the secretary of state post, and both Canada and Spain have had two female foreign affairs ministers (see Table 9.2). Women have held the justice portfolio at least once in all seven countries. Significantly, three women have served as justice minister in Canada and Chile, and two women have served as attorney general in the United States.

---

[4] Women were excluded by law from the US service academies—public, taxpayer-funded, free tuition universities—until 1975; the first class to include women matriculated in 1976 and the first women graduated in 1980 (nearly 40 years ago). Of the 119 women admitted to West Point, only 62 graduated. The first women were not promoted to "general officer" ($n = 2$) until 2004. In 2008, "Lieutenant General Ann Dunwoody [became] the First Female Four-Star General in the U.S. Armed Forces" ("History of Women in the Military," http://www.usma.edu/corbin/sitepages/history%20of%20women%20in%20the%20military.aspx). Dunwoody did not graduate from a service academy but enlisted in the Women's Army Corps in 1975 ("History of Women in the Military," http://www.usma.edu/corbin/sitepages/history%20of%20women%20in%20the%20military.aspx). It took Dunwoody more than three decades to reach the rank of four-star general. For data on women in the US military and among those in the top ranks, see http://www.cnn.com/2013/01/24/us/military-women-glance/.

[5] All have college degrees; four have doctorates (PhD degrees) and two have law degrees. Two were Eagle Scouts; six had military experience; three had been elected to the US House of Representatives and another two had been US senators.

Women face the greatest obstacles accessing the finance portfolio. None of our countries had a female treasury minister during our study (see Table 9.1). In many countries, the experiential criteria needed for the post include professional experience in the corporate or financial sectors, two areas of the economy where women's presence remains low. An alternative route to the treasury ministry, however, is available in the United Kingdom and Australia, where *ministrables* can qualify as shadow ministers instead. Serving as shadow treasury minister can suffice to provide the necessary experience that would justify the *ministrable*'s appointment to the position in a governing cabinet. This was the case for the former UK chancellor of the exchequer George Osborne. Osborne had no background in economics or finance but had served as shadow chancellor for five years (2005–2010) before his appointment as chancellor. A similar route to a treasury minister appointment is theoretically available in Australia, although no woman has ever served in that position. An additional route to the treasury ministership has been available to Australian Labor Party *ministrables*, insofar as deputy prime ministers have the freedom to choose their portfolio. Male deputy prime ministers often pick treasury, yet when Julia Gillard was deputy prime minister, she chose to lead the employment and workplace relations portfolio instead.

Given that our media data consistently demonstrate that political experience is strongly valorized across all countries, it is important to note that women are still kept out of political leadership positions in parliaments or parties that set up ministerial opportunities (see also Verge and Claveria 2016). An interviewee in Chile, a former party president, said, "In the parties, among the leadership, there aren't enough women with the political capacity and preparation to be ministers."[6] When asked what sorts of things presidents looked for in potential ministers, interviewees mentioned things like leadership skills, political influence, or management capacity. When pressed further on what these qualities mean in practice, it became clear how gendered they are. A former minister said that presidents are looking to appoint people who "know how to manage things." He explained those qualities by identifying past office-holding experience: "someone who has been a minister before, or a senator, or someone who has been a president of a party."[7] Women, however, are rare among senators or party presidents and,

[6] Interview with former party leader, August 18, 2014, Santiago.
[7] Interview, August 6, 2014, Santiago.

until Bachelet's parity cabinet, they were under-represented in cabinet, too. Between 1990 and 2006, men held 83.9 percent of all cabinet posts (Altman 2008, 264); women's representation in the Senate has ranged between 6 and 18 percent since 1989; and the overwhelming majority of party presidents have been men (Franceschet 2018). In 2009, each of Chile's five largest parties was headed by a man, and women comprised between 8 and 22 percent of party executives.[8] If having held one of these positions is an important type of political experience that selectors seek in potential ministers, such posts are gendered in ways that favor men and disadvantage women.

In Chile, this gendered disadvantage is evident in the patterns of appointment to the four portfolios that are part of the cabinet's inner circle, the Political Committee (finance, interior, SEGOB, SEGPRES): between 1990 and 2014, 44 individuals have served in these four posts. Just five of them (11 percent) were women, and all of them were appointed after 2006. Prior to Bachelet's election as president, no woman occupied a cabinet post on the Political Committee (Dumas, Lafuente, and Parrado 2013).

In Spain, too, there is evidence that where political experience is equated with leadership in parties, men are advantaged in appointment to cabinet. Recall from Chapter 5 that the party leadership is a key recruiting ground for ministers in Spain. Yet there are significantly fewer women among the political bosses or party heavyweights. Virtually all the regional party leaders, commonly known as *barones*, are men. Not surprisingly, a political expert noted that female ministers are more likely to qualify for cabinet through their policy expertise than through political experience. He added that female ministers, especially under former prime ministers like Felipe González and María José Aznar, were also more likely to be independents, and therefore to have less influence or power in the party.[9]

Experiential criteria are flexible: appointments can be justified by any of the three criteria we have identified. It is implausible that there are not 10 women who meet these criteria in each of our country cases, a number that would be sufficient in many countries to construct a cabinet with gender parity. Therefore, women's experience is either (1) invisible to the selector, or (2) the selector exploits the flexibility inherent in experiential criteria strategically, to identify qualified men rather than women.

---

[8] http://www.iadb.org/es/investigacion-y-datos/geppal/detalles-del-pais,17693.html?country=CHL.

[9] Interview, May 28, 2012, Madrid.

The Invisibility of Women's Experience and Expertise

Ministrables are not permitted to self-nominate for cabinet and therefore rely on their talent and experience being noticed by selectors. There is strong evidence that women's experience is routinely not seen. Evidence of women's relative invisibility among the politically experienced comes from a feature newspaper story that appeared after Chile's 2013 election. The country's leading newspaper, *El Mercurio*, contracted a headhunting firm to identify 25 likely ministers. The firm used the president's stated criteria for cabinet appointment, which included seemingly objective qualities like "strategic vision, leadership, and capacity to establish networks." Women were noticeably absent from the list compiled: of the 25 names offered, just four (16 percent) were women, despite the newspaper's certain knowledge that the president had promised to appoint a gender parity cabinet.[10] In an interview, a former minister explained how difficult it was to find qualified women to appoint to cabinet: "The problem is finding women who have the capacity [to be minister]. Normally, there are 10 men and one woman." He went on to admit that ultimately, the problem was sexism: "Women have had less participation in the political parties. This is a conservative society that has relegated women to the home or to certain professions." He noted that women tended not to be in those professions that prepared one for a political career.[11]

Being seen as qualified by the selector is challenging, given prohibitions against self-nomination and active lobbying for a post. This is particularly disadvantageous for women. To become visible, a female *ministrable* must actively make herself visible to the selector, but in so doing will violate informal rules of recruitment. In the United Kingdom, we found evidence of women being criticized for playing by the rules prohibiting self-nomination. Former prime minister John Major categorized ministerial lobbying or self-nomination as "unthinkable behavior" (Major 2000, 347). At the same time, his excuse for not appointing women to cabinet in 1990 was that "there was no obvious candidate banging on the Cabinet door demanding entry" (Major 2000, 214). This exposes how informal rules about self-nomination criteria are gendered to women's disadvantage: aspirant female politicians who are not otherwise visible in important parliamentary networks were

---

[10] M. Vega, R. Fernández, and M. Herrera, "Fortalezas y debilidades de quienes prodrían estar en el nuevo gobierno," *El Mercurio*, December 22, 2013.

[11] Interview, August 6, 2014, Santiago.

expected to self-nominate, to "bang on the door" demanding entry to cabinet, but this practice is strongly frowned upon. Indeed, Major also dismissed one female MP "who was open about her desire to become a minister" as "too much of a maverick" (Major 2000, 354). If female *ministrables* are not already visible to the selector, there is no clear route to becoming visible and making one's experience and expertise evident.[12] Later in the chapter, we discuss how women's exclusion from affiliational networks reinforces the likelihood that women's experience will not be seen.

Experiential Criteria Are Deployed Strategically

Even when women do have extensive political skills, their talent risks being strategically downplayed or disregarded. This often manifests itself as a discussion about how appointments generally must be made on "merit," or questioning the merit of a particular individual. As the media data show, the flexibility of experiential criteria can be deployed to keep women out, as well as to justify an individual's appointment.

When cabinets with few women are appointed, selectors or the media often justify this outcome in terms of how ministers should be appointed on "merit," rather than tokenism or gender. Conservative Party prime minister John Major appointed an all-male cabinet when he took over from Thatcher in 1990, despite advice from advisors (Hogg and Hill 1996, 11) and lobbying from feminists in the party. In his memoirs he recalled that "one Conservative backbencher, Teresa Gorman, said what she thought about that very plainly;" nevertheless, he "decided not to cave in to tokenism or to Teresa's pleas" (Major 2000, 213), and waited until 1992 to appoint two women to cabinet. He notes, "with the promotion of Virginia Bottomley to Health and Gillian Shephard to Employment, *both on merit*, I was able to bring women into Cabinet" (2000, 309; emphasis added).[13] In 2013 Australian prime minister

---

[12] This is not to argue that the burden of being visible should be borne only by female *ministrables*. As Juanita Kreps informed President Jimmy Carter at the announcement of her appointment as US secretary of commerce, "you have to look harder for qualified women" (Interview with Juanita Kreps, January 17, 1986; Interview C-0011. Southern Oral History Program Collection (#4007); http://docsouth.unc.edu/sohp/html_use/C-0011.html). Kreps was the first woman to serve as secretary of commerce, as well as the first economist (Robert D. McFadden, "Juanita M. Kreps, Commerce Secretary, Dies at 89," *New York Times*, July 7, 2010.

[13] We acknowledge that Major followed a prime minister who included no women in her cabinet for over a decade. According to a former advisor, "his inheritance from Mrs Thatcher of a lack of women with strong middle-level ministerial experience was the cause of the problem" (interview with former special advisor, August 12, 2016).

Tony Abbott appointed just one woman to his cabinet. A senior member of his party is quoted as saying, "I would always support the best person for cabinet, but I would hope consideration would be given to the relative merits of some women who have done a good job as shadows."[14]

Similarly, when female ministers are appointed, their experience or credentials are routinely called into question. In the United Kingdom, Theresa May's appointment as home secretary in 2010 was met with "surprise."[15] While journalists are fond of listing ministers' political credentials, noting, for example, that they ran a campaign, served as shadow minister or chairman of the party,[16] or simply noting that someone was appointed because they were "a clever chap,"[17] May's political credentials were systematically downplayed, trivialized, or disregarded by the press. Instead of being recognized for her skills, she was "known for her large collection of shoes"[18] and her "love of footwear."[19] One columnist went further and asked "how well qualified is Mrs May to take it on? Not at all, as it happens. Her career as a shadow minister has ranged across much of Whitehall—education, employment, women's issues, transport, culture, local government—just about everything, in fact, except home affairs."[20] May's qualifications for the job were called into question despite abundant generalist political experience: she had been an MP since 1997, served as chairman of the Conservative Party in 2002–2003, and shadowed six different portfolios in the period 1999–2010.

In Germany, both political experience and policy expertise (*Fachkompetenz*) are very important in the process of qualifying for cabinet. Gender quotas within parties make it easier for women to accumulate requisite experience at federal or *Land* level, but nevertheless there is evidence that women's experience can be overlooked or trivialized. As one female former minister put it, it is very easy for selectors to overlook women: "they would say 'no, she doesn't quite fit, he would be better or he would be better.' "[21] In a newspaper interview with Renate Schmidt, Germany's incoming minister for family affairs, senior citizens, women and youth, her extant political experience and policy expertise were questioned: "do you even have the capabilities

---

[14] "Libs 'Shocked' by Lack of Women in Cabinet," *The Australian*, September 13, 2013.
[15] "A Special Relationship; Cameron at No 10," *The Telegraph*, May 13, 2010.
[16] "Ministers Begin Work with a 5pc Pay Cut," *The Telegraph*, May 14, 2010.
[17] "Theresa May Strikes the Only Clunky Cabinet Note So Far," *The Telegraph*, May 12, 2010.
[18] "Five Lib Dems, a Big Beast and a Kitten-Heeled Home Secretary," *The Telegraph*, May 13, 2010.
[19] "Ministers Begin Work with a 5pc Pay Cut, *The Telegraph*, May 14, 2010.
[20] "Theresa May Strikes the Only Clunky Cabinet Note So Far," *The Telegraph*, May 12, 2010.
[21] Interview with former minister, October 29, 2014.

needed for this department?"[22] It is also proposed to her in the interview that she is the "nice, maternal balance to the men of action" in the cabinet.[23] A comparison of the evaluations of Ursula von der Leyen and Franz Josef Jung's experiential qualifications, both appointed to Angela Merkel's first federal cabinet in 2005 from regional governments, demonstrates the gendered assessment of "merit." News reports question the adequacy of von der Leyen's ministerial experience at *Land* level, noting how even her "party friends" will look on with suspicion at her rapid promotion from *Land* to federal cabinet.[24] In contrast, Jung's self confidence is noted: "though a *Land* level politician, he would dare to take on almost any office at federal level [...] He is tough enough to assert himself in a difficult ministry."[25]

Experiential criteria for appointment to cabinet positions are numerous, various, and flexible and, by their nature, can be used strategically, as evidenced in the preceding. Different evaluative criteria, employed strategically, can function to exclude women from cabinets, or can undermine them once appointed. The signal of a woman appointed to cabinet often activates public questioning about her experiential credentials, initiating a media discussion about merit, where such discussion is rare for male appointees. Nonetheless, the flexibility of experiential criteria in cabinet appointments may facilitate the appointment of women to cabinet.

Flexible Experiential Criteria Create Opportunities to Select Women

There is considerable evidence that some portfolios offer greater opportunities for women to be appointed to cabinet. Cross-national studies

---

[22] "Aus allen Wolken gefallen," *Süddeutsche Zeitung*, October 17, 2002.

[23] Ibid.

[24] "Lohn der Treue," *Süddeutsche Zeitung*, October 17, 2005.

[25] "Die Zähmung der Tiger," *Der Spiegel*, 17, October 2005. An example from the United States, recently re-publicized, makes a similar point. At the outset of the George W. Bush administration, Fred Barnes lamented, "about 30 percent of the president's picks so far have been women and about 50 percent white males," and reported that "[t]here have been some private complaints by white males" about the lack of merit of the appointment of women to positions in the new administration (Fred Barnes, "The Bush Quotas: Now Look Who's Counting by Race and Gender," *The Weekly Standard*, April 16, 2001). Barnes offered Michele Davis as an example of an underqualified woman, although Davis had served twice as assistant secretary in the Treasury Department. Davis has since claimed that, despite her experience and qualifications, "she was described as a token in the early days of the George W. Bush administration" (Elise Viebeck, "Where Are All the High-Ranking GOP Women?" *Washington Post*, August 2, 2016.

of gender and cabinet appointments show a consistent trend wherein women are more likely to be appointed to portfolios associated with women's caring roles, like education, children and youth, social services, or health (Escobar-Lemmon and Taylor-Robinson 2009; Krook and O'Brien 2012). We note a similar pattern among our country cases: in five of the seven cases, the first women to hold cabinet posts were appointed to posts stereotypically considered to be "feminine." The first female ministers to be appointed to cabinet in both Germany and Spain were given the health portfolios, and in the United Kingdom and the United States, the first female ministers were given the labor portfolio. Australia's first female minister with portfolio was minister for education, and subsequently minister for social security.

In sum, our data confirm existing gender and politics research: experiential criteria are strongly gendered to men's advantage. Since men have traditionally performed the roles of politician and leader that are markers of experience, masculine rather than feminine traits and characteristics are precisely those employed to indicate the talent, skills, and experience relevant to appointment to cabinet. It is not, and has never been, the case that there are no qualified women. Instead, women's experience is not seen, or the flexibility of qualifying criteria is deployed strategically to question women's merit and keep them out of office—or both.

Gendered Consequences of Affiliational Criteria

What are the gendered consequences of affiliation as a criterion for cabinet appointment? Feminist political scientists have documented the ways that elite political networks are gendered to men's advantage; even if women are not formally excluded, their presence in places where network ties are forged is rarely welcomed (Culhane 2017; Franceschet and Piscopo 2014). Indeed, when ties are forged through traditionally male-only activities, like sports or drinking, gender norms actively discourage women's participation. To the extent that individuals prefer to spend time with members of their own sex, this tendency is further heightened in political networks where favors, power, and status are important currency (Bjarnegård 2013, 22, 25). Chapter 6 identified five areas of selector–*ministrable* affiliation: (1) personal friendship, (2) membership in the selector's personal political network, (3) a *ministrable*'s political service to or campaign support for the selector, (4) shared personal connection through university, and (5) as a party competitor or rival. We discuss the gendered consequences of the first four affiliational criteria in the following.

We find that the affiliational criteria that play a role in allocating ministerial opportunities are traditionally strongly gendered in favor of men. To reiterate from Chapter 6, we identify three patterns of affiliational criteria across our cases: (1) strong and *consistent* affiliational linkages, with more than half of cabinet appointees meeting at least one of the affiliational relationships, (2) *occasional* affiliational linkages (between 20 and 50 percent), and (3) *rare* affiliational links (fewer than a fifth of all appointees). Overall, we find is that where affiliation is a strong and consistent criterion, women's presence in cabinet remains low for longer and does not reach high magnitudes (see Table 9.3). Three countries where affiliational criteria are strong and consistent—Australia, the United Kingdom, and the United States—fit this pattern. In none of these three countries have women constituted more than a third of cabinet—high magnitude—and parity has not been reached in any cabinet.

Table 9.3 Impact of Affiliational Criteria on Women's Representation in Cabinet, from Date of Last All-Male Cabinet to 2016

Reliance on Affiliational Criteria	Country	Date of Last All-Male Cabinet	Year of Highest Number of Women in Cabinet	Highest Female Representation N (%)
Strong and consistent[a]	Australia	1993	2016	5 (22.7)
	Spain	1986	2008	9 (56.3)
	United Kingdom	1987	2015	7 (33.3)
	United States	1981	1997	4 (28.6)
Occasional[b]	Chile	1970	2006	10 (50.0)
	Germany	1957	2002	6 (46.2)
Rare[c]	Canada	1968	2015	15 (50.0)

[a] More than half of all appointees have an affiliational relationship with the selector.

[b] Between 20 and 50 percent of appointees have an affiliational relationship with the selector.

[c] Fewer than 20 percent of appointees have affiliational relationships with the selector.

Where selectors have routinely and consistently relied on affiliational criteria for cabinet appointments, male ministers are more likely to be appointed, and women's inclusion in cabinets has been slow and modest. In short, affiliational relationships between the selector and *ministrables* gender the appointment process to the advantage of men.

The one outlier in this category is Spain. In Spain, where affiliational criteria are strong and consistent, at least two women have been included in every post-election cabinet since 1989, and until 2016, gender parity has been reached on two occasions (2004 and 2008). As we show in the following, the emergence of gender as a strong representational criterion limits a selector's capacity to appoint exclusively from affiliational networks. Also, some selectors in Spain have more diverse affiliational networks.

In Chile and Germany, the application of affiliational criteria as a way to qualify for cabinet is employed occasionally rather than consistently. Although there are no prohibitions on selectors appointing their political allies and friends as ministers in either country, German chancellors are constrained by coalition co-selectors, and more prescriptive representational criteria in both countries pose additional constraints. All-male cabinets were last formed in 1970 in Chile[26] and 1957 in Germany; in each country, parity cabinets have been formed on at least one occasion. Finally, in Canada, ministers are rarely appointed on the basis of affiliational criteria, largely because representational criteria are so numerous and strongly institutionalized. The last all-male cabinet in Canada was appointed in 1968, and parity has been achieved once since then, in 2015.

Overall, where no strongly prescriptive rules counteract the strategic incentives for selectors to appoint ministers on affiliation criteria, selectors will continue to employ such criteria in forming governing cabinets; as a result, women's presence remains stuck at lower magnitudes.

These general patterns are confirmed in our media data. We analyzed media reports of ministerial recruitments in two processes of cabinet formation for each country. For all new governments, we established the number of ministers who are linked to the selector by at least one of the five affiliational criteria, and then we identified how many of these ministers are women.

As Table 9.4 illustrates, in most cases of new cabinet formation, far fewer women than men qualify through affiliational criteria. There are two notable cases where women comprise a comparatively high proportion of ministers

---

[26] Chile has had no all-male cabinets since the return of democracy in 1990.

Table 9.4 Affiliational Criteria and Gendered Patterns of Appointment to Cabinet (New Governments Only, through 2016)

Reliance on Affiliational Criteria	Country	Selector (Year)	Total Number of Ministers	All Ministers with Affiliational Links N (%)	Male Ministers with Affiliational Links N (%)	Female Ministers with Affiliational Links N (%)
Strong and consistent[a]	Australia	Abbott (2013)	18	17 (94.4)	16 (94.1)	1 (5.9)
	Spain	Zapatero (2004)	16	13 (81.3)	8 (61.5)	5 (38.5)
		Rajoy (2011)	13	10 (76.9)	7 (70.0)	3 (30.0)
	United Kingdom	Cameron* (2010)	22	15 (68.2)	12 (80.0)	3 (20.0)
	United States	Obama (2009)	15	10 (66.7)	7 (70.0)	3 (30.0)
	Chile	Bachelet* (2006)	20	12 (60.0)	6 (50.0)	6 (50.0)
Occasional[b]	Chile	Piñera* (2010)	23	8 (34.8)	7 (87.5)	1 (12.5)
	Germany	Merkel* (2005)	14	3 (21.4)	1 (33.3)	2 (66.7)
Rare[c]	Canada	Trudeau (2015)	30	3 (10.0)	2 (66.7)	1 (33.3)

*Coalition government.

[a] More than half of all appointees have an affiliational relationship with the selector.

[b] Between 20 and 50 percent of appointees have an affiliational relationship with the selector.

[c] Fewer than 20 percent of appointees have affiliational relationships with the selector.

with affiliational links. In Chile, half of ministers with identified affiliational links to President Bachelet were women; in Germany, three of Chancellor Merkel's ministers shared an affiliational link with her, and two of them were women. Overall, women's lack of access to affiliation with a selector (or potential selectors in their party's elite) disadvantages them in appointment to cabinet.

Our interview data, media data, and analysis of memoirs expose in more fine-grained detail the mechanisms through which elite political networks around selectors have traditionally been gendered in favor of men, foreclosing women's participation. In this section, we provide evidence of the gendered consequences of selectors being permitted to appoint ministers on grounds of (1) friendship, (2) membership in their inner circle, (3) political service or support for campaign, or (4) broader university links. We also show, however, that a selector's sex does not automatically determine whether his or her network will include women or not. We identify three cases where male and female selectors have women in their personal networks—Michelle Bachelet, José Luis Rodríguez Zapatero, and Angela Merkel—and discuss how these personal network affiliations affect gendered outcomes of cabinets. We also find evidence of change when selectors are actively encouraged by intra-party feminists to bring more women into their networks.

Presidents and prime ministers are permitted to appoint their close friends to cabinet, with the caveat that they can also justify their friends' appointment publicly in terms of experiential criteria (political experience or policy expertise). This *appointment of friends* is strongly gendered. While we find evidence of political friendships between women, it is hard to imagine women developing intense personal friendships with male political colleagues without coming under severe scrutiny. An exception may be the close personal relationship between George W. Bush and his second-term secretary of state, Condoleezza Rice.

Take, for example, the friendship between UK prime minister Tony Blair and his chancellor of exchequer for 10 years, Gordon Brown. Although this friendship turned notoriously hostile, Blair's account of his relationship with Brown before becoming leader in 1994 is characterized by some intensity. In his autobiography Blair describes how the two were "well-nigh inseparable for over ten years. [. . .] as close as two people ever are in politics" (Blair 2011, 68), even traveling from time to time to New York together "essentially just to get away and think" (Blair 2011, 55). Blair's account of being locked away with Brown in a friend's house in Edinburgh to thrash out who should become party leader reads like romantic fiction:

> The conversations were long, but there were few wasted moments. Our minds moved and at that point in sync. When others were present, we felt the pace and power diminish, until, a bit like lovers desperate to get to love making but disturbed by old friends dropping round, we would try to bustle them out, steering them doorwards with a hearty slap on the back. (Blair 2011, 71)

Chapter 6 includes several instances of male selectors appointing close male friends to cabinet. For example, UK prime minister David Cameron appointed his long-term friend George Osborne as chancellor of the exchequer. In our media data, Osborne is described as Cameron's "closest ally"[27] and as a fellow "former member of the [all-male] Bullingdon club, the elitist Oxford University drinking and dining clique."[28] In Spain, José Antonio Alonso, appointed as interior minister, is described as a childhood friend and university classmate of Zapatero.[29] And in Chile, the links between President Piñera and several of his ministers were forged in the prestigious Universidad Católica and in close-knit business circles.[30]

Affiliational criteria for ministerial recruitment also apply when a selector appoints from his *personal political network*, where the selector and *ministrable* have a history of shared political work and mutual support. There is significant evidence that women benefit less than men from this as a qualifying route into cabinet because women are routinely excluded from such inner circles. This exclusion means that they have not had the opportunity to demonstrate trust and loyalty to the prime minister or president.

For example, in Chile, elite political networks are notoriously closed to women, making it hard for women to qualify for cabinet through affiliational criteria. Recall from Chapter 3 that in Chile, although presidents ultimately decide who will be in their cabinet, all presidents solicit lists of recommendations from their coalition partners. In 1990, when the first post-dictatorship president, Patricio Aylwin, formed his cabinet, he consulted with the party leaders of his coalition partners, all of whom were men. The complete absence of women from the party leaders' personal networks meant that all of the names proposed by the parties were men. A former minister explained in an interview that President Aylwin actually wanted to appoint at least one woman to his cabinet, namely, to head the newly created National Women's Service. In the absence of any recommendations from the party leaders, he ended up appointing Soledad Alvear, who, although politically active herself, was also the wife of the president of the Christian

[27] "Power Play; As the UK Election Result Became Clear, the Secret Meetings Began," *Sunday Times*, May 16, 2010.

[28] "The New Establishment; With the New Government Comes a New Elite," *Sunday Times*, May 23, 2010.

[29] "Magistrado progresista y amigo de Zapatero," *El País*, April 1, 2004.

[30] Mónica González, "Las redes de amistad y negocios del gabinete de Sebastián Piñera," https://ciperchile.cl/2010/02/10/las-redes-de-amistad-y-negocios-del-gabinete-de-pinera/. February 10, 2010.

Democratic Party.[31] While emphasizing that Alvear was indeed highly qualified for the post of National Women's Service Director, the former minister observed that "there were also many other women [who were qualified]. But they were simply not seen."[32] The only women who were "seen" were those linked through marriage to other men in the selector's personal network.

Given the important role of the party elite in submitting recommendations to presidents during cabinet appointment in Chile, the absence of women among party leaders is consequential. One interviewee explained, "of those who are responsible for sending recommendations [for cabinet] to the president, as far as I know, it's always men. Women are not in the places where power is distributed." When talking about the "strong men" and the informal process of making recommendations for appointed posts in government, a political expert said, "I say 'men' because it's very rare that there are women; it's generally men."[33] Our media data bear this out as well. In mid-January 2006, a journalist writing about which party notables would be involved in the process of identifying names of *ministrables* within the parties said, "The men who will negotiate . . . are party presidents, members of the party directives, and members of the blocs of deputies and senators who demand 'quotas of power.'" She added that, since President Bachelet's wish for a gender parity cabinet was well known in the parties, one party, the Party for Democracy (PPD), had invited a female deputy, María Antonieta Saa, to participate in the discussions. The article identifies 15 other individuals, some of whom are listed as certain to be negotiating, while others are identified as possibly participating in the discussions. Among the other 15 names, only one other woman appears, Alejandra Sepúlveda, from the Christian Democratic Party.[34]

The prevalence of personal political networks for cabinet appointments clearly works to men's advantage in the United Kingdom as well. For example, former prime minister John Major describes the parliamentary dining clubs that emerged after the 1979 election. He explains, "The new Members soon formed their own alliances. Within weeks, like-minded Conservative colleagues set up dining clubs. The Blue Chips included those

[31] Interview with former minister, August 11, 2014, Santiago. Notably, the woman whom Alywin appointed as deputy director of the National Women's Service was also the wife of the president of one of the other coalition parties.

[32] Interview with former minister, August 11, 2014, Santiago.

[33] Interview, August 13, 2014, Santiago.

[34] Meche Garrido, "Listos equipos negociadores," *El Mercurio*, January 13, 2006.

new MPs with most experience of the inner ring of government, often gained through working at Central Office or as a front-bench aide" (Major 2000, 67). Former minister and diarist Alan Clark referred to the Blue Chip Club as "that tight little masonic group [. . .] determined to monopolise the allocation of higher office."[35] These Clubs were composed exclusively of men, whose meetings, according to one member, were raucous affairs where the language was "most unladylike."[36] There is overt evidence that affiliations created in these all-male dining clubs served as a mechanism for cabinet recruitment. In his autobiography, John Major justifies his choice of one minister in his first post-election cabinet thus: "I put my fellow Blue Chip Club member John Patten in education" (2000, 308). Note that Major did not deem it necessary to justify this appointment any further with experiential criteria, thereby reinforcing the strength of affiliation as a route to ministerial office.

In Germany, too, our interview data reveal that membership in such networks is gendered to men's advantage. A former minister explains, "over centuries informal networks have worked for men. They knew each other, they always nominated each other."[37] Another said, "Among men there is a high degree of male solidarity and that's a type of male solidarity for men who lose their seats as state prime ministers or who are not re-elected as minsters and—bam—they are in cabinet. This is something that women don't have. When Heide Simonis failed as minister-president of Schleswig-Holstein, not one person asked Simonis—who was a competent woman—if she wanted to be finance minister. And she would have been able to do that. Hans Eichel failed as minister-president of Hesse and immediately he was federal finance minister. But no one cared about the women. They had to look out for themselves."[38] Similarly, the CDU's Andenpakt discussed in Chapter 6 is also referred to as a "Männerbund"—a closed male group, with only male members and explicit goals to promote their male allies in politics.

If *ministrables* are not close friends of the selector or part of the selectors' inner political circle, they can still meet affiliational criteria by demonstrating *political service or support for the selector's campaign*. *Ministrables* need to be noticed by the selector and seen to be trustworthy and loyal; political service

---

[35] http://archive.spectator.co.uk/article/12th-december-1998/12/when-the-chips-are-up.
[36] https://www.theguardian.com/theguardian/1999/feb/02/features11.g26.
[37] Interview, October 29, 2014.
[38] Interview, October 27, 2014.

and campaign support constitute an effective strategy for increasing one's visibility. Recall that ministrables cannot self-nominate for a spot in cabinet but need to await the call. We find evidence that women are less likely than men to meet these affiliational criteria as women's service is routinely not "seen" by the selector or selectors, or they are not given the opportunity to demonstrate service in the first place.

A good example comes from the United Kingdom. New Labour is described in interviews as a tight male network led by men: Tony Blair, Gordon Brown, and Peter Mandelson. As much as Tony Blair "liked to be surrounded by women,"[39] these women were not necessarily on his radar for high-profile positions (Annesley and Gains 2010). In the United Kingdom and Australia, inclusion in shadow cabinet is the prominent mechanism for accessing ministerial office. Not only does it allow *ministrables* to accumulate political experience and policy expertise, it also allows them to demonstrate political service and loyalty toward the incoming prime minister. Historically, it has been challenging for women to access shadow cabinets in the UK Labour Party and the Australian Labor Party, as shown in Chapter 8.

In the United States, women entered Barack Obama's affiliational network by supporting his candidacy for president in 2008, joining his campaign, providing him with key endorsements, and actively campaigning for him. Of the four women appointed to Obama's first-term initial cabinet, two were early supporters of his nomination: Kathleen Sebelius, governor of Kansas, and Janet Napolitano, governor of Arizona. Both candidacy endorsements came early in Obama's campaign, and Napolitano had to disappoint a long-standing political friend, Hillary Clinton, in supporting Obama instead. Both endorsements were crucial for Obama, who won the majority of delegates in the Kansas primary election[40] and who split the primary election delegate count with Clinton in Arizona.[41] Such early campaign support, providing the political service connection with the (eventual) president, while important, is not equally available to women and men. To the extent that women are not placed in high political office, giving power to a campaign endorsement or making political service evident and valuable to an eventual selector, women cannot leverage those positions into entry into an affiliational relationship

---

[39] Interview with former special advisor, July 11, 2016.
[40] "Kansas Caucus Results," *New York Times*, https://www.nytimes.com/elections/2008/primaries/results/states/KS.html.
[41] "Arizona Primary Results," *New York Times*, https://www.nytimes.com/elections/2008/primaries/results/states/AZ.html.

with a selector. The small numbers of women in US governorships (9 of 50 governors)[42] and Senate seats (23 of 100 in 2018)[43] mean that the campaign and political support necessary for developing an affiliational relationship with a future selector will be disproportionately available to men as a route to qualifying for cabinet on affiliational grounds.

In some countries, the homogeneity of the political elite provides men with opportunities to develop affiliational relationships that can lead to cabinet appointments—opportunities that are unavailable to women. In Australia, Chile, and the United Kingdom, the political elite is strikingly homogeneous, often having attended the same elite single-sex private and preparatory schools. Elsewhere, networks emerge through universities, and particularly fraternities or elite clubs that are composed exclusively of men. In many countries, the ties that bind members of the political elite are strengthened through living in the same city, like Washington, D.C., Santiago, or London, and often in particular neighborhoods in those cities. We find evidence that affiliational criteria of this type are gendered when the associations and patronage run through all-male school and university clubs and fraternities.

Evidence of important affiliational networks appear in our media data for the 2010 election of David Cameron and, significantly, no female ministers are mentioned as members of such networks. Journalists and columnists made repeated reference to the "Notting Hill set," a reference to the neighborhood in London where Cameron lived, noting as well that many of the members of the Notting Hill set also shared backgrounds in elite public schools and had studied at either Oxford or Cambridge. Journalists also referenced the all-male Bullingdon Club, described as "the elitist Oxford University drinking and dining clique," in which David Cameron, George Osborne, and Boris Johnson all participated.[44]

Shared university experience was a common affiliational connection among cabinet appointees in Barack Obama's first-term initial cabinet—although only for male cabinet members. Two members of cabinet shared Harvard connections with Obama (Shaun Donovan, housing and urban development, and Arne Duncan, education); Attorney General Eric Holder

---

[42] "Women in Statewide Elective Executive Office," http://cawp.rutgers.edu/women-statewide-elective-executive-office-2018.

[43] Only "52 women have ever served in the Senate"; in 2018, the 23 female senators constituted a historic record high number. "Women in the US Senate, 2018," http://www.cawp.rutgers.edu/women-us-senate-2018.

[44] "The New Establishment," *The Sunday Times*, May 23, 2010.

shared a Columbia University connection with Obama. No female cabinet member in Obama's first-term initial cabinet enjoyed this type of affiliational connection with the president who appointed her.[45] Again, to the extent that women are under-represented in the venues in which men forge or confirm affective relationships, women will be disadvantaged in opportunities for cabinet posts where affiliational criteria are employed by selectors in forming their cabinets.

Gendered Change in Affiliational Criteria over Time

Affiliational criteria have historically been gendered in ways that strongly favor men. Nevertheless, the exclusionary power of affiliational criteria can change. Among our cases, we find evidence of female selectors—including Michelle Bachelet and Angela Merkel—having more heterogeneous networks than men, and examples of male selectors with diverse networks, such as José Luis Rodríguez Zapatero. We also find evidence of feminists in political parties working proactively to ensure that qualified female *ministrables* secure access to the prime minister's or president's inner circle or to reward women's service and loyalty.

A female minister who served in Bachelet's initial cabinet in 2006 said that the president appointed many women, not just to cabinet, but also to the upper echelon of decision-making throughout the state, "because she *knew* more women and she *saw* more women."[46] Unlike her male predecessors, Bachelet had women in her networks. Other interviews, along with our media data, confirm that affiliational criteria were gendered to women's advantage when Bachelet was the selector. The president personally knew all of the women whom she appointed to her initial cabinet in 2006, mostly through prior working or political relationships. Scholarly accounts of Bachelet's emergence as presidential candidate and her victory in the 2006 election emphasize the fact that she was not part of the traditional party elite in Chile (Siavelis 2014; Thomas 2011). Media accounts of Bachelet's political

---

[45] Obama appointed Penny Pritzker as secretary of commerce in his second-term initial cabinet; Pritzker received her BA degree from Harvard. Sylvia Mathews Burrell replaced Katheleen Sebelius as health and human services secretary in 2014; she also received her BA degree from Harvard. Loretta Lynch, Obama's second attorney general, was appointed to the post in 2015; like Obama, she holds a law degree from Harvard.

[46] Interview, August 11, 2014, Santiago, Chile.

networks contrast the characteristics (for example, social class, school ties, and neighborhood) of her network to the traditional political elite in Chile. The most significant difference is that Bachelet's network is more diverse than had been the case for previous Chilean presidents, in terms of sex, class, education, age, and even political affiliation, that is, to the extent that her network has been more open to independents.[47]

Spain's former prime minister José Luis Rodríguez Zapatero is likewise described in interviews as someone who actively invited and promoted women in his political networks. A former minister recounted in an interview that as soon as he won the party leadership, Zapatero began to incorporate women into the front lines of the party leadership;[48] some of those women were ultimately appointed to his 2004 cabinet. The team that Zapatero put together to work with him most closely during the 2004 electoral campaign included four women (out of 10 individuals). Prior to the election, these 10 people were referred to as Zapatero's "cabinet," and three of the four women in the group were subsequently appointed to his initial cabinet.[49]

During Prime Minister Tony Blair's time in office, feminists in the party worked hard to ensure that female *ministrables* made it onto Blair's radar and into cabinet. Blair's political secretary, Sally Morgan, is mentioned on numerous occasions in interviews as someone who worked hard to bring aspirant, experienced female MPs to Blair's attention. She was actively involved in the process of ministerial recruitment and reshuffles, a part of the job he hated.[50] For example, she made sure that there was at least one woman in each ministerial team so as to set up women's chances for selection in cabinet, and she initiated regular meetings between backbench MPs and Blair after Prime Minister's Questions, reserving some slots just for women.

In sum, affiliational criteria have historically been gendered to advantage men's inclusion in cabinet. Selectors, in the absence of prohibitions on appointing all-male cabinets, appointed only men to their cabinets when their networks of friendship, trust, and loyalty were exclusively composed of men. As political networks in some countries, or for some selectors, become more diverse, affiliational criteria may be a basis for including women in cabinet as well.

---

[47] Ximena Pérez and Paula Coddou, "El estilo del bacheletismo," *El Mercurio*, January 21, 2006.
[48] Interview, May 22, 2012. Madrid.
[49] Zapatero encarga a diez notables su modelo de gobierno, *El País*, January 9, 2004.
[50] Interview with former political advisor, July 11, 2016, London.

Conclusion: Gendered Consequences of Experience and Affiliation

Two sets of criteria for qualifying for cabinet—experiential and affiliational—have clearly gendered consequences. These criteria have historically worked together to justify the appointment of specific (male) ministers or the exclusion of female *ministrables*, and to construct cabinets whose members can be trusted to be loyal to the selector. We do not argue here that either set of criteria determine the appointment of specific cabinet ministers; rather, we argue that these criteria intersect in practice as selectors construct cabinets of known, trusted confidants and justify their choices on the basis of publicly acceptable criteria of political experience and policy expertise. These criteria have historically served to disadvantage women in access to cabinet or to exclude women completely.

Nonetheless, our data demonstrate that female *ministrables* have the necessary policy expertise and substantial political experience relevant to the cabinet appointment; women have been increasingly included in selectors' affiliational networks as such networks have diversified. The numbers of women appointed to cabinet posts have increased to higher magnitudes in all of our country cases, and gender parity cabinets have been appointed in Canada, Chile, Germany, and Spain (in Spain, more than once). Have experiential and affiliational criteria sufficiently re-gendered the pool of *ministrables* and increased the number of women qualified for cabinet appointment?

We argue that experiential and affiliational criteria are insufficient in and of themselves to re-gender the cabinet formation process and to explain women's increasing inclusion in cabinets. Although experiential criteria are prescribed by the rules about qualifying for cabinet, they are flexible and non-specific. Given the flexibility of the criteria, there are multiple grounds on which *ministrables* can demonstrate experience and expertise relevant for cabinet appointment. Affiliational criteria, while permitted for cabinet formation, cannot be publicly justified as qualifying *ministrables* in the absence of experiential criteria, and ministers appointed solely on the basis of an affiliational relationship with the selector face legitimacy challenges and media criticism.

The gendered consequences of experiential and affiliational criteria are activated by the presence of strong representational criteria for qualifying for cabinet appointment. Representational criteria for cabinet qualification are strongly prescribed in all our country cases, and they function to leverage experiential and affiliational qualification for cabinet. Although the specifics of representational criteria vary across our country cases, in each of our cases, the inclusion of women in cabinet has become a strong prescriptive rule. The emergence of prescriptive rules about representation, where gender requirements now mean "include women," has heightened female *ministrables'* qualification for cabinet, has made eligible women visible to selectors, and now constrains selectors to diversify their networks and to appoint women to cabinet. A strong prescriptive representational rule of sex has leveraged affiliational criteria, even as experiential criteria remain the justificatory foundation for women's qualification for cabinet and for selectors' appointment of female ministers. The power of the representational criterion of gender has put an end to all-male cabinets, has increased the magnitude of women's presence in cabinet across all our cases, has served to establish concrete floors of female ministers, and has contributed to the rise of gender parity cabinets. We discuss the impact of representational criteria on women's cabinet inclusion in the following chapter.

10

Gendered Representational Criteria

Including Women

The normative principles underlying democratic governance mean that representation is an important dimension of all cabinets. Among all three types of qualifying criteria, representational criteria are the most strongly prescriptive. Unlike experiential criteria, which are flexible and non-specific, and affiliational criteria, which are permitted rather than prescribed, representational criteria are prescriptive in force and establish specific characteristics that must be present within the cabinet team. What differs over time and across countries, however, are the specifics of what must be represented. Including women in cabinet has only recently emerged as a prescriptive rule. Historically, the presence of *gender* as a representational criterion meant that it was permissible to compose cabinets entirely of *men*. In all of our country cases, the inclusion of *women* in the gender representational criterion emerged at different points in time from two separate processes that ultimately reinforce each other.

First, feminists, particularly those in political parties, mobilize broad public support for the idea that women's political inclusion is a central ingredient of democracy. Second, individual selectors use their power to act on this idea, bringing more women into their cabinet teams. Selectors respond to demands by feminist activists to increase the number of women they appoint, and in so doing, they initiate new minima, what we term *concrete floors*, that recast public expectations about women's inclusion in cabinet. As these processes interact over time, leaders find it increasingly difficult to generate public legitimacy for cabinets that are perceived to fall short in respecting inclusionary norms about gender.

We anticipated that in countries with multiple representational criteria, such as Canada and Germany, creating an additional representational criterion for the inclusion of women would be difficult. In fact, our data show that the opposite is the case. As we demonstrate in this chapter, in countries with a strong tradition of appointing ministers on representational grounds, the inclusion of women has been uncontroversial. In such cases where representational criteria include things like religious affiliation, territory, region, or ethnicity, for example, it has not been contentious to add women to the list. In countries with a weaker tradition of appointing on representational grounds, transforming the gender criterion to prescribe women's inclusion has been resisted, most commonly evidenced by a strategy of challenging women's "merit" for appointment to cabinet.

In Canada, as demonstrated in Chapter 7, representational criteria with respect to region have always been paramount. But Canada was also among the first of our cases where a strong and persistent inclusionary norm emerged that re-gendered the representational criterion to include women. Conservative prime minister John Diefenbaker appointed Canada's first female minister in 1958. Writing about this historic milestone in his memoirs, Diefenbaker wrote, "over the years, I had taken the position that the women of Canada deserved and had the right to expect representation in cabinet" (Diefenbaker 1976, 39). It would take more than two decades, however, for post-election cabinets to include more than just one female minister. The turning point came in 1984, when another Conservative prime minister, Brian Mulroney, was first elected. Mulroney's predecessor, Liberal prime minister Pierre Trudeau, had appointed Canada's last all-male cabinet when he was first elected in 1968; after being elected to his final term in 1980, he appointed just one woman to his 27-member cabinet. When Mulroney took office in 1984, he quadrupled the number of women in cabinet, appointing four women in a 27-member cabinet. In his memoirs, Mulroney (2007, 40) confessed to being "inspired by [Diefenbaker's] progressiveness" in being the first to appoint a female minister. On the night of his election in 1984, he promised "the advancement of women's rights will be one of the major concerns of the Government of Canada" (Mulroney 2007, 40). One of the ways Mulroney acted on this promise was by appointing a record number of women to cabinet (as well as to other important posts such as judge, deputy minister, and senator). Upon forming a second government in 1988, Mulroney appointed even more women: seven in a 38-member cabinet.

When the Conservatives lost government in 1993, the newly elected Liberal government of Jean Chretién did not revert to the record of male-dominated cabinets set by previous Liberal prime ministers, none of whom ever appointed more than one woman to cabinet. Instead, Chretién matched the new inclusionary bar set by Mulroney; his first cabinet included virtually the same proportion of women, 18.1 percent, as Mulroney's previous initial cabinet (18.4).[1] Subsequent Liberal governments formed by Chretién included even greater proportions of women: 25.0 percent in 1997 and 26.9 percent in 2000. In sum, since 1984, a clear inclusionary norm with respect to women has been present in Canada.

Further evidence that women's inclusion is needed for cabinets to be perceived as sufficiently representative is that declines in women's presence are criticized in the media. In 2006, Conservative prime minister Stephen Harper appointed just six women to his 26-member cabinet. Although the percentage of women in his (much smaller) cabinet (23 percent) was virtually the same as that of his Liberal predecessor, Paul Martin (23.6 percent), there were three fewer women sitting at Harper's cabinet table, and political commentators noted and criticized the decline.[2] In 2008, when Harper went on to win a second term in office, he matched the record of Conservative Brian Mulroney, by crossing a new threshold in terms of women's cabinet representation. Harper's initial cabinet in 2008 included two more women than his 2006 cabinet, reaching the 30 percent threshold for the first time in Canadian history. Journalists, columnists, and commentators noted that Harper was "sending a strong message to women," that the cabinet was "more representative," and that the move was "very public, very symbolic."[3]

In Germany, with strong rules about representational balance in politics, referred to as *Proporz*, an informal rule about gender balance emerged relatively early as well. The last all-male initial cabinet was appointed in 1957, and the last post-election cabinet with just one woman was formed in 1983. Since 1987, German cabinets have displayed a consistent upward trajectory: women's inclusion ranged between two and four ministers from 1987 to 1994, and between four and six ministers since 1998. The inclusionary norm that applies system-wide in Germany has its origins in the principle of *Proporz*, but the push for gender inclusion as part of this formula has its origins in the parties. In the German Social Democratic Party (SPD), a formal party rule applies: "at least 40 percent of each gender in boards and

---

[1] In numerical terms, women's inclusion looks different because each leader had cabinets of a different size (i.e., numbers of ministers). Mulroney's 1988 cabinet was the largest initial cabinet in Canadian history, with 38 members (seven of whom were women). Chretién's initial cabinet in 1993 included four women, but in a much smaller (by Canadian standards) cabinet of just 22 ministers.

[2] Heather Mallick, "Harper's No Ladies' Man," *Chatelaine*, November 8, 2006. http://www.chatelaine.com/living/harpers-no-ladies-man/. Retrieved August 9, 2016.

[3] "Harper's Cabinet Strategy," *Globe and Mail*, October 31, 2008; Jeffrey Simpson, "Harper's Improved Cabinet," *Globe and Mail*, October 31, 2008; Peter Donolo, quoted in Jane Taber, "The New Cabinet, Gender Equity," *Globe and Mail*, October 30, 2008.

lists" (Party Statutes, Article 11 [2][4]). As noted in Chapter 7, this rule has been interpreted as applying to cabinet spots as well. When discussing the SPD party quota, a former minister said, "men and women are equal and should be equally positioned in the party. If we have six ministries, then it should be three women and three men [. . .]. The SPD always pays attention to at least 40 percent women. If we got seven ministries then it could be four women and three men, mostly it was four men and three women."[5] Another former minister confirmed, "An SPD Chancellor must definitely have a gender balance. He could not afford to have, say 80 percent men and 20 percent women [. . .]. These days no SPD Chancellor would be able to afford to put up a cabinet that didn't have 35–40 percent women. That is a law, that's how it is."[6] A former SPD minister confirmed the power of this rule by referring to sanctions: "if the leader of our party appointed five men and just one women then there would be a riot in the party, that wouldn't be on."[7] Similar party gender quotas apply in the Greens, which was in government with the SPD from 1998 to 2005. The Greens introduced a rule on gender equality for all lists in the 1980s.[8]

Although the strong gender component of *Proporz* has its origins in the SPD and the Greens, there has been a broader diffusion effect, meaning that it would now be inconceivable for a CDU/CSU government to fall below around one-third women; the public criticism would be too strong.[9] Asked if the SPD's gender norm now has broader application across all parties, a former minster said, "No one would dare propose an all-male cabinet. And even the FDP, a party that is against quotas, wrings its hands to make sure that a least one woman is in the executive (*Vorstand*) and would probably entrust one woman to a ministry."[10]

The importance of the formal party rule on gender as a mechanism for facilitating women's inclusion in cabinet was made clear in interviews. A former minister said, "if we didn't have the quota women would always lose out [. . .] now they are forced to say, I can't just put forward men, I also have to nominate women and I have to have women on my radar. Without

[4] http://www.quotaproject.org/uid/countryview.cfm?CountryCode=DE#sources.
[5] Interview with former minister, October 29, 2014.
[6] Interview with former minister, October 27, 2014.
[7] Interview with former minister, October 29, 2014.
[8] Interview with former minister June 30, 2016.
[9] Interviews with former ministers, October 27, 2014, October 29, 2014, June 30, 2016; interview with political journalist, October 30, 2014.
[10] Interview with former minister, October 29, 2014.

the quota they would say 'no, she doesn't quite fit, he would be better, he would be better, he would be better. The quota is the precondition for women even having a chance to demonstrate their talents in politics."[11]

The representational rule about gender now requires that German selectors actively look for women. One former minister was clear about the role that gender played in her selection for cabinet: "I got it because, first, they definitely needed a woman [. . .] I embodied the gender with competence and a biography that fit."[12] Another expert gave the appointment of Barbara Henricks as an example: "[she] got her post because a minister was needed from the *Land* of North Rhine-Westphalia, plus she is a woman."[13] That said, the questioning of women's "merit" has not completely gone away. A former minister said, "that argument about merit always comes up. But it never comes up when we say we need someone from the trade union, we need someone from that region, we need someone from there. In those cases, no one thinks about saying 'only the qualified, only the best.'"[14]

Similar evidence that representational criteria have been re-gendered to women's inclusion appears in Chile and Spain, countries where legacies of dictatorship have produced deeply entrenched norms about the inclusionary aspects of democracy. Socialist president Salvador Allende formed Chile's last all-male cabinet in 1970, but three years later his government was brutally overthrown in a military coup that led to 17 years of dictatorship. Following the return to democracy, however, every Chilean cabinet included at least one woman. In 1990, the first post-dictatorship president, Patricio Aylwin, only included one woman, but over the next decade, women's movements and feminists in the political parties of the *Concertación* coalition put the issue of gender equality in politics firmly on the public agenda, making a clear link between Chile's status as a modern democracy and the need to fully incorporate women into arenas of power (Franceschet 2005). Women's lobbying efforts paid off in 2000 when Socialist president Ricardo Lagos appointed a record number of women to his post-election cabinet (five women in a 17-member cabinet). His successor, Michelle Bachelet, appointed a parity cabinet. What is notable, however, is that even when the center-left *Concertación* lost government to the political right for the first time, the new president, Sebastián Piñera, while not matching Bachelet's record of appointing female

[11] Interview with former minister, October 29, 2014.
[12] Interview with former minister, October 27, 2014.
[13] Interview with country expert, October 28, 2014.
[14] Interview with former minister, October 29, 2014.

ministers, still managed to construct an initial cabinet in which women held 27.1 percent of portfolios.[15] Indeed, such behavior by Piñera was anticipated in the media: after his election, some columnists speculated that he would be looking for women to include in his cabinet, although Piñera himself said that he "was not going to marry himself to the idea of total gender parity as did Bachelet."[16]

In Spain, no women were appointed to the first four post-election cabinets after the end of the Franco dictatorship.[17] Felipe González, leader of the leftist PSOE, appointed two all-male post-election cabinets, in 1982 and 1986. It was not until González formed his third and fourth governments that he began to include women in initial cabinets, after feminists in the party mobilized around and won internal party quotas for women (Verge 2007, 2010). In 1989, González's post-election cabinet included two women (of 18 posts, or 11 percent), and his final cabinet in 1993 included three women (of 17 posts, or 17.6 percent). As in Canada, it was a selector on the right—in this case José María Aznar (PP)—who appointed a record number of women (four) to a much smaller cabinet (with just 14 posts). To a great extent, Aznar's actions were driven by electoral competition with the PSOE, and by the conservative leader's wish to demonstrate symbolically that the People's Party (PP) was a modern and democratic political party. Setting a new record for women's inclusion in cabinet was a relatively easy way to signal to Spanish citizens that the PP embraced a modern and inclusionary view of democracy. A strong inclusionary norm was further entrenched when Zapatero appointed two successive gender parity cabinets (2004 and 2008). When the PP returned to government again after eight years in opposition, its leader, Mariano Rajoy, appointed a record number of women for his party, surpassing the record set by Aznar. Although Rajoy's initial cabinet in 2011 was the smallest in the post-Franco era, with just 13 ministers, he nonetheless appointed women to four of the portfolios (30.7 percent).

In the United States, although the first woman was appointed to cabinet as early as 1933, only recently has gender representation shifted from "only men" to "include women." Beginning with the Carter administration, there has been increasing attention to women's inclusion in cabinet and moves toward the regular appointment of women—and more than one—to cabinet posts.

---

[15] Sabina Drysdale and Paula Coddeu, "Los Sebastián boys," *El Mercurio*, January 23, 2010.
[16] Quoted in Eduardo Sepúlveda, "Ningún padrino, ningún cacique nos va a imponer a ninguna autoridad ni funcionario en nuestro gobierno," *El Mercurio*, January 24, 2010.
[17] Some women were brought in during cabinet shuffles, however.

The last all-male post-election cabinet was appointed by Ronald Reagan in his first presidential term (1981), but the Carter cabinet (1977) had already included two women from the outset. Reagan subsequently included one woman in his second post-election cabinet (1985), and President George H. W. Bush, succeeding Reagan, similarly appointed one woman to his initial (1989) cabinet.

With Bill Clinton, the numbers of women appointed to cabinet increased. Clinton was the first president to appoint more than two women, appointing three women to his first post-election cabinet (1993), and four women to his second-term post-election cabinet (1997).[18] George W. Bush appointed three female cabinet secretaries in his first post-election cabinet and matched Clinton by similarly appointing four women to his second-term initial cabinet.[19] Barack Obama appointed four women to his initial cabinet,[20] dropping back to three in his second-term post-election cabinet.[21] Obama's appointment of eight women to cabinet posts, although they did not serve concurrently, demonstrates that a sufficient number of women can be found in the United States to construct a gender parity cabinet.[22]

Across the three most recent two-term US presidencies, presidents of different parties have appointed at least three women in every initial cabinet. They have done so in the absence of any formal party rules that require such inclusion (as in the UK Labour Party; see discussion in the following); in the absence of any gender quotas for legislative candidacies; and, since Bill Clinton, in the absence of any appointment promises.[23] Women's inclusion in cabinet based on a gendered representational criterion has become firmly established.

In the United Kingdom, party rules in the Labour Party set new expectations about gender as representational criterion. As set out in Chapter 7,

[18] Clinton also appointed the first women to three cabinet posts that had historically been held only by men: attorney general (Janet Reno), secretary of energy (Hazel O'Leary), and secretary of state (Madeleine Albright).

[19] G. W. Bush appointed a woman as secretary of state (Condoleezza Rice) and appointed the first (and still only) woman to lead the Department of Agriculture (Ann Veneman).

[20] Obama appointed women as secretaries of state (Hillary Clinton) and homeland security (Janet Napolitano), among others.

[21] Obama appointed the second woman ever to serve as attorney general, Loretta Lynch, in 2015.

[22] The US cabinet is currently at its largest size: 15. Gender parity, defined as 50 percent $\pm/-1$, requires only seven or eight women to achieve.

[23] Mitchell Locin, "Clinton Finishes Cabinet of Diversity, Appointments Make History," *Chicago Tribune*, December 25, 1992. It is worth noting that as Democratic presidential candidate in 2016, Hillary Clinton promised to appoint a cabinet that "looks like America," confirming that women would have been nominated for half of her cabinet posts.

during the 1980s and 1990s a series of changes were made to the Standing Orders of the Parliamentary Labour Party (PLP) which govern the process of shadow cabinet elections. These PLP rules about gender were directly responsible for the record number of women appointed to UK cabinet in 1997.[24] Labour prime minister Tony Blair appointed five women to his 21-member cabinet (or 28.5 percent), up from the previous high of two women under Harold Wilson (1974–1979) and John Major (1992–1997). Once in government, Prime Minister Tony Blair was permitted by his party to appoint future cabinets. It is clear that the party rules on gender set new expectations, with his two subsequent cabinets either equaling or increasing the number of women in cabinet (six in 2001 and five in 2005). Feminist lobbying of Blair from within his party, for example, by his political secretary Sally Morgan, served to sustain the number of female ministers at this magnitude for subsequent cabinets.[25] Labour Party leaders since Blair have committed to gender parity in ministerial appointments.

In the Conservative Party, expectations about gender representation in cabinet changed significantly when the party returned to office in 2010 after 13 years of Labour Party governments. Such change is clearly visible in David Cameron's overt pledge in 2008 that, if elected, he would appoint women to one-third of his government's cabinet posts by the end of his first term in office.[26] Notably, the pledge was not a response to any feminist pressure from within the Conservative Party,[27] but rather part of Cameron's strategic pitch to change the image of the Conservative Party (Childs and Webb 2011) and to compete with Labour for female voters (Annesley and Gains 2014). In our media data we find evidence of Cameron being sanctioned through criticism for his failure to produce a more diverse team, despite his pledge. When Cameron was elected in 2010, the share of women in cabinet dropped from 25 percent in 2005 to 18 percent (Annesley and Gains 2010), because no women were appointed by the Liberal Democrats, the Conservatives' coalition partners. One commentator noted that, despite promises of a new politics of Coalition, "the right school and university, a palatable public manner and the xy chromosome remain the vital determinants of power. . . . [A]ll the governing coalition has to offer is the arcane spectacle, more tribal than class or credo, of male supremacy."[28] At the same time, criticism of Cameron's

---

[24] Interview with former special advisor, July 11, 2016.
[25] Interviews with former minister December 17, 2013 and former special advisor, July 11, 2016.
[26] "Cameron Vow on Women Ministers," *The Guardian*, March 2, 2008.
[27] Interview with former minister, June 7, 2016.
[28] "This Far But No Further?" *The Telegraph*, May 14, 2010.

one-third pledge reveals the persistence of the old narratives about appointment on merit rather than gender. For example, former Conservative minister Ann Widdecombe said she would have been "grossly insulted" to be promoted on such grounds, adding, "I just don't see how you can say what proportion of your government will be male or female, over or under 40, or ginger or blonde. When I was made a minister, it was presumably because I had convinced somebody somewhere I had earned it."[29] One newspaper commentator wrote, "I want the best people in the job, whether they are male, female or hermaphrodite, not mediocrities who have been picked to satisfy a quota mentality."[30]

When re-elected with a single-party majority government in 2015, Cameron delivered on the one-third pledge, appointing seven women to his 21-member cabinet (33.3 percent), an act that met with overt praise.[31] When Theresa May became prime minister in June 2016, she initially maintained women's presence at seven, though this then fell to five following the 2017 general election, despite media speculation that she might set a new UK standard by appointing a gender parity cabinet. Overall, there is clear evidence that gender as a representational criterion has become firmly established across both parties of government in the United Kingdom.

Australia is the outlier among our seven cases, where a gendered representational rule regarding women's inclusion is weakly institutionalized and not strongly enforced, meaning that selectors can ignore this rule. This happened in 2013 with Prime Minister Tony Abbott. Despite sanctions in the form of criticism and disapproval, he proceeded to appoint just one woman to his cabinet. The inclusion of women is nonetheless an extant representational criterion. Following the 2013 election, media reports insisted that the new prime minister must assure "adequate representation in the ministry by state of origin, gender, membership of the upper or lower house, and party—as between the Liberal and National parties."[32] In Australia, there are numerous advocates for the principle of including women as part of the gender representational criterion. As Liberal MP Margaret Fitzherbert observed at the time, a cabinet with only one or two women is "just not representative" of

[29] Cited in "Cameron Vow on Women Ministers," *The Guardian*, March 2, 2008.

[30] "Few Women in the Cabinet, beyond Theresa May: Does This Matter?" *Telegraph Online*, May 12, 2010.

[31] See, for example, http://www.bloomberg.com/news/articles/2015-05-11/cameron-says-johnson-to-attend-cabinet-as-he-promotes-women.

[32] "Abbott Told to Drop Also-Rans from Team," *The Age*, September 11, 2013.

the nation.[33] However, the weaker institutionalization of the gender representational criterion in Australia is evidenced by the continuing presence of
preexisting stronger narratives that counter women's inclusion with claims
about "merit," arguments that are particularly strong in the Liberal Party.
Liberal foreign minister Julie Bishop said her party "appoints and promotes
on merit, not gender. That's what women are looking for: recognition of their
talents, not of their chromosomes."[34] In contrast, an Australian Labor Party
politician rejected "merit" and appointment of women as conflicting criteria,
explaining in an interview that "[the ALP] absolutely appoint on merit as
well but we are missing out on half the population if we don't give proper regard to [women's] merit."[35]

Moreover, the gendered representational criterion of including women
in cabinet often competes with, and loses out to other, more forceful representational criteria. Put another way, the appointment of women is on the
checklist, but it is not a priority in the Liberal Party, and therefore can be
ignored—or disparaged. As one former Coalition minister Kay Patterson put
it, the prime minister "has to take into account a lot more than gender."[36]
The competitive rather than complementary nature of representational
criteria is apparent in both parties, despite the claim that the Labor Party is
concerned about not "missing out on half the population." Indeed, women
within the party have forcefully documented how women's inclusion in cabinet is crowded out by strong competition between two party factions: the
right, "influenced by Catholic social teaching," and the left, "influenced by
traditional labour-market protectionist beliefs" (Kent 2009, 145). Labor
Party caucus control over elections for ministerial positions have been
flagged by insiders as one of the biggest hurdles to women in executive office (Ryan 1999a; Summers 2003).[37] The first female Labor minister, Susan
Ryan, appointed in 1983, stated that "factional party power stymied more
women than parliament" (1999a, 138). More recently, the former speaker of
the Australian House of Representatives, Anna Burke, criticized Labor Party
faction leaders as "faceless men [who are] firmly in control" of the ministerial
selection process, to the detriment of women who hope for a "meritorious
selection."[38]

[33] Cited in "Libs 'Shocked' by Lack of Women in Cabinet," *The Australian*, September 12, 2013.
[34] Cited in *The Australian Magazine*, September 28, 2013.
[35] Interview, March 23, 2010.
[36] Cited in "Libs 'Shocked' by Lack of Women in Cabinet," *The Australian*, September 13, 2013.
[37] Interview with former minister, March 23, 2010.
[38] "Fraction Too Much Faction in Labor 'Cabal,'" *The Australian*, October 13, 2013.

Table 10.1 Number of Representational Qualifying Criteria, and Women's Presence in Cabinet, by Country and Date of Last All-Male Cabinet

Country	Representational Criteria	N of Criteria	Year of Last All-Male Cabinet	Highest % of Women in Cabinet
Australia	Sex, region, party/party faction, chamber of parliament	3	1993	22.7
Canada	Sex, region, language, race/ethnicity	4	1968	50.0
Chile**	Sex, party	2	1970	50.0
Germany	Sex, region, party, religion*	4	1957	46.2
Spain	Sex, region*	2	1986	56.0
United Kingdom	Sex, region, race/ethnicity	3	1987	33.3
United States	Sex, race/ethnicity	2	1981	26.7

*Varies by party.

**Includes democratic governments only.

Conclusion: The Power of Representational Criteria

We find that a strong predictor of women's inclusion in cabinet is the presence of an institutionalized representational rule on gender that insists on such inclusion. As Table 10.1 shows, across our country cases, such a rule clearly exists: the era of all-male cabinets has decisively ended across our cases. Contrary to our expectation, however, we find that even in the countries with an established tradition of appointing ministers on general representational grounds, recasting gender to include women has been relatively easy and uncontroversial; there is no apparent impact of the number of representational criteria in a country on its inclusion of women in cabinet. Table 10.1 summarizes the extent to which the inclusion of women in cabinet has been institutionalized as a representational criterion. Operationalizing institutionalization of this informal rule as the year of a country's last all-male cabinet, we anticipated that the experience of women's cabinet inclusion in a comparatively greater distance across time would erode the novelty of female cabinet ministers. As Table 10.1 shows, Germany and Canada were first to relinquish the practice of appointing all-male cabinets. These same two countries have embraced the continued, uninterrupted inclusion of women and are among those to have achieved the highest magnitude of women in cabinet.

Although women's inclusion as a representational criterion is clear across all our cases, the number of female ministers needed to satisfy the inclusionary rule varies. Moreover, in countries with weaker requirements to balance ministerial appointments on representational grounds, rewriting the representational rule on gender to include women has met with resistance, often couched in the language of "merit." In the next chapter we show how such inclusionary gains, or concrete floors, develop and become locked in for each of our cases.

11
Concrete Floors and
Cabinet Appointments
Explaining Gendered Outcomes and Change

Cabinet appointments matter because cabinets and "the core executive [are] the most significant venue for achieving the substantive representation of women" (Annesley and Gains 2010, 909). Around the world, however, women are less likely to achieve ministerial office than are men, which prompted the three research questions of this book: Why are more men than women appointed to cabinet? Why do women's appointments to cabinet vary cross-nationally? And why have gendered patterns of appointment changed over time? This chapter summarizes our answers to these three questions and develops and explains one of this book's most important findings and conceptual contributions: namely, the emergence of concrete floors that establish enduring minimum thresholds for women's cabinet representation. We conclude the chapter by outlining the book's main theoretical contributions and the practical implications that emerge from our findings.

Why Have More Men Than Women Been Appointed to Cabinet?

More men than women become ministers not because there is a dearth of eligible or qualified women, but because rules for cabinet appointments generally allow presidents and prime ministers significant agency when choosing their ministers, thus permitting them to employ qualifying criteria that advantage men. Our research shows that rules about selection and qualifying criteria empower selectors to follow strategic incentives to appoint ministers on the basis of trust and loyalty and to interpret experiential criteria flexibly to support such selection. There are no prohibitions on selectors appointing from their personal and political network of friends and allies, and although rules also prescribe that each minister meets experiential criteria, Chapter 5 demonstrates that such criteria are flexible and non-specific. Chapter 9 showed that these rules have gendered consequences and produce gendered outcomes. The gendered outcome of predominantly male cabinets is not, however, the consequence of prescriptive rules about appointing men. Rather, men's over-representation among ministers owes to the absence of prohibitions on appointing mostly men, the fact that (male) selectors' networks tend to be primarily populated by men, and flexibility in interpreting experiential criteria. In other words, all-male and mostly male cabinets are the product of rules that permit affiliational criteria and prescribe experiential criteria, but do not prescribe gender as a representational criterion. We find that the presence of representational criteria that prescribe women's inclusion in cabinet is the key factor prohibiting selectors' use of affiliational and experiential criteria to appoint all-male cabinets exclusively from their networks of trust and loyalty. Our research finds, however, that a representational criterion relating to gender is a relatively recent phenomenon, and, more important, varies in strength cross-nationally.

What Explains Cross-National Variation?

Many of the factors found to affect women's parliamentary representation and the process of legislative recruitment are not appropriate for understanding the gendered nature of cabinet formation. We find that cross-national variation in women's cabinet appointments cannot be explained by political system type, the number of selectors and/or veto players, or the individual characteristics of the selectors, such as whether they come from a left or right party, or whether they are male or female. Instead, our study finds that variation across countries can be explained by differences in qualifying criteria and differences in how selectors have used their political agency and autonomy to exploit the flexibility in qualifying criteria.

Chapter 6 showed that all selectors face strategic incentives to use affiliation as a *ministrable* qualifying criterion. Doing so is permitted, but only insofar as experiential and representational criteria leave room for selectors to choose ministers on the basis of trust and loyalty. Because experiential criteria are generally flexible, as evidenced in Chapter 5, such criteria allow selectors significant latitude; all ministers will meet some experiential criteria, whether in the form of political experience, policy expertise, or educational credentials that can be linked to the cabinet portfolio.

Representational criteria, on the other hand, do not permit such latitude. Representational criteria, albeit taking the form of informal rules, are specific and prescriptive, requiring selectors to include ministers with particular characteristics like sex, race, ethnicity, or region of origin. In two of our country cases, Canada and Germany, representational criteria are plentiful and strongly institutionalized, giving selectors less latitude to employ affiliational criteria. Where representational criteria are only weakly institutionalized, as is the case in Australia, affiliational relationships with selectors remain a powerful route to ministerial office. As we showed in Chapter 9, however, the predominance of affiliational criteria do not neatly predict cross-national patterns in women's appointment to cabinet. Canada and Germany have high proportions of women in cabinet, but so too does Spain, where membership in the prime minister's affiliational network is a strong predictor of cabinet appointment.

If the prevalence of affiliational criteria does not explain cross-national variation on its own, what does? Our study finds that the political agency exercised by certain selectors plays a key role in establishing new representational criteria prescribing women's inclusion. Where presidents or prime ministers exploit the absence of prohibitions on increasing the number of female ministers and/or use their agency to respond to lobbying from feminists in their political party, they are able to appoint women to cabinet and reconfigure the gender representational criterion to include women. Such selectors may be deviating from past practices of appointing mostly men, but we find no evidence that such leaders are sanctioned for appointing women. On the contrary, selectors who include more women are praised by journalists, by political commentators, and by feminists in the parties for their actions. In all our country cases, presidents and prime ministers face few rules that prohibit them from appointing women to cabinet, including in large numbers. Those country cases with few women in cabinet, such as Australia and the United States, have not yet had selectors willing to act on their agency and autonomy to include equitable numbers of women in cabinet.

What Explains Change over Time?

Our data on women's appointment to initial cabinets across seven countries show long periods where all-male or mostly male cabinets were regularly formed. Over time, the number of women appointed has grown steadily across all countries, reaching high magnitudes of 30 percent or more in several. The change in gendered patterns is clear, however: all-male cabinets have disappeared, with countries like Germany leaving them behind in 1958, while others, like Australia, forming an all-male cabinet as late as 1993. We argue that cross-time and cross-national variation share a similar dynamic: namely, the interaction of rules about selection and rules about who can be selected. Both sets of rules create space for political agency that some selectors use to initiate an increase in the number of women appointed. As noted earlier, such selectors are not sanctioned, but are generally praised for such actions. This means that political learning plays an important role in generating new representational criteria that prescribe women's inclusion. Political leaders learn lessons "about the costs and benefits that accrue from choosing one alternative over another" (Mershon 1994, 51). When a selector earns public praise for substantially increasing women's presence, subsequent leaders may likewise wish to enjoy those same benefits and may even fear the costs of public criticism for not continuing with the practice of women's inclusion. Over time, therefore, women's inclusion becomes a new representational criterion for cabinet appointments. In the following, we illustrate this dynamic for each of our seven cases through the development of the concept of the concrete floor.

The Concrete Floor

We developed the concept of a concrete floor to help make sense of our main empirical finding, namely, that once a certain threshold of women's ministerial inclusion is firmly established, it does not decrease. We define a concrete floor as the minimum number or proportion of women in cabinet for that ministerial team to be perceived as legitimate. We find both terms in the metaphor helpful. First, concrete, once set, is strong and nearly permanent, and can only be broken with difficulty.[1] Second, floors can be raised over time.[2]

We operationalize the establishment of a concrete floor as a three-step process that can only be evidenced retrospectively (see Figure 11.1). That is, we can only conclude that a concrete floor has been established when a specific

---

[1] One would need to a jackhammer to destroy an actual concrete floor.

[2] For a more detailed discussion of the metaphor of the concrete floor, see Beckwith, Franceschet, and Annesley (2017).

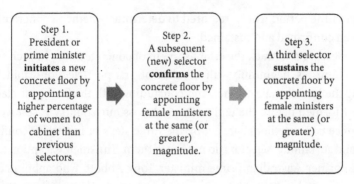

Figure 11.1. Initiating, confirming, and sustaining concrete floors.

level of women's inclusion in cabinet is sustained across three iterations of post-election cabinets by three successive selectors or sets of selectors. One selector *initiates* a new concrete floor by appointing a number of women to an initial cabinet; the next selector *confirms* it by appointing the same number of women to his or her cabinet; and a third selector *sustains* it by continuing women's inclusion in cabinet at the same (or higher) level. We further specify that a concrete floor must be initiated, confirmed, and sustained by three different selectors, forming a post-election cabinet, to increase our confidence that we are identifying the effect of something more than individual behavior or personal preference on the part of returning selectors, thereby identifying rules and not regularities (Mershon 1994). A concrete floor does not require a change of party government to be confirmed or sustained, but it does require a change of selector following an election and is based on that selector's initial cabinet. Finally, our concept is conservatively operationalized. Although a president or prime minister may increase the number of women included in a newly formed cabinet, compared to a previous cabinet, the initial number of women in cabinet sets the floor, regardless of simple increases above that number, unless confirmed and sustained by subsequent selectors.[3]

Note that our approach to operationalizing a concrete floor means that it will be easier to identify the floor in some countries than in others. Where there is a high turnover of selectors, it may be possible to identify a concrete floor sooner. In other cases, where the same selector forms several cabinets,

---

[3] For example, Barack Obama appointed four women to his first-term initial cabinet in 2009, but only three to his second-term cabinet in 2013, sustaining a concrete floor of three for women's US cabinet inclusion.

a longer time period will be required to determine whether a concrete floor has been confirmed and sustained.

We measure and track the establishment of concrete floors in each of our seven countries, beginning with the date of first post-election cabinet following the last all-male cabinet, and concluding with the final post-election cabinet formed before the end of 2016. Across our country cases, we find that, once concrete floors are set by the three steps of initiation, confirmation, and sustaining, selectors do not break them. The single exception to this rule is former Australian prime minister Tony Abbott, who appointed just one woman to his 2013 cabinet, therein breaking the existing concrete floor of three (and at least 15 percent). Abbott was strongly criticized by politicians and the media, and his successor, Malcolm Turnbull, formed a cabinet in 2016 that restored the concrete floor by appointing at least three women to his cabinet.[4]

For each country, we measure the concrete floor in two ways: by magnitude and by number. Recall from Chapter 1 that the magnitude of women's presence in cabinet is measured as an ordinal variable of five categories: very low (0 to 9 percent of cabinet), low (10 to 19 percent), medium (20 to 29 percent), high (30 percent or more), and parity (50 percent +/−1).[5] We developed these categories to accommodate the comparatively small size of cabinets (15–25 ministers) and the fact that once two or more women are appointed to cabinet, most country cases move into the "low" or "medium" magnitude category of women's representation in cabinet. We also establish the concrete floor as a number but recognize that numerical values are less helpful in a comparative study where cabinet size varies. A concrete floor of six female ministers tells us nothing comparatively: in the United States, where cabinets comprise 15 ministers, having a concrete floor of six means that women are close to parity; but in Canada, where cabinets often include 25 to 30 ministers, a concrete floor of six is less impressive. Nonetheless, absolute numbers matter: they

---

[4] In fact, Turnbull appointed five women to his initial cabinet. We argue that a concrete floor is only irreparable when a selector's disregard of a concrete floor is met (1) with media silence or consent from the governed, and (2) is not immediately corrected by a selector. For example, President Donald Trump broke the concrete floor ($n = 3$) in the United States, appointing only two women to his initial cabinet. His actions were met with sanctions in the form of extensive criticism; before the end of the first year of his presidency, Trump had restored the US concrete floor by appointing Kirstjen Nielsen as secretary of homeland security, bringing the number of women in cabinet back to three.

[5] We recognize that the two categories at the high end of the range are not mutually exclusive.

are frequently reported and debated in media discussions; they serve as targets for selectors (and their critics); and they influence national discourse. The requisite number of women for appointment to cabinet (a numerical concrete floor) may be firmly in the awareness of the new prime minister or president.

In the following, we explain how concrete floors develop in each of our seven countries, identifying when, where, and how rules of ministerial recruitment create opportunities for the initiation, confirmation, and sustaining of a concrete floor for women's inclusion in cabinet. Following the theoretical assumptions set out in our account of institutional change in Chapter 2, we identify the crucial roles played by agency, ambiguity, and ideational change in this process. We also identify what has constrained change in some cases. We begin with four countries with higher concrete floors where parity has been achieved at least once—Canada, Germany, Chile, and Spain—and then turn to three countries with lower concrete floors where parity has not yet been achieved—Australia, the United Kingdom, and the United States (see Table 11.1).

Table 11.1 Concrete Floors by Country, through 2016

Country	Concrete Floor (Magnitude)	Highest Magnitude Reached	Highest Number of Female Ministers (%) Reached
Australia	Low ~ broken	Medium	5 (22.7)
United Kingdom	Low	High	7 (33.3)
United States	Medium	Medium	4 (26.7)
Canada	Medium	Parity	15 (50)
Chile	Medium	Parity	10 (50)
Germany	Medium	Parity	6 (46.2)
Spain	Medium	Parity	9 (56)

Categories: very low 0%–9%; low 10%–19%; medium 20%–29%; high 30% or higher; parity.

Canada: Rules Empower Selectors to Initiate New Concrete Floors and Eventually Achieve Parity

Canada's concrete floor is the product of a combination of rules that empower selectors and rules about representational criteria. Today, the concrete floor in Canada is that women hold 20–29 percent of seats in cabinet (a medium magnitude concrete floor). Women's presence in cabinet has reached parity once, in 2015 when Prime Minister Justin Trudeau appointed an equal number of men and women to cabinet. As explained in Chapter 3, Canadian prime ministers enjoy extensive autonomy when selecting ministers. Although they are constrained by strong informal rules about qualifying criteria, prime ministers do not share selection powers or consult with party elites in making their cabinet choices. The main source of change, therefore, can be located in a system of rules that confers agency on prime ministers to initiate dramatic increases in women's cabinet inclusion.

Three distinct moments of change can be identified. The first occurred in 1984, when Conservative prime minister Brian Mulroney abandoned the practice of appointing only one woman to cabinet. Mulroney initiated a concrete floor of four female ministers, dramatically increasing the number of women in cabinet from one female minister to four (from 3.7 to almost 15 percent). No subsequent leader appointed fewer women in terms of number or proportion. In initiating the concrete floor, Mulroney exploited rules that empower prime ministers in cabinet formation.

In his memoirs, Mulroney attributes his concern for women's inclusion to his Conservative predecessor, Prime Minister John Diefenbaker, who appointed the country's first female minister. Mulroney recalls promising to promote women's rights upon his election and delivering on the promise "by appointing more women ministers, deputy ministers, senators, and judges than any other prime minister up to that time."[6] The concrete floor initiated by Mulroney was confirmed in 1993, when newly elected Liberal prime minister Jean Chretién matched the bar set by Mulroney. Chretién's 1993 post-election cabinet included virtually the same proportion of women, 18.1 percent, as Mulroney's previous post-election cabinet (18.4). Chretién then initiated a higher concrete floor, raising the floor from the low to the medium magnitude for the first time in Canadian history. By appointing seven women in his next two post-election cabinets, the concrete floor rose

---

[6] Brian Mulroney, *Memoirs, 1939–1993* (Toronto: McClelland & Stewart, 2007) (quote is on first page of Chapter 4, location 887).

from low to medium magnitude. With a party change in government in 2006, newly elected Prime Minister Stephen Harper confirmed the new medium magnitude concrete floor, appointing six women in a 26-member cabinet (23 percent).

When Harper won a parliamentary majority in 2008, he initiated a new concrete floor for women's cabinet representation, appointing eight women, hitting the 30 percent threshold, or high magnitude, for the first time in Canadian history. Journalists, columnists, and commentators praised Harper's cabinet as "more representative."[7] Although a slight decline occurred when Harper formed his third post-election cabinet in 2011, which included only seven women (26.6 percent), another historic milestone came a few years later when the Liberals returned to government. In 2015, Prime Minister Justin Trudeau named the country's first gender parity cabinet with 15 female ministers. Trudeau's cabinet was widely applauded for its gender balance and ethnic diversity. Criticisms in the national print media were notable for their absence.

Parity is not the new concrete floor in Canada. According to our operationalization of the concrete floor, Trudeau confirmed a concrete floor at a high magnitude (30 percent). At this writing, Trudeau is still in his first term as prime minister, and we will not know if the floor is sustained at that magnitude until he is replaced by another prime minister. Hence, the concrete floor remains at medium rather than high magnitude. Although we cannot be entirely certain what a new selector will do, our concept of the concrete floor leads us to believe that no matter which party wins the next parliamentary election, women's cabinet inclusion will likely be sustained at the high magnitude set by Prime Minister Harper in 2008. Given that strongly prescriptive rules about representation in Canadian cabinets have always existed, and leaders who increase women's presence are praised rather than criticized, future leaders are unlikely to risk the sanction of public criticism by moving backward in terms of women's inclusion.

Germany: Progress Driven by Parties and *Proporz*

The concrete floor in Germany currently stands at medium in magnitude and four in number. Parity was reached in 2002, by the SPD-Green coalition,

[7] "Harper's Cabinet Strategy," *Globe and Mail*, October 31, 2008; Jeffrey Simpson, "Harper's Improved Cabinet," *Globe and Mail*, October 31, 2008; Peter Donolo, quoted in Jane Taber, "The New Cabinet, Gender Equity," *Globe and Mail*, October 30, 2008.

but was not confirmed as a new concrete floor. Similarly, a high magnitude in women's representation was initiated in 1998 by SPD-Green and confirmed in 2005 by the Grand Coalition, but it reverted to medium by the next set of CDU-FDP selectors in 2008 and so was not sustained.

In Germany, the formal rules of ministerial recruitment empower chancellors to choose ministers, but strong informal rules always constrain them through the requirements (1) to share some powers of selection with co-selectors in their own party, and (2) to relinquish powers over some ministerial selections to their coalition partners. In other words, in contrast to Canada, it is not the selector acting alone who has initiated a new concrete floor. Rather, the agents of change who initiate a higher concrete floor are in political parties. The SPD and the Greens both introduced formal party rules that mandated women's representation across all internal positions. Ambiguity about the applicability of these quota rules led to their being applied to cabinet as well as other internal party positions when the two parties first formed a coalition government in 1998. This initiated Germany's first high magnitude cabinet of five ministers (31.25 percent).

Unlike the SPD, the CDU did not have a similarly prescriptive party rule. It had a softer 30 percent *Kannbestimmung* instead. Nevertheless, interviewees reported that an informal rule of 30–40 percent women now applies across all parties. Thus, when the Grand Coalition was formed between the CDU/CSU and SPD in 2005, a high magnitude of 33 percent was confirmed. That high magnitude was not sustained with the next change of selectors, as the CDU/CSU's next partner, the FDP, a party with no rules on gender representation, appointed just one female minister among its allocation. Interview data indicate that there would now be sanctions in the form of public and political disapproval if women's representation were not to reach 40 percent in cabinet.[8]

The establishment of a higher concrete floor was relatively uncontroversial in Germany. This can be explained by the long-established tradition of using representational criteria when making public appointments—known as *Proporz*. This tradition meant that it was comparatively easy to map on gender as a component of *Proporz* following a process of ideational change, largely driven by feminists within parties. With gender as a component of *Proporz*, selectors across all parties were required to find women to meet

---

[8] Interviews with former ministers, October 27, 2014, October 29, 2014; country expert, October 28, 2014; and broadcast journalist, October 30, 2014.

the representational criteria. Women's cabinet appointments have not been strongly contested on grounds of experiential "merit." As one minister said, "the women are just as good as the men. The argument that we need qualified people has run its course."[9] Rather, gender as a component of *Proporz* appears to be increasingly accepted: part of a female *ministrable*'s qualification is the very fact that she helps selectors to fulfill representational criteria.

Spain: Steady Progress Driven by Empowered Selectors and Feminists in Political Parties

Since 2004, all post-election cabinets in Spain have included women at high magnitudes (30 percent or more), reaching gender parity in initial cabinets in 2004 and 2008. Given that there have been few changes in prime ministers in Spain between 2004 and 2016, our operationalization of the concrete floor does not yet permit us to conclude that a high-magnitude concrete floor has been sustained. A medium-magnitude concrete floor (20 to 29 percent, with three female ministers) was initiated in 1996, confirmed in 2004, and sustained in 2011. The trajectory in Spain, however, is one of steady gains driven primarily by ideational change, feminists in the leftist parties, and empowered prime ministers committed to gender equality. A former minister explained in an interview that one of the long-term effects of Zapatero's two consecutive parity cabinets was that any future regression would have to be justified. In her view, equality was now the norm, and any deviation would need to be accounted for.[10]

Both major Spanish political parties have initiated new concrete floors. After winning a third term in office in 1989, Felipe González initiated a concrete floor of two women, thereby moving Spain from zero to low magnitude (10 to 19 percent) for women's cabinet inclusion. Prime Minister José María Aznar, of the People's Party (PP), set a new bar, appointing four women (28.6 percent) to a much smaller cabinet with just 14 posts, moving Spain for the first time from low to medium magnitude. When the Socialists returned to power in 2004, Spain got its first gender parity government, led

---

[9] Interview with former minster, October 29, 2014, Berlin.

[10] Interview, May 21, 2012, Madrid. The minister may have been correct. Although falling outside of our time-frame, Pedro Sánchez, a new prime minister from the PSOE, took office in June 2018, after the government of Mariano Rajoy lost a confidence motion in parliament. Sánchez appointed the world's first cabinet in which women hold a super majority (11 of 17 posts).

by José Luis Rodríguez Zapatero (and upon re-election in 2008, Zapatero appointed a female majority cabinet). When the conservative PP returned to power in 2011, Prime Minister Mariano Rajoy appointed a cabinet with 30 percent female ministers (high magnitude), adding yet another woman to his post-election 2016 cabinet, putting women's cabinet representation at 38 percent.

The steady gains in women's inclusion in Spain owe primarily to the significant autonomy enjoyed by prime ministers to select ministers and to broader ideational changes at the societal level in favor of gender equality. Feminists in the PSOE were successful in having a party quota adopted in 1988, and even though leaders in the People's Party rejected gender quotas, electoral incentives led them to include women in an effort to present itself as a modern conservative party. Feminists in the PSOE had a strong ally when Zapatero became PSOE leader in 2000. In the lead-up to the 2004 general election, Zapatero promised to appoint a gender-equal cabinet if elected. Given the lack of constraints on selectors in Spain, and the fact that Zapatero had many women in his political networks, it was easy for him to keep that promise.

Chile: The Power of Pledges and Feminist Lobbying

Chile's concrete floor currently stands at medium magnitude (20 to 29 percent), with a clear upward trajectory. The floor was initiated in 2000 by Socialist president Ricardo Lagos, with five women in a 17-member cabinet (29.4 percent). A decade after the return of democracy, women in the center and left parties of the *Concertación* were frustrated by the slow progress women were making in elected and appointed office. At the time, efforts to build support for gender quotas for elected office were going nowhere. Feminists in the parties realized they might be more successful if they lobbied presidents to use their powers of appointment to improve women's political representation. After Lagos' election, women in the parties lobbied the incoming president to appoint a cabinet in which women made up at least one-third of ministers, even handing him a list of names of women as potential cabinet appointments (Franceschet 2005). In this regard, activists made female *ministrables* visible to the selector. These efforts were successful: President Lagos came very close to meeting that target, approaching 30 percent.

President Lagos' successor, Michelle Bachelet, confirmed the concrete floor initiated by Lagos, but went even further, appointing the country's first gender parity cabinet. Even though Bachelet represented the same coalition of political parties that had governed Chile since 1990, she effectively used her gender as a strategic advantage, positioning herself outside of the country's elite male political networks. In a further effort to signal political renewal, she promised gender equality in cabinet, a promise that she easily kept since Chilean presidents do not share selection powers with other political actors. In 2010, the government changed hands and, for the first time since 1990, a coalition of parties of the right won the presidency. President Piñera sustained the concrete floor initiated by Lagos, appointing six female ministers in a cabinet of 22 (27.2 percent). In sum, since 2000, women's inclusion has been firmly established at this medium magnitude, and there is no reason to expect regression, given that Chilean presidents from both left and right have respected the concrete floor they have built.

United States: Empowered Selectors, Slow to Respond to Feminists in Political Parties

The United States, like Chile, has a medium magnitude concrete floor (20 to 29 percent magnitude). Republican President Reagan appointed the country's last all-male post-election cabinet in 1981, but included Elizabeth Dole as transportation secretary in his second-term cabinet in 1985, thereby initiating a concrete floor of one (of very low magnitude). This floor was confirmed by Republican George H. W. Bush in 1989 and sustained by Democratic president Bill Clinton in 1993. Not only did Clinton sustain this concrete floor, he also initiated a new floor, increasing the number of women in the US cabinet to three (or medium magnitude). This new concrete floor was confirmed by Republican president George W. Bush in 2001 and in 2005 and was sustained by Democratic president Barack Obama in 2009. Unlike the Chilean case, however, no US selector has initiated a higher concrete floor.

US presidents are empowered to appoint their cabinet ministers; although constitutional rules formally permit the Senate to reject the president's choices, the Senate does not routinely use that power (and certainly not to block women from cabinet appointment simply on the grounds of sex). Effectively, there are no co-selectors to prevent US presidents from appointing women to cabinet in higher magnitudes. President Clinton used his autonomy to push for stronger gender representation in 1992, making a campaign promise to appoint a cabinet "that looks like America" or at least "more like America than previous administrations" (Christopher 2001, 163); Clinton asked his transition team to seek qualified women and members of minority groups to add to the list of potential nominees (Christopher 2001, 163). Following Clinton, Presidents Bush and Obama sustained a US concrete floor of three female ministers, with Obama appointing a total of seven women to his post-election cabinets during his two terms of office. Nonetheless, even as Bush and Obama matched Clinton's appointment record, they made no promise to do so, and did not increase the number of women in cabinet during their terms of office. The US concrete floor has been stagnant across the past three decades, functioning as a cap as well as a floor.

Representational criteria are generally weak in the United States compared to other countries. In a political culture that is suspicious of representational criteria, only sex and race/ethnicity criteria are prescriptive: cabinets must include women and they must include persons of color. Despite a US concrete floor of three women, there is no prescription for a gender parity cabinet; there is only a representational rule prohibiting all-male cabinets. As a result, presidents are permitted to appoint their close male friends and allies to cabinet posts, and they consistently do so. With weak prescription regarding the number of women in cabinet and a stagnant concrete floor of three women, permission to employ affiliational criteria for cabinet appointments perpetuates the practice of presidents appointing predominantly male cabinets.

United Kingdom: Slow Progress, Hindered by Affiliational Qualifying Criteria

The concrete floor in the United Kingdom is low in magnitude (10 to 19 percent), although a high magnitude category was reached once, in 2015. Since the last all-male cabinets of the Thatcher era, progress has been uneven. Conservative prime minister John Major initiated a concrete floor of two women (9.52 percent) in 1992, following three successive all-male post-election cabinets formed by Margaret Thatcher. When Major became prime minister in 1990, he noted, "One [. . .] area of discrimination stared out at me every day" (Major 2000, 213). Made aware of issues of representation and presentation by his press secretary Gus O'Donnell (Hogg and Hill 1995, 11), and lobbied by backbench feminists in his party (Major 2000, 213), Major appointed two women to the junior ministerial ranks in 1990, subsequently promoting them to cabinet following the 1992 election, in his words, "both on merit" (Major 2000, 308).

Prime Minister Tony Blair's first Labour Party government, elected in 1997, confirmed Major's concrete floor at the low magnitude category, and initiated a new concrete floor at the medium magnitude (23.8 percent). A new floor was not initiated because Blair used his selection powers to promote women's inclusion. Rather, party rules governing Parliamentary Labour Party (PLP) shadow cabinet elections produced a cabinet with more women. In this case, the agents of change were feminists within the Labour Party who pushed, against strong resistance from their male counterparts, for rule change within their party. The number of women and the medium magnitude concrete floor were confirmed by two subsequent post-election Labour governments[11] for which Blair did have unconstrained powers of selection. Feminists within the Labour Party continually pressured Blair to appoint women. The medium magnitude concrete floor was not sustained, however. During the 2010 parliamentary election campaign, in the absence of any party requirement, Conservative leader David Cameron pledged that one-third of his future cabinet ministers would be women. Facing the formation of a coalition government, however, Cameron kept his promise, but the overall proportion of women in cabinet dropped back to a lower magnitude (18.8 percent) because his co-selector, Liberal Democrat Nick Clegg, appointed no women to the four cabinet spots allotted to his party.

As is the case for the United States, a higher concrete floor has not been sustained in the United Kingdom because the ideational change needed to secure a representational criterion of women's inclusion at higher numbers has not happened. Although the representational criterion of including women in cabinet is strong—all-male cabinets or cabinets with only one female minister are prohibited—the prescribed number of women in cabinet continues to be low, permitting prime ministers to continue the United Kingdom's strong tradition of using affiliational criteria as the primary route to qualifying for cabinet.

Moreover, there is no strong tradition of appointments on representational criteria in the United Kingdom upon which gender as a criterion can

---

[11] Blair appointed six women in his 2001 cabinet and five in his 2005 cabinet.

be mapped. Diversity in cabinet is certainly becoming a desideratum and, without doubt, the Coalition government was strongly criticized in the media for its lack of diversity in terms of both gender and class. But in equal measure, the media data are still replete with reference to how ministers should be appointed on "merit" and not gender. One commentator argued, "the assumption that Parliament or Cabinet should fully 'reflect the diversity of the electorate' is ridiculous."[12] In the absence of established representational criteria generally and of gender specifically, rules permit selectors to continue appointing on affiliational grounds, which reinforces the advantage of men in appointment to cabinet.

Australia: A Low, Slow, and Broken Concrete Floor Due to Weak Representational Criteria

The concrete floor in Australia is low in magnitude (10 to 19 percent) and is the only one among our cases to have been broken. The Australian concrete floor was established by three successive selectors as ranging between 10 and 19 percent (or three female ministers). The floor of three was initiated by Liberal prime minister John Howard in 2001, confirmed by Labor prime minister Kevin Rudd in 2007, and sustained by Labor prime minister Julia Gillard in 2010. This floor was then broken by Liberal prime minister Tony Abbott following the 2013 election, when he appointed only one female minister to cabinet. Australia is the only country in our study where a concrete floor, once initiated, confirmed, and sustained across three successive selectors, is not respected by the next. For Australia, the three questions to answer with our model are as follows: (1) How was a low concrete floor established? (2) How was possible for it to be broken? (3) Why has it not been possible to establish a higher magnitude of women's representation in the country?

Australia's concrete floor was initiated by Liberal prime minister John Howard in 1996, and then was increased in 2001. As shown in previous chapters, Liberal prime ministers always form a Coalition with the Nationals and so can reckon with predictable constraints on their capacity to appoint ministers. John Howard, who described himself as a "staunch coalitionist," opted to form a Coalition with the National Party in 1996, even though his

[12] Libby Purves, "Too Few Women? Read My Lips: I Don't Care," *The Times*, May 17, 2010.

party could have theoretically governed in its own right (Howard 2010, 275). In 1996, he was the first prime minister to raise the floor and appoint more than one woman to cabinet. Both recent Australian Labor Party prime ministers, Kevin Rudd and Julia Gillard, were permitted to bypass the party rule that empowers the party caucus to elect ministers. In other words, recent Australian prime ministers have all had strong agency to select women to cabinet, but have chosen not to use it, and there is no evidence of the selector pledge being deployed. Australia has only twice moved into medium magnitude, and even then, only barely—20 percent under Labor prime minister Kevin Rudd in 2007, and 22.7 percent under Liberal prime minister Malcolm Turnbull in 2016.

Australia lacks strong representational criteria that require selectors to include women among their ministers: the current concrete floor is three female ministers in a cabinet of around 20 ministers. Other representational criteria are also in play in Australia, relating to states, their relative electoral performance, and chamber of parliament. In contrast to Canada and Germany, however, these representational rules do not appear to be strongly prescriptive, and discretion and ambiguity play a role in limiting their impact.[13] Mapping gender onto existing representational criteria to include women is therefore contested, rather than accepted. As former minister Kay Patterson remarked when Tony Abbott was compiling his cabinet in 2013, "He has to take into account a lot more than gender," citing a fair balance between states as well as between the lower and upper houses as the most significant representational criteria.[14] The ideational change required to include women as a strong representational rule has not yet happened in Australia. It has not been successfully driven by feminists within parties or by the women's movement. As a consequence, the "merit" argument continues to be used as a strategic device to question the qualifications of female *ministrables*, and prime ministers continue to be permitted to appoint on affiliational grounds.

In the absence of an established representational rule on gender, Prime Minister Tony Abbott was permitted to appoint just one woman to his cabinet in 2013, thereby breaking the already low concrete floor. Appointments were made on affiliational grounds as Abbott stated that his trusted shadow team would continue in government. Abbott also used merit as a strategic

---

[13] As former prime minister John Howard stated (2010, 276), "Cabinets should never mathematically reflect state balance, but nor should they be ignored."

[14] "Libs 'Shocked' by Lack of Women in Cabinet," *The Australian*, September 13, 2013.

device by claiming that this would be the experienced team that the electorate deserved. Abbott's choice met with some sanctions in the form of political, media, and public criticism. More significantly, his Liberal successor, Prime Minister Malcolm Turnbull, subsequently appointed a record high of five women to his cabinet in 2016, a strong indication that one woman was, in fact, not enough.

Gendered Process and Outcomes of Cabinet Formation

In all our cases, concrete floors are established in strongly institutionalized and rule-bound contexts. They come about through a process that combines selector agency, the interpretation of ambiguity inherent in informal rules about qualification, and ideational change that resets representational criteria and prescribes rules for future selectors. The combination of factors varies across cases to explain the different magnitudes of concrete floors that have been initiated, confirmed, and sustained in each country. With few exceptions, the pattern across all cases is similar: (1) inclusion of women in cabinet, (2) a consistent, modest upward trajectory, and (3) a common concrete floor at a medium magnitude of inclusion (20 to 29 percent). Even our outlier case at the low end, Australia, repaired its broken floor at the first opportunity. Although there are multiple instances of cabinets exceeding this magnitude, no country has sustained a concrete floor of more than 30 percent.[15] Four countries have had gender parity cabinets: Canada (2015), Chile (2006), Germany (2002), and Spain (2004, 2008), but gender parity has not yet been confirmed or sustained as a concrete floor by a subsequent selector in any of our cases. The upward trajectory in all of these countries, however, offers hope that, with time, high-magnitude concrete floors will be sustained.

Rules for qualifying for cabinet interact in similar ways in all cases, powered primarily by representational criteria requiring women's inclusion in the cabinet team. Once such criteria are confirmed and sustained, selectors

[15] In the United Kingdom, 33.3 percent of members of David Cameron's single-party post-election cabinet were women; this level has not been sustained by a subsequent prime minister. Post-2016, Spain has confirmed a concrete floor, initiated by previous selectors, higher than the medium magnitude reported in Table 11.1. In 2011, Mariano Rajoy confirmed the high magnitude concrete floor of José Zapatero's parity cabinets at 30.8 percent and, in 2016, at 38.0 percent. In June 2018, Pedro Sánchez, replacing Mariano Rajoy as Spanish prime minister, following a vote of no confidence, appointed a female-majority cabinet. Because Sánchez came into the prime ministership without a parliamentary election, we cannot yet consider a high magnitude to have been sustained.

comply, appointing women to cabinet at the appropriate (and sometimes higher) number. Rules about women's inclusion are enforced by feminists in the selector's party (or coalition) and the media. Representational criteria requiring women's inclusion also change selector behavior in regard to experiential and affiliational criteria, as described in the following.

Established concrete floors, matched by a newly elected president's or prime minister's cabinet choices, free selectors from the burden of justifying women's appointments on experiential grounds and of denying the importance of gender diversity in cabinet. Our previous chapters offer examples of media and opponents' criticisms of women's appointments on the grounds that those ministers were appointed on the basis of gender rather than merit. Yet this book includes multiple examples of the concomitant defense, wherein selectors justify women's appointments on experiential grounds. Such debate positions sex and merit as competing criteria, even though no empirical evidence supports such juxtaposition. The establishment of concrete floors across time and across three different selectors undergirds the representational criterion of cabinet qualification and shifts selector behavior in regard to experiential criteria. Selectors no longer need to justify women's presence in (relatively) high numbers in cabinet. To reiterate the Canadian example, Liberal prime minister Justin Trudeau justified his appointment of a gender parity cabinet by saying simply, "It's 2015."

The representational criterion also appears to change selector behavior in regard to affiliational criteria. Presidents and prime ministers continue to appoint trusted friends, political allies, and even former opponents to cabinet. Selectors in some countries also increasingly include women in their affiliational networks. Recognizing the need to appoint (more) women to cabinet, selectors do not seek female *ministrables* randomly or universally; rather, selectors continue to seek *ministrables* qualified for appointment on affiliational grounds while striving to find women who meet this criterion. Selectors are assisted in this search by activist women, inside and outside political parties, who make female *ministrables* visible to them. Presidents and prime ministers work to extend their affiliational networks to include women, increasing women's chances of cabinet appointment, and meeting their country's concrete floor for women's inclusion.

We show this relationship in Figure 11.2, reiterating the model we developed in Chapter 2 (presented there as Figure 2.1). The model posits an interactive relationship between formal and informal rules about who selects ministers and rules about who is eligible and qualified for selection. The

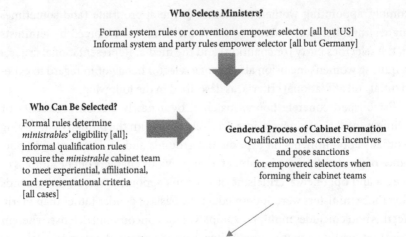

Who Selects Ministers?

Formal system rules or conventions empower selector [all but US]
Informal system and party rules empower selector [all but Germany]

Who Can Be Selected?

Formal rules determine
ministrables' eligibility [all];
informal qualification rules
require the *ministrable* cabinet team
to meet experiential, affiliational,
and representational criteria
[all cases]

Gendered Process of Cabinet Formation
Qualification rules create incentives
and pose sanctions
for empowered selectors when
forming their cabinet teams

Gendered Composition of Cabinet

Figure 11.2. The cabinet appointment process: formal and informal rules interact to produce gendered process and outcomes.

findings confirm our original model as useful for understanding the rules shaping the process and outcome of cabinet formation. As this chapter and Chapters 8, 9, and 10 confirm, our original model serves to explain not only the gendered outcomes of cabinet formation but the *process* of cabinet formation as well.

First, in all our country cases, with the exception of the United States, formal rules empower presidents or prime ministers to form their cabinet, with no formal system rules requiring intervention or participation of other actors. Second, informal rules at the system level serve to further support selectors' powers, with the exception of Germany. In the United States, presidents constrained by the formal rules of Senate consent nonetheless almost always get approval for their nominees. In Chile, Canada, and Spain, where selectors are unrestrained by formal powers in constructing their cabinet, informal rules further undergird their selection powers, underscoring the complete independence of the selector even from her or his own party. Formal and informal rules at the party level historically constrained selectors in the Australian Labor Party and the UK Labour Party, but such rules have weakened over time. Third, formal system rules or strongly institutionalized informal rules establish who is eligible to be appointed to cabinet in every country. More specifically, informal rules determine the set of qualifications

that define the eligibility pool for ministerial office. Such rules require potential and aspiring ministers to bring some combination of experiential,
affiliational, and representation credentials to the cabinet team.

Rules about who selects intersect in practice with rules about who can be
selected to shape and to gender the process of cabinet formation. Empowered
selectors are free to choose ministers, but they are not free to choose whomever they wish. Rather, their substantive choice is conditioned by the range
of incentives that reassure (affiliational) and reward (representational) the
selector as he or she forms the cabinet team. Presidents and prime ministers
have strong incentives to appoint known, reliable, trustworthy supporters
and allies to their cabinet, but they have equally strong incentives to avoid
sanctions for appointing only men or very few women. In all cases, selectors
work to identify *ministrables* with the combined range of policy expertise
and political experience that strengthen the cabinet team and deter criticism.
The interaction of these rules governing selectors and qualifying *ministrables*
regenders the process of cabinet formation and produces the gendered outcome of women in cabinet.

Contributions to Research on Gender and Cabinets

Cabinets, Ministers, and Gender makes four main contributions to research
on politics and gender and to the scholarship on cabinets and ministerial recruitment more generally. First, it illustrates the value of moving beyond the
common dichotomy of formal versus informal institutions, revealing a more
nuanced understanding of how complex sets of rules interact to empower,
constrain, and create different opportunities and obstacles for women's inclusion as ministers. Second, it demonstrates how institutional change emerges
from a complex iterative process through which political actors use their
agency to interpret and exploit ambiguity in rules to deviate from past practice, thereby contributing to the development of new rules, which in turn
constrain future political actors. Third, it shows that although political parties
play an important role in women's cabinet appointment, party ideology does
not predict gendered patterns in women's ministerial appointments. Finally,
our study finds representational imperatives to be the most strongly prescriptive and determinative of positive gendered outcomes. In the following,
we elaborate on these contributions and conclude by indicating some future
research directions that emerge from our study.

Moving beyond the Formal versus Informal Dichotomy

One of the most important conceptual innovations in comparative politics in recent years has been to focus on the informal dimensions of political institutions (Helmke and Levitsky 2006). As noted in Chapter 2, gender scholars played a leading role in moving the literature forward by refining and further specifying the concept of informal institutions (Bjarnegard and Kenny 2015; Chappell and Waylen 2013; Gains and Lowndes 2014; Lowndes 2014; Waylen 2017). Our study of cabinet appointments and gender, however, reveals the limitations of a binary conceptual framework that includes just two categories: formal versus informal institutions. We think that greater nuance is needed, and that much can be gained from different ways of categorizing rules to understand how they produce unequal outcomes for women.

Research on cabinet formation and ministerial recruitment emphasizes the relative absence of formal rules (de Winter 1991; Dogan 1989; Dowding and Dumont 2014). We have argued throughout the book, however, that although the process of ministerial recruitment is undeniably rule bound, virtually all of the rules are unwritten and therefore not legally enforceable. But simply conceptualizing the rules surrounding cabinet appointment as informal neglects the most important ways in which rules differ and why they produce varying gendered outcomes cross-nationally and over time. Our research provides a framework for making sense of predominantly informal institutions and their gendered effects. The book's findings demonstrate the value in paying attention to four additional dimensions of informal rules: (1) the *number* of informal rules at play in an institutional setting; (2) whether rules *prescribe* or permit; (3) whether rules are *specific* or flexible; and (4) the degree of *institutionalization* of the rules.

For any institutional setting, it is important to identify all the rules in play, both formal and informal. Identifying whether rules are plentiful or few matters since a context structured by few rules gives political actors more latitude than those faced with multiple rules. In contrast, while multiple rules may create more constraints, such a context could also imply more ambiguity and scope for interpretation. That is why it is important not just to count all the rules in play, but also to indicate whether they prescribe, prohibit, or permit certain courses of action. When it comes to rules establishing who is qualified for cabinet appointment, our study finds that prescriptive rules are far more consequential than rules that permit, even when the permitted course of action is more in keeping with the strategic incentives of political actors.

Affiliational criteria are permitted by the rules, but experiential and representational criteria are prescriptive in nature. This means that where representational criteria are plentiful, they will limit opportunities for selectors to appoint trusted friends and allies to cabinet, unless those *ministrables* also meet a representational criterion. Another relevant dimension of rules is their degree of specificity, which determines how much latitude selectors have to interpret the rule. In Chapters 5 and 7, we showed that rules establishing experiential criteria are flexible and non-specific—either political or policy experience will do—while rules about representational criteria are specific and fixed, identifying precisely which socio-demographic characteristics must be present on the cabinet team. Selectors thus have more latitude when interpreting experiential criteria, but very little latitude when faced with rules about representation.

Finally, we need to know how strongly institutionalized a rule is, and how this varies cross-nationally and over time. A rule is strongly institutionalized if political actors face costly sanctions for non-compliance and therefore almost always choose to comply with the rule. Rules about representation, for example, achieving party balance in Chile and ensuring the representation of each province in Canada are good examples of strongly institutionalized rules that are consistently followed over time, regardless of which party holds office. In sum, our research provides a blueprint to guide scholars in how to analyze institutional settings that are largely devoid of formal rules.

Further research is needed to identify the informal rules of cabinet recruitment, including affiliational, experiential, and representational criteria, in other regions of the world not covered in this study, in countries with semi-presidential systems, and those with strong traditions of coalition government. We also see scope for further research on the consequences of affiliational and representational criteria for qualification. For example, if selectors are restricted in their capacity to appoint trusted allies to their cabinets because of competing representational criteria, then what happens to trusted political allies? Are they appointed elsewhere? What impact might this have on cabinet's status and operation? Some researchers have noted the irony that women's presence in cabinets may be expanding precisely when cabinets are becoming less powerful (Siavelis 2009; Sykes 2009). Do selectors strive to expand and diversify their affiliational networks, knowing that they need broader networks from which to recruit ministers?

Institutional Change Emerges from Iterative and Interactive Processes

Most studies seeking to explain cross-national variation in women's cabinet presence take a cross-sectional approach, with fewer studies seeking to explain change over time (Claveria 2015; Krook and O'Brien 2012; Scherpereel, Adams, and Jacob 2018). This book takes an even longer-term view, featuring periods in which women's cabinet presence was nonexistent or very low, as well as the periods when women's presence began to increase. As a result, we are able to explain both cross-national variation and cross-time change. Using an institutionalist approach focused on rules, actors, and processes, we find that change in women's cabinet representation emerges from an iterative process involving the interaction of rules and political agency over time. The model we developed in Chapter 2 conceptualizes the outcome of a team of ministers as determined by the interaction of rules about who selects ministers and who can be a minister. As discussed earlier, we find that both sets of rules create space for political actors to exploit ambiguity in rules, and thereby deviate from the practice of appointing all-male or mostly male cabinets. Selectors who increase the number of women in cabinet are applauded for their actions, creating incentives for future selectors to do the same. Over time, concrete floors are confirmed and sustained, creating new representational rules that prescribe a specific threshold for women's inclusion. Significantly, we find that male selectors are as likely, if not more likely, as female selectors to make the first move to increase women's presence. In some cases, selectors do so in response to pressures from women in the parties, but in recent years, selectors who form gender parity cabinets have committed themselves to doing so through a pre-election pledge.

We think that digging more deeply into the role of presidents and prime ministers is a fertile area for future research. More research is needed on why some selectors decide to form gender parity cabinets and why selectors confirm and sustain the concrete floors set by first movers. We did not interview former prime ministers or presidents for this book, but perhaps future researchers will be able to seek interviews or read memoirs of selectors who initiated new concrete floors or formed gender parity cabinets to get a stronger sense of their motivations. Future research could also explore in greater depth the role of social movement activism in creating new norms surrounding women's inclusion, and the role of the media in creating pressure on selectors to include women in their cabinet teams.

Political Parties Are Important, but Party Ideology Is Not

The scholarship on cabinet formation and ministerial recruitment focuses on whether ministers are party members or not (see Amorim Neto and Samuels 2010; Costa Pinto et al. 2018), paying less attention to the role of party rules in structuring the process of ministerial recruitment. In seeking to explain changes in women's representation in cabinet, researchers often highlight party ideology as an explanatory factor, hypothesizing that selectors from left parties will appoint more women than other parties. Our data show instead that left parties are not always the first movers when it comes to increasing the magnitude of women's representation. In Australia, Canada, and Spain, leaders from conservative and centrist rather than leftist parties initiated historic increases in women's cabinet inclusion. And even though leftist leaders like Bachelet and Zapatero were the first to form parity cabinets in Chile and Spain, in Canada it was a prime minister from a center party, Liberal leader Justin Trudeau, who formed the first parity cabinet at the federal level.

Our book shows that political parties nonetheless play an important role in women's cabinet appointment in several ways. In some of our country cases, political parties differ in terms of rules about who selects ministers, and rules about what criteria qualify individuals for appointment to cabinet. The UK Labour Party and Australian Labor Party have at times required party leaders and prime ministers to hand over selection power entirely to the parliamentary caucus; in Germany, political parties share powers of selection with the chancellor. In other countries, representational criteria for qualifying for cabinet vary by party. Across all our cases, party membership or allegiance is an important criterion for eligibility as a *ministrable*. Political parties are the incubator of ministerial careers. In terms of qualifying for a cabinet post, we found that political experience is the most frequently cited type of experience across all cases, meaning that service in parties remains an important way to accumulate relevant experience and demonstrate political skills and competence that lead to cabinet appointment.

Parties remain gendered institutions, and the rules and practices in political parties affect women and men's chances of joining cabinet differently. Gender gaps in party membership, activity, and office holding remain skewed toward men. As gendered institutions, political parties have historically blocked women's access to ministerial office. More recently, however, we find evidence that parties, alongside selectors, have become important actors in the process of initiating and locking in institutional change in favor of more equal outcomes for women. Parties are key sites for women's mobilization, providing opportunities for feminists to lobby party leaders to include more women. In Chapters 7 through 10, we offer evidence that party feminist lobbying for more gender equality in cabinet played a crucial role in initiating new concrete floors for women's cabinet inclusion.

We therefore see scope for further bringing parties into the analysis of ministerial recruitment and cabinet formation. We particularly encourage more research on gender in political parties, and the mechanisms for internal change in political parties, along the lines of research undertaken by Bjarnegård and Kenny (2015, 2016), Verge (2015), and Verge and Claveria (2016).

Rules about Representation Determine Positive Outcomes for Women

One of the most striking (and surprising) findings of our study is that representational imperatives are the most strongly prescriptive rules of cabinet formation, and thus the most determinative of positive gendered outcomes. Ultimately, this book tells an optimistic story. When representational criteria include women, rule changes become locked in and women's cabinet representation does not regress significantly. Although scholars often acknowledge that cabinets are sites of representation and selectors use cabinet appointments to send symbolic messages to social groups whose support they wish to ensure (Franceschet, Annesley, and Beckwith 2017), research on cabinet formation has not yet systematically examined the role of representational criteria in the selection of ministers. In contrast, our analysis of qualifying criteria across seven countries shows that where they exist, rules that prescribe representational criteria are among the most consistently followed and thus the most strongly institutionalized of all rules. Moreover, across all of our cases, such rules about representation are informal, thereby providing further evidence that informal rules can be powerful in bringing about positive outcomes for women. Although formal rules like candidate gender quotas have been key to improving women's parliamentary representation, our study makes clear that formal rule changes are unnecessary for improving women's cabinet representation. Concrete floors have as powerful an effect as formal rules.

Because representational criteria emerge from a complex iterative process of political actors working with various types of rules, we encourage future researchers to explore in greater detail how this process unfolds in different countries around the world, and the role that feminist movements or feminists in political parties play in the creation of new rules about women's representation. We also think there is scope for further expanding research on the emergence of other representational criteria to explain the inclusion or exclusion of other under-represented groups based on social class, race, ethnicity, sexual orientation, or gender identity. A second line of research might explore cross-national differences in representational criteria. Why have some countries, like the United States and Canada, developed stronger rules about race and ethnicity than countries like Germany and Spain?

Practical Implications of Our Findings

Our research exposes the process of appointing ministers to cabinets, and in this final section, we offer some practical guidance on how to make ministerial teams more diverse. We think these lessons have broader applicability for how to make all types of leadership teams more diverse. Significantly, our research offers a blueprint for how to do so quickly and without recourse to formal quotas. Formal quotas are no doubt an important and effective tool in the process of parliamentary recruitment, where appointment is dependent on multiple processes and sets of actors: party selectors, opponents, and the electorate. In the case of cabinets, fewer actors are involved in the selection process. We conclude our book with some recommendations for what advocates of gender equity and diversity in political leadership can do to accelerate and lock in progress.

The Power of Promising a Gender Parity Cabinet

We find that the most rapid progress in women's ministerial appointments occurs when aspirant prime ministers or presidents make a public pledge during an election campaign to include women in cabinet. Such pledges take the form of promising to appoint a gender parity cabinet or, less specifically, to form a cabinet that "looks like the country." US presidential candidate Bill Clinton was the first such candidate to issue this kind of pledge during the 1992 campaign. Subsequent candidates made similar promises: José Luis Rodríguez Zapatero did so in Spain (2004), Michelle Bachelet in Chile (2006), and Justin Trudeau in Canada (2015). In the United Kingdom, candidate David Cameron promised a government in which women would comprise at least one-third of ministers (2005). Such pledges are evidence that, in these countries, the representational criterion of including women is established.

Pledges are powerful mechanisms for women's inclusion in cabinet, because the individual who makes the pledge is identifiable, holds the necessary institutional power to fulfill the promise, and can be held accountable for delivering on the promise (or not). Our media data reveal that selectors who pledge to appoint a gender parity cabinet are praised for delivering on the promise, and we found no evidence that any selectors have been sanctioned for pledging and delivering parity. It is also worth noting that we found no selector pledging to appoint *fewer* women to cabinet than had previously been the case (for an opposing party or in the same party's government).

Pledges are powerful mechanisms for advocates of gender equality within and outside of political parties. Selectors with appointment powers are clear targets for equality activists. By exercising their agency to make and deliver on a pledge for gender equality, selectors change the norms about gender representation, which subsequent selectors feel obliged to follow and, over time, a higher concrete floor becomes sustained. The reasons behind each pledge may differ—feminist conviction, response to intra-party feminist lobbying, and/or electoral consideration—but, without fail, each case triggers a step change for women's representation in cabinet.

Pledges are effective mechanisms for increasing women's numbers in cabinets. Pledges, once given, can easily be implemented by selectors. Pledges are also the responsibility of an empowered individual, who can be sanctioned through negative publicity, criticism of general commitment to women's issues, and electoral challenge in the next election, by activists and the media. In response to such sanctions, selectors can also quickly make adjustments to ensure a gender parity cabinet by means of a cabinet reshuffle. While we always would encourage feminist activists and women in political parties to lobby candidates for executive office, we specifically encourage members of the media and of the public to use occasions like press conferences and leaders' debates to ask presidential candidates and party leaders whether they will appoint a gender-balanced cabinet—and, if not, to explain why.

Interrogate and Contest Common Understandings
of "Merit"

We advocate challenging the term "merit" or "best person for the job," as if "merit" is objective and singular.[16] Our evidence shows that all cabinet ministers need to be able to demonstrate some modicum of political or policy experience, but the specific credentials required to qualify for a spot in cabinet are flexible and open to interpretation. We argue that assertions of "merit" or questioning an appointee's merit are not in fact a debate about qualification for office. Rather, such assertions evidence a political strategy to retain an unequal status quo, a strategy most often deployed against women (or other under-represented groups) by those who resist practices that challenge men's historic dominance in cabinets.

In relation to cabinets, meritorious qualifications for cabinet are manifested in a number of ways. As well as political or policy experience, a *ministrable's* "merit" may be that she is loyal and can be trusted by the prime minister or president, or it may be that he represents a political or socio-demographic group that needs to be included in cabinet in order to bring the positive benefits of diversity to the government, to make it "look like the country," and to enhance the government's legitimacy. In this regard, merit relates not just to an individual's personal credentials, but also the individual's contributions and strengths in relation to the rest of the cabinet team.

Instead of focusing on individual merit, we conceive of merit in the broader terms of what each person brings to the team. We advocate replacing individual merit with consideration of the merit of the entire cabinet, including the prescribed criteria of relevant experience (experiential criteria) and national diversity (representational criteria), recognizing that meaningful qualification for cabinet depends not only on individuals, but also on how those individuals combine to create a balanced and diverse cabinet team. We recommend challenging selectors to explain why their party has no "meritorious" women. For the United States, with more than 325 million persons, a claim by any party that there are insufficient numbers of "meritorious" women to constitute a gender parity cabinet is preposterous. Only seven or eight women are necessary for a US gender parity cabinet. Finally, we also recommend the Trudeau strategy of declining to engage in the merit

---

[16] Our argument echoes Murray (2014), who exposes the gendered assumptions in using "merit" as a yardstick for selecting parliamentary candidates.

versus gender pseudo-debate in regard to women's inclusion in cabinets.[17] At our time of writing, it's already 2019.

Continue Feminist Mobilization

In conclusion, we recommend that organized women, inside and outside the state, continue to be vigilant and remain mobilized to bring pressure on selectors. Feminist activists have succeeded in creating the political context for the rise of gender parity cabinets in several countries. A recent example is Spanish prime minister Pedro Sánchez's female-super-majority cabinet, appointed in 2018. Moreover, Sweden has initiated, confirmed, and sustained a concrete floor of gender parity,[18] as has France.[19] Such cabinets, however, are far from permanent for any of the country cases in this book. Concrete floors were recently broken in Australia (2013) and the United States (2017); although both were repaired,[20] it is clear that the rules empowering selectors can be used to exclude women from cabinet or to diminish their numbers. The rules, apparently gender-neutral, depend primarily (and sometimes exclusively) on the selector's political will to appoint female cabinet ministers and to appoint them in equitable numbers. Empowerment of the selector is a tool that activist women can leverage to increase women's presence in cabinet governance, but it is a tool that can be used against women as well.

Concerted feminist activism directed at selectors can ensure continuity in women's equitable inclusion in cabinet. As we note elsewhere in this book, cabinets are important loci of policymaking, and women's inclusion in this powerful arena is crucial in policy terms. Perhaps more important, however, women's cabinet membership is also the means by which women's presence at the highest levels of democratic governance is normalized. Although cabinets are institutions of small size, women's presence within them provides a foothold by which women's equitable inclusion in all arenas of government can be advanced.

---

[17] See Franceschet, Beckwith, and Annesley (2015).
[18] Data and research by Frida Gustafsson, University of Sussex.
[19] Data and research by Kirsten Costedio and Rita Maricocchi, Case Western Reserve University.
[20] In the United States, by the same selector within a year of taking office, with the appointment of Kirstjen Nielsen as secretary of homeland security in December 2017.

List of Interviews

Interviewee Category: Former minister (1), Advisor, political elite, party leader (2); Country expert (3)	Date	Location	Type of interview	Recorded (Yes/No)	Confidentiality assured (Yes/No)
Category 1	March 20, 2010	Sydney, Australia	In person	Yes	Yes
Category 1	March 23, 2010	Sydney, Australia	In person	Yes	Yes
Category 1	May 21, 2012	Madrid, Spain	In person	Yes	Yes
Category 1	May 22, 2012	Madrid, Spain	In person	Yes	Yes
Category 1	May 29, 2012	Madrid, Spain	In person	Yes	Yes
Category 1	May 29, 2012	Madrid, Spain	In person	Yes	Yes
Category 1	January 8, 2013	Santiago, Chile	In person	Yes	Yes
Category 1	January 15, 2013	Santiago, Chile	In person	No	Yes
Category 1	December 17, 2013	London, UK	In person	No	Yes
Category 1	May 6, 2014	Madrid, Spain	In person	Yes	Yes
Category 1	May 13, 2014	Madrid, Spain	In person	Yes	Yes
Category 1	August 6, 2014	Santiago, Chile	In person	Yes	Yes
Category 1	August 11, 2014	Santiago, Chile	In person	Yes	Yes

Interviewee Category: Former minister (1), Advisor, political elite, party leader (2); Country expert (3)	Date	Location	Type of interview	Recorded (Yes/No)	Confidentiality assured (Yes/No)
Category 1	August 12, 2014	Santiago, Chile	In person	No	Yes
Category 1	October 27, 2014	Bavaria, Germany	In person	Yes	Yes
Category 1	October 29, 2014	Berlin, Germany	In person	Yes	Yes
Category 1	September 23, 2014		Email	Email	Yes
Category 1	October 22, 2014		Email	Email	Yes
Category 1	June 7, 2016,	London, UK	In person	Yes	Yes
Category 1	June 7, 2016	London, UK	In person	No	Yes
Category 1	June 30, 2016		Phone	No	Yes
Category 2	March 24, 2010	Sydney, Australia	In person	Yes	Yes
Category 2	December 17, 2013	London, UK	In person	No	Yes
Category 2	May 13, 2014	Madrid, Spain	In person	Yes	Yes
Category 2	May 16, 2014	Madrid, Spain	In person	Yes	Yes
Category 2	May 19, 2014	Madrid, Spain	In person	Yes	Yes
Category 2	August 19, 2014	Santiago, Chile	In person	Yes	Yes
Category 2	August 19, 2014	Santiago, Chile	In person	Yes	Yes
Category 2	July 13, 2015	Santiago, Chile	In person	No	Yes

Interviewee Category: Former minister (1), Advisor, political elite, party leader (2); Country expert (3)	Date	Location	Type of interview	Recorded (Yes/No)	Confidentiality assured (Yes/No)
Category 2	July 15, 2015	Santiago, Chile	In person	Yes	Yes
Category 2	July 17, 2015	Santiago, Chile	In person	Yes	Yes
Category 2	July 11, 2016	London, UK	In person	No	Yes
Category 2	August 12, 2016		Email	Email	Yes
Category 2	June 12, 2018		Email	Email	Yes
Category 3	May 16, 2012	Madrid, Spain	In person	Yes	Yes
Category 3	May 21, 2012	Madrid, Spain	In person	Yes	Yes
Category 3	May 28, 2012	Madrid, Spain	In person	Yes	Yes
Category 3	May 28, 2012	Madrid, Spain	In person	Yes	Yes
Category 3	January 10, 2013	Santiago, Chile	In person	Yes	Yes
Category 3	January 14, 2013	Santiago, Chile	In person	Yes	Yes
Category 3	January 15, 2013	Santiago, Chile	In person	Yes	Yes
Category 3	May 6, 2014	Madrid, Spain	In person	Yes	Yes
Category 3	May 8, 2014	Madrid, Spain	In person	Yes	Yes
Category 3	May 13, 2014	Madrid, Spain	In person	Yes	Yes
Category 3	May 14, 2014	Madrid, Spain	In person	Yes	Yes
Category 3	May 14, 2014	Madrid, Spain	In person	Yes	Yes

Interviewee Category: Former minister (1), Advisor, political elite, party leader (2); Country expert (3)	Date	Location	Type of interview	Recorded (Yes/No)	Confidentiality assured (Yes/No)
Category 3	May 20, 2014	Madrid, Spain	In person	Yes	Yes
Category 3	August 12, 2014	Santiago, Chile	In person	Yes	Yes
Category 3	August 13, 2014	Santiago, Chile	In person	Yes	Yes
Category 3	October 28, 2014	Bavaria, Germany	In person	Yes	Yes
Category 3	October 30, 2014	Berlin, Germany	In person	Yes	Yes
Category 3	June 30, 2015	Santiago, Chile	In person	No	Yes
Category 3	July 3, 2015	Santiago, Chile	In person	Yes	Yes
Category 3	July 6, 2015	Santiago, Chile	In person	Yes	Yes
Category 3	July 10, 2015	Santiago, Chile	In person	Yes	Yes
Category 3	July 22, 2015	Santiago, Chile	In person	Yes	Yes
Category 3	July 14, 2016	Sussex, UK	In person	No	Yes

Total number of interviews: 57

Category 1 Former ministers: 21

Category 2: Advisors, political elites, and party leaders: 13

Category 3: Country experts: 23

Women Holding High-Status Cabinet Posts, by Country, through 2016

Australia: Amanda Vanstone served as Australia's justice minister from 1997 to 1998, appointed by Liberal prime minister John Howard. Julie Bishop was appointed minister of foreign affairs in 2013 by Liberal prime minister Tony Abbott, and Marise Payne was appointed defense minister in 2015 by Liberal prime minister Malcolm Turnbull.

Canada: Only one woman has held the defense portfolio in Canada. In January 1993, Conservative prime minister Brian Mulroney appointed Kim Campbell to the post, a post she held for less than six months. No other woman has ever held the post.

Prior to 2017,two women served as foreign affairs ministers in Canada, both of them appointed by Conservative prime ministers. Flora Macdonald was appointed to the post in Joe Clarke's initial cabinet in June 1979, but the government fell less than a year later. Barbara McDougall was appointed by Prime Minister Brian Mulroney in a cabinet shuffle in 1991. She held the post for two years. Between 1993 and 2017, no woman held the foreign affairs portfolio. In January 2017, Prime Minister Justin Trudeau appointed Chrystia Freeland to the post.

Three women have served as justice ministers in Canada: the first, Kim Campbell, received the post in a cabinet shuffle in 1990, but the second two were appointments to post-election cabinets. Anne McLellan was appointed justice minister in 1997 after Liberal prime minister Chretién won a second majority government, and Jody Wilson-Raybould was appointed to Justin Trudeau's initial cabinet in 2015.

Chile: Chile has had two female defense ministers. The first, Michelle Bachelet, was appointed to the post in a cabinet shuffle in 2002 during Ricardo Lagos' presidency. The second, Vivianne Blanlot, was appointed to President Bachelet's initial cabinet in 2006, but was shuffled out just over a year later.

Only one woman, Soledad Alvear, has served as foreign affairs minister in Chile. She was appointed to President Lagos' initial cabinet, after having served as justice minister in the previous cabinet of Eduardo Frei.

Three women have been appointed to the justice post in Chile. The first, Adriana Olguín Baltra, was the country's first woman appointed to any ministerial post. She was appointed as justice minister just before the 1952 election. The second, Soledad Alvear, was appointed to President Eduardo Frei's initial cabinet in 1994. The third female justice minister, Javiera Blanca, was appointed by President Bachelet in a cabinet shuffle in 2015.

Germany: Ursula von der Leyen was appointed defense minister by Angela Merkel in 2013.

Three women have served as minister for justice. Sabine Leutheusser-Schnarrenberger, from the liberal Free Democratic Party, held the post twice: from 1992 to 1996 in the CDU-FDP coalition led by Chancellor Helmut Kohl and 2009 to 2013 in the coalition led by Chancellor Angela Merkel. Herta Däubler-Gmelin, a Social Democrat, was minister of justice during 1998–2002 in the SPD-Green Coalition led by Chancellor Gerhardt

Schröder, and Brigitte Zypries, also a Social Democrat, held the post in 2002–2009, spanning coalitions led by Chancellor Gerhardt Schröder and Chancellor Angela Merkel.

Spain: Only one woman has been appointed minister of defense in Spain: Carme Chacón, who was appointed by Prime Minister Zapatero after he won his second term in office.

In the post-Franco era, two women have served as foreign affairs minister, but neither was appointed to an initial cabinet. Ana Palacios was appointed to the post by Prime Minister Aznar in 2002 and she served until 2004. Prime Minister Zapatero appointed Trinidad Jiménez to the post partway through his second government. She held the post from 2010 to 2011.

Margarita Mariscal de Gante y Mirón was appointed justice minister by Prime Minister Aznar in 1996 and she served in the post until 2000.

United Kingdom: Margaret Beckett was secretary of state for foreign and Commonwealth affairs from 2006 to 2007, appointed by Labour prime minister Tony Blair. Liz Truss was appointed secretary of state for justice and lord chancellor by Conservative prime minister Theresa May in 2016.

United States: The United States has had three female secretaries of state: Madeleine Albright (1997–2001, appointed by Bill Clinton), Condoleezza Rice (2005–2009, appointed by George W. Bush), and Hillary Clinton (2009–2013, appointed by Barack Obama).

Only two women have served as US attorney general: Janet Reno, appointed by President Clinton in 1993, and Loretta Lynch, appointed by President Obama in 2015.

Summary of Rules for Cabinet Appointments, All Countries in Data Set

Country	Rules about Who Selects Ministers	Rules about Eligibility and Qualifying Criteria
Australia	There are no formal rules outlining the prime minister's authority to form cabinet. Selectors are empowered by strongly institutionalized informal rules. Formal party rules in the Australian Labor Party (ALP) empower the parliamentary caucus to select ministers. For most recent ALP governments, powers of selection have been transferred from the ALP to the prime minister.	Australia's constitution requires cabinet ministers to hold a parliamentary seat within three months of appointment to cabinet. Experiential criteria are prescribed by informal rules, but are flexible. Affiliational criteria are permitted and are consistently employed. Representational criteria are relatively easy to meet, and include region, party, party faction, chambers of parliament, and sex.
Canada	The governor general formally appoints all cabinet ministers on the recommendations of the prime minister; the cabinet is not subject to parliamentary approval. There are no formal rules outlining the prime minister's authority to form cabinet. Constitutional convention, however, fully empowers prime ministers to form their cabinets.	Constitutional convention prescribes that cabinet ministers be elected members of parliament. Experiential criteria are prescribed by informal rules, but are flexible. Affiliational criteria are permitted. Representational criteria are prescribed and extensive: each of the country's 10 provinces must have representation in cabinet, and sex, linguistic, racial, and ethnic diversity are also prescribed.

Chile	The president appoints all cabinet ministers; the cabinet is not subject to congressional approval. Formal and informal rules fully empower selectors.	Formal rules prohibit members of Congress from retaining their congressional seat if appointed to cabinet. Experiential criteria are prescribed by informal rules, but are flexible. Affiliational criteria are permitted but are not employed consistently, largely due to requirements to meet representational requirements for parties. Representational criteria are prescribed, and include party and sex.
Germany	Formal constitutional rules empower the chancellor to select ministers. Article 64 of the Basic Law states, "Federal Ministers shall be appointed and dismissed by the Federal President upon the proposal of the Federal Chancellor." However, informal rules at the party level prescribe that regional party leaders are always consulted. Coalitions mean that chancellors hand over some selection powers to the leaders of their coalition partner.	Cabinet ministers may be drawn from within or outside of parliament. Experiential criteria are prescribed by informal rules, but are flexible. Affiliational criteria are permitted, but are not consistently employed due to representational criteria emerging from coalition constraints. Representational criteria for public appointments, referred to as *Proporz*, have a strong tradition in Germany. Some representational criteria, like region, party, and sex, are required by all parties, but religion as a representational criterion is only relevant in the CDU and CSU and is declining in significance.
Spain	According to Spain's constitution, the king formally appoints ministers on the recommendation of the prime minister. Although there is an investiture vote in parliament for the prime minister, the cabinet is not subject to parliamentary approval or approval by the monarch. Selectors are fully empowered by both formal and informal rules.	Cabinet ministers may be drawn from within or outside of parliament. Experiential criteria are prescribed by informal rules, but are flexible. Affiliational criteria are permitted and are consistently employed in both parties. Representational criteria are minimal: sex is a representational criterion across the two major parties, but region is more salient in the Socialist Workers Party (PSOE) than in the People's Party (PP).

| United Kingdom | With a largely unwritten constitution, there are no formal rules outlining the prime minister's authority to form cabinet. Constitutional convention, however, fully empowers selectors. The prime minister selects all cabinet ministers; the cabinet is not subject to parliamentary approval or approval by the monarch, although the monarch formally appoints ministers on the prime minister's recommendations.

Party-level rules for the Labour Party required that, when in opposition, the Parliamentary Labour Party would elect shadow ministers, who would move to cabinet once the party won office. | Constitutional convention prescribes that cabinet ministers be elected members of parliament.
Experiential criteria are prescribed by informal rules, but are flexible.
Affiliational criteria are permitted and are consistently employed by selectors of the two major parties.
Representational criteria are minimal and include region, race/ethnicity, and sex. |
| United States | Formal rules constrain selectors; the president nominates ministers, the Senate confirms or denies the appointment by majority vote on each nominee (US Constitution, Art. II, Sec. 2). Congressional legislation establishes cabinet departments. Informal rules fully empower selectors, since the Senate rarely blocks qualified *ministrables*, and unqualified nominees remove themselves from consideration if it becomes clear they cannot be confirmed. | Formal rules prohibit members of Congress from retaining their congressional seat if appointed to cabinet.
Experiential criteria are prescribed by informal rules, but are flexible, with some modest exceptions. Active members of the US military are ineligible for appointment as Secretary of Defense (10 U.S. Code § 113 (a)). A federal anti-nepotism law (1967) prohibits nomination of the president's family members (5 U.S. Code § 3110).
Affiliational criteria are permitted and are consistently employed by selectors of both parties.
Representational criteria are prescribed but are minimal and include race/ethnicity and sex. |

Bibliography

Aberbach, Joel. D., and Bert A. Rockman. 2002. "Conducting and Coding Elite Interviews." *PS: Political Science and Politics* 35 (4): 673–676.

Acker, Joan. 1992. "From Sex Roles to Gendered Institutions." *Contemporary Sociology* 21 (5): 565–569.

Adams, Melinda, John Scherpereel, and Suraj Jacobs. 2016. "The Representation of Women in African Legislatures and Cabinets: An Examination with Reference to Ghana." *Journal of Women, Politics and Policy* 37 (2): 145–167.

Albright, Madeleine. 2003. *Madam Secretary: A Memoir.* New York: Harper Perennial.

Aldridge, John. 2010. "The New Establishment." *The Sunday Times*, May 23.

Allen, Peter. 2016. "Achieving Sex Equality in Executive Appointments." *Party Politics* 22 (5).

Altman, David. 2008. "Political Recruitment and Candidate Selection in Chile, 1990–2006: The Executive Branch." In *Pathways to Power: Political Recruitment and Candidate Selection in Latin America*, eds. Peter M. Siavelis and Scott Morgenstern. University Park: Pennsylvania State University Press, 240–270.

Amorim Neto, Octavio. 2006. "The Presidential Calculus: Executive Policymaking and Cabinet Formation in the Americas." *Comparative Political Studies* 39 (4): 415–440.

Amorim Neto, Octavio, and David Samuels. 2010. "Democratic Regimes and Cabinet Politics: A Global Perspective." *Revista Ibero-americana de Estudos Legislativos* 1 (1): 10–23.

Anderssen, Erin. 2015. "We Have a Record Number of Female MPs but Hold the Applause." *Globe and Mail*, October 20.

Andeweg, Rudi B. 2014. "Cabinet Ministers, Leaders, Team Players, Followers." In *The Oxford Handbook of Political Leadership*, eds. R.A.W. Rhodes and Paul t'Hart. Oxford: Oxford University Press, 532–546.

Annesley, Claire. 2015. "Rules of Ministerial Recruitment." *Politics & Gender* 11 (4): 618–642.

Annesley, Claire, and Susan Franceschet (eds.). 2015. "Gender and the Executive Branch." *Politics & Gender* 11 (4): 613–617.

Annesley, Claire, and Francesca Gains. 2010. "The Core Executive: Gender Power and Change." *Political Studies* 58 (5): 909–929.

Annesley, Claire, and Francesca Gains. 2014. "Can Cameron Capture Women's Votes? The Gendered Impediments to a Conservative Majority in 2015." *Parliamentary Affairs* 67 (1): 767–782.

Atchison, Amy. 2015. "The Impact of Female Cabinet Ministers on a Female-Friendly Labor Environment." *Journal of Women, Politics, and Policy* 36 (4): 388–414.

Atchison, Amy, and Ian Downs. 2009. "Women Cabinet Ministers and Female-Friendly Social Policy." *Poverty and Public Policy* 1 (2): 1–23.

Atkins, Judi, Timothy Heppell, and Kevin Theakston. 2013. "Party Leaders Are Getting Younger, but Cabinet Ministers Are Not." *Democratic Audit*, November 4, http://eprints.lse.ac.uk/view/year/2013.html.

Baldez, Lisa. 2002. *When Women Protest: Women's Movements in Chile*. New York: Cambridge University Press.

Balls, Ed. 2016. *Speaking Out: Lessons in Life and Politics*. London: Hutchinson.

Bar, Antonio. 1988. "Spain." In *Cabinets in Western Europe*, eds. Jean Blondel and Ferdinand Müller-Rommel. Houndsmill, Basingstoke, Hampshire: Macmillan, 102–119.

Barnes, Fred. "The Bush Quotas: Now Look Who's Counting by Race and Gender." *The Weekly Standard*, April 16, 2001, http://www.weeklystandard.com/the-bush-quotas/article/12605.

Barnes, Tiffany, and Diana O'Brien. 2018. "Defending the Realm: The Appointment of Female Defense Ministers Worldwide." *American Journal of Political Science* 62 (2): 355–368.

Bashevkin, Sylvia. 2018. *Women as Foreign Policy Leaders: National Security and Gender Politics in Superpower America*. New York: Oxford University Press.

Bauer, Gretchen, and Faith Okpotor. 2013. "'Her Excellency': An Exploratory Overview of Women Cabinet Ministers in Africa." *Africa Today* 60 (1): 77–97.

Bauer, Gretchen, and Manon Tremblay (eds.). 2011. *Women in Executive Power: A Global Overview*. New York: Routledge.

Beckmann, Matthew N., and Richard L. Hall. 2013. "Elite Interviewing in Washington, DC." In *Interview Research in Political Science*, ed. Layna Mosley. Ithaca, NY: Cornell University Press, 196–208.

Beckwith, Karen. 2005. "A Common Language of Gender?" *Politics & Gender* 1 (1): 128–137.

Beckwith, Karen. 2014. "Women, Gender, and Conservative Parties in the 21st Century." Paper presented at the Workshop on Women, Gender, and Conservative Parties in the 21st Century, Case Western Reserve University, October 9–11.

Beckwith, Karen. 2015. "Before Prime Minister: Margaret Thatcher, Angela Merkel and Gendered Party Leadership Contests." *Politics & Gender* 11 (4): 718–745.

Bego, Ingrid. 2014. "Accessing Power in New Democracies: The Appointment of Female Ministers in Postcommunist Europe." *Political Research Quarterly* 67 (2): 347–360.

Berlinksi, Samuel, Torun Dewan, Keith Dowding. 2012. *Accounting for Ministers: Scandal and Survival in British Government, 1945–2007*. Cambridge: Cambridge University Press.

Berry, Jeffrey M. 2002. "Validity and Reliability Issues in Elite Interviewing." *PS: Political Science and Politics*, 35 (4): 679–682.

Beyeler, Michelle, and Claire Annesley. 2010. "A Feminist Institutionalist Perspective on the Welfare State." In *Gender, Politics, and Institutions: Towards a Feminist Institutionalism*, eds. Fiona Mackay and Mona Lena Krook. Basingstoke: Palgrave, 79–94.

Bjarnegård, Elin. 2013. *Gender, Informal Institutions, and Political Recruitment: Explaining Male Dominance in Parliamentary Representation*. New York: Palgrave Macmillan.

Bjarnegård, Elin, and Meryl Kenny. 2015. "Revealing the 'Secret Garden': The Informal Dimensions of Political Recruitment." *Politics and Gender* 11 (4): 748–753.

Bjarnegård, Elin, and Meryl Kenny. 2016. "Comparing Candidate Selection: A Feminist Institutionalist Approach." *Government and Opposition* 51 (3): 370–392.

Blair, Tony. 2011. *A Journey*. London: Arrow.

Bleich, Erik, and Robert Pekkanen. 2013. "How to Report Interview Data." In *Interview Research in Political Science*, ed. Layna Mosley. Ithaca, NY: Cornell University Press, 85–105.

Blondel, Jean. 1985. *Government Ministers in the Contemporary World*. London: Sage Publications.

Blondel, Jean, 1991a. "Are Ministers Representatives or Managers, Amateurs, or Specialists?" In *Politische Klasse und politische Institutionen*, eds. Hans-Dieter Klingemann, Richard Stöss, and Bernhard Weßel. Wiesbaden: Westdeutscher Verlag, 187–207.

Blondel, Jean. 1991b. "Cabinet Government and Cabinet Ministers." In *The Profession of Government Minister in Western Europe*, eds. Jean Blondel and Jean-Louis Thiebault. New York: St. Martin's Press, 5–18.

Blondel, Jean, and Ferdinand Müller-Rommel (eds.). 1988. *Cabinets in Western Europe*. Houndsmill, Basingstoke, Hampshire: Macmillan.

Blondel, J., and J. L. Thiébault (eds.). 1991. *The Profession of Government Minister in Western Europe*. Houndsmills, Basingstoke: Macmillan.

Bonvecchi, Alejandro, and Carlos Scartascini. 2011. *The Presidency and the Executive Branch in Latin America: What We Know and What We Need to Know*. Washington, DC: Inter-American Development Bank. Working Paper No. IDB-WP-283.

Borrelli, MaryAnne. 2002. *The President's Cabinet*. Boulder, CO; London: Lynne Rienner.

Borrelli, MaryAnne. 2010. "Gender Desegregation and Gender Integration in the President's Cabinet, 1933–2010." *Presidential Studies Quarterly* 40 (4): 734–748.

Borrelli, MaryAnne, and Janet M. Martin (eds.). 1997. *The Other Elites: Women, Politics and Power in the Executive Branch*. Boulder, CO: Lynne Reiner.

Brown, Gordon. 2017. *My Life, Our Times*. London: Bodley Head.

Calvo, Kerman. 2007. "Sacrifices That Pay: Polity Membership, Political Opportunities, and the Recognition of Same-Sex Marriage in Spain." *South European Politics and Society* 12 (3): 295–315.

Camerlo, Marcelo, and Cecilia Martínez-Gallardo (eds.). 2017. *Government Formation and Minister Turnover in Presidential Cabinets*. London; New York: Routledge.

Capoccia, Giovanni. 2016. "When Do Institutions 'Bite'? Historical Institutionalism and the Politics of Institutional Change." *Comparative Political Studies* 49 (8): 1095–1127.

Chappell, Louise. 2006. "Comparing Political Institutions: Revealing the Gendered Logic of Appropriateness." *Politics & Gender* 2 (2): 223–235.

Chappell, Louise, and Georgina Waylen. 2013. "Gender and the Hidden Life of Institutions." *Public Administration* 91 (3): 599–615.

Childs, Sarah, and Paul Webb. 2011. *Sex, Gender and the Conservative Party: From Iron Lady to Kitten Heels*. London: Routledge.

Chretién, Jean. 2007. *My Years as Prime Minister*. Toronto: Alfred A. Knopf.

Christopher, Warren. 2001. *Chances of a Lifetime*. New York: Scribner.

Clark, Alan. 2010. "A Life in His Own Words: The Complete Diaries 1972–1999." London: Weidenfeld & Nicolson.

Claveria, Silvia. 2014. "Still a Male Business? Explaining Women's Presence in Executive Office." *West European Politics* 37 (5): 1156–1176.

Conradt, David P., and Eric Langenbacher. 2013. *The German Polity*. Plymouth: Rowman & Littlefield.

Costa Pinto, António, Maurizio Cotta, and Pedro Tavares de Almeida. 2018. "Beyond Party Government? Technocratic Trends in Society and in the Executive." In *Technocratic Ministers and Political Leadership in European Democracies*, eds. António Costa Pinto, Maurizio Cotta, and Pedro Tavares de Almeida. New York: Palgrave Macmillan, 1–27.

Culhane, Leah. 2017. "Local Heroes and 'Cute Hoors': Informal Institutions, Male Over-Representation and Candidate Selection in the Republic of Ireland." In *Gender and Informal Institutions*, ed. Georgina Waylen. Lanham, MD: Rowman & Littlefield, 45–66.

Curtin, Jennifer. 1997. "Women in the Australian Federal Cabinet." Research Note no 40, Department of the Parliamentary Library, http://www.aph.gov.au/library/pubs/rn/1996-97/97rn40.pdf, accessed September 30, 2010.

Curtin, Jennifer. 2006. "Gendering Political Representation in the Old and New Worlds of Westminster." In *Representing Women in Parliament*, eds. Marian Sawer, Manon Tremblay, and Linda Trimble. London: Routledge, 236–251.

Curtin, Jennifer. 2010. "Feminism, Power and the Representation of Women." In *Government, Politics, Power and Policy in Australia*, 9th ed., eds. Dennis Woodward, Andrew Parkin, and John Summers. Frenchs Forest, NSW: Longman/Pearson Education Australia, 394–414.

Dahlerup, Drude. 2006. "The Story of the Theory of Critical Mass." *Politics & Gender* 2 (4): 511–522.

Dahlerup, Drude, and Monique Leyenaar. 2013. "Introduction." In *Breaking Male Dominance in Old Democracies*, eds. Drude Dahlerup and Monique Leyenaar. New York: Oxford University Press, 1–23.

Dausend, Peter. 2013. "Basteln mit dem Hammer." *Die Zeit*. No. 47.

Dávila, Mireya. 2011. *Governing Together: The Concertación Administrations in Chile, 1990–2009*. PhD dissertation, University of North Carolina, Chappel Hill.

Dávila, Mireya, and Octavio Avendaño. 2018. "Together We Govern: Portfolio Allocation in Chile (1990–2014)." In *Government Formation and Minister Turnover in Presidential Cabinets: Comparative Analysis in the Americas*, eds. Marcelo Camerlo and Cecilia Martínez-Gallardo. London and New York: Routledge.

Davis, Rebecca Howard. 1997. *Women and Power in Parliamentary Democracies: Cabinet Appointments in Western Europe, 1968–1992*. Lincoln; London: University of Nebraska Press.

De Winter, Lieven. 1995. "The Role of Parliament in Government Formation and Resignation." In *Parliaments and Majority Rule in Western Europe*, ed. Herbert Döring. New York: St. Martin's Press, 115–151.

De Winter, Lieven. 1991. "Parliamentary and Party Pathways to Cabinet." In *The Profession of Government Minister in Western Euope*, eds. Jean Blondel and Jean-Louis Thiébault. Houndsmill, Basingstoke: Macmillan, 44–69.

Diefenbaker, John G. 1976. *One Canada: Memoirs of the Right Honourable John G. Diefenbaker, The Years of Achievement, 1956–1962*. Toronto: Macmillan Company of Canada.

Dogan, Mattei. 1989. "Selecting Cabinet Ministers." In *Pathways to Power: Selecting Rulers in Pluralist Democracies*, ed. Mattei Dogan. Boulder, CO: Westview Press, 1–18.

Donno, Daniela, and Anne-Kathrin Kreft. 2018. "Authoritarian Institutions and Women's Rights." *Comparative Political Studies* 52 (5): 720–753.

Dowding, Keith, and Patrick Dumont (eds.). 2009. *The Selection of Ministers in Europe: Hiring and Firing*. London; New York: Routledge.

Dowding, Keith, and Patrick Dumont (eds.). 2014. *The Selection of Ministers around the World*. London; New York: Routledge.

Dowding, Keith, and Chris Lewis. 2015. "Australia: Ministerial Characteristics in the Australian Federal Government." In *The Selection of Ministers around the World*, eds. Keith Dowding and Patrick Dumont. Abingdon: Routledge, 44–60.

Duerst-Lahti, Georgia, and Rita Mae Kelly. 1995. "On Governance, Leadership, and Gender." In *Gender Power, Leadership, and Governance*, eds. Georgia Duerst-Lahti and Rita Mae Kelly. Ann Arbor: University of Michigan Press, 11–37.

Dumas, Víctor, Mariano Lafuente, and Salvador Parrado. 2013. *Strengthening the Centre of Government for Results in Chile*. Inter-American Development Bank, Technical Note.

Eason, Christina. 2011. *Their Lordship Is Divided: The Representation of Women in the Transitional House of Lords, 1999–2009*. Doctoral Thesis, The University of Manchester.

Encarnación, Omar G. 2009. "Spain's New Left Turn: Society Driven or Party Instigated?" *South European Politics and Society* 14 (4): 399–415.

Escobar-Lemmon, Maria, and Michelle Taylor-Robinson. 2005. "Women Ministers in Latin American Government: When, Where, and Why?" *American Journal of Political Science* 49 (4): 829–844.

Escobar-Lemmon, Maria, and Michelle M. Taylor-Robinson. 2009. "Getting to the Top: Career Paths of Women in Latin American Cabinets." *Political Research Quarterly* 62 (4): 685–699.

Escobar-Lemmon, Maria, and Michelle M. Taylor-Robinson. 2016. *Women in Presidential Cabinets: Power Players or Abundant Tokens?* New York: Oxford University Press.

Escobar-Lemmon, Maria, Leslie Schwindt-Bayer, and Michelle Taylor-Robinson. 2014. "Representing Women: Empirical Insights from Legislatures and Cabinets in Latin America." In *Representation: The Case of Women*, eds. Maria Escobar-Lemmon and Michelle Taylor-Robinson. New York: Oxford University Press, 205–224.

Fernández, María de los Angeles, and Eugenio Rivera. 2013. "Instituciones Informales, Coaliciones y Gabinetes en el Presidencialismo." *Política: Revista de Ciencia Política* 51 (1): 155–184.

Field, Bonnie N. 2009. "A 'Second Transition' in Spain? Policy, Institutions, and Interparty Politics under Zapatero (2004–8)." *South European Society and Politics* 14 (4): 379–397.

Field, Bonnie. 2016. *Why Minority Governments Work: Multilevel Territorial Politics in Spain*. New York: Palgrave Macmillan.

Fischer, Jörn. 2011. *Deutsche Bundesminister: Wege ins Amt und wieder hinaus. Selektions- und Deselektionsmechanismen im Bundeskabinett unter besonderer Berücksichtigung von Push-Rücktritten*. PhD thesis, Universität zu Köln.

Fischer, Jörn, and André Kaiser. 2009. "Hiring and Firing Ministers Under Informal Constraints." In *The Selection of Ministers in Europe: Hiring and Firing*, eds. Keith Dowding and Patrick Dumont. New York: Routledge, 21–40.

Fleisher, Julia, and Markus Seyfried. 2015. "Drawing from the Bargaining Pool: Determinants of Ministerial Selection in Germany." *Party Politics* 21 (4): 503–514.

Foster, Nigel, and Satish Sule. 2010. *German Legal System and Laws*. 4th ed. Oxford: Oxford University Press.

Fox, Richard L., and Jennifer L. Lawless. 2004. "Entering the Arena? Gender and the Decision to Run for Office." *American Journal of Political Science* 48 (2): 264–280.

Franceschet, Susan. 2005. *Women and Politics in Chile*. Boulder, CO: Lynne Rienner.

Franceschet, Susan. 2011. "Gendered Institutions and Women's Substantive Representation: Female Legislators in Chile and Argentina." In *Gender, Politics, and Institutions: Towards a Feminist Institutionalism*, eds. Mona Lena Krook and Fiona Mackay. London: Palgrave Macmillan, 58–78.

Franceschet, Susan. 2018. "Informal Institutions and Women's Political Representation in Chile (1990–2015)." In *Gender and Representation in Latin America*, ed. Leslie Schwindt-Bayer. New York: Oxford University Press, 140–155.

Franceschet, Susan, Claire Annesley, and Karen Beckwith. 2017. "What Do Women Symbolize? Symbolic Representation and Cabinet Appointments." *Politics, Groups and Identities* 5 (3): 488–93.

Franceschet, Susan, and Jennifer M. Piscopo. 2014. "Sustaining Gendered Practices? Power, Parties, and Elite Political Networks in Argentina." *Comparative Political Studies* 47 (1): 85–110.

Franceschet, Susan, and Gwynn Thomas. 2010. "Renegotiating Political Leadership: Michelle Bachelet's Rise to the Chilean Presidency." In *Cracking the Highest Glass Ceiling: A Global Comparison of Women's Campaigns for Chief Executive Office*, ed. Rainbow Murray. Thousand Oaks, CA: Praeger, 177–195.

Franceschet, Susan, and Gwynn Thomas. 2015. "Resisting Parity: Gender and Cabinet Appointment in Chile and Spain." *Politics & Gender* 11 (4): 643–664.

Friedland, Steven I. 2015. "'Advice and Consent' in the Appointments Clause: From Another Historical Perspective." *Duke Law Journal Online* 64 (May): 173–192.

Gains, Francesca, and Vivien Lowndes. 2014. "How Is Institutional Formation Gendered, and Does It Make a Difference? A New Conceptual Framework and a Case Study of Police and Crime Commissioners in England and Wales." *Politics and Gender* 10 (4): 524–548.

Gates, Robert M. 2014. *Duty: Memoirs of a Secretary at War*. New York: Vintage Books.

George, Alexander L., and Andrew Bennett. 2005. *Case Studies and Theory Development in the Social Sciences*. Cambridge, MA: MIT Press.

Gerhardt, Michael J. 2003. *The Federal Appointments Process: A Constitutional and Historical Analysis*. Chicago: The University of Chicago Press.

Gillard, Julia. 2014. *My Story*. London: Bantam Press.

Gómez, Raúl, and Tània Verge. 2012. "Party Patronage in Spain: Appointments for Party Government." *Party Patronage and Party Government in European Democracies*, eds. Petre Kopecky, Peter Mair, and Maria Spirova. Oxford: Oxford University Press, 316–334.

Gussow, David. 2006. "Crossing the Floor, Conflict of Interest, and the Parliament of Canada Act." *Canadian Parliamentary Review* (Summer 2006): 9–11.

Hall, Peter A. 1986. *Governing the Economy: The Politics of State Intervention in Britain and France*. Oxford: Oxford University Press.

Hall, Peter A., and Rosemary C. R. Taylor. 1996. "Political Science and the Three New Institutionalisms." *Political Studies* 44 (5): 936–957.

Harman, Harriet. 2017. *A Woman's Work*. London: Allen Lane.

Helmke, Gretchen, and Steven Levitsky. 2004. "Informal Institutions and Comparative Politics: A Research Agenda." *Perspectives on Politics* 2 (4): 725–740.

Helmke, Gretchen, and Steven Levitsky (eds.). 2006. *Informal Institutions and Democracy: Lessons from Latin America*. Baltimore, MD: Johns Hopkins University Press.

Hinojosa, Magda. 2012. *Selecting Women, Electing Women*. Philadelphia: Temple University Press.

Hogg, Sarah, and Jonathan Hill. 1996. *Too Close to Call*. London: Time Warner Paperbacks.

Howard, John. 2010. *Lazarus Rising: A Personal and Political Autobiography*. Sydney: Harper Collins.

Jacobs, Suraj, John Scherpereel, and Melinda Adams. 2013. "Gender Norms and Women's Political Representation: A Global Analysis of Cabinets." *Governance* 27 (2): 321–345.

Johnson, Carol. 2015. "Playing the Gender Card: The Uses and Abuses of Gender in Australian Politics." *Politics and Gender* 11 (2): 291–319.

Johnson, Niki. 2016. "Keeping Men In, Shutting Women Out: Gender Biases in Candidate Selection Processes in Uruguay." *Government & Opposition* 51 (3): 339–415.

Joignant, Alfredo, Lucas Perello, and Javier Torres. 2014. "Political Capital and the Unequal Career Origins of the Political Elite in Chile." In *Political Inequality in an Age of Democracy: Cross-national Perspectives*, ed. Joshua Kjerulf Dubrow. London; New York: Routledge, 87–94.

Kaiser, André, and Jörn Fischer. 2009. "Linkages between Parliamentary and Ministerial Careers in Germany, 1949–2008: The Bundestag as Recruitment Pool." *German Politics* 18 (2): 140–154.

Kam, Christopher, and Indridi Indridason. 2009. "Cabinet Dynamics and Ministerial Careers in the French Fifth Republic." In *The Selection of Ministers in Europe*, eds. Keith Dowding and Patrick Dumont. Abingdon: Routledge, 41–57.

Katz, Richard S., and Peter Mair. 1995. "Changing Models of Party Organization and Party Democracy: The Emergence of the Cartel Party." *Party Politics* I (1): 5–28.

Kaufman, G. 1997. *How to Be a Minister*. London: Faber and Faber.

Kenny, Meryl. 2013. *Gender and Political Recruitment: Theorizing Institutional Change*. London: Palgrave.

Kenny, Meryl. 2014. "A Feminist Institutionalist Approach." *Politics & Gender* 10 (4): 679–684.

Kenny, Meryl, and Tània Verge. 2016. "Opening Up the Black Box: Gender and Candidate Selection in a New Era." *Government and Opposition* 51 (3): 351–369.

Kerby, Matthew. 2009. "Worth the Wait: The Determinants of Ministerial Appointment in Canada, 1935–2008." *Canadian Journal of Political Science* 42 (3): 593–691.

Kerby, Matthew. 2015. "Canada." In *The Selection of Ministers Around the World*, eds. Keith Dowding and Patrick Dumont. London; New York: Routledge, 264–282.

Krook, Mona Lena. 2009. *Quotas for Women in Politics*. New York: Oxford University Press.

Krook, M. L., and F. Mackay (eds.). 2011. *Gender, Politics and Institutions: Towards a Feminist Institutionalism*. New York: Palgrave Macmillan.

Krook, Mona Lena, and Diana O'Brien. 2012. "All the President's Men? The Appointment of Female Cabinet Ministers Worldwide." *Journal of Politics* 74 (3): 840–855.

Krook, Mona Lena, and Pär Zetterberg (eds.). 2016. *Gender Quotas and Women's Representation: New Directions in Research*. New York: Routledge.

Kumar, Martha Joynt. 2009. "The 2008–2009 Presidential Transition through the Voices of Its Participants." *Presidential Studies Quarterly* 39 (4): 823–858.

Laver, Michael. 1994. "Models of Government Formation." *Annual Review of Political Science Review* 1: 1–25.

Laver, Michael, and Kenneth A. Shepsle. 1994. "Cabinet Ministers and Government Formation in Parliamentary Democracies." In *Cabinet Ministers and Parliamentary Government*, eds. Michael Laver and Kenneth A. Shepsle. New York: Cambridge University Press, 3–12.

Laver, Michael, and Kenneth A. Shepsle. 1996. *Making and Breaking Governments: Cabinets and Legislatures in Parliamentary Democracies*. Cambridge: Cambridge University Press.

Laver, Michael, and Kenneth A. Shepsle. 2000. "Ministrables and Government Formation: Munchkins, Players, and Big Beasts of the Jungle." *Journal of Theoretical Politics* 12 (1): 113–124.

Levi, Margaret, and Laura Stokes. 2000. "Political Trust and Trustworthiness." *Annual Review of Political Science* 3 (1): 475–507.

Lieberman, Robert. 2002. "Ideas, Institutions, and Political Order: Explaining Political Change." *American Political Science Review* 96 (4): 697–712.

Light, Paul. 2015. "Back to the Future on Presidential Appointments." *Duke Law Journal* 64 (8): 1499–1512.

Loomis, Burdett. 2001. "The Senate and Executive Branch Appointments: An Obstacles Course on Capitol Hill?" *The Brookings Review* 19 (2): 32–36.

Lovecy, Jill. 2007. "Framing Claims for Women." In *Women and New Labour*, eds. Claire Annesley and Francesca Gains. Bristol: Policy Press, 63–92.

Lovenduski, Joni. 1998. "Gendering Political Research." *Annual Review of Political Science* 1: 333–356.

Lovenduski, Joni. 2005. *Feminizing Politics*. Cambridge, UK: Polity Press.

Lovenduski, Joni. 2016. "The Supply and Demand Model of Candidate Selection: Some Reflections." *Government and Opposition* 51 (3): 513–528.

Lowndes, Vivien. 2014. "How Are Things Done Around Here? Uncovering Institutional Rules and Their Gendered Effects." *Politics & Gender* 10 (4): 685–691.

Lowndes, Vivien, and Mark Roberts. 2013. *Why Institutions Matter: The New Institutionalism and Political Science*. London: Palgrave.

Lynch, Julia F. 2013. "Aligning Sampling Strategies with Analytic Goals." In *Interview Research in Political Science*, ed. Layna Mosley. Ithaca, NY: Cornell University Press, 31–44.

Mackay, Fiona. 2014. "Nested Newness, Institutional Innovation, and the Gendered Limits of Change." *Politics & Gender* 13 (2): 232–252.

Mackay, Fiona, Meryl Kenny, and Louise Chappell. 2010. "New Institutionalism through a Gender Lens: Towards a Feminist Institutionalism?" *International Political Science Review* 31: 573–588.

Mahoney, James, and Kathleen Thelen. 2010. "A Theory of Gradual Institutional Change." In *Explaining Institutional Change: Ambiguity, Agency, and Power*, eds. James Mahoney and Kathleen Thelen. New York: Cambridge University Press, 1–37.

Mahoney, James, and Kathleen Thelen (eds.). 2010. *Explaining Institutional Change: Ambiguity, Agency, and Power*. Cambridge: Cambridge University Press.

March, James G., and Johan P. Olsen. 1989. *Rediscovering Institutions: The Organizational Basis of Politics*. New York: Free Press.

March, James G., and Johan P. Olsen. 2011. "The Logic of Appropriateness." In *The Oxford Handbook of Political Science*, ed. Robert E. Goodin. New York: Oxford University Press, 478–497.

Martinez-Gallardo, Cecilia. 2014. "Designing Cabinets: Presidential Politics and Ministerial Stability." *Journal of Latin American Politics* 6 (2): 3–38.

Martinez-Gallardo, Cecilia, and Petra Schleiter. 2015. "Choosing Whom to Trust: Agency Risks and Cabinet Partisanship in Presidential Democracies." *Comparative Political Studies* 48 (2): 231–264.

Mason, Jennifer. 2006. "Mixing Methods in a Qualitatively Driven Way." *Qualitative Research* 6 (1): 9–25.

McHenry, Dean E. 1955. "The Origins of Caucus Selection of Cabinet." *Historical Studies: Australia and New Zealand* 7 (25): 37–43.

Mershon, Carol. 1994. "Expectations and Informal Rules in Cabinet Formation." *Comparative Political Studies* 27 (1): 40–79.

Moon, Jeremy, and Imogen Fountain. 1997. "Keeping the Gates? Women as Ministers in Australia 1970–96." *Australian Journal of Political Science* 32 (3): 455–466.

Mulroney, Brian. 2007. *Memoirs, 1939–1993*. Toronto: McClelland & Stewart.

Murray, Rainbow (ed.). 2010. *Cracking the Highest Glass Ceiling: A Global Comparison of Women's Campaigns for Chief Executive Office*. Santa Barbara, CA: Praeger.

Murray, Rainbow. 2014. "Quotas for Men: Reframing Gender Quotas as a Means of Improving Representation for All." *American Political Science Review* 108 (3): 520–532.

Norris, Pippa, and Joni Lovenduski. 1995. *Political Recruitment: Gender, Race, and Class in the British Parliament*. New York: Cambridge University Press.

O'Brien, Diana, Matthew Mendez, Jordan Carr Peterson, and Jihyun Shin. 2015. "Letting Down the Ladder or Shutting the Door? Female Prime Ministers, Party Leaders, and Cabinet Ministers." *Politics & Gender* 11 (4): 689–717.

Olivares, Alejandro, Bastián González, Javiera Meneses, and Matías Rodríguez. 2014. "Los think-tanks en el gabinete: una exploración del caso chileno, 2006–2014." *Revista de Sociología* 29: 37–54.

Ostrom, Elinor. 1986. "An Agenda for the Study of Institutions." *Public Choice* 48 (1): 3–25.

Ostrom, Elinor. 2005. *Understanding Institutional Diversity*. Princeton, NJ: Princeton University Press.

Parry, Keith, and Lucinda Maer. 2012. "Ministers in the House of Lords." House of Commons Library, Standard Note SN/PC/05226.

Pierson, Paul. 2000. "Increasing Returns, Path Dependence, and the Study of Politics." *American Political Science Review* 94 (2): 251–267.

Piscopo, Jennifer M. 2016. "When Informality Advantages Women: Quota Networks, Electoral Rules, and Candidate Selection in Mexico." *Government and Opposition* 51 (3): 487–512.

Poguntke, Thomas, and Paul Webb, eds. 2005. *The Presidentialization of Politics: A Comparative Study of Modern Democracies*. Oxford: Oxford University Press.

Pruysers, Scott, and Julie Blais. 2017. "Why Won't Lola Run? An Experiment Examining Stereotype Threat and Political Ambition." *Politics & Gender* 13 (2): 232–252.

Punnett, R. M. 1964. "The Labour Shadow Cabinet, 1955–64." *Parliamentary Affairs* 18 (1): 61–70.

Rasch, Björn Erik, Shane Martin, and José Antonio Cheibub (eds.). 2015. *Parliaments and Government Formation: Unpacking Investiture Rules*. Oxford: Oxford University Press.

Real-Dato, José, and Miguel Jerez-Mir. 2009. "Cabinet Dynamics in Democratic Spain (1977—2008)." In *The Selection of Ministers in Europe: Hiring and Firing*, eds. Keith Dowding and Patrick Dumont. London: Routledge, 110–124.

Reyes-Housholder, Catherine. 2016. "*Presidentas* Rise: Consequences for Women in Cabinet?" *Latin American Politics & Society* 58 (3): 3–25.

Reynolds, Andrew. 1999. "Women in the Legislatures and Executives of the World: Knocking at the Highest Glass Ceiling?" *World Politics* 51 (4): 547–572.

Rhodes, R. A. W. 2006. "Executives in Parliamentary Government." In *The Oxford Handbook of Political Institutions*, eds. R.A.W. Rhodes, Sarah A. Binder, and Bert A. Rockman. New York: Oxford University Press, 322–343.

Rhodes, R. A. W, John Wanna, and Patrick Weller. 2009. *Comparing Westminster*. Oxford: Oxford University Press.

Riddel, Peter, Zoe Gruhn, and Liz Carolan. 2011. *The Challenge of Being a Minister*. London: Institute for Government.

Rodríguez Teruel, Juan. 2011a. "Ministerial and Parliamentary Elites in Multi-level Spain: 1977–2009." *Comparative Sociology* 10: 877–907.

Rodríguez Teruel, Juan. 2011b. *Los Ministros de la España Democrática: Reclutamiento político y carrera ministerial de Suárez a Zapatero (1976–2010).* Madrid: Centro de Estudios Políticos y Constitucionales.

Rodríguez Teruel, Juan, and Miguel Jerez Mir. 2018. "The Selection and Deselection of Technocratic Ministers in Democratic Spain." In *Technocratic Ministers and Political Leadership in European Democracies*, eds. António Costa Pinto, Maurizio Cotta, and Pedro Tavares de Almeida. New York: Palgrave Macmillan, 139–171.

Ryan, Susan. 1999a. *Catching the Waves: Life in and Out of Politics.* New York: Harper Collins.

Ryan, Susan. 1999b. "Rollers and Dumpers: Life as a Cabinet Minister." *The Sydney Papers* (Winter): 21–27.

Sawer, Marian. 2013. "Misogyny and Misrepresentation: Women in Australian Parliaments." *Political Science* 65 (1): 105–117.

Sawer, Marian, and Marian Simms. 1993. *A Woman's Place: Women and Politics in Australia.* St. Leonards: Allen and Unwin.

Scherpereel, John, Melinda Adams, and Suri Jacobs. 2018. "Ratchets and Seesaws: Exploring Temporal Patterns in Women's Political Representation." *Socius: Sociological Research for a Dynamic World* 4: 1–13.

Schmidt, Vivien. 2010. "Taking Ideas and Discourses Seriously: Explaining Change through Discursive Institutionalism as the Fourth 'New Institutionalism.'" *European Political Science Review* 2 (1): 1–25.

Schwindt-Bayer, Leslie. 2010. *Political Power and Women's Representation in Latin America.* New York: Oxford University Press .

Seawright, Jason, and John Gerring. 2008. "Case Selection Techniques in Case Study Research." *Political Research Quarterly* 61 (2): 294–308.

Siaroff, Alan. 2000. "Women's Representation in Legislatures and Cabinets in Industrial Democracies." *International Political Science Review* 21 (2): 197–215.

Siavelis, Peter M. 2000. *The President and Congress in Postauthoritarian Chile: Institutional Constraints to Democratic Consolidation.* University Park, PA: The University of Pennsylvania State Press.

Siavelis, Peter M. 2006. "Accommodating Informal Institutions in Chilean Politics." In *Informal Institutions and Democracy in Latin America*, eds. Gretchen Helmke and Steven Levitsky. Baltimore, MD: Johns Hopkins University Press, 33–55.

Siavelis, Peter M. 2014. "The Fault Lines of Coalitional Presidentialism: Cabinets, Quotas, and the Second Floor in Chile." Paper presented at the 23rd World Congress of the International Political Science Association, Montreal, Canada, July 19–24.

Smooth, Wendy. 2006. "Intersectionality in Electoral Politics: A Mess Worth Making." *Politics & Gender* 2 (3): 400–414.

Smooth, Wendy. 2011. "Standing for Women? Which Women? The Substantive Representation of Women's Interests and the Research Imperative of Intersectionality." *Politics & Gender* 7 (3): 436–441.

Steinmo, Sven. 2008. "Historical Institutionalism." In *Approaches in the Social Sciences*, eds. Donatella Della Porta and Michael Keating. Cambridge: Cambridge University Press, 118–138.

Stockemer, Daniel. 2017. "The Proportion of Women in Legislatures and Cabinets: What Is the Empirical Link?" *Polity* 49 (3): 434–460.

Streeck, Wolfgang, and Kathleen Thelen (eds.). 2005. *Beyond Continuity Institutional Change in Advanced Political Economies*. Oxford: Oxford University Press.

Strom, Kaare, Ian Budge, and Michael J. Laver. 1994. "Constraints on Cabinet Formation in Parliamentary Democracies." *American Journal of Political Science* 38 (2): 303–335.

Sykes, Patricia L. 2009. "Incomplete Empowerment: Female Cabinet Ministers in Anglo-American Systems." In *Dispersed Democratic Leadership: Origins, Dynamics, and Implications*, eds. John Kane, Haig Patapan, and Paul 't Hart. New York: Oxford University Press, 37–58.

Thelen, Kathleen, and Sven Steinmo. 1992. "Historical Institutionalism in Comparative Politics." In *Structuring Politics: Historical Institutionalism in Comparative Analysis*, eds. Sven Steinmo, Kathleen Thelen, and Frank Longstreth. New York: Cambridge University Press, 1–32.

Thomas, Gwynn. 2011. "Michelle Bachelet's Liderazgo Feminino (Feminine Leadership): Gender and Redefining Political Leadership in Chile's 2005 Presidential Campaign." *International Feminist Journal of Politics* 13 (1): 63–82.

Thomas, Melanee, and Marc André Blodet. 2013. "Sacrificial Lambs, Women's Candidates, and District Competitiveness in Canada." *Electoral Studies* 32 (1): 153–166.

Thomas, Melanee, and Lisa Young. 2014. "Women (Not) in Politics." In *Canadian Politics*, 6th ed., eds. James Bickerton and Alain Gagnon. Toronto: University of Toronto Press, 373–394.

Tremblay, Manon, and Réjean Pelletier. 2001. "More Women Constituency Party Presidents: A Strategy for Increasing the Number of Women Candidates in Canada?" *Party Politics* 7 (2): 157–190.

Tremblay, Manon, and Daniel Stockemer. 2013. "Women's Ministerial Careers in Cabinet, 1921–2010: A Look at Socio-Demographic Traits and Career Experiences." *Canadian Public Administration* 56 (4): 523–541.

Tripp, Aili Mari, and Alice Kang. 2008. "The Global Impact of Quotas: On the Fast Track to Increase Female Legislative Representation." *Comparative Political Studies* 41 (3): 338–361.

Van Acker, Elizabeth. 1999. *Different Voices: Gender and Politics in Australia*. South Yarra: Macmillan.

Verge, Tània. 2007. *Partidos y Representación Política: Las Dimensiones del Cambio en los Partidos Políticos Españoles, 1976–2006*. Madrid: Centros de Investigaciones Sociológicas.

Verge, Tània. 2010. "Gendering Representation in Spain: Opportunities and Limits of Gender Quotas." *Journal of Women, Politics, and Policy* 31 (2): 166–190.

Verge, Tània. 2012. "Institutionalizing Gender Equality in Spain: Incremental Steps from Party to Electoral Gender Quotas." *West European Politics* 35 (2): 395–414.

Verge, Tània. 2015. "The Gender Regime of Political Parties: Feedback Effects between 'Supply' and 'Demand.'" *Politics & Gender* 11 (4): 754–759.

Verge, Tània, and Sílvia Claveria. 2016. "Gendered Political Resources: The Case of Party Office." *Party Politics* 24 (5): 536–548.

Vogel, Lars. 2009. *Der Weg ins Kabinett. Karrieren von Ministern in Deutschland*. Frankfurt am Main: Peter Lang.

Waylen, Georgina. 2007. *Engendering Transitions: Women's Mobilization, Institutions, and Gender Outcomes*. Oxford: Oxford University Press.

Waylen, Georgina. 2014. "Informal Institutions, Institutional Change, and Gender Equality." *Political Research Quarterly* 67 (1): 212–223.

Waylen, Georgina (ed.). 2017. *Gender and Informal Institutions*. Lanham, MD: Rowman & Littlefield.

Weldon, S. Laurel. 2011. *When Protest Makes Policy: How Social Movements Represent Disadvantaged Groups*. Ann Arbor: University of Michigan Press.

Weller, Patrick. 2005. "Investigating Power at the Centre of Government: Surveying Research on the Australian Executive." *Australian Journal of Public Administration* 64 (1): 35–42.

Weller, Patrick. 2007. *Cabinet Government in Australia, 1901–2006: Practice, Principles, Performance*. Sydney: University of New South Wales.

White, Graham. 2005. *Cabinets and First Ministers*. Vancouver: University of British Columbia Press.

Whitford, Andrew B., Vicky M. Wilkinson, and Mercedes Ball. 2007. "Descriptive Representation and Policymaking Authority: Evidence from Women in Cabinets and Bureaucracies." *Governance* 20 (4): 559–580.

Young, Iris Marion. 1998. *Justice and the Politics of Difference*. Princeton, NJ: Princeton University Press.

Yuan, Y. Connie, Inga Carboni, and Kate Ehrlich. 2014. "The Impact of Interpersonal Affective Relationships and Awareness on Expertise Seeking: A Multilevel Network Investigation." *European Journal of Work and Organizational Psychology* 23 (4): 554–569.

Zussman, David. 2013. *Off and Running: The Prospects and Pitfalls of Government Transitions*. Toronto: University of Toronto Press.

Index